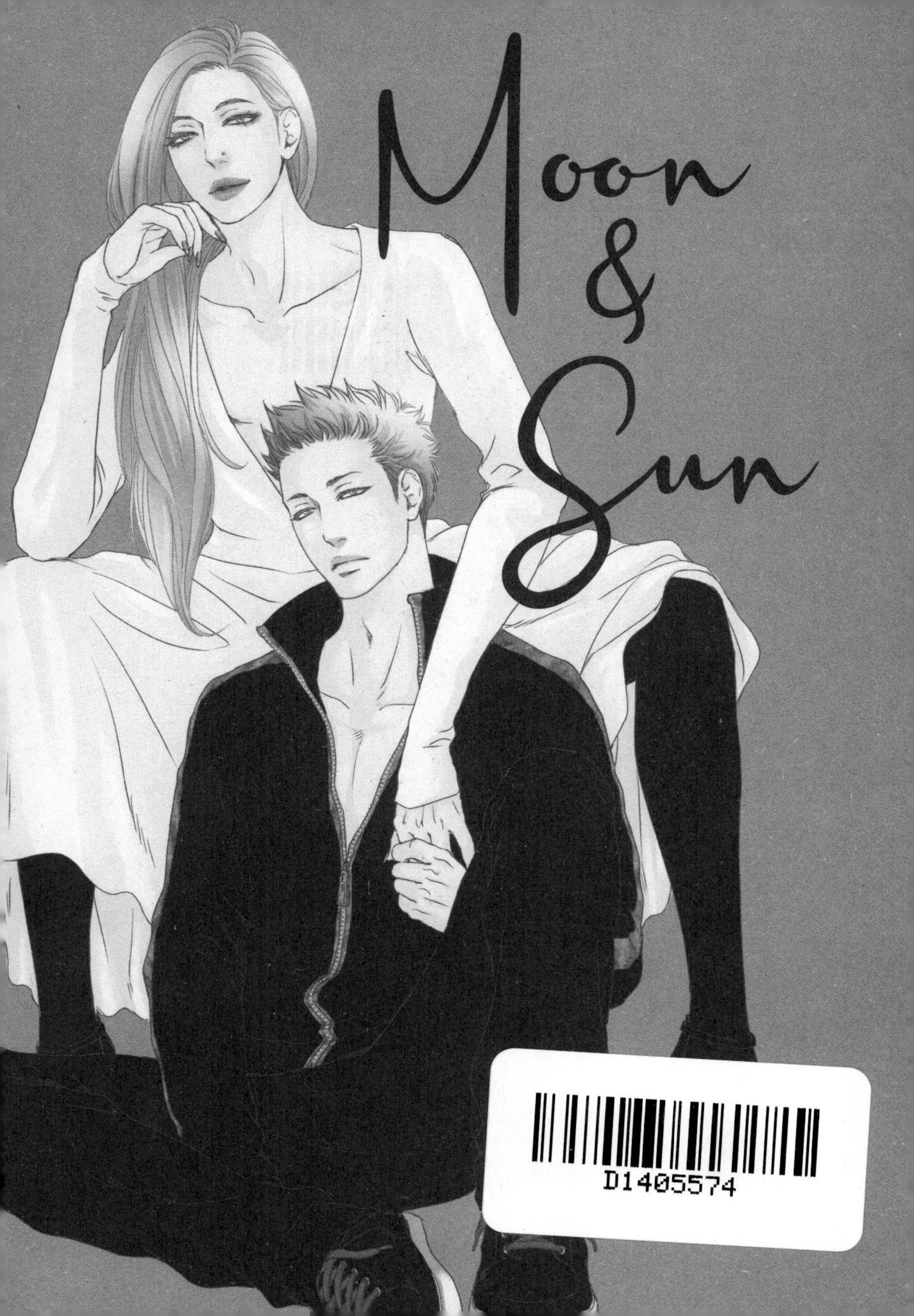
Moon
&
Sun

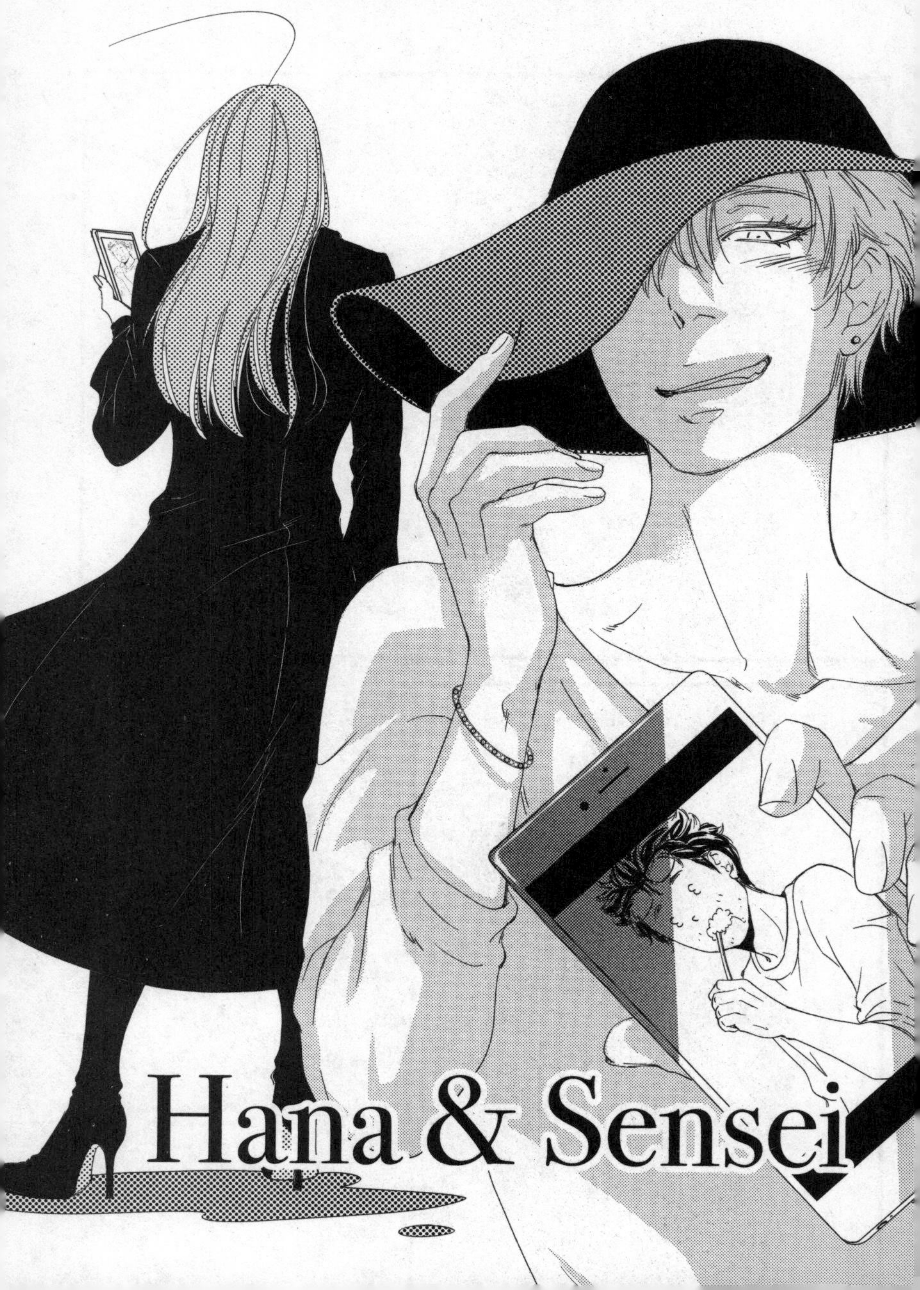
Hana & Sensei

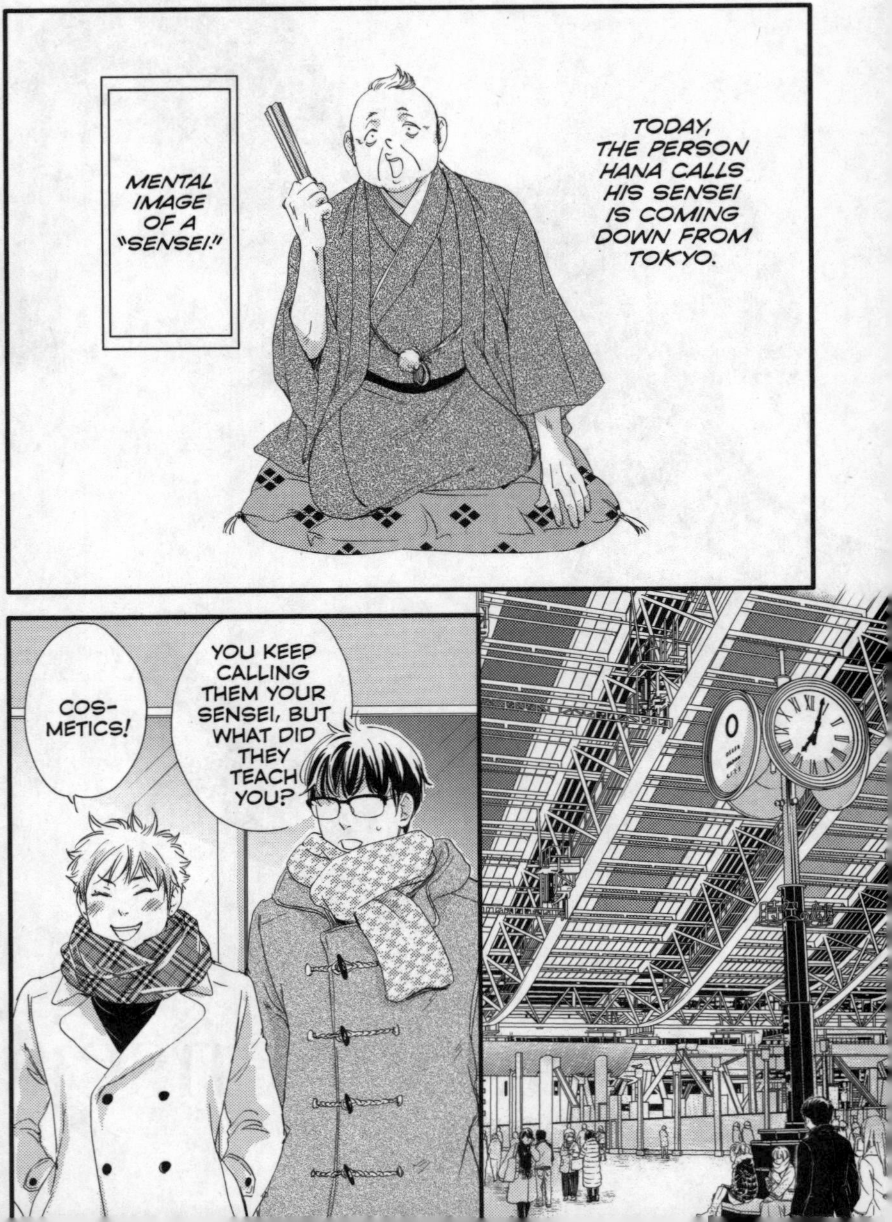
TODAY, THE PERSON HANA CALLS HIS SENSEI IS COMING DOWN FROM TOKYO.
MENTAL IMAGE OF A "SENSEI."
YOU KEEP CALLING THEM YOUR SENSEI, BUT WHAT DID THEY TEACH YOU?
COS-METICS!

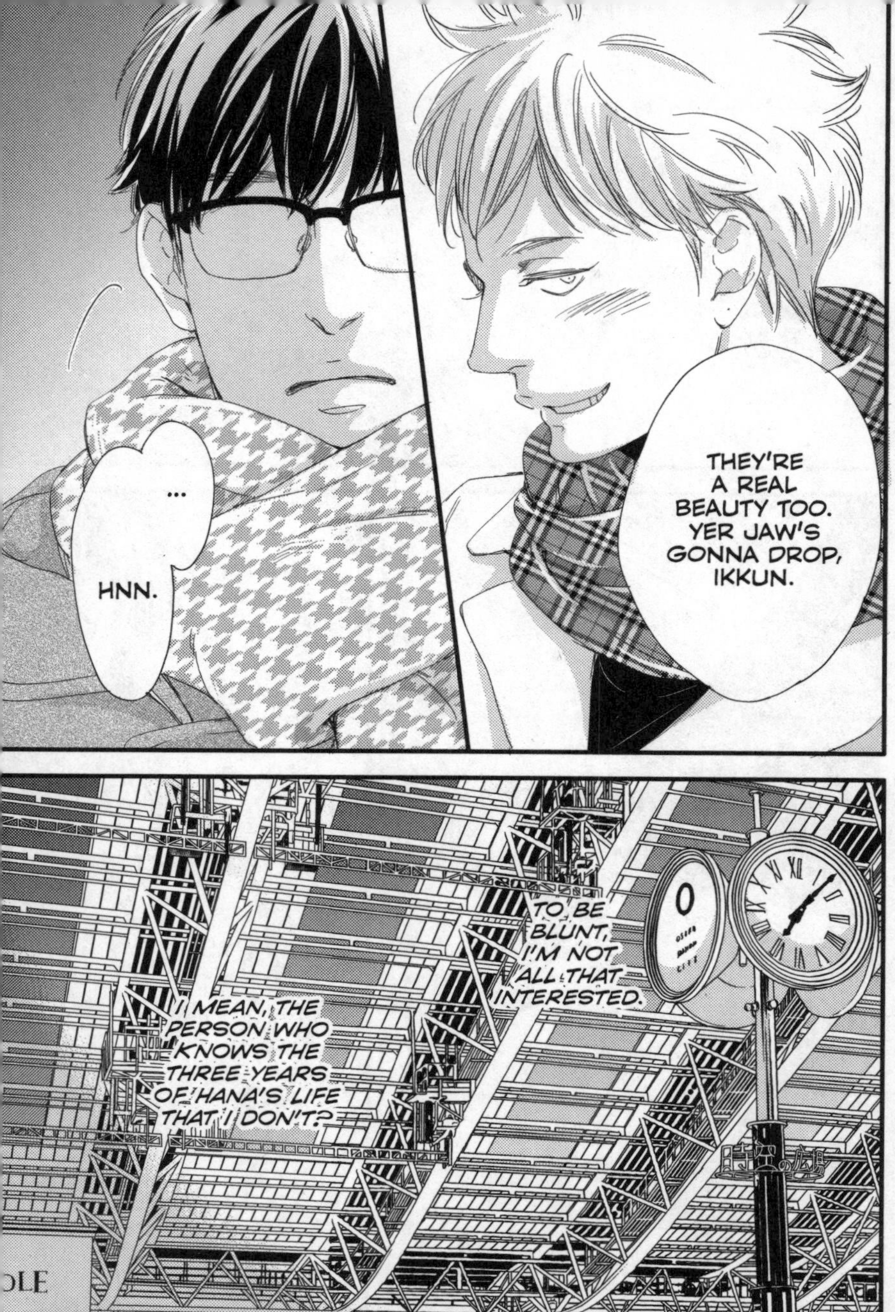
THEY'RE A REAL BEAUTY TOO. YER JAW'S GONNA DROP, IKKUN.
...
HNN.
TO BE BLUNT, I'M NOT ALL THAT INTERESTED.
I MEAN, THE PERSON WHO KNOWS THE THREE YEARS OF HANA'S LIFE THAT I DON'T?
OLE

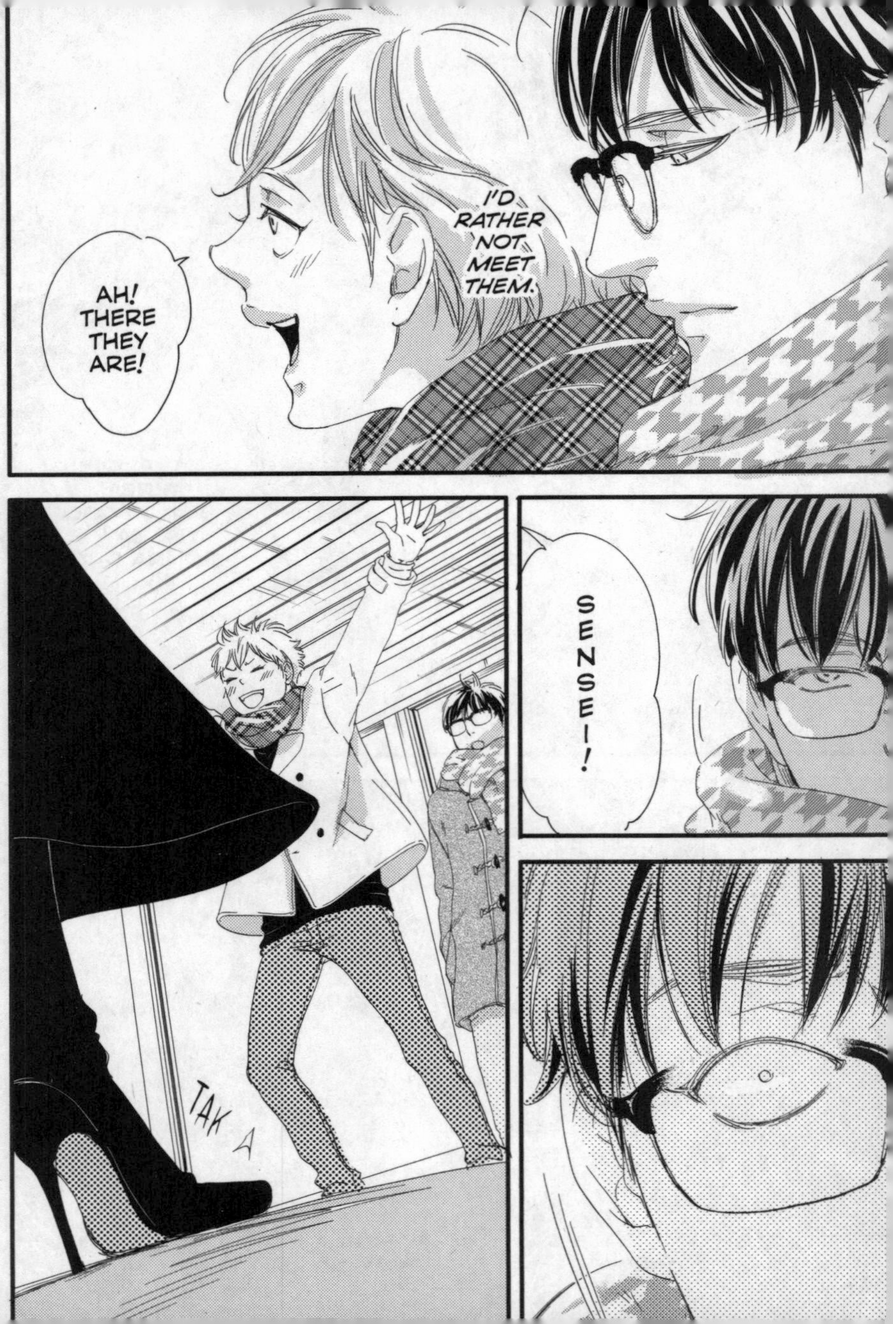
I'D RATHER NOT MEET THEM.
AH! THERE THEY ARE!
SENSEI!
TAK

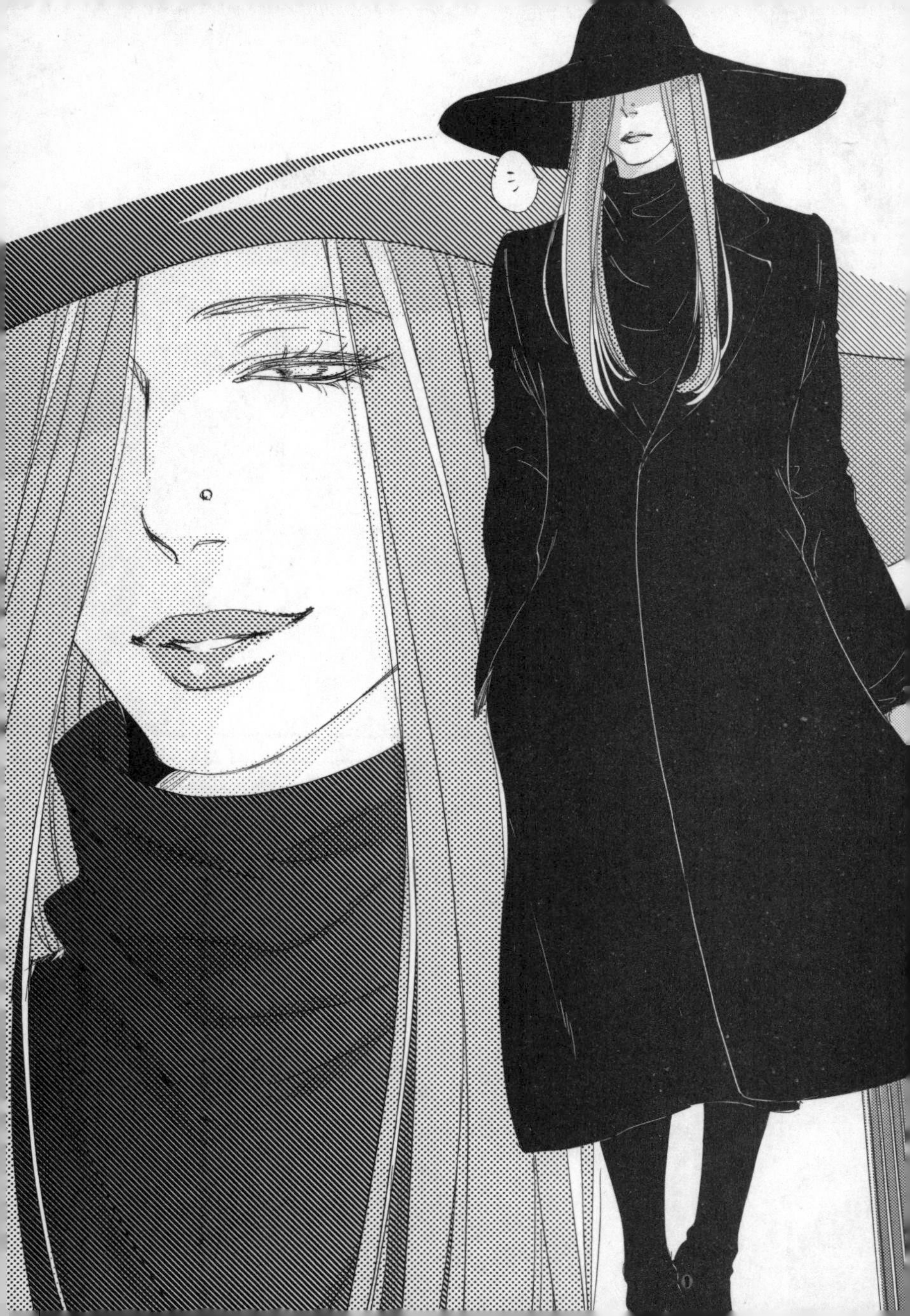

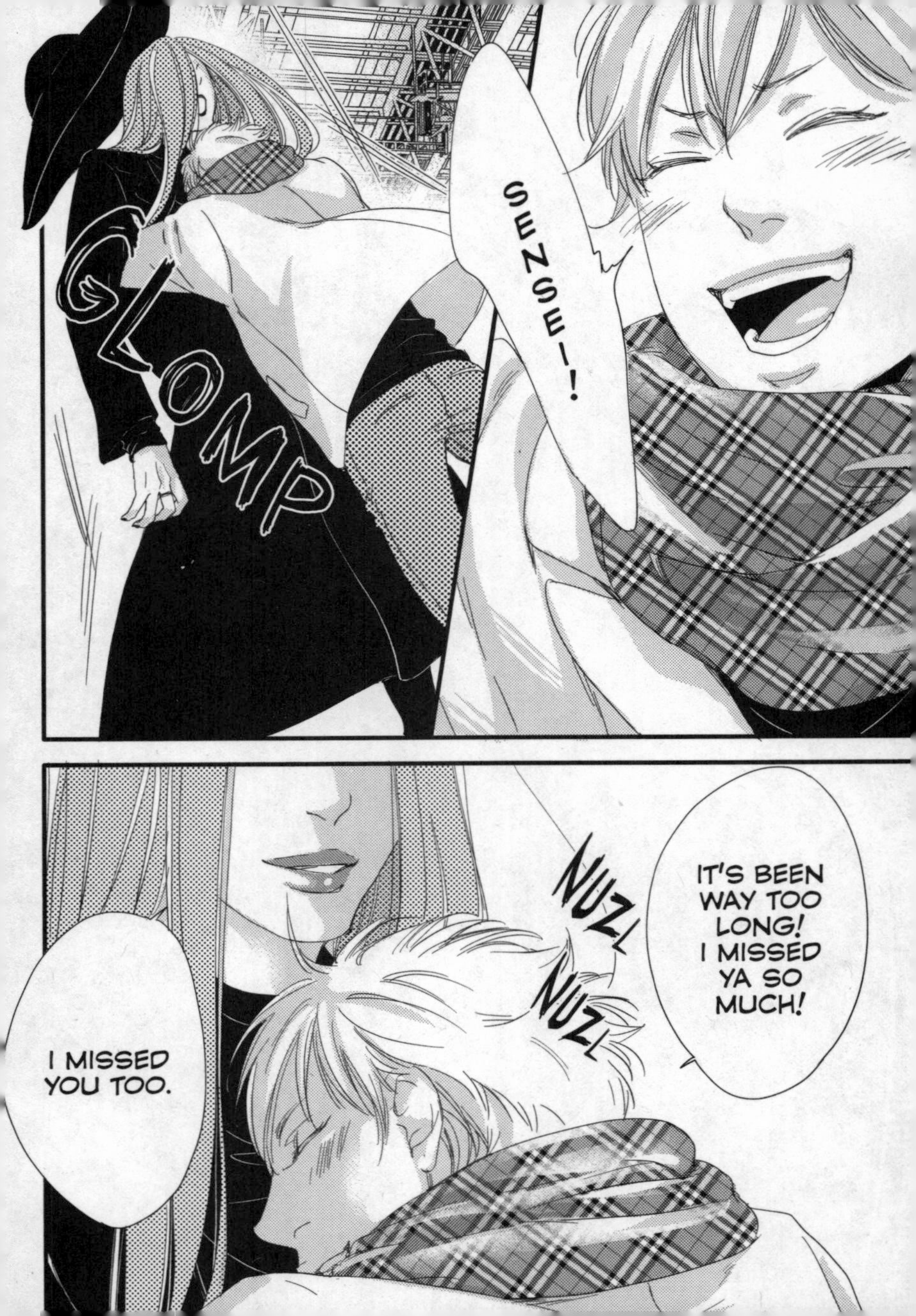
SENSEI!
GLOMP
IT'S BEEN WAY TOO LONG! I MISSED YA SO MUCH!
NUZL NUZL
I MISSED YOU TOO.

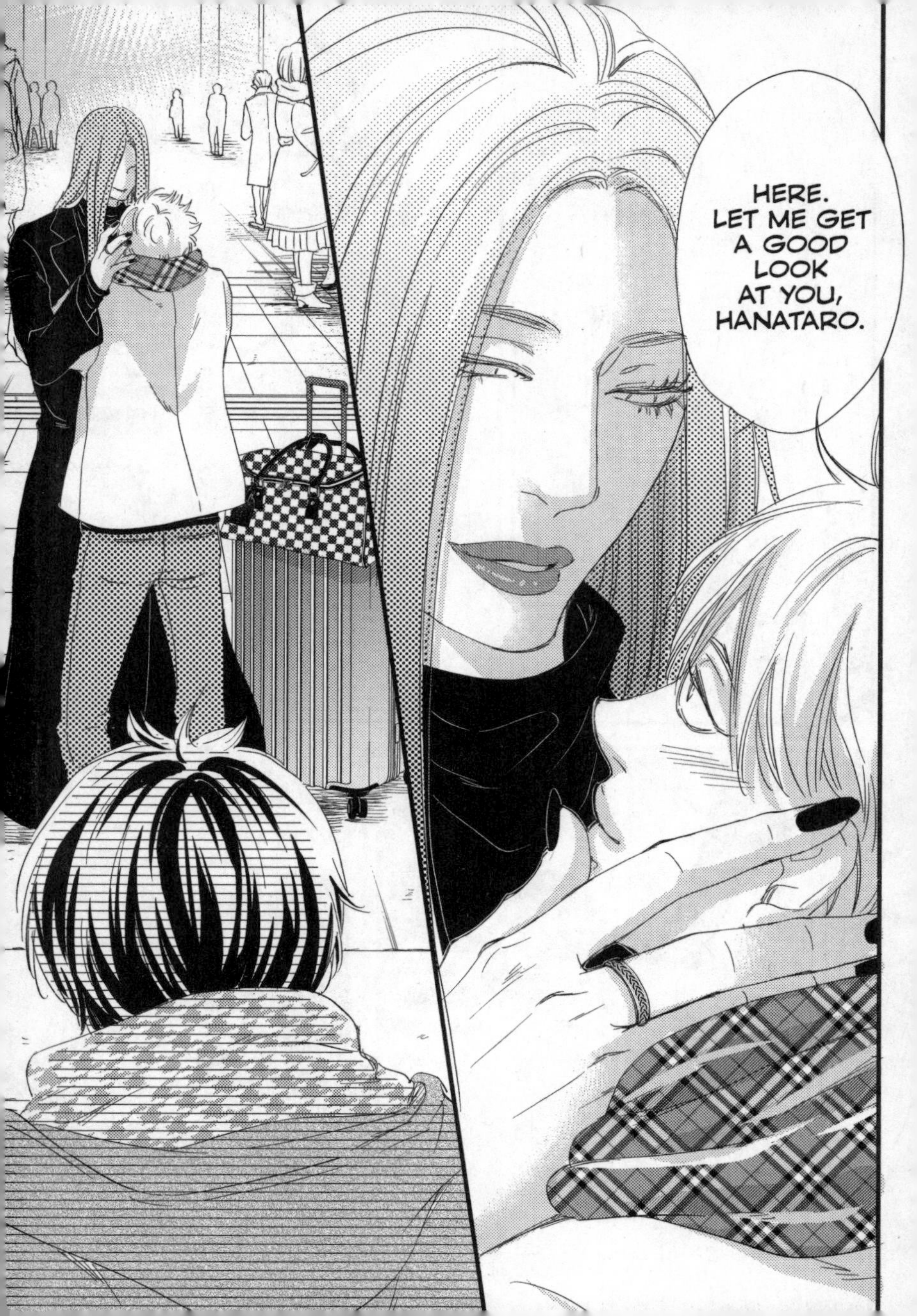
HERE. LET ME GET A GOOD LOOK AT YOU, HANATARO.

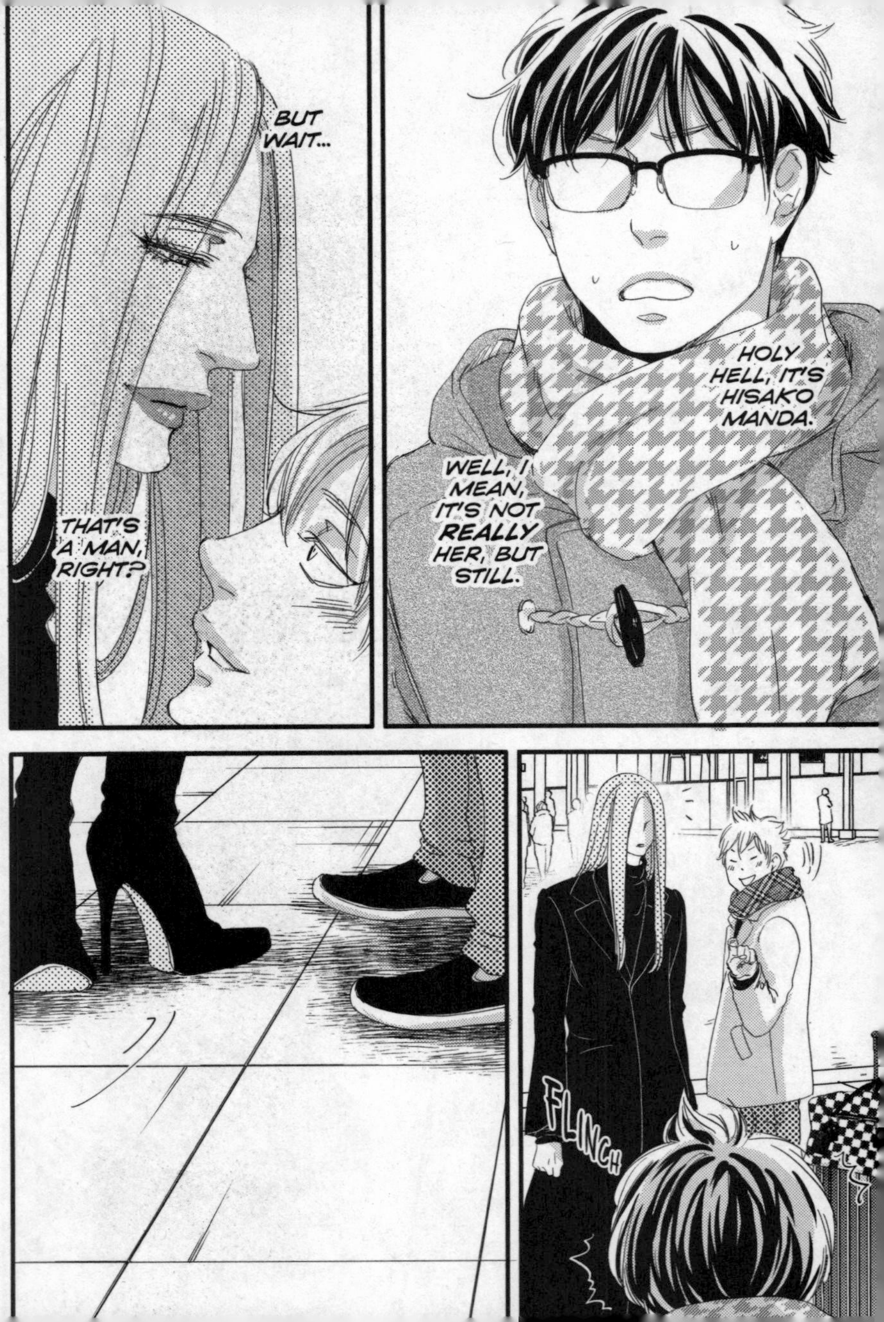
HOLY HELL, IT'S HISAKO MANDA.
WELL, I MEAN, IT'S NOT REALLY HER, BUT STILL.
BUT WAIT...
THAT'S A MAN, RIGHT?
FLINCH

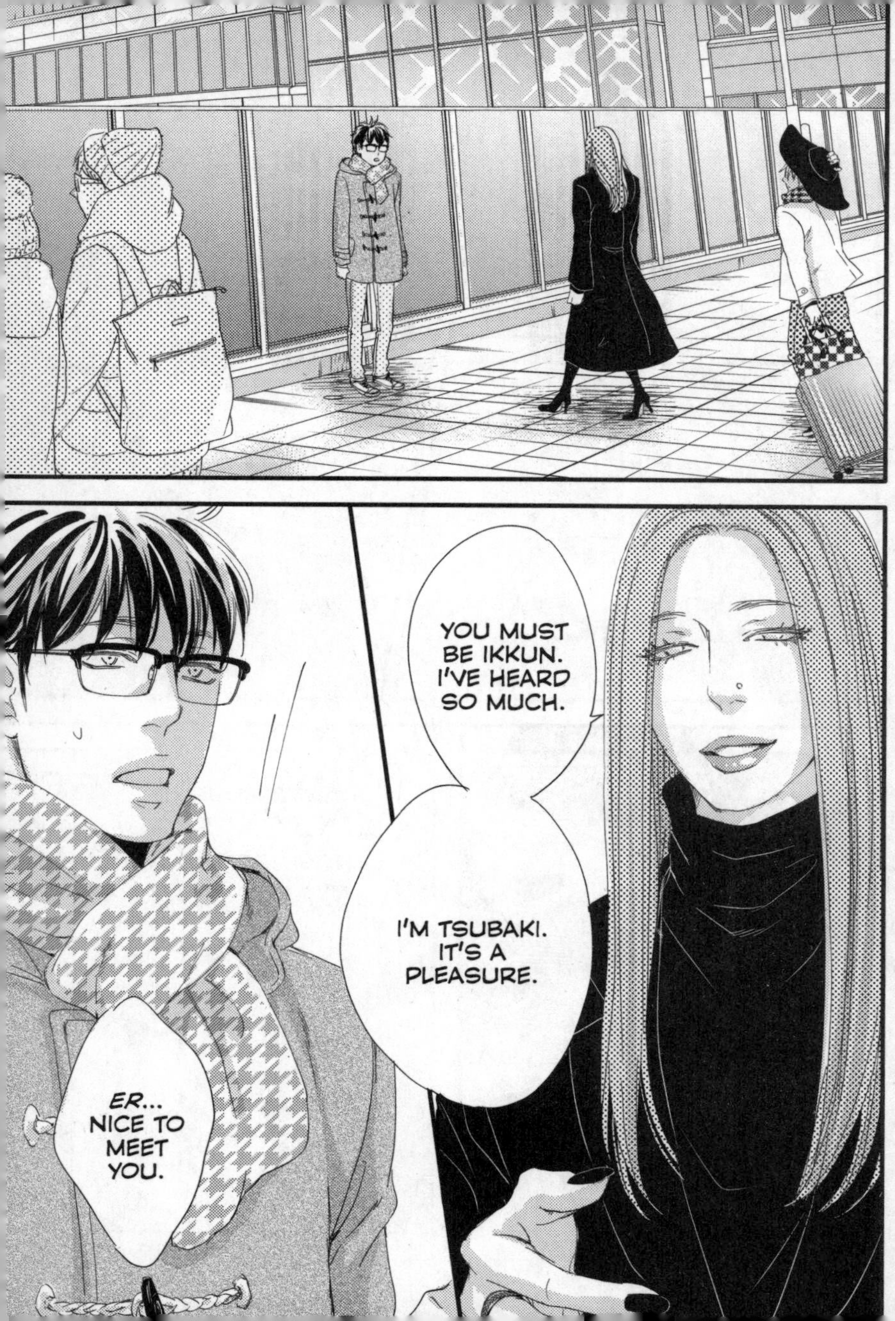
YOU MUST BE IKKUN. I'VE HEARD SO MUCH.
I'M TSUBAKI. IT'S A PLEASURE.
ER... NICE TO MEET YOU.

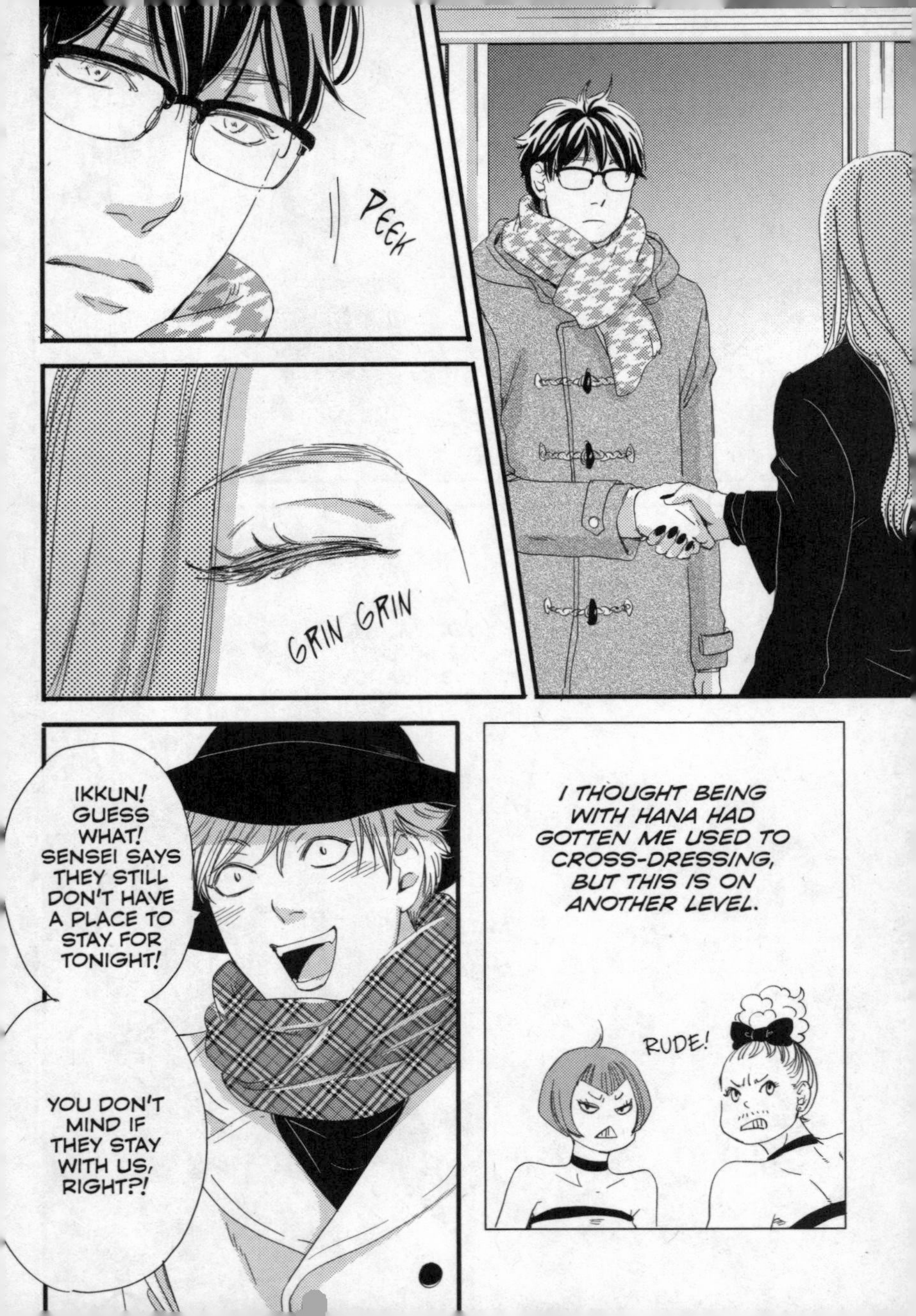
PEEK
GRIN GRIN
I THOUGHT BEING WITH HANA HAD GOTTEN ME USED TO CROSS-DRESSING, BUT THIS IS ON ANOTHER LEVEL.
RUDE!
IKKUN! GUESS WHAT! SENSEI SAYS THEY STILL DON'T HAVE A PLACE TO STAY FOR TONIGHT!
YOU DON'T MIND IF THEY STAY WITH US, RIGHT?!

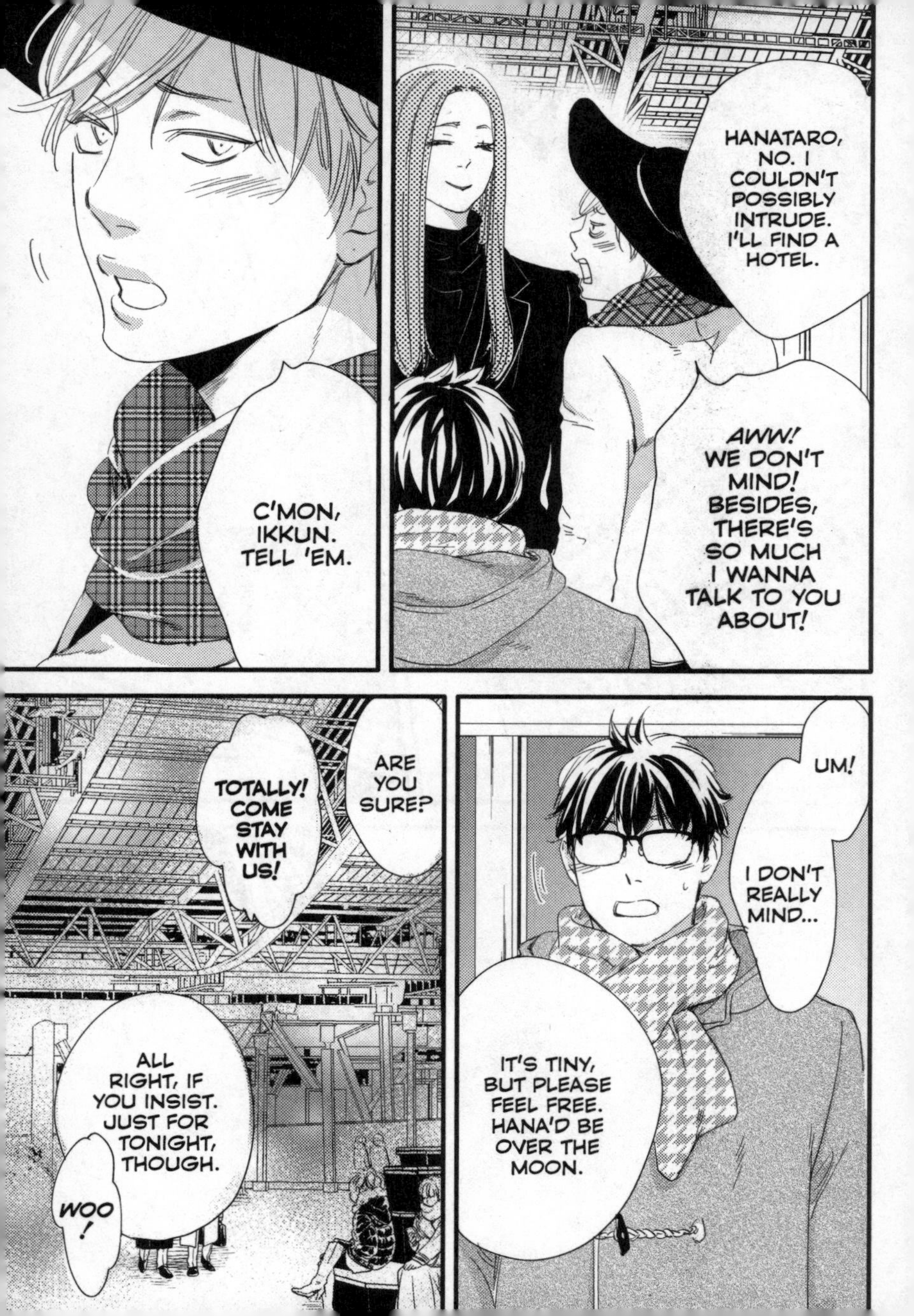
HANATARO, NO. I COULDN'T POSSIBLY INTRUDE. I'LL FIND A HOTEL.
AWW! WE DON'T MIND! BESIDES, THERE'S SO MUCH I WANNA TALK TO YOU ABOUT!
C'MON, IKKUN. TELL 'EM.
UM!
I DON'T REALLY MIND...
IT'S TINY, BUT PLEASE FEEL FREE. HANA'D BE OVER THE MOON.
ARE YOU SURE?
TOTALLY! COME STAY WITH US!
ALL RIGHT, IF YOU INSIST. JUST FOR TONIGHT, THOUGH.
WOO!

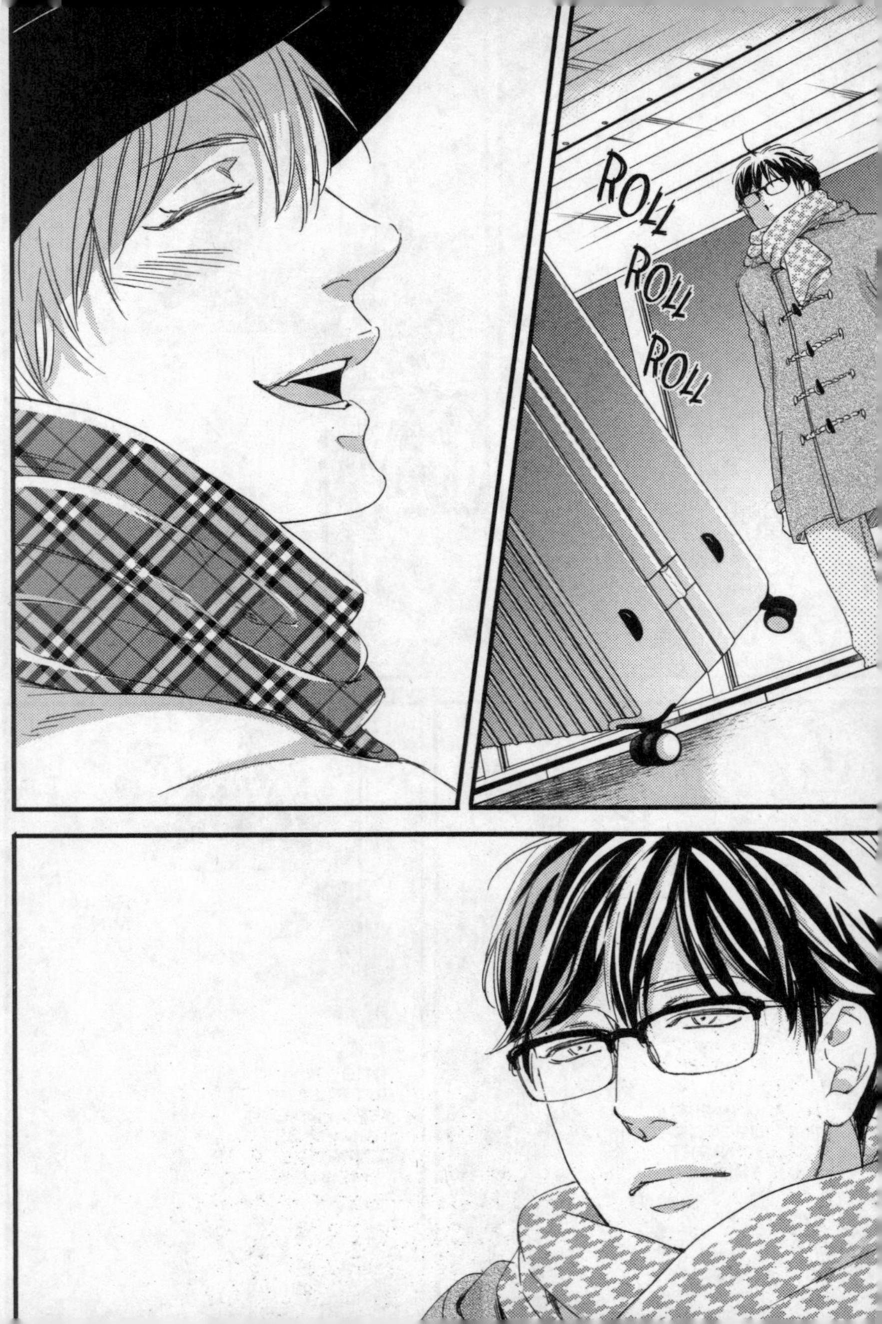
ROLL
ROLL
ROLL

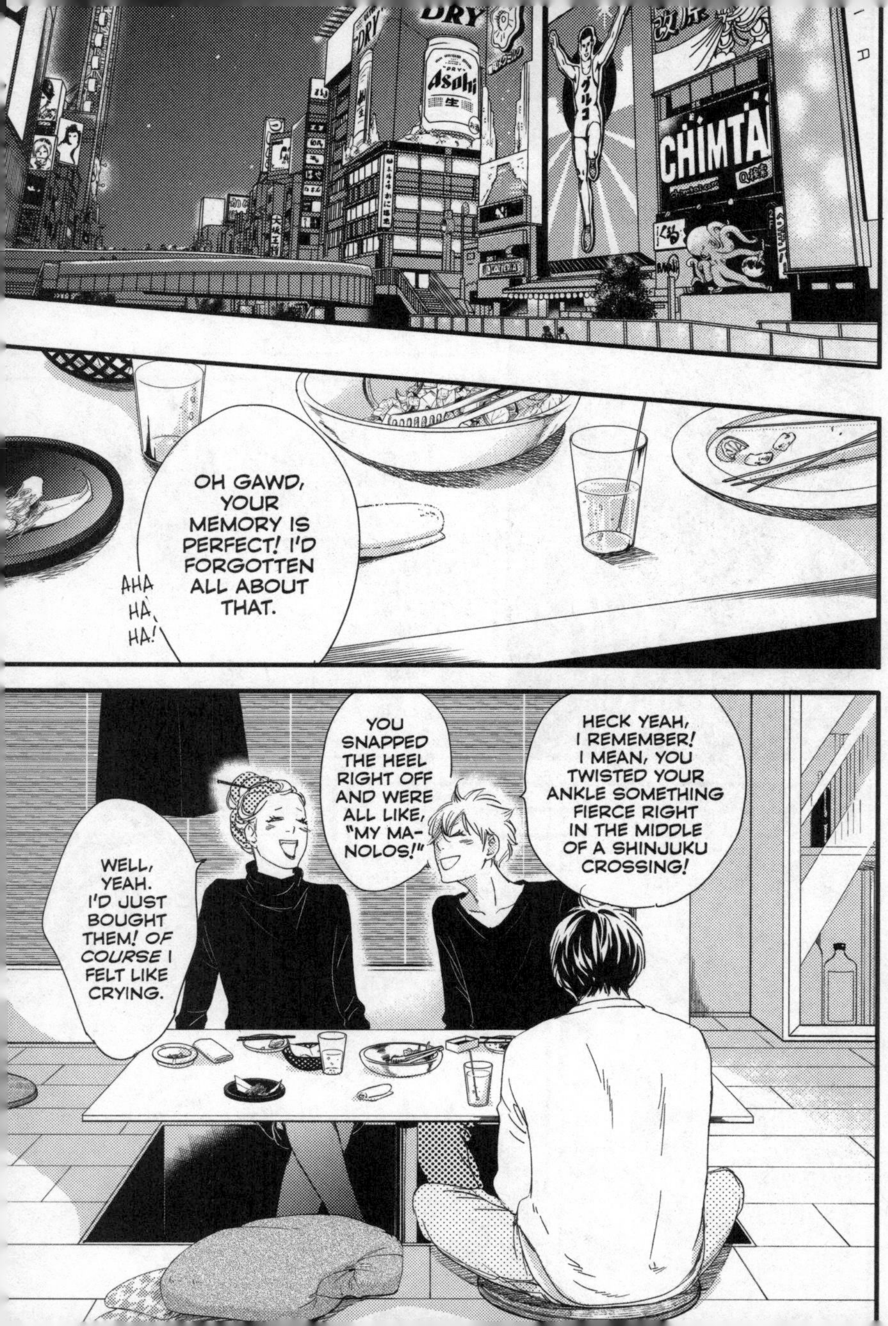
DRY
Asahi
CHIMTA
OH GAWD, YOUR MEMORY IS PERFECT! I'D FORGOTTEN ALL ABOUT THAT.
AHA HA HA!
HECK YEAH, I REMEMBER! I MEAN, YOU TWISTED YOUR ANKLE SOMETHING FIERCE RIGHT IN THE MIDDLE OF A SHINJUKU CROSSING!
YOU SNAPPED THE HEEL RIGHT OFF AND WERE ALL LIKE, "MY MA-NOLOS!"
WELL, YEAH. I'D JUST BOUGHT THEM! *OF COURSE* I FELT LIKE CRYING.

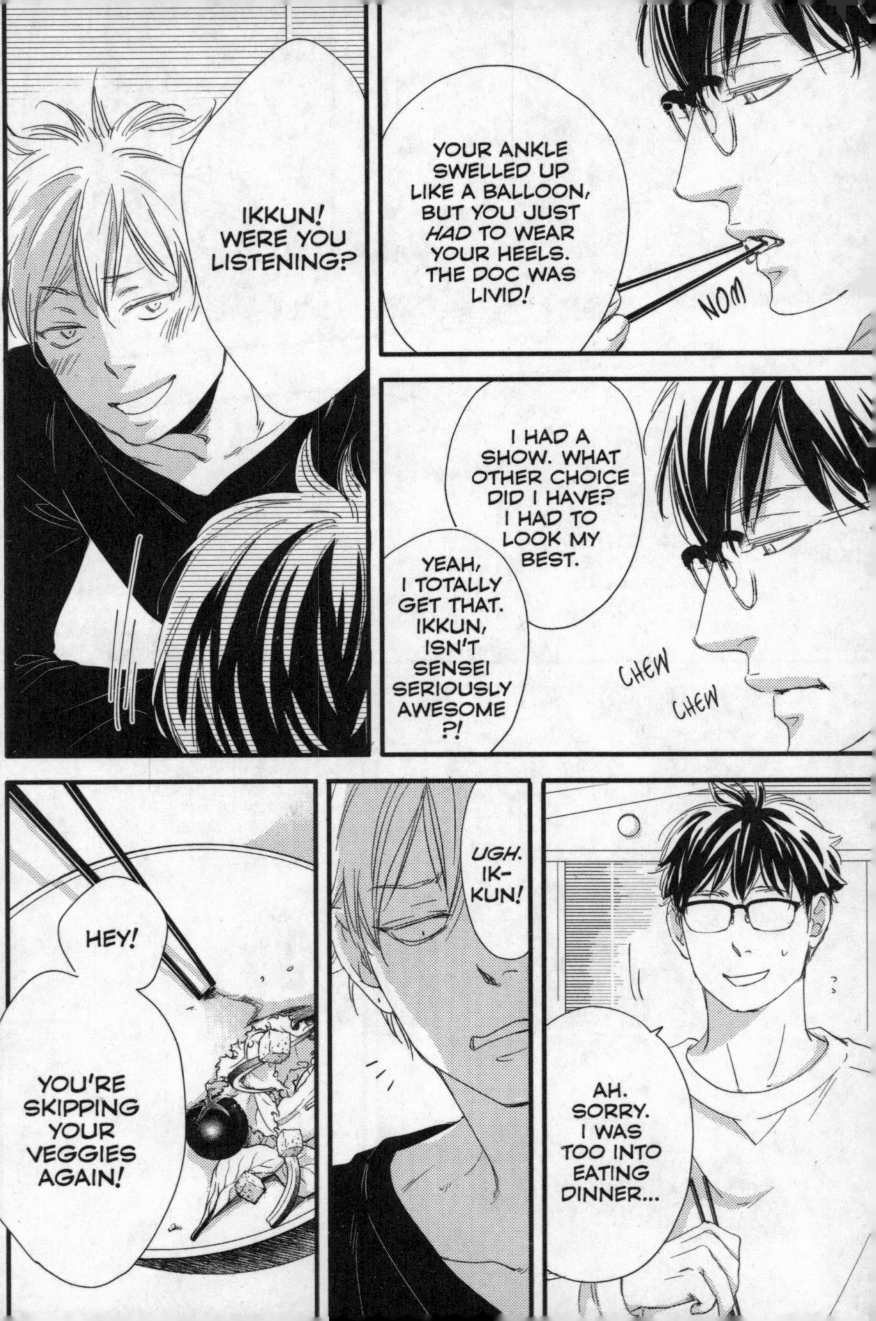
YOUR ANKLE SWELLED UP LIKE A BALLOON, BUT YOU JUST *HAD* TO WEAR YOUR HEELS. THE DOC WAS LIVID!
NOM
I HAD A SHOW. WHAT OTHER CHOICE DID I HAVE? I HAD TO LOOK MY BEST.
YEAH, I TOTALLY GET THAT. IKKUN, ISN'T SENSEI SERIOUSLY AWESOME ?!
CHEW
CHEW
IKKUN! WERE YOU LISTENING?
AH. SORRY. I WAS TOO INTO EATING DINNER...
UGH. IK-KUN!
HEY!
YOU'RE SKIPPING YOUR VEGGIES AGAIN!

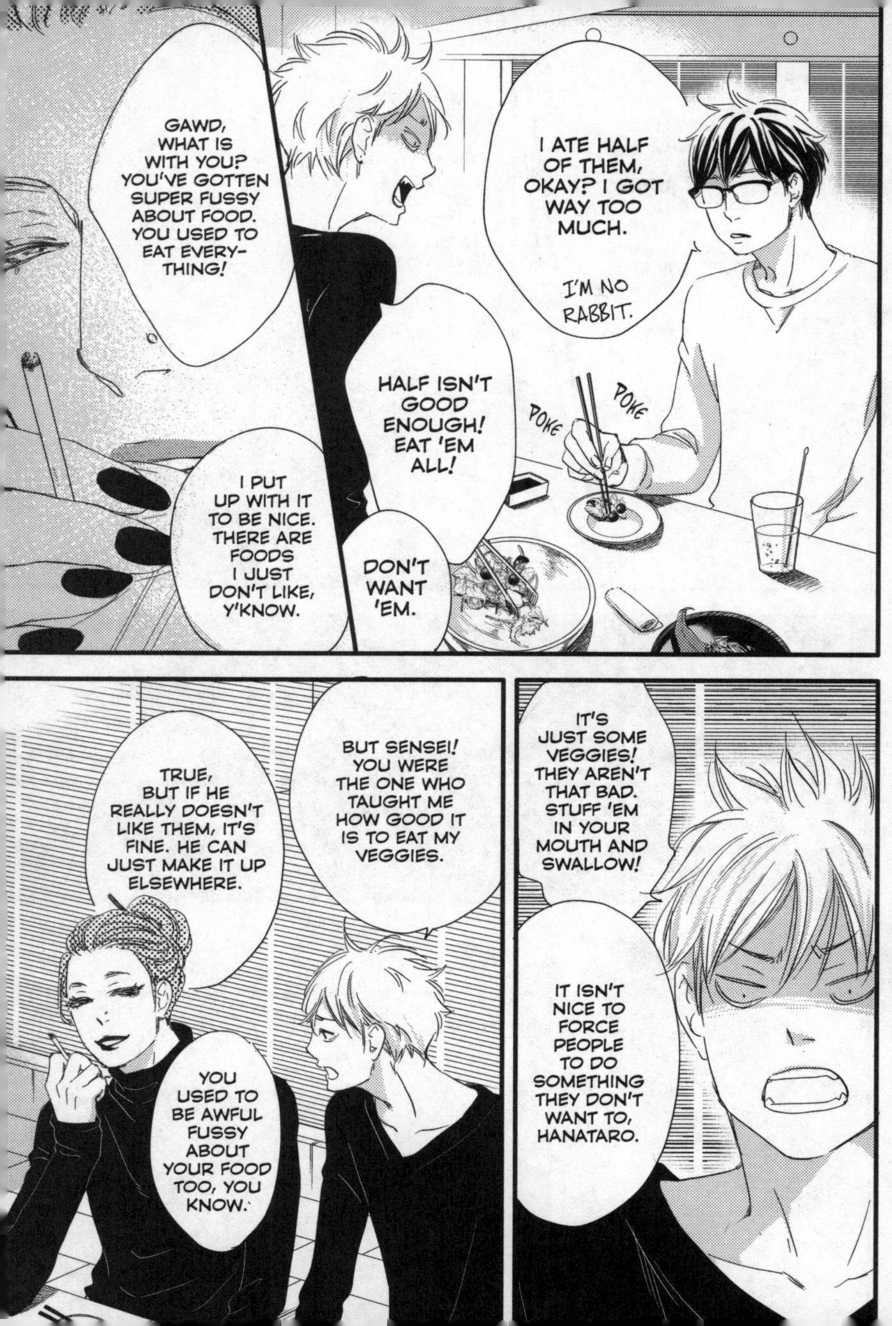
GAWD, WHAT IS WITH YOU? YOU'VE GOTTEN SUPER FUSSY ABOUT FOOD. YOU USED TO EAT EVERY-THING!
I ATE HALF OF THEM, OKAY? I GOT WAY TOO MUCH.
I'M NO RABBIT.
POKE
POKE
HALF ISN'T GOOD ENOUGH! EAT 'EM ALL!
DON'T WANT 'EM.
I PUT UP WITH IT TO BE NICE. THERE ARE FOODS I JUST DON'T LIKE, Y'KNOW.
IT'S JUST SOME VEGGIES! THEY AREN'T THAT BAD. STUFF 'EM IN YOUR MOUTH AND SWALLOW!
IT ISN'T NICE TO FORCE PEOPLE TO DO SOMETHING THEY DON'T WANT TO, HANATARO.
BUT SENSEI! YOU WERE THE ONE WHO TAUGHT ME HOW GOOD IT IS TO EAT MY VEGGIES.
TRUE, BUT IF HE REALLY DOESN'T LIKE THEM, IT'S FINE. HE CAN JUST MAKE IT UP ELSEWHERE.
YOU USED TO BE AWFUL FUSSY ABOUT YOUR FOOD TOO, YOU KNOW.

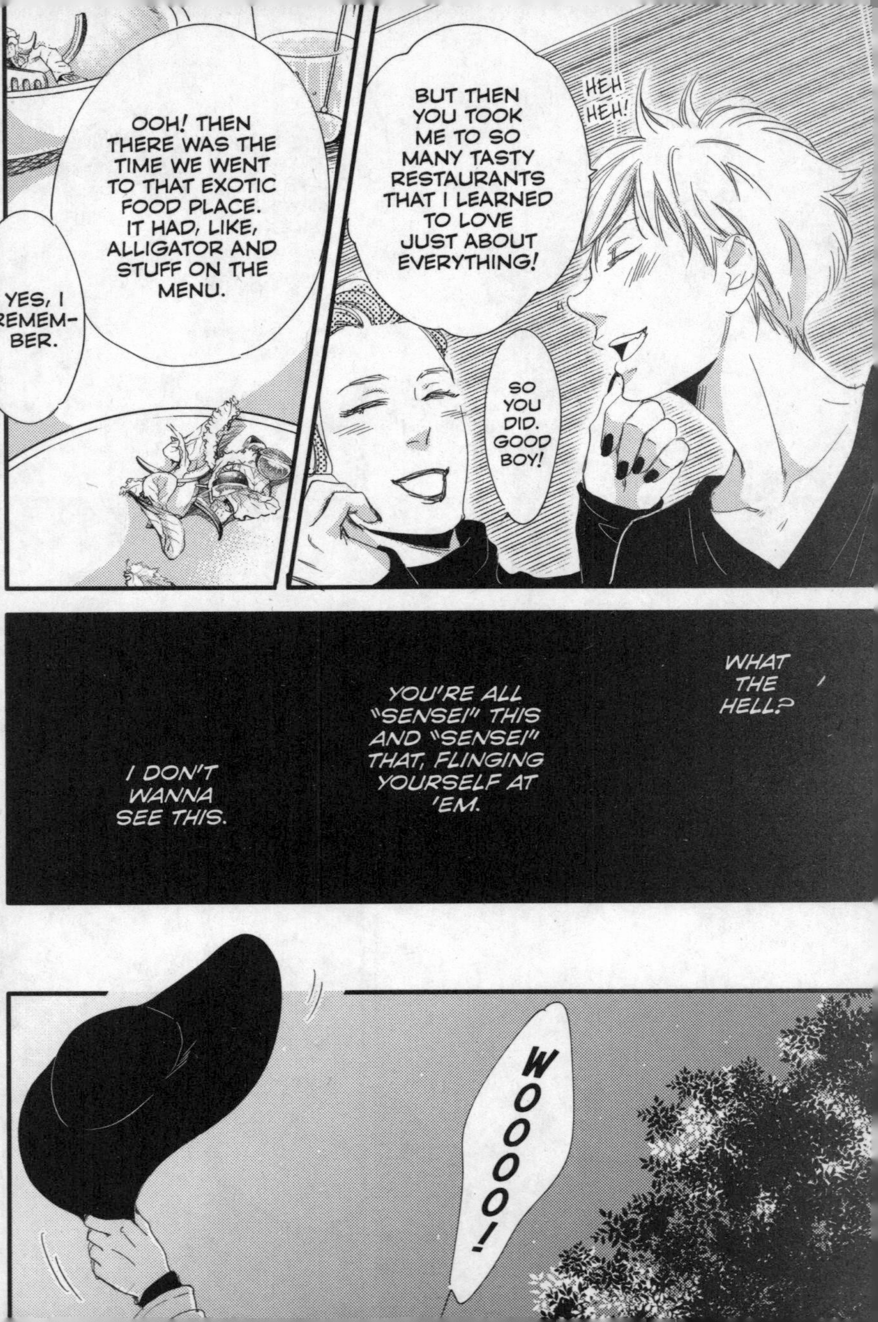
HEH HEH!
BUT THEN YOU TOOK ME TO SO MANY TASTY RESTAURANTS THAT I LEARNED TO LOVE JUST ABOUT EVERYTHING!
SO YOU DID. GOOD BOY!
OOH! THEN THERE WAS THE TIME WE WENT TO THAT EXOTIC FOOD PLACE. IT HAD, LIKE, ALLIGATOR AND STUFF ON THE MENU.
YES, I REMEMBER.
WHAT THE HELL?
YOU'RE ALL "SENSEI" THIS AND "SENSEI" THAT, FLINGING YOURSELF AT 'EM.
I DON'T WANNA SEE THIS.
WOOOOO!

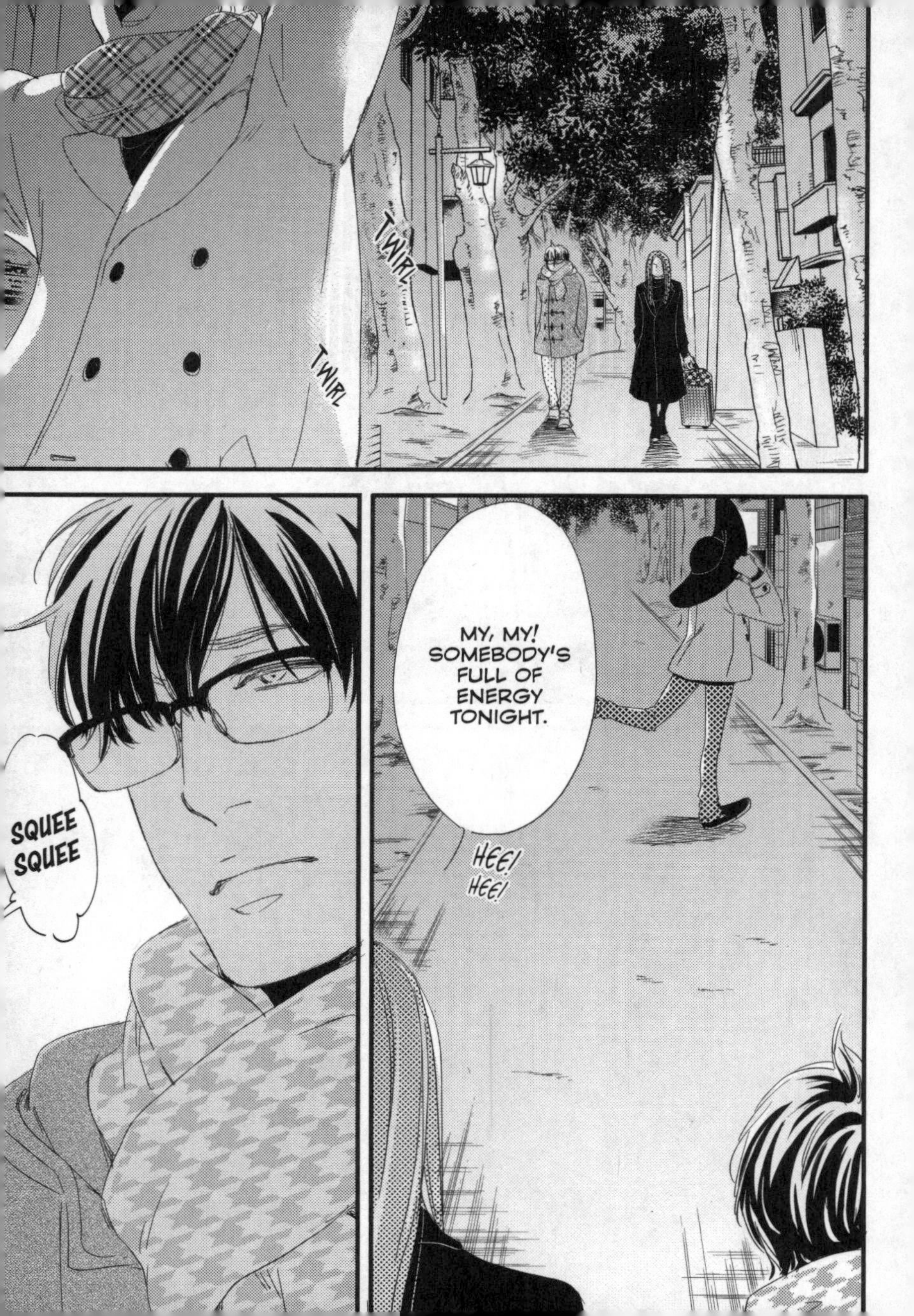
TWIRL
TWIRL
MY, MY! SOMEBODY'S FULL OF ENERGY TONIGHT.
HEE! HEE!
SQUEE SQUEE

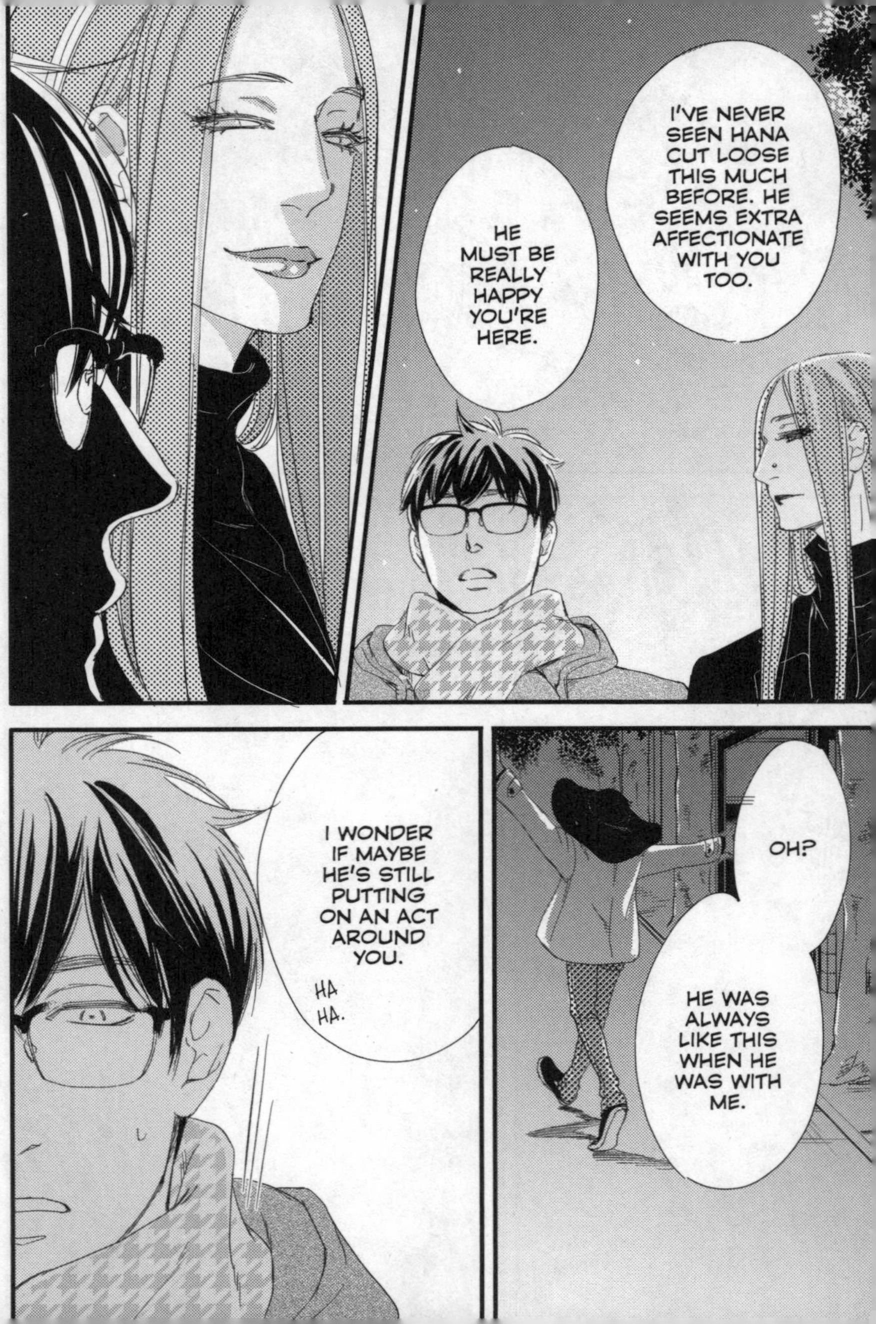
I'VE NEVER SEEN HANA CUT LOOSE THIS MUCH BEFORE. HE SEEMS EXTRA AFFECTIONATE WITH YOU TOO.
HE MUST BE REALLY HAPPY YOU'RE HERE.
OH?
HE WAS ALWAYS LIKE THIS WHEN HE WAS WITH ME.
I WONDER IF MAYBE HE'S STILL PUTTING ON AN ACT AROUND YOU.
HA HA.

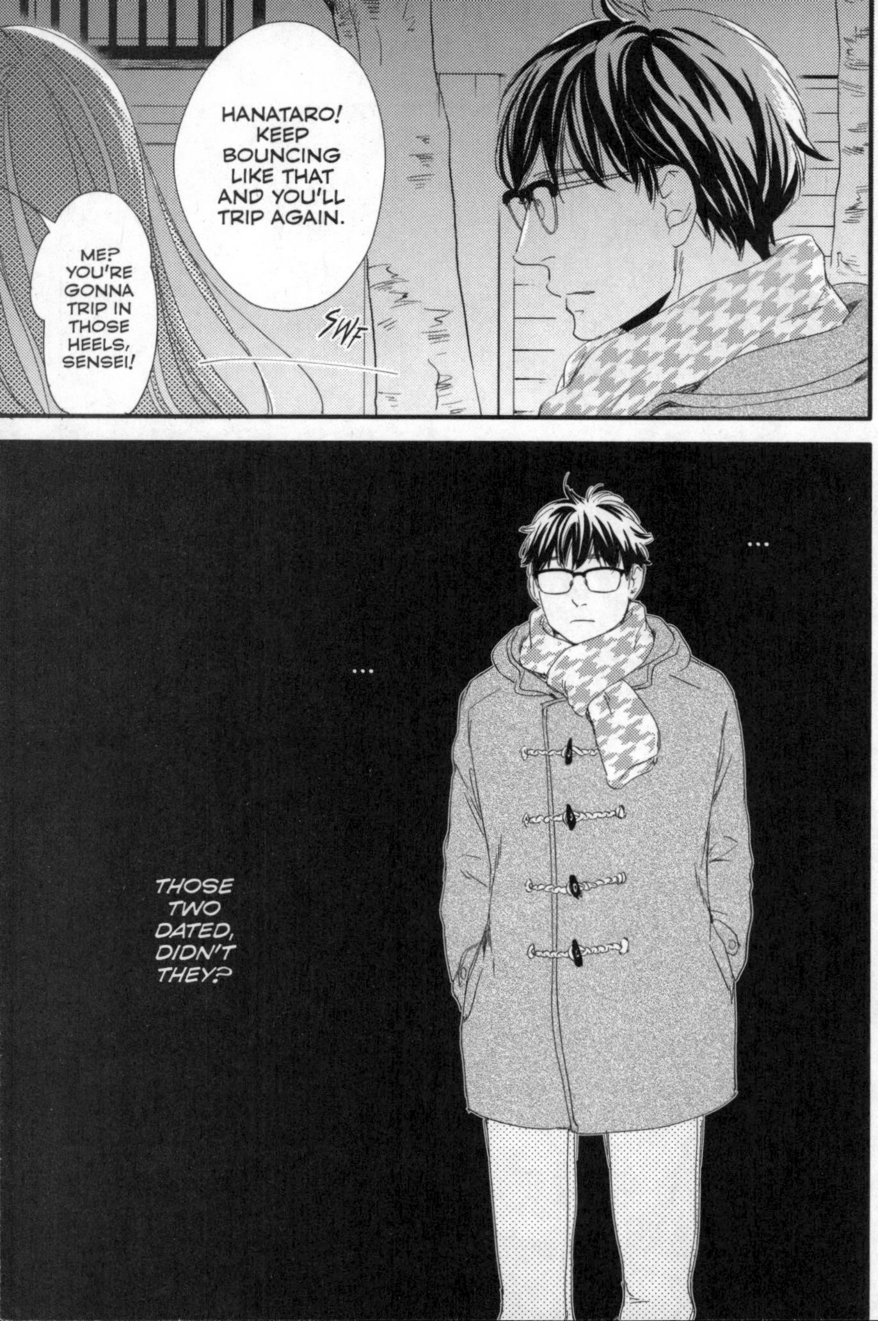
HANATARO! KEEP BOUNCING LIKE THAT AND YOU'LL TRIP AGAIN.
SWF
ME? YOU'RE GONNA TRIP IN THOSE HEELS, SENSEI!
...
...
THOSE TWO DATED, DIDN'T THEY?

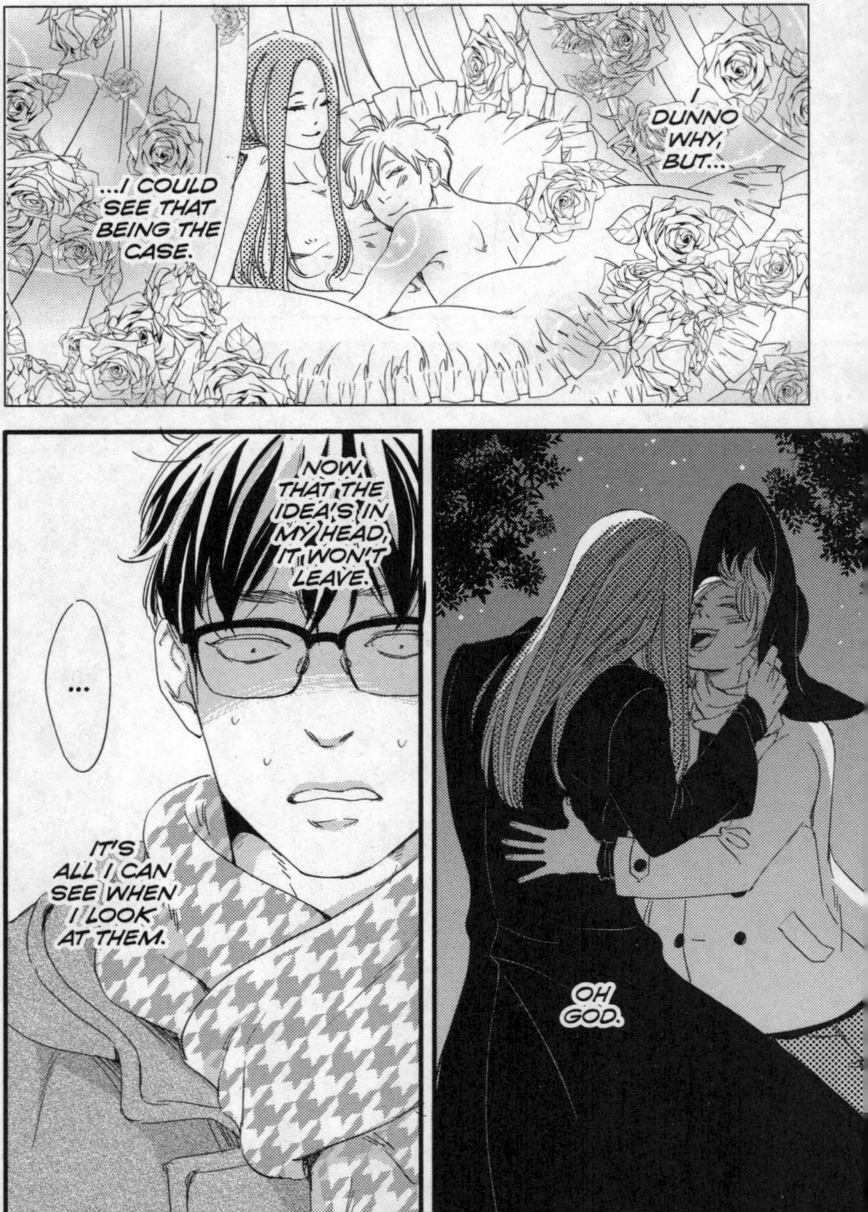
I DUNNO WHY, BUT...
...I COULD SEE THAT BEING THE CASE.
OH GOD.
NOW THAT THE IDEA'S IN MY HEAD, IT WON'T LEAVE.
...
IT'S ALL I CAN SEE WHEN I LOOK AT THEM.

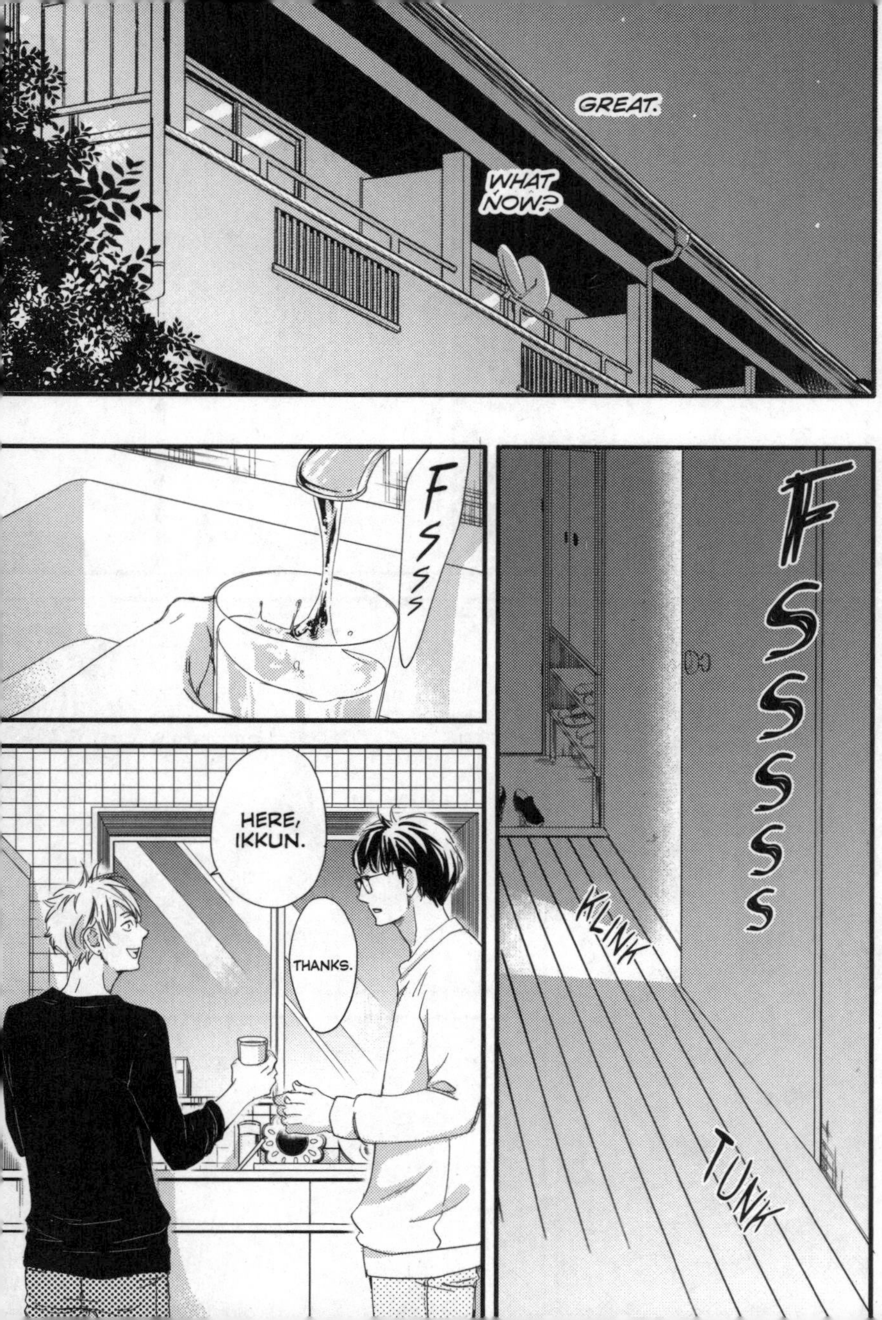
GREAT.
WHAT NOW?
FSSSSSS
KLINK
TUNK
FSSS
HERE, IKKUN.
THANKS.

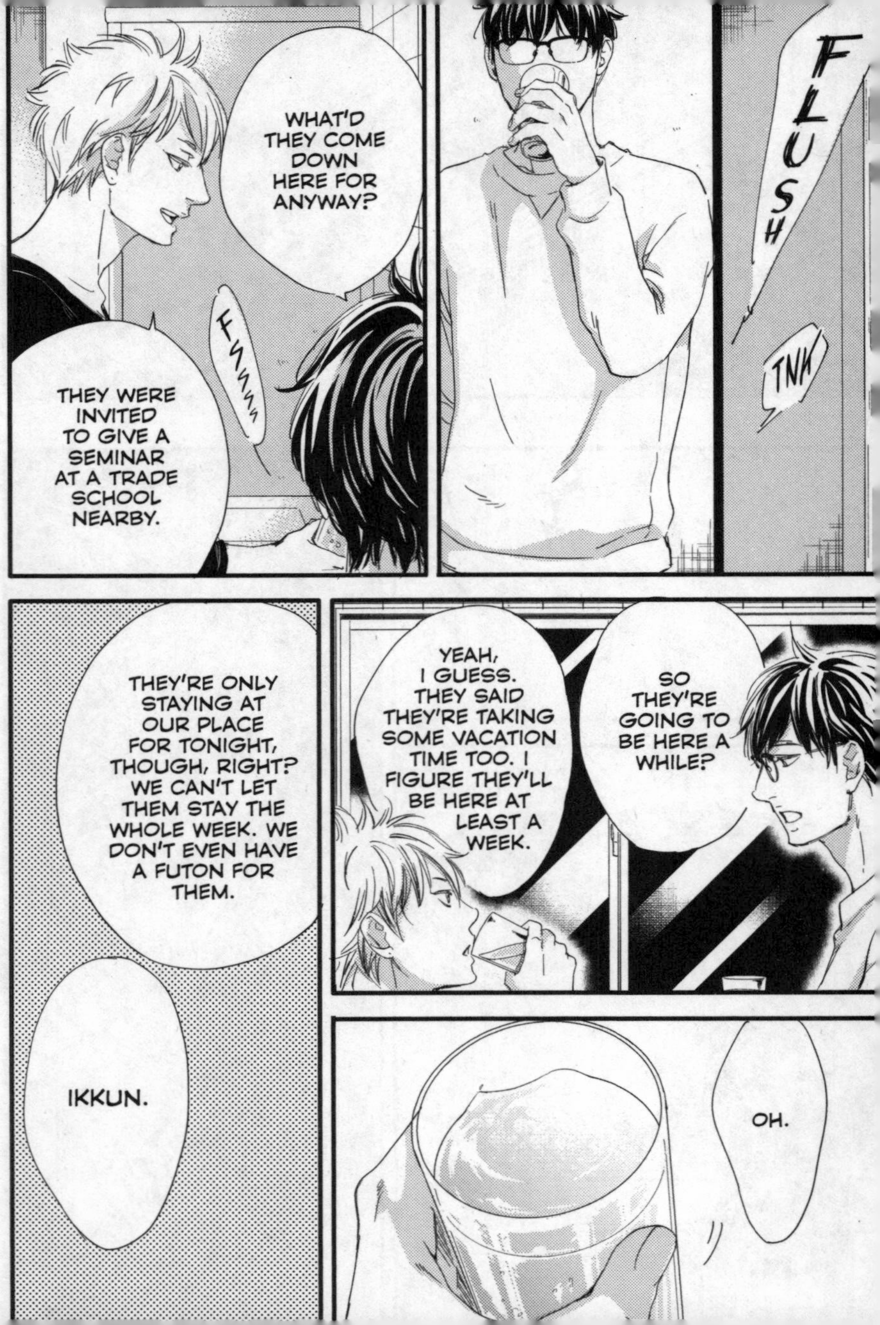
FLUSH
TNK
WHAT'D THEY COME DOWN HERE FOR ANYWAY?
FSSSS
THEY WERE INVITED TO GIVE A SEMINAR AT A TRADE SCHOOL NEARBY.
SO THEY'RE GOING TO BE HERE A WHILE?
YEAH, I GUESS. THEY SAID THEY'RE TAKING SOME VACATION TIME TOO. I FIGURE THEY'LL BE HERE AT LEAST A WEEK.
OH.
THEY'RE ONLY STAYING AT OUR PLACE FOR TONIGHT, THOUGH, RIGHT? WE CAN'T LET THEM STAY THE WHOLE WEEK. WE DON'T EVEN HAVE A FUTON FOR THEM.
IKKUN.

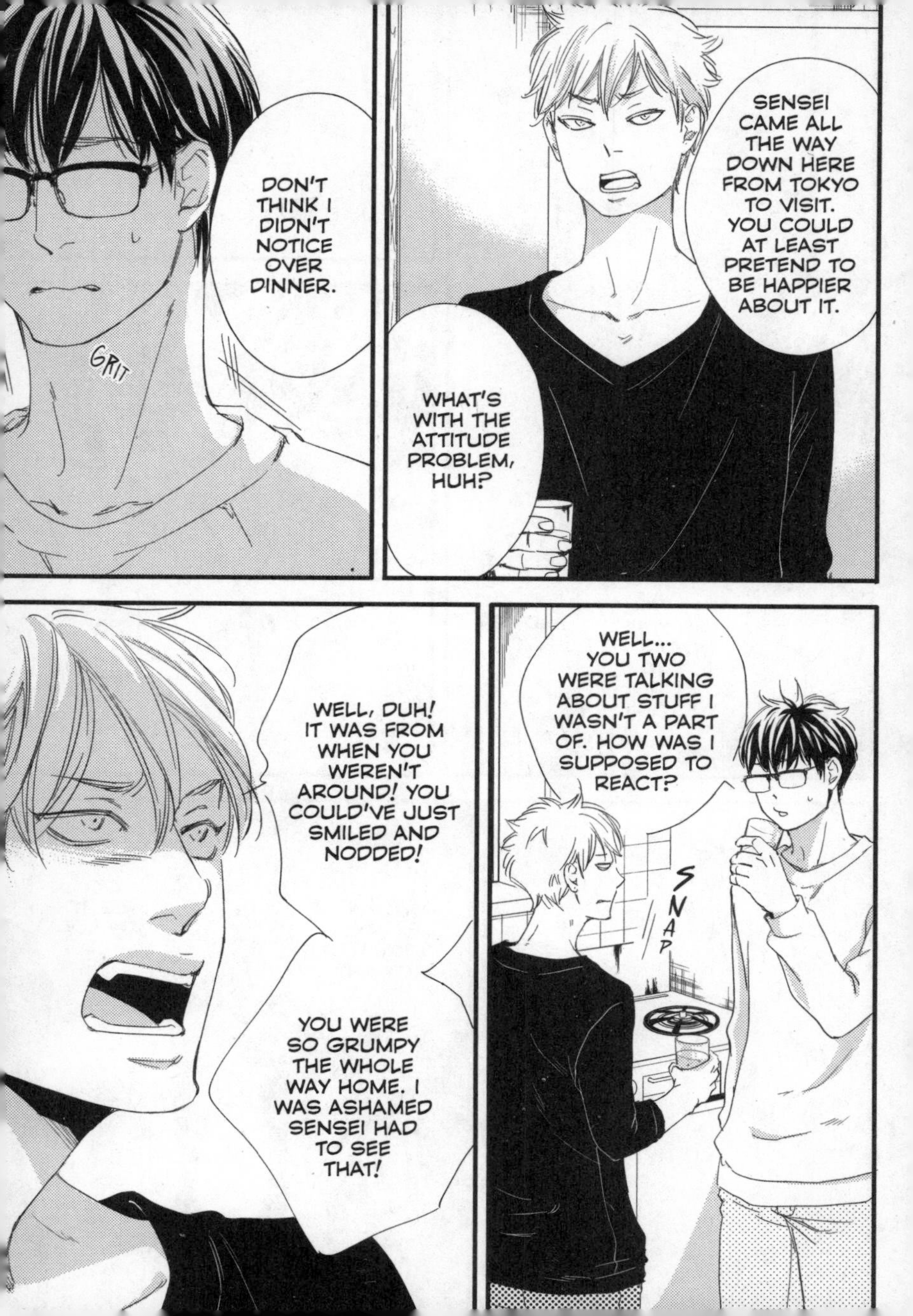
SENSEI CAME ALL THE WAY DOWN HERE FROM TOKYO TO VISIT. YOU COULD AT LEAST PRETEND TO BE HAPPIER ABOUT IT.
WHAT'S WITH THE ATTITUDE PROBLEM, HUH?
DON'T THINK I DIDN'T NOTICE OVER DINNER.
GRIT
WELL... YOU TWO WERE TALKING ABOUT STUFF I WASN'T A PART OF. HOW WAS I SUPPOSED TO REACT?
SNAP
WELL, DUH! IT WAS FROM WHEN YOU WEREN'T AROUND! YOU COULD'VE JUST SMILED AND NODDED!
YOU WERE SO GRUMPY THE WHOLE WAY HOME. I WAS ASHAMED SENSEI HAD TO SEE THAT!

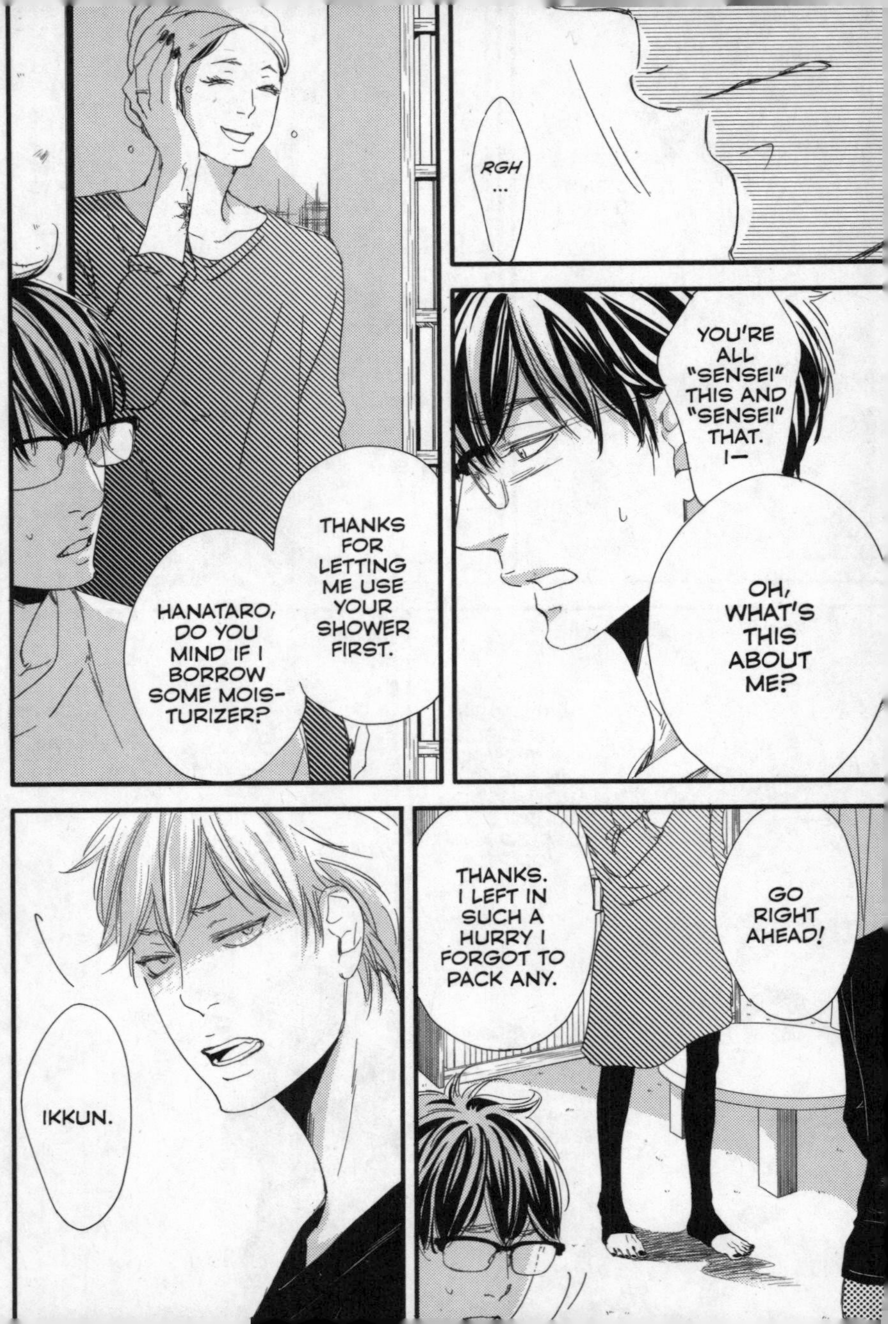
RGH ...
YOU'RE ALL "SENSEI" THIS AND "SENSEI" THAT. I—
OH, WHAT'S THIS ABOUT ME?
THANKS FOR LETTING ME USE YOUR SHOWER FIRST.
HANATARO, DO YOU MIND IF I BORROW SOME MOIS-TURIZER?
GO RIGHT AHEAD!
THANKS. I LEFT IN SUCH A HURRY I FORGOT TO PACK ANY.
IKKUN.

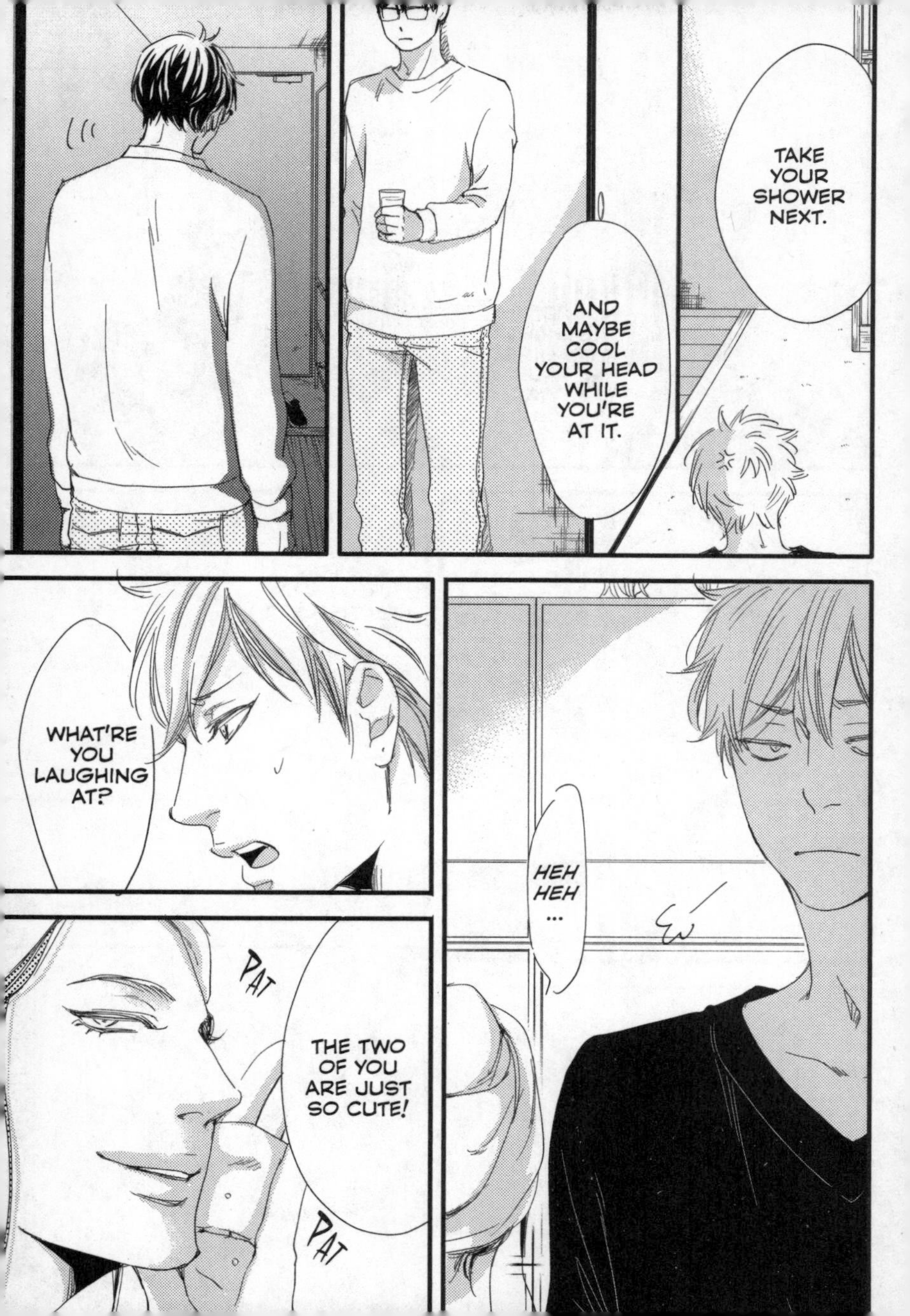
TAKE YOUR SHOWER NEXT.
AND MAYBE COOL YOUR HEAD WHILE YOU'RE AT IT.
HEH HEH ...
WHAT'RE YOU LAUGHING AT?
PAT
THE TWO OF YOU ARE JUST SO CUTE!
PAT

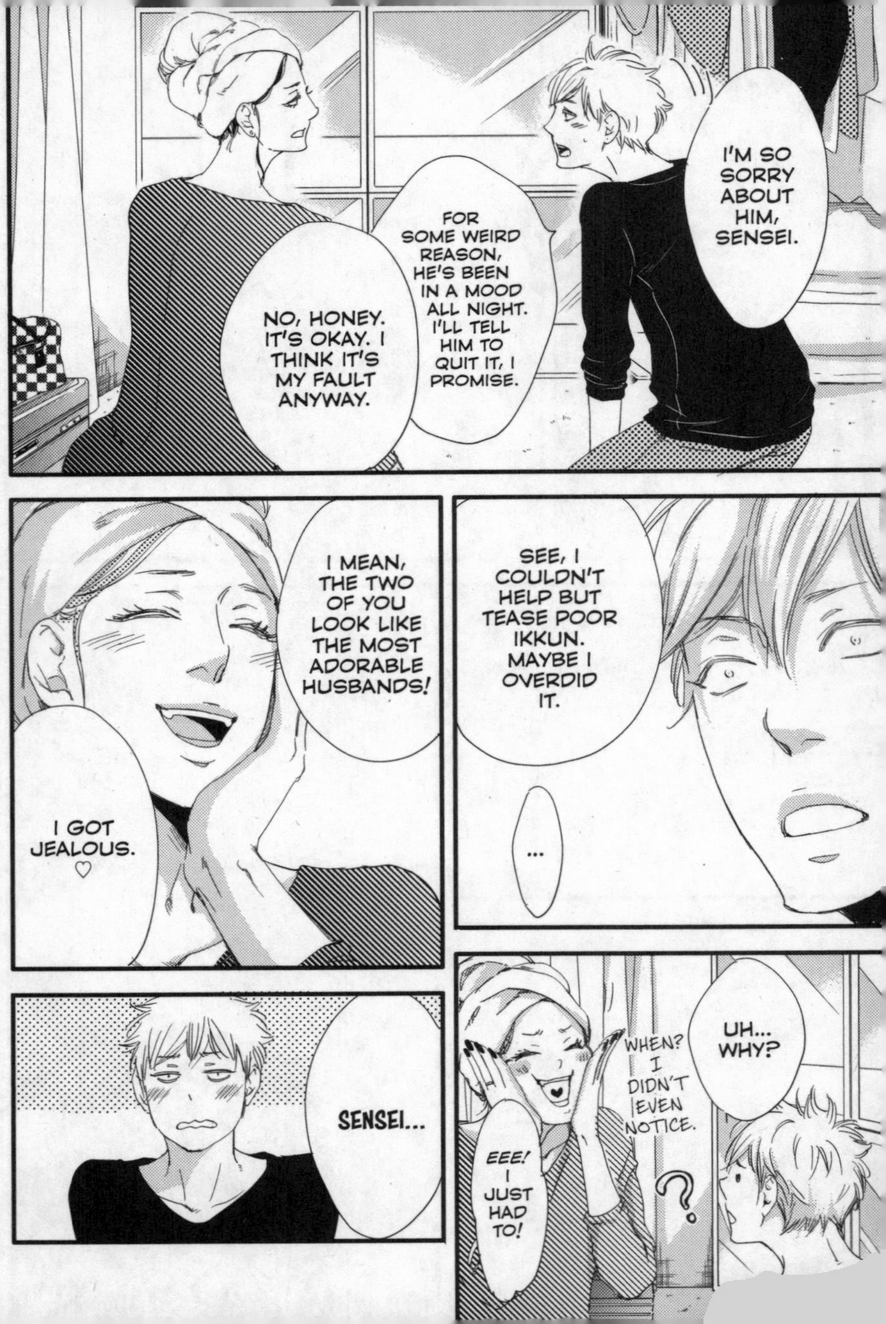
I'M SO SORRY ABOUT HIM, SENSEI.
FOR SOME WEIRD REASON, HE'S BEEN IN A MOOD ALL NIGHT. I'LL TELL HIM TO QUIT IT, I PROMISE.
NO, HONEY. IT'S OKAY. I THINK IT'S MY FAULT ANYWAY.
SEE, I COULDN'T HELP BUT TEASE POOR IKKUN. MAYBE I OVERDID IT.
...
I MEAN, THE TWO OF YOU LOOK LIKE THE MOST ADORABLE HUSBANDS!
I GOT JEALOUS. ♡
UH... WHY?
WHEN? I DIDN'T EVEN NOTICE.
EEE! I JUST HAD TO!
?
SENSEI...

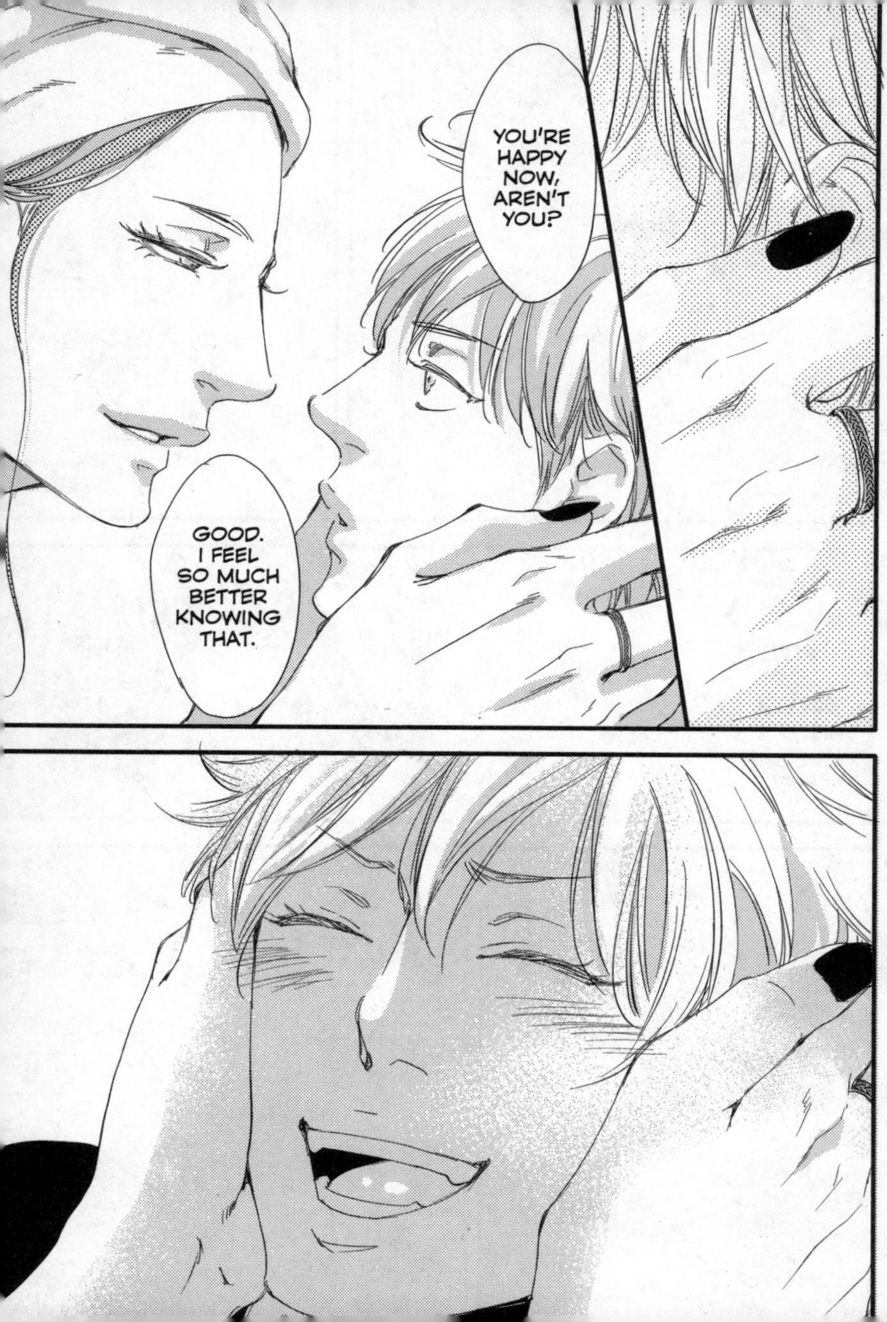
YOU'RE HAPPY NOW, AREN'T YOU?
GOOD. I FEEL SO MUCH BETTER KNOWING THAT.

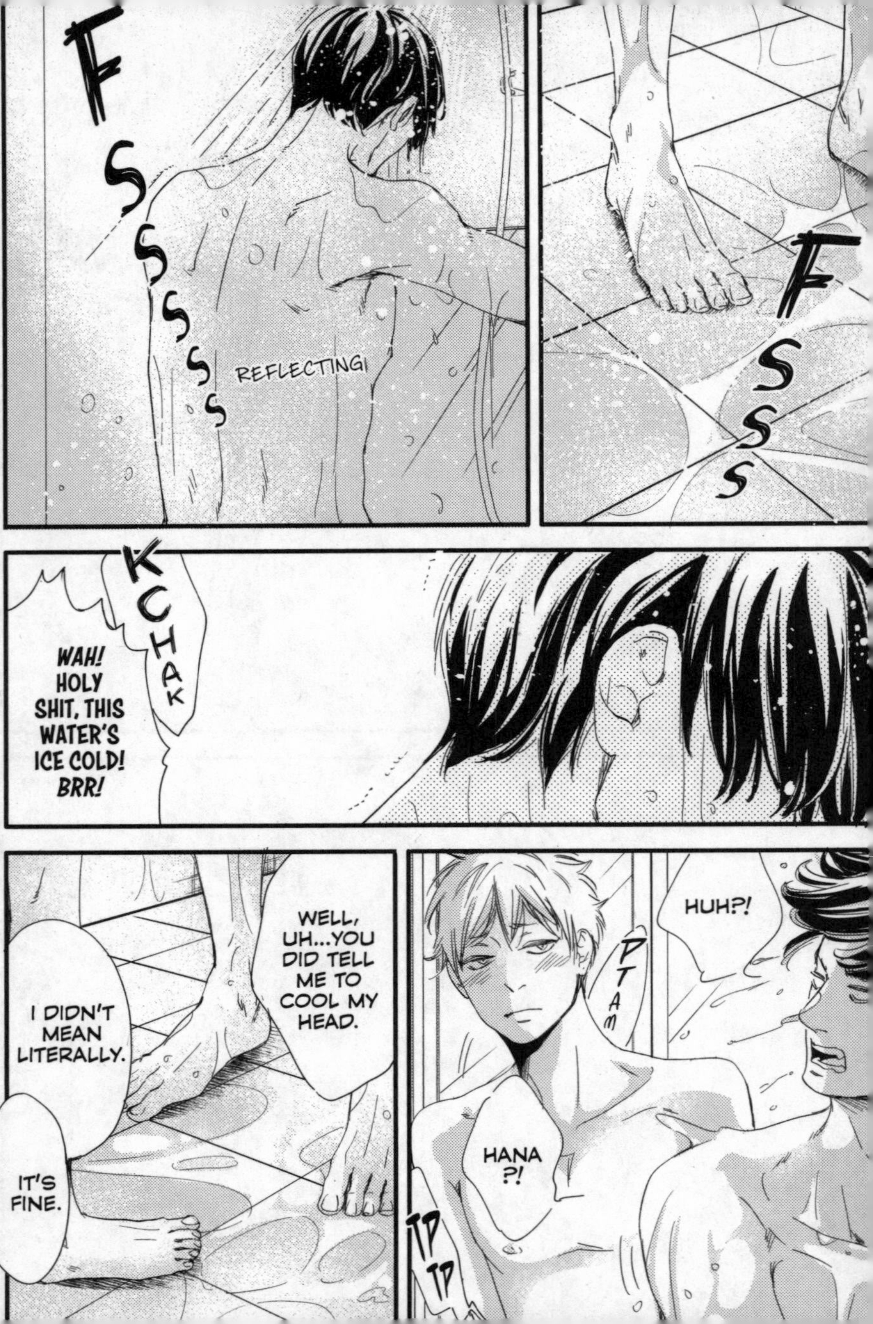
FSSS
FSSSSSS
REFLECTING!
KCHAK
WAH! HOLY SHIT, THIS WATER'S ICE COLD! BRR!
HUH?!
PTAM
HANA?!
TP TP
WELL, UH...YOU DID TELL ME TO COOL MY HEAD.
I DIDN'T MEAN LITERALLY.
IT'S FINE.

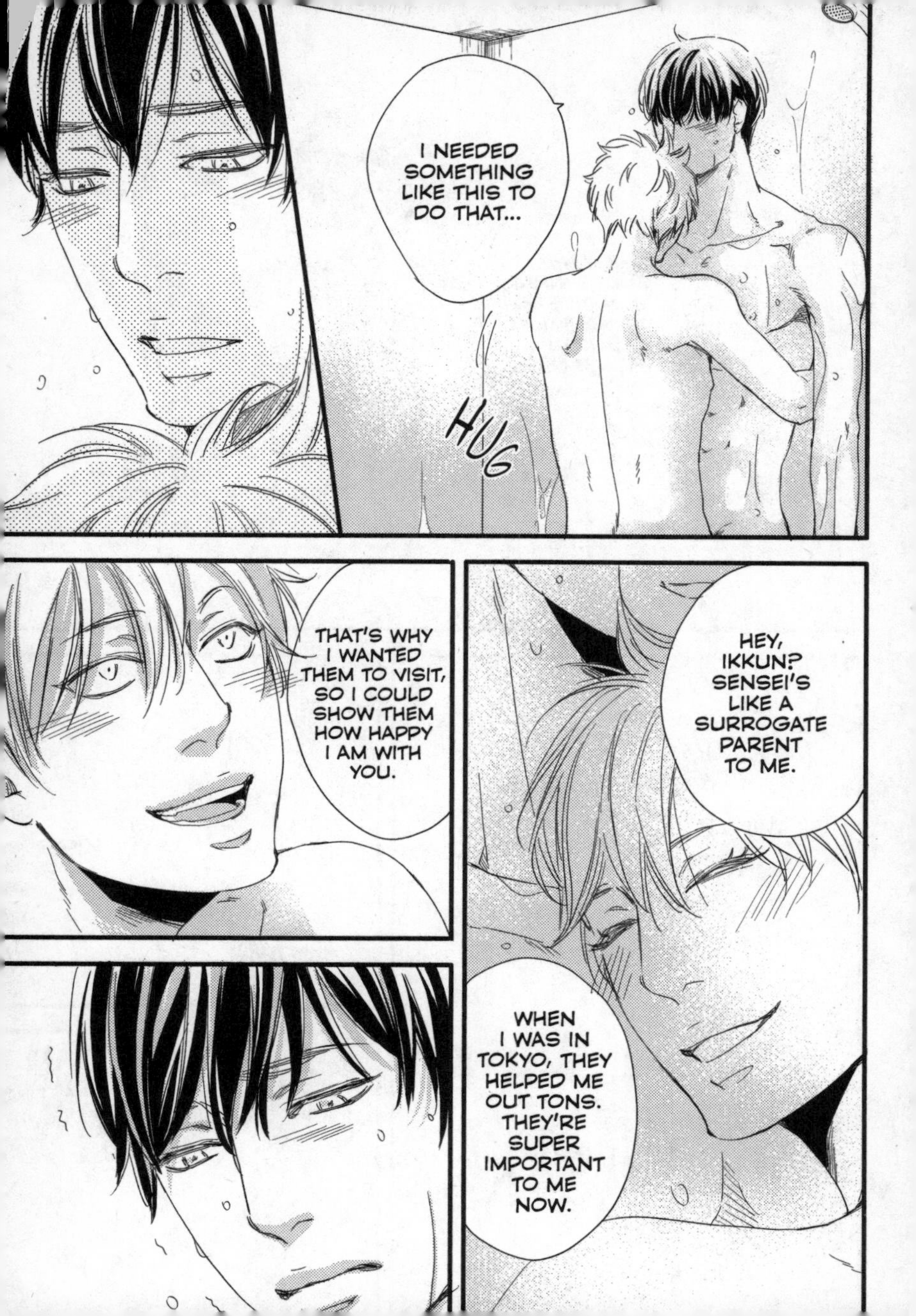
I NEEDED SOMETHING LIKE THIS TO DO THAT...
HUG
HEY, IKKUN? SENSEI'S LIKE A SURROGATE PARENT TO ME.
WHEN I WAS IN TOKYO, THEY HELPED ME OUT TONS. THEY'RE SUPER IMPORTANT TO ME NOW.
THAT'S WHY I WANTED THEM TO VISIT, SO I COULD SHOW THEM HOW HAPPY I AM WITH YOU.

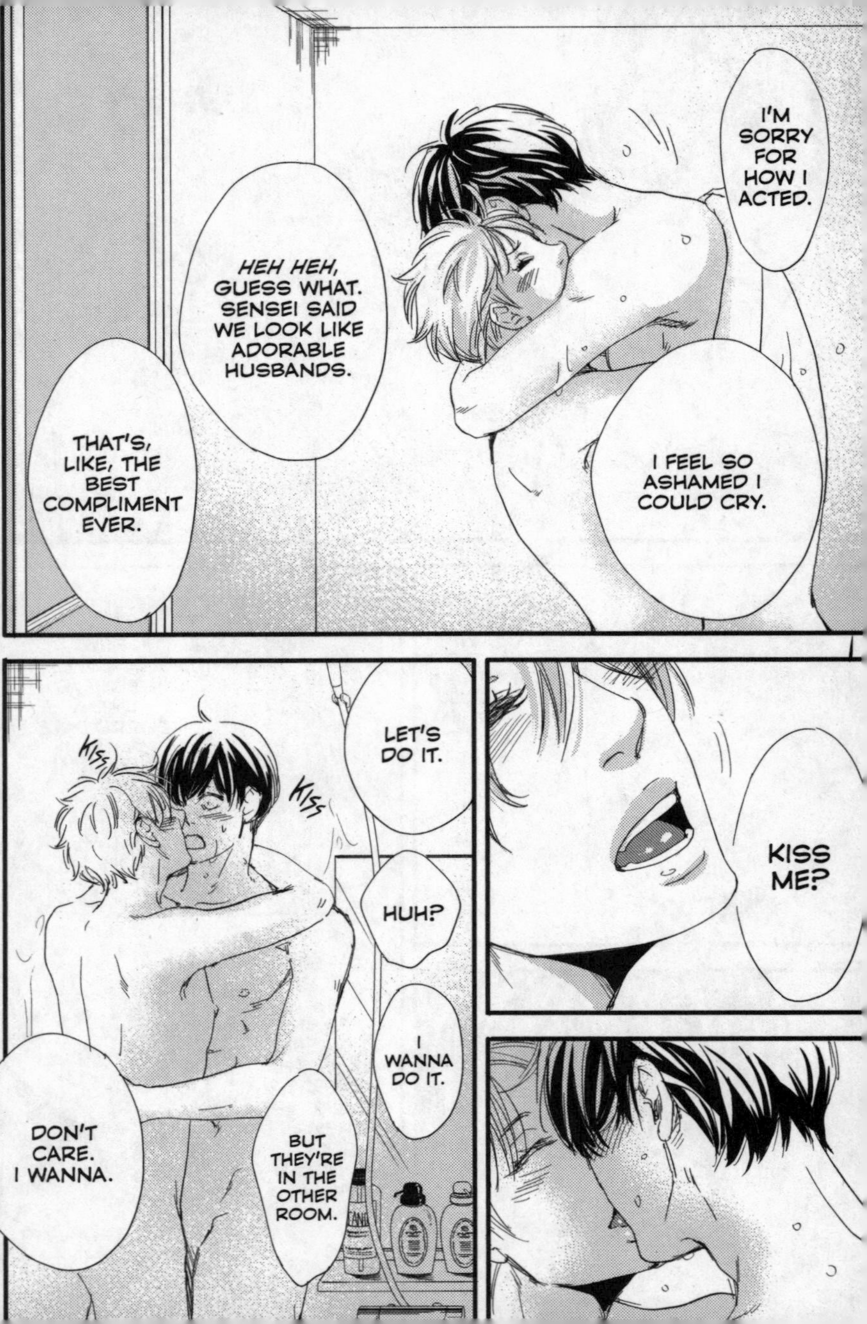
I'M SORRY FOR HOW I ACTED.
I FEEL SO ASHAMED I COULD CRY.
HEH HEH, GUESS WHAT. SENSEI SAID WE LOOK LIKE ADORABLE HUSBANDS.
THAT'S, LIKE, THE BEST COMPLIMENT EVER.
KISS ME?
LET'S DO IT.
KISS
KISS
HUH?
I WANNA DO IT.
BUT THEY'RE IN THE OTHER ROOM.
DON'T CARE. I WANNA.

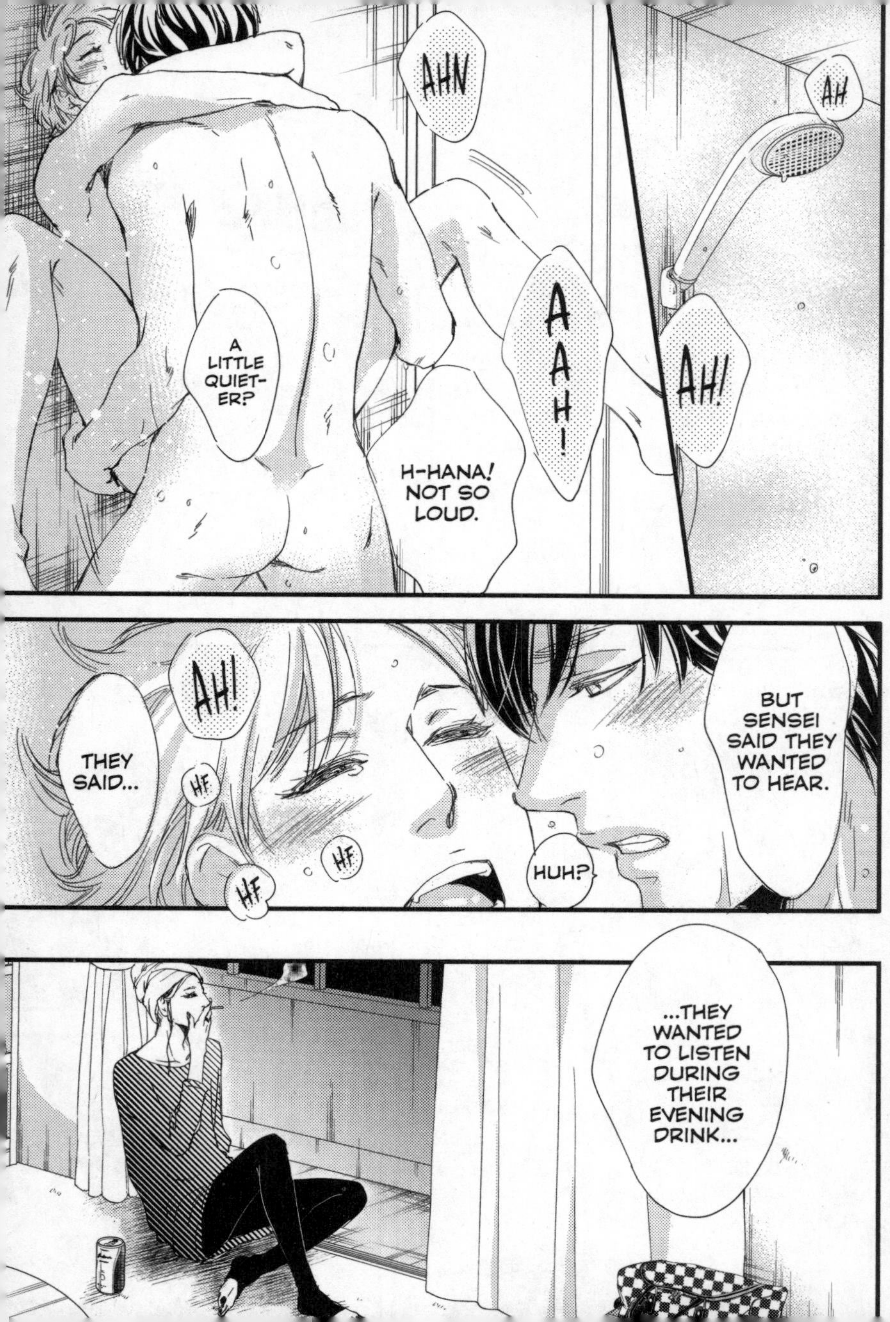

AH
AHN
AAH!
AH!
H-HANA! NOT SO LOUD.
A LITTLE QUIET-ER?
BUT SENSEI SAID THEY WANTED TO HEAR.
HUH?
AH!
THEY SAID...
HF
HF
HF
...THEY WANTED TO LISTEN DURING THEIR EVENING DRINK...

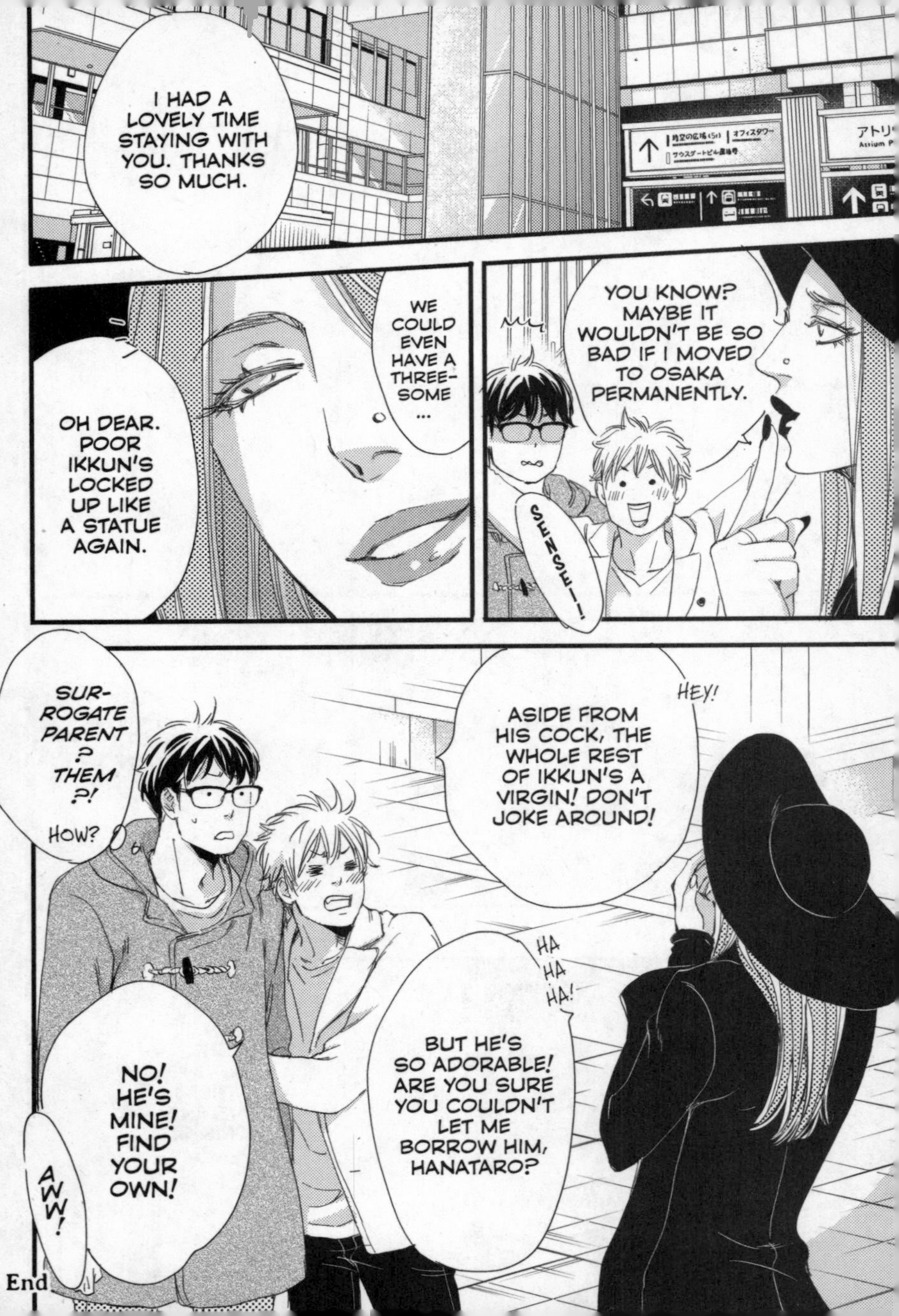
I HAD A LOVELY TIME STAYING WITH YOU. THANKS SO MUCH.
YOU KNOW? MAYBE IT WOULDN'T BE SO BAD IF I MOVED TO OSAKA PERMANENTLY.
SENSEI!!
WE COULD EVEN HAVE A THREE-SOME ...
OH DEAR. POOR IKKUN'S LOCKED UP LIKE A STATUE AGAIN.
HEY!
ASIDE FROM HIS COCK, THE WHOLE REST OF IKKUN'S A VIRGIN! DON'T JOKE AROUND!
SUR-ROGATE PARENT? THEM?!
HOW?
HA HA HA!
BUT HE'S SO ADORABLE! ARE YOU SURE YOU COULDN'T LET ME BORROW HIM, HANATARO?
NO! HE'S MINE! FIND YOUR OWN!
AWW!
End

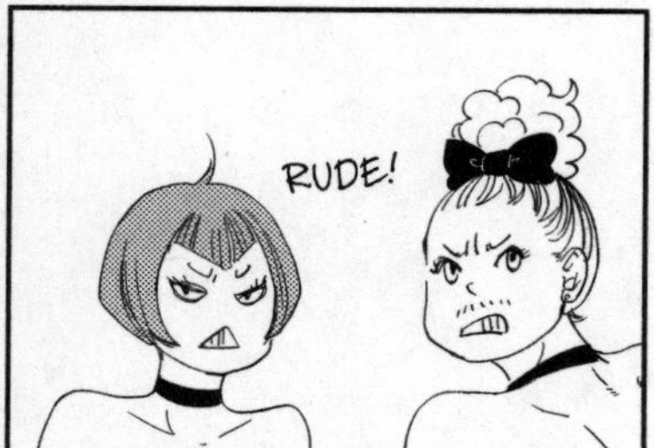
RUDE!

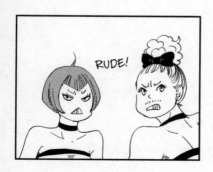

Chapter 1

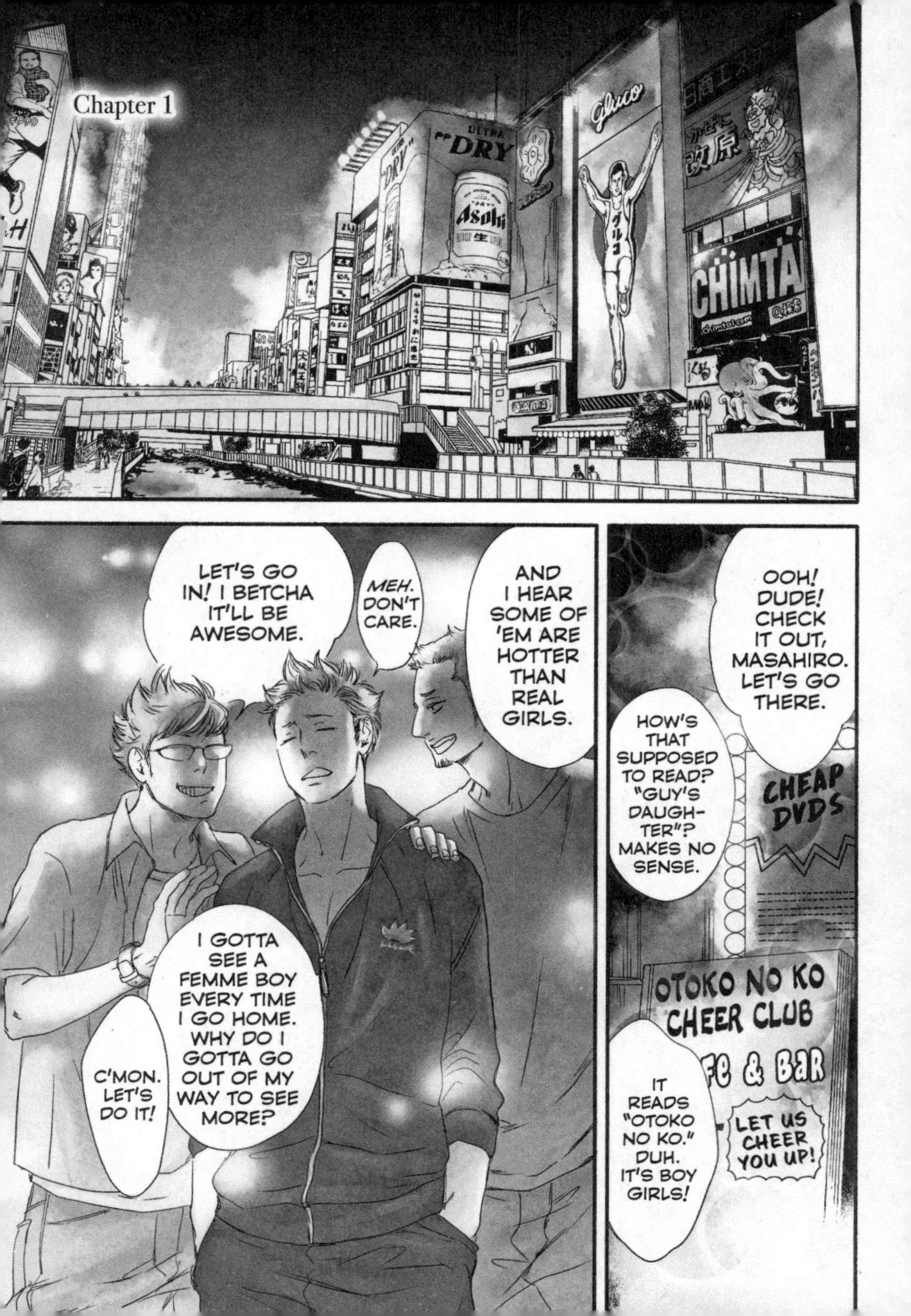
ULTRA "DRY"
Asahi
CHIMTA
OOH! DUDE! CHECK IT OUT, MASAHIRO. LET'S GO THERE.
HOW'S THAT SUPPOSED TO READ? "GUY'S DAUGHTER"? MAKES NO SENSE.
CHEAP DVDS
OTOKO NO KO CHEER CLUB
IT READS "OTOKO NO KO." DUH. IT'S BOY GIRLS!
LET US CHEER YOU UP!
AND I HEAR SOME OF 'EM ARE HOTTER THAN REAL GIRLS.
MEH. DON'T CARE.
LET'S GO IN! I BETCHA IT'LL BE AWESOME.
I GOTTA SEE A FEMME BOY EVERY TIME I GO HOME. WHY DO I GOTTA GO OUT OF MY WAY TO SEE MORE?
C'MON. LET'S DO IT!

Moon & Sun

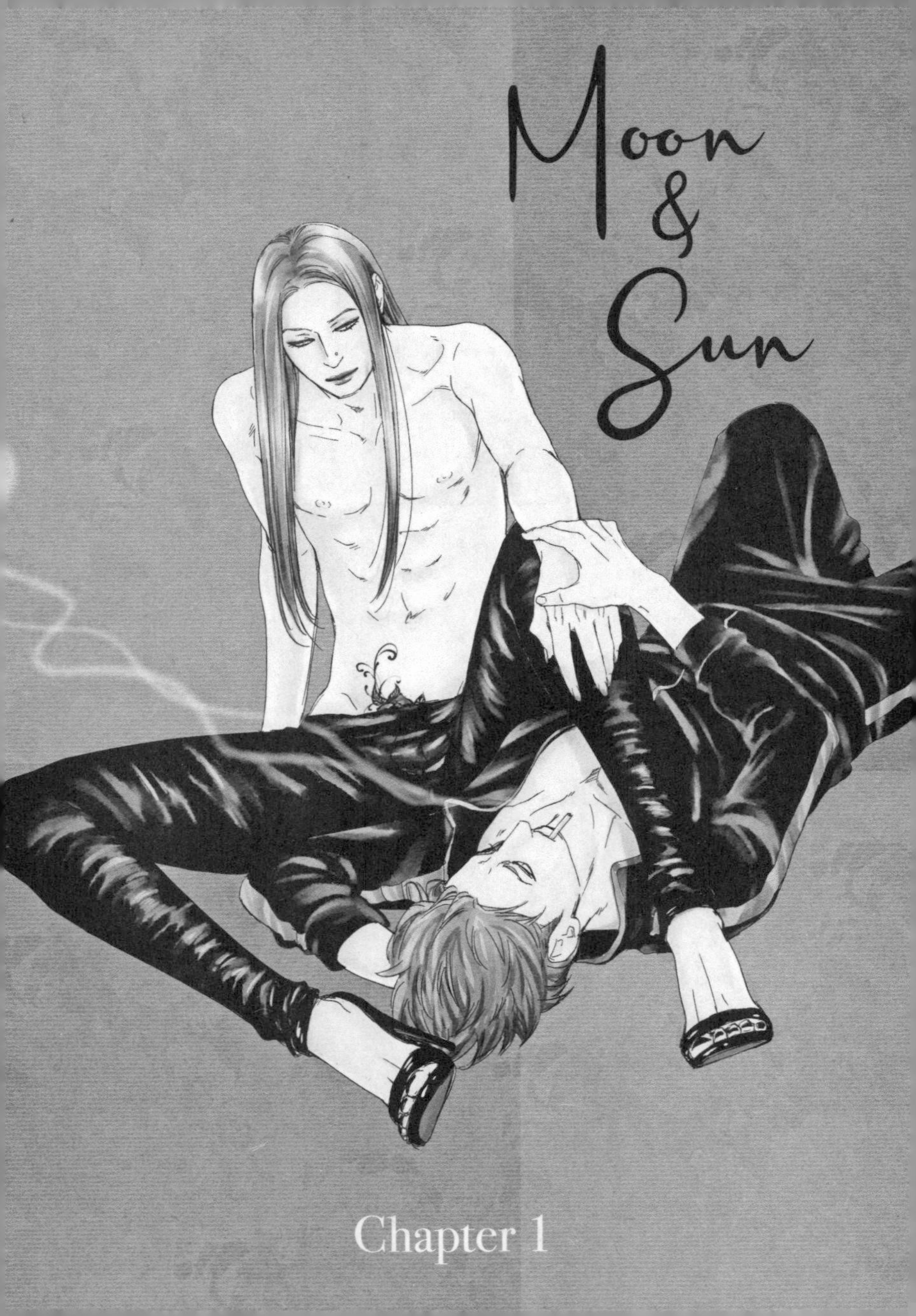

Chapter 1

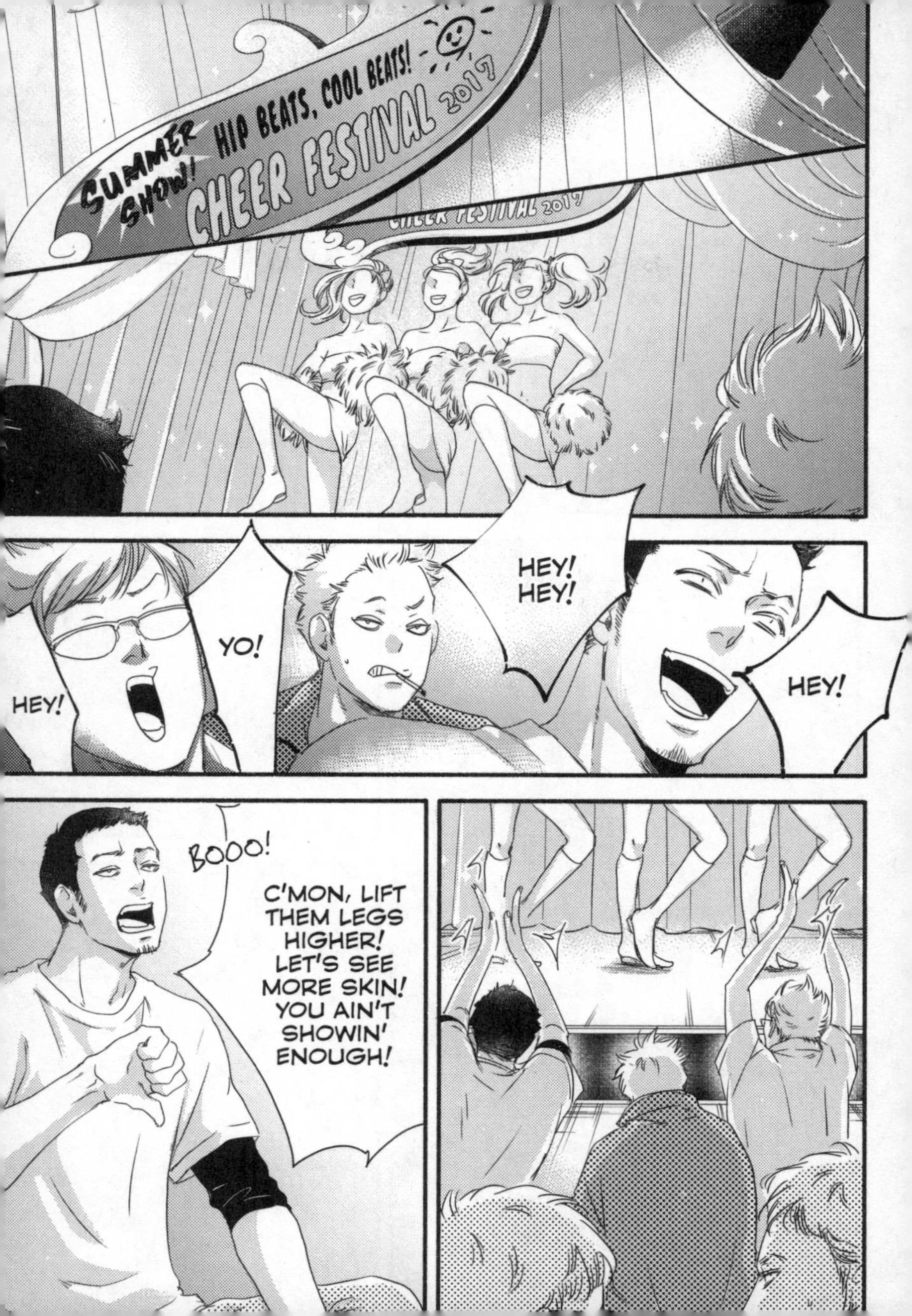
SUMMER SHOW!
HIP BEATS, COOL BEATS!
CHEER FESTIVAL 2017
HEY! HEY!
HEY!
YO!
HEY!
BOOO!
C'MON, LIFT THEM LEGS HIGHER! LET'S SEE MORE SKIN! YOU AIN'T SHOWIN' ENOUGH!

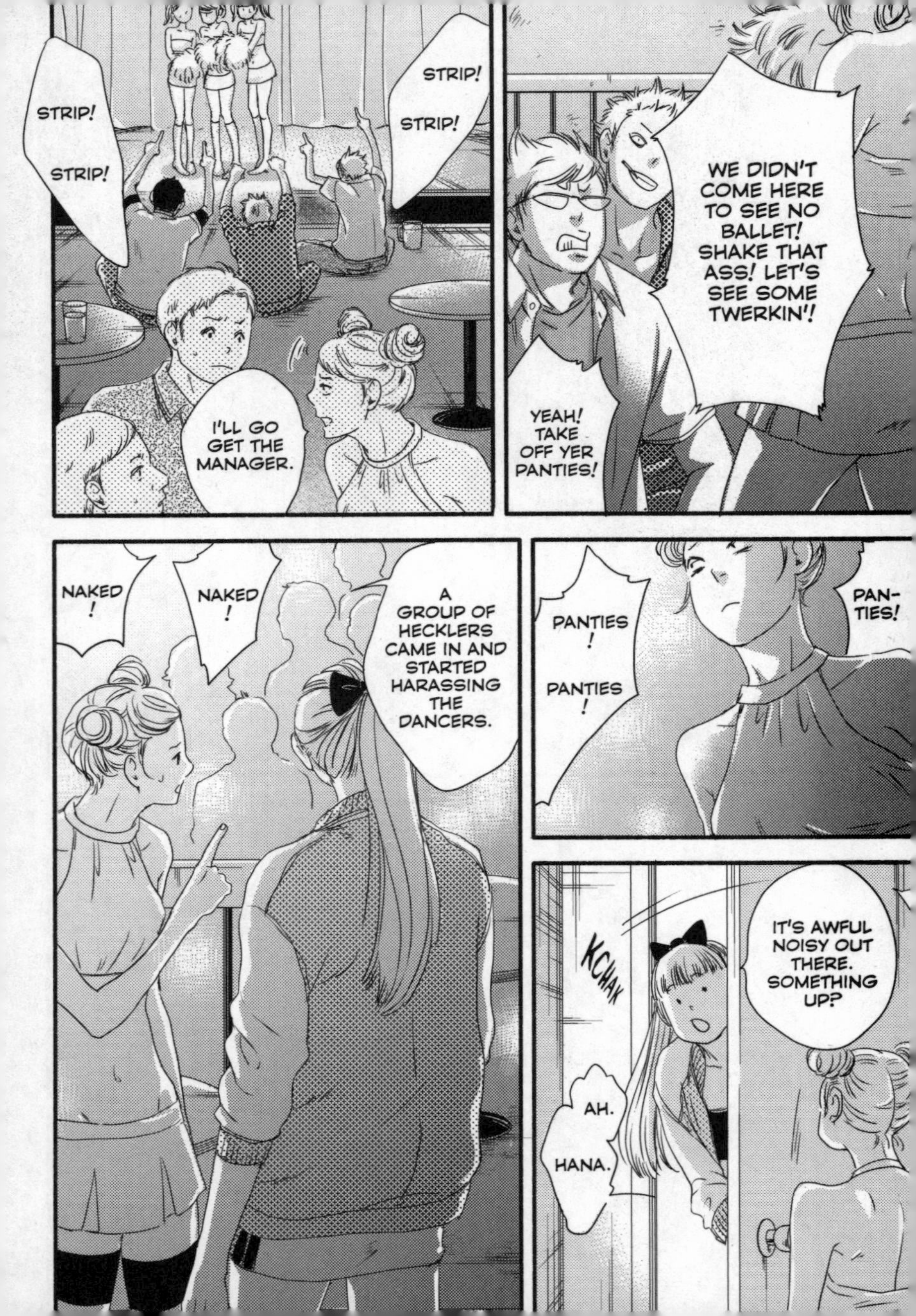
WE DIDN'T COME HERE TO SEE NO BALLET! SHAKE THAT ASS! LET'S SEE SOME TWERKIN'!
YEAH! TAKE OFF YER PANTIES!
STRIP! STRIP!
STRIP! STRIP!
I'LL GO GET THE MANAGER.
PAN-TIES!
PANTIES! PANTIES!
IT'S AWFUL NOISY OUT THERE. SOMETHING UP?
KCHAK
AH. HANA.
A GROUP OF HECKLERS CAME IN AND STARTED HARASSING THE DANCERS.
NAKED!
NAKED!

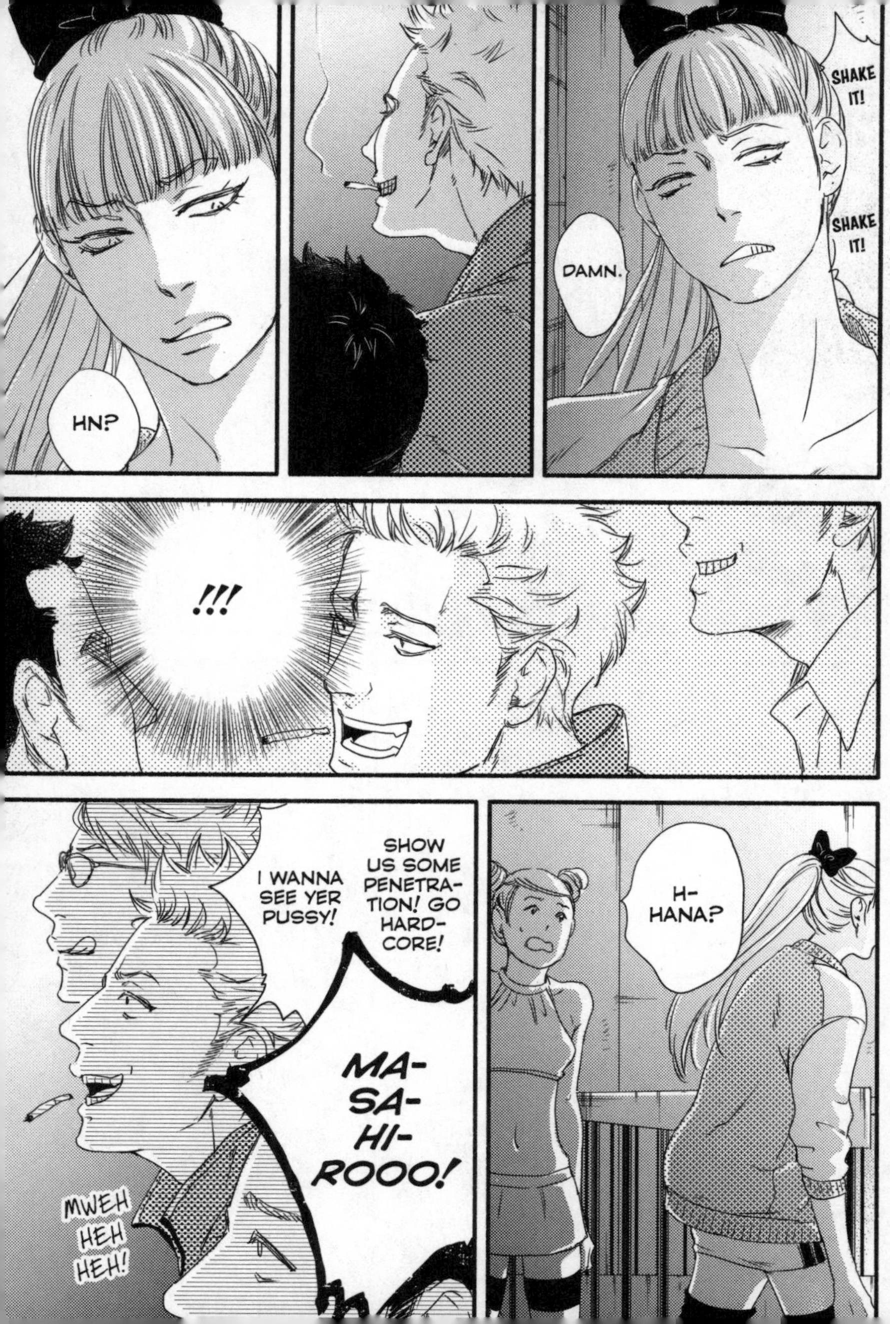
SHAKE IT!
SHAKE IT!
DAMN.
HN?
!!!
H- HANA?
SHOW US SOME PENETRATION! GO HARDCORE!
I WANNA SEE YER PUSSY!
MA-SA-HI-ROOO!
MWEH HEH HEH!

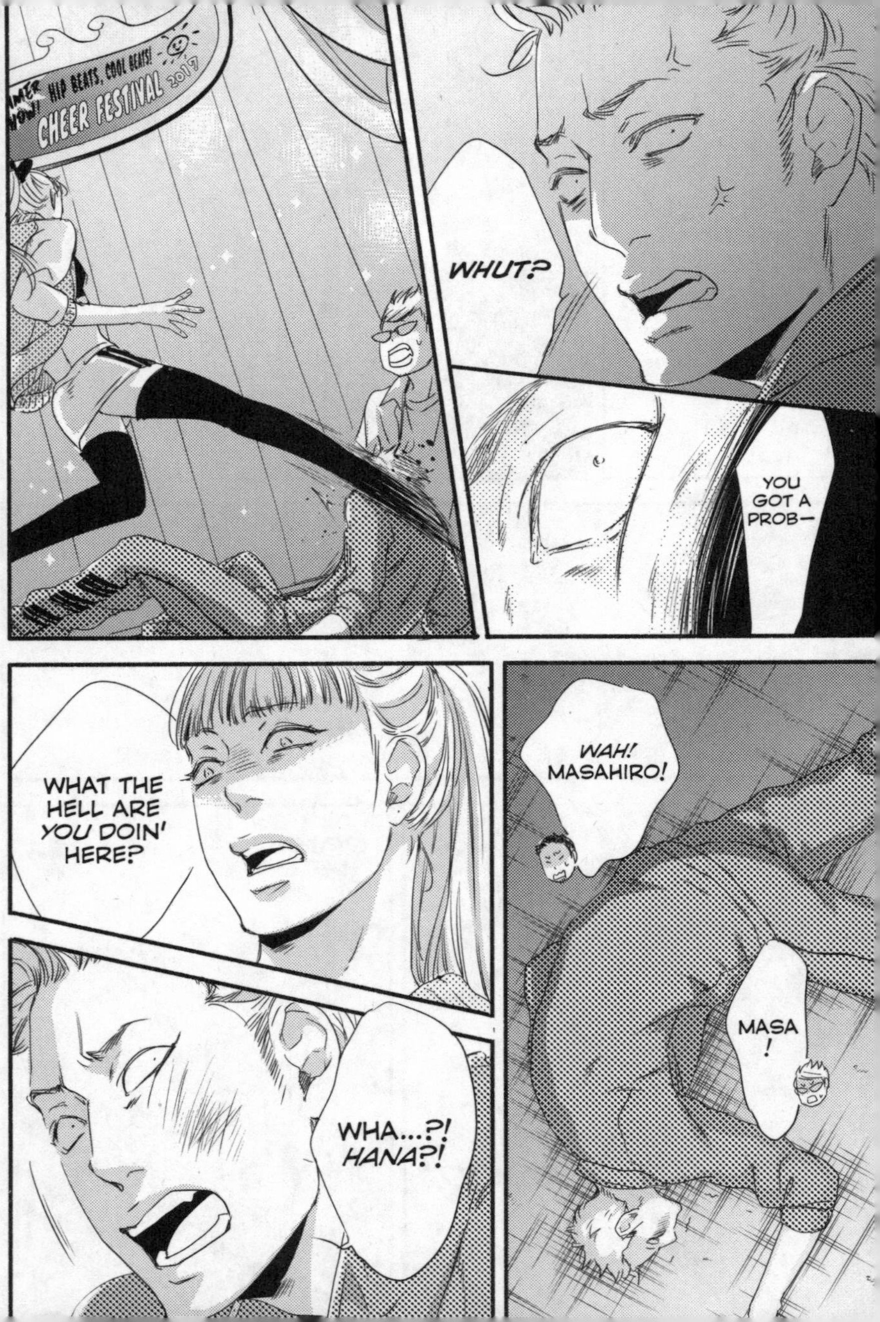
WHUT?
YOU GOT A PROB—
HIP BEATS, COOL BEATS!
CHEER FESTIVAL 2017
WAH! MASAHIRO!
MASA!
WHAT THE HELL ARE *YOU* DOIN' HERE?
WHA...?! *HANA?!*

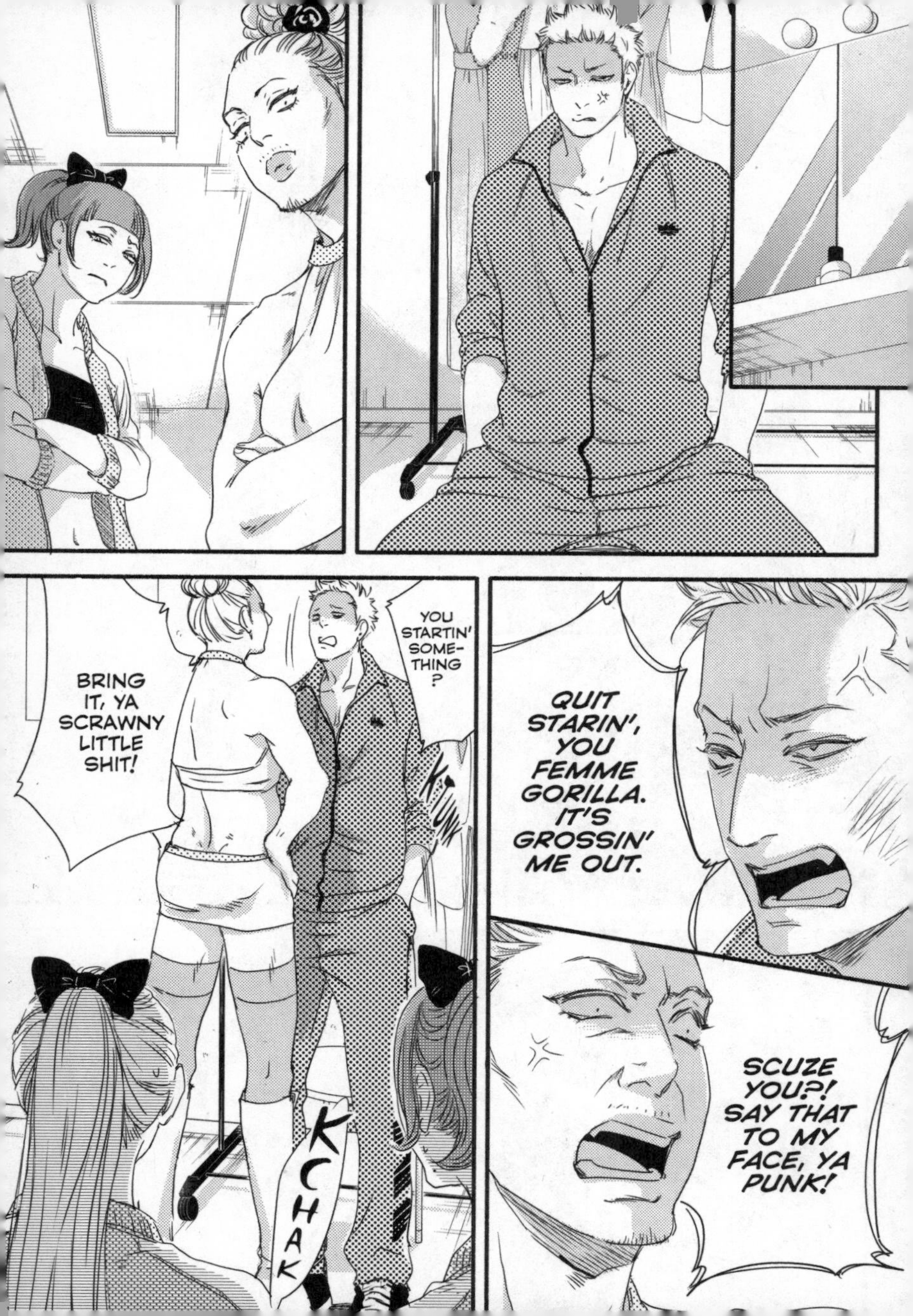
QUIT STARIN', YOU FEMME GORILLA. IT'S GROSSIN' ME OUT.
SCUZE YOU?! SAY THAT TO MY FACE, YA PUNK!
YOU STARTIN' SOME-THING?
BRING IT, YA SCRAWNY LITTLE SHIT!
KCHAK

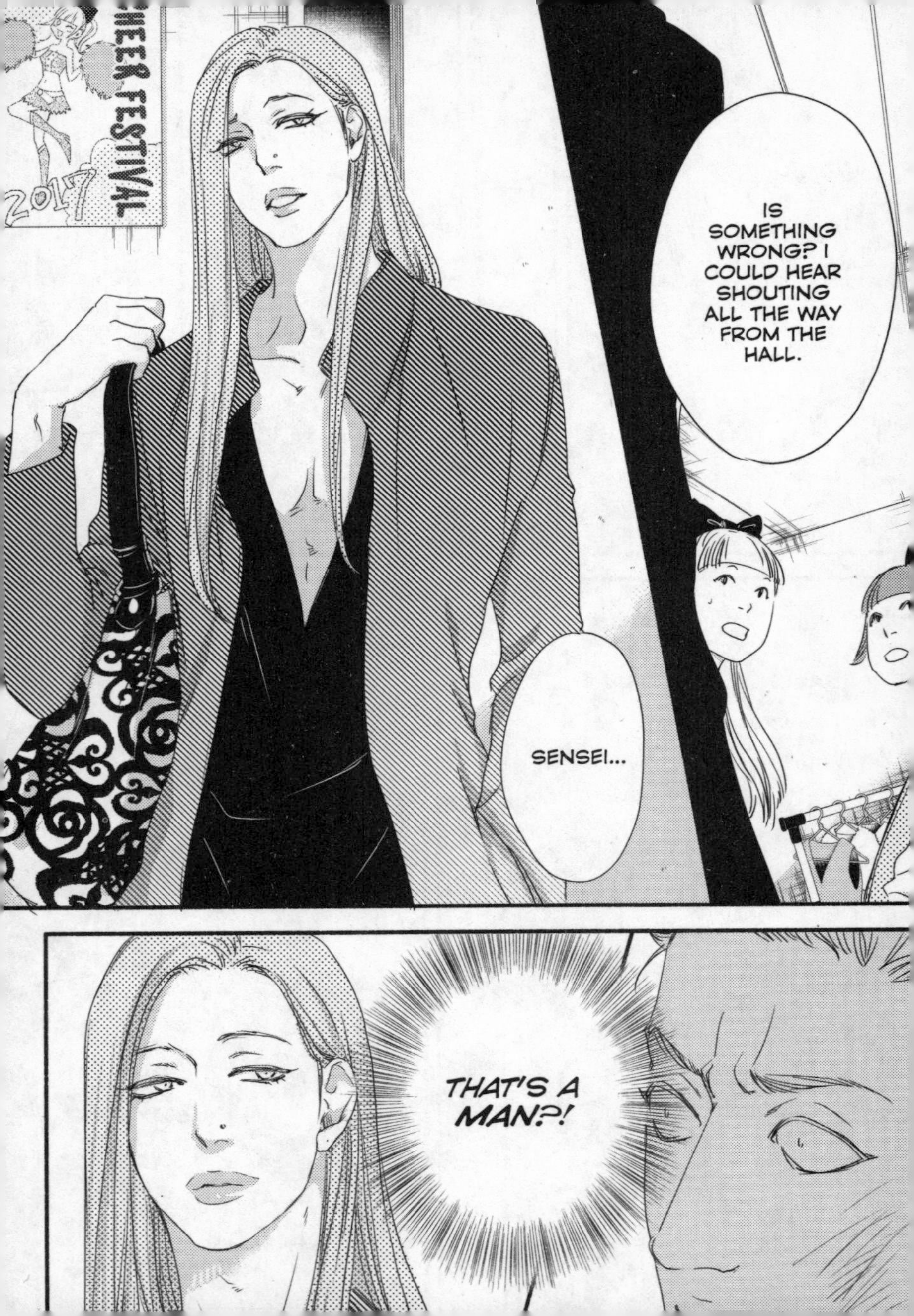
IS SOMETHING WRONG? I COULD HEAR SHOUTING ALL THE WAY FROM THE HALL.
SENSEI...
HEER FESTIVAL
2017
THAT'S A MAN?!

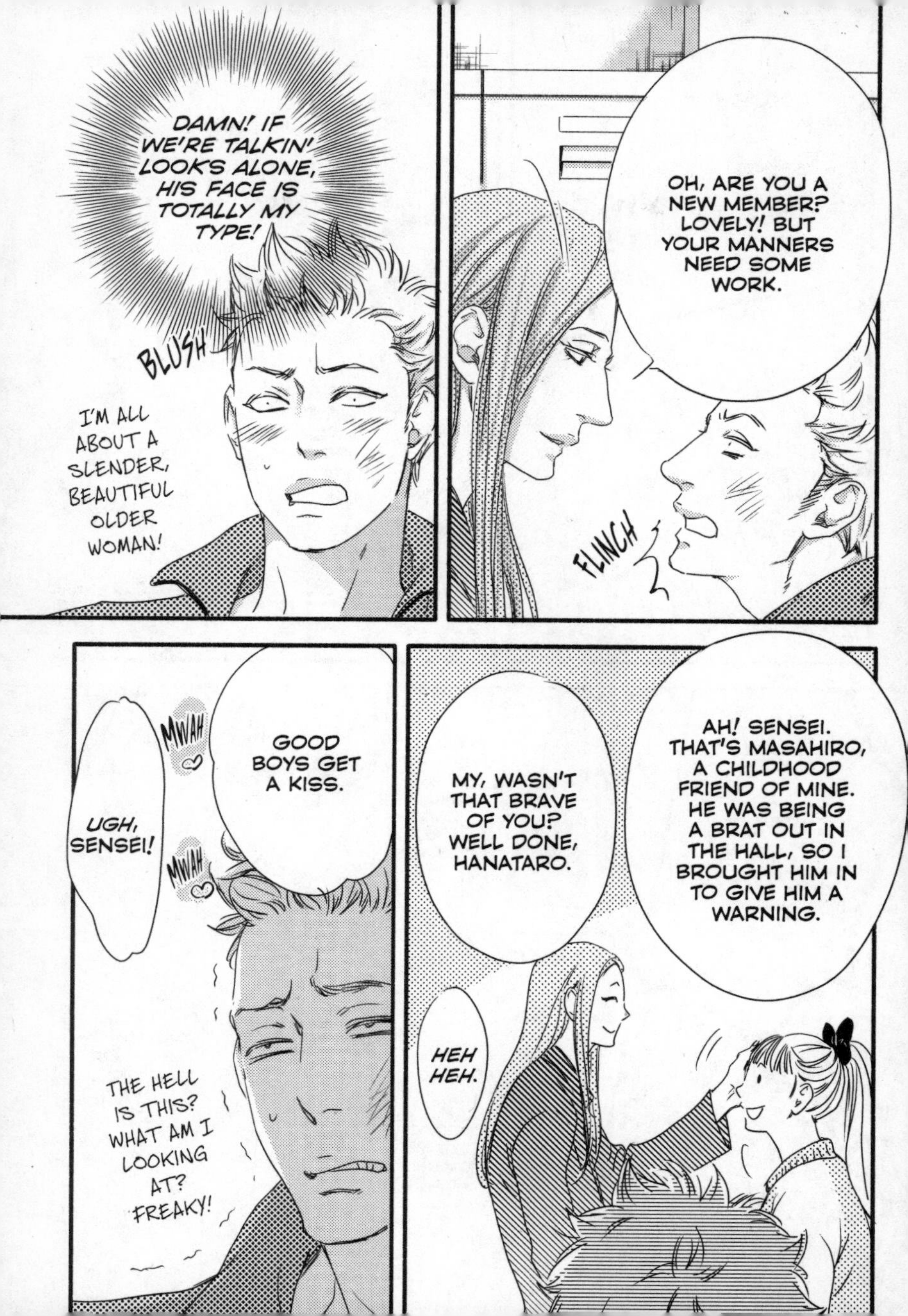
OH, ARE YOU A NEW MEMBER? LOVELY! BUT YOUR MANNERS NEED SOME WORK.
FLINCH
DAMN! IF WE'RE TALKIN' LOOKS ALONE, HIS FACE IS TOTALLY MY TYPE!
BLUSH
I'M ALL ABOUT A SLENDER, BEAUTIFUL OLDER WOMAN!
AH! SENSEI. THAT'S MASAHIRO, A CHILDHOOD FRIEND OF MINE. HE WAS BEING A BRAT OUT IN THE HALL, SO I BROUGHT HIM IN TO GIVE HIM A WARNING.
MY, WASN'T THAT BRAVE OF YOU? WELL DONE, HANATARO.
HEH HEH.
GOOD BOYS GET A KISS.
MWAH
UGH, SENSEI!
MWAH
THE HELL IS THIS? WHAT AM I LOOKING AT? FREAKY!

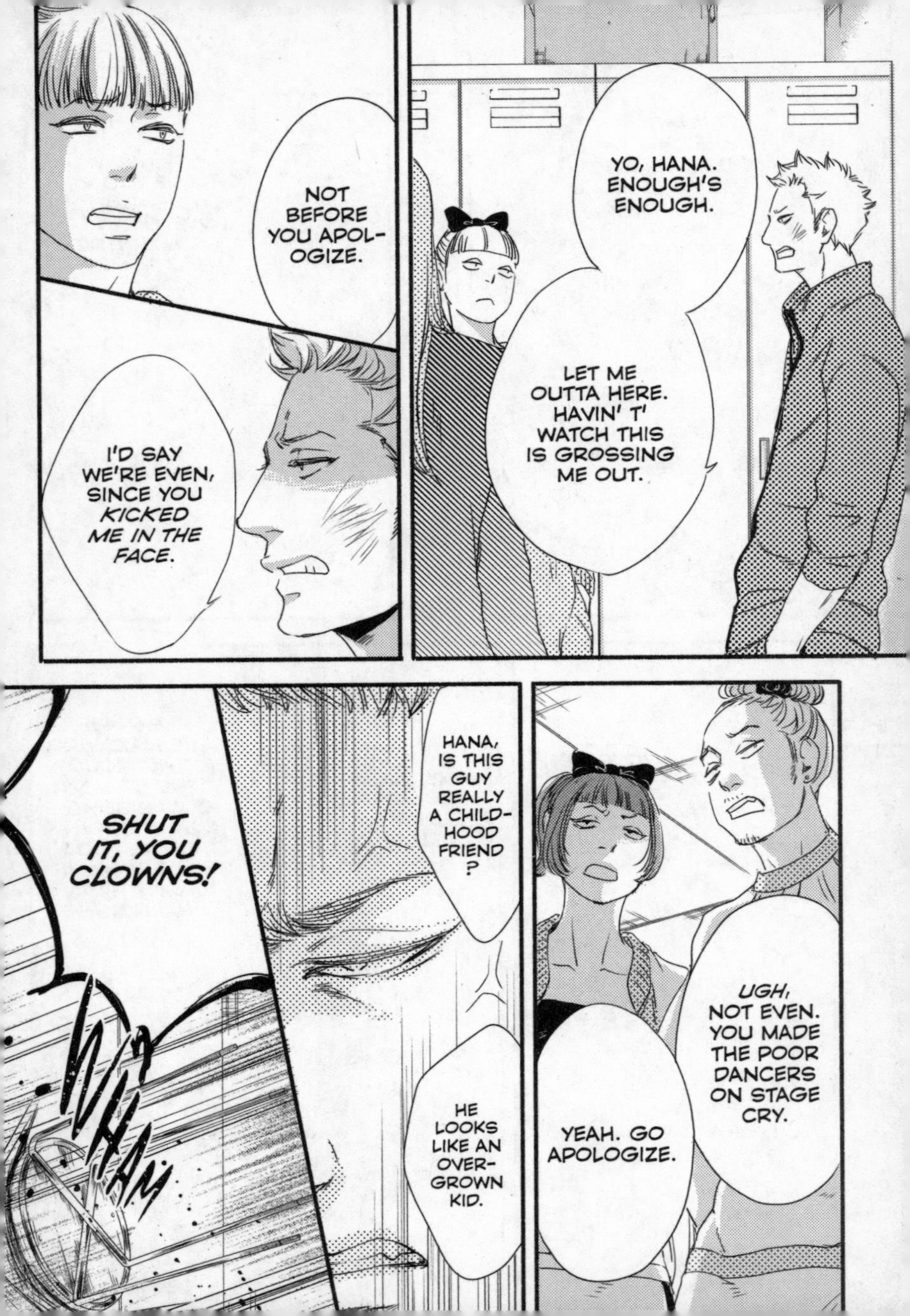
YO, HANA. ENOUGH'S ENOUGH.
LET ME OUTTA HERE. HAVIN' T' WATCH THIS IS GROSSING ME OUT.
NOT BEFORE YOU APOLOGIZE.
I'D SAY WE'RE EVEN, SINCE YOU *KICKED* ME IN THE FACE.
UGH, NOT EVEN. YOU MADE THE POOR DANCERS ON STAGE CRY.
YEAH. GO APOLOGIZE.
HANA, IS THIS GUY REALLY A CHILDHOOD FRIEND?
HE LOOKS LIKE AN OVERGROWN KID.
SHUT IT, YOU CLOWNS!
WHAM

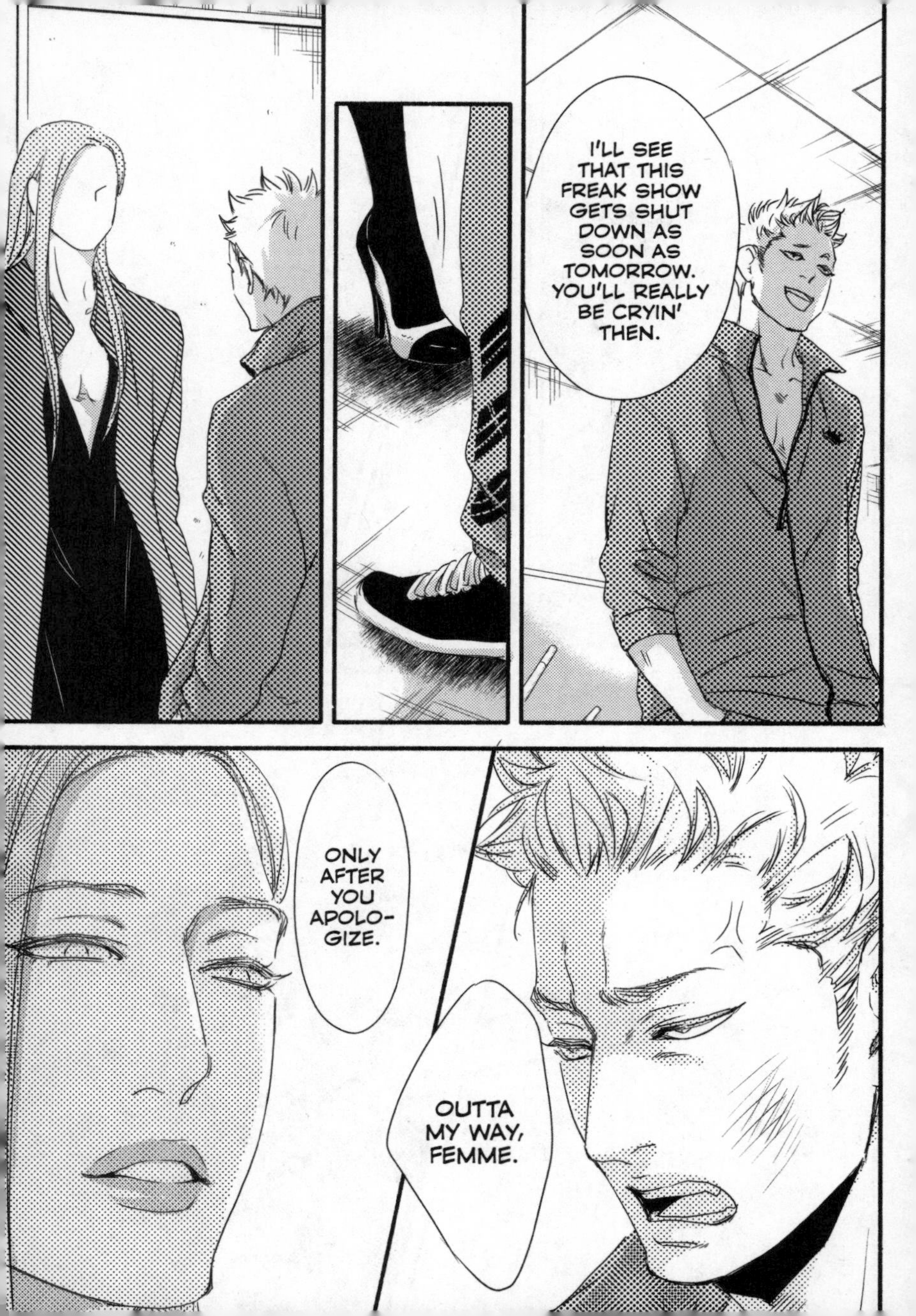
I'LL SEE THAT THIS FREAK SHOW GETS SHUT DOWN AS SOON AS TOMORROW. YOU'LL REALLY BE CRYIN' THEN.
ONLY AFTER YOU APOLO-GIZE.
OUTTA MY WAY, FEMME.

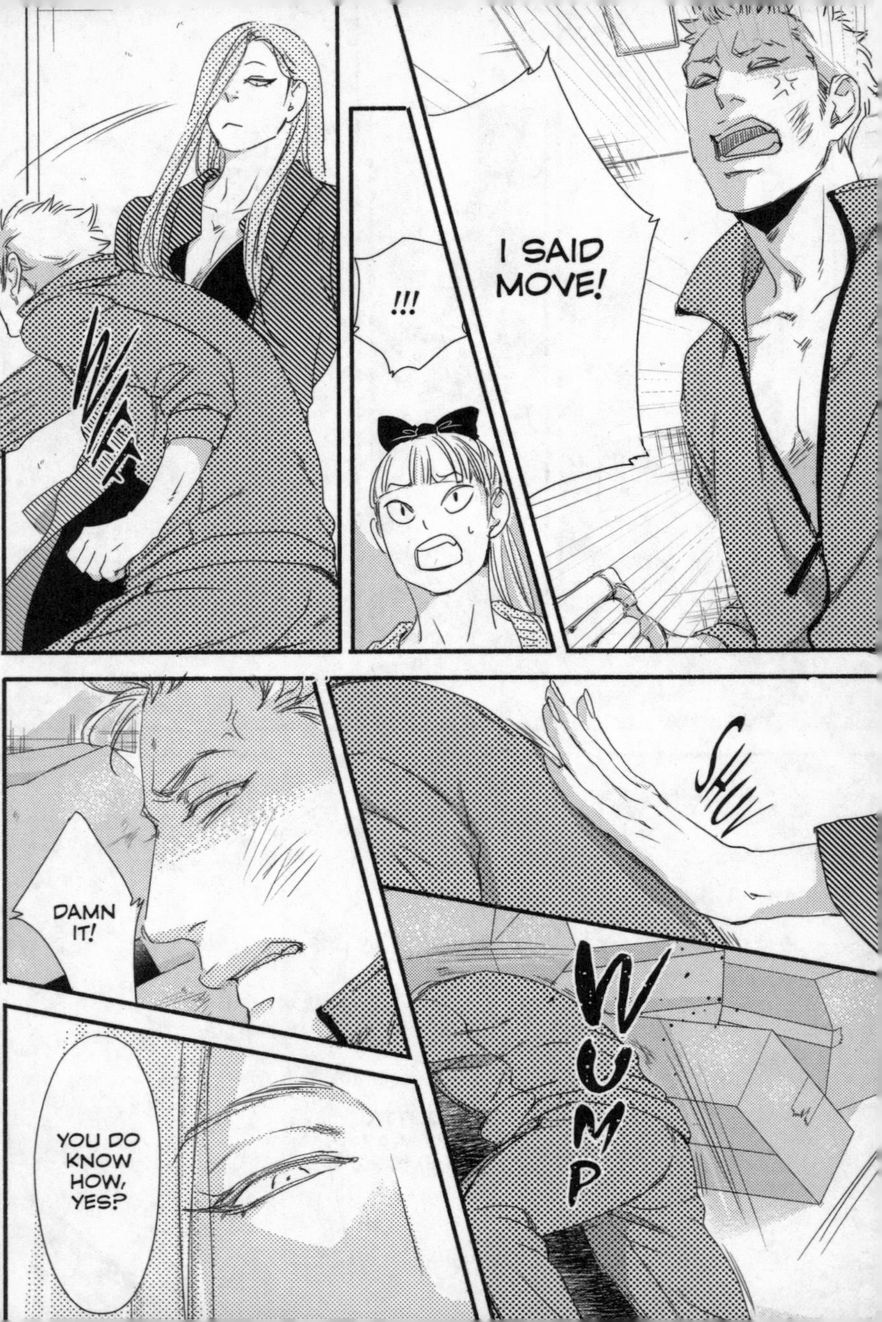
I SAID MOVE!
!!!
SHUV
WUMP
DAMN IT!
YOU DO KNOW HOW, YES?

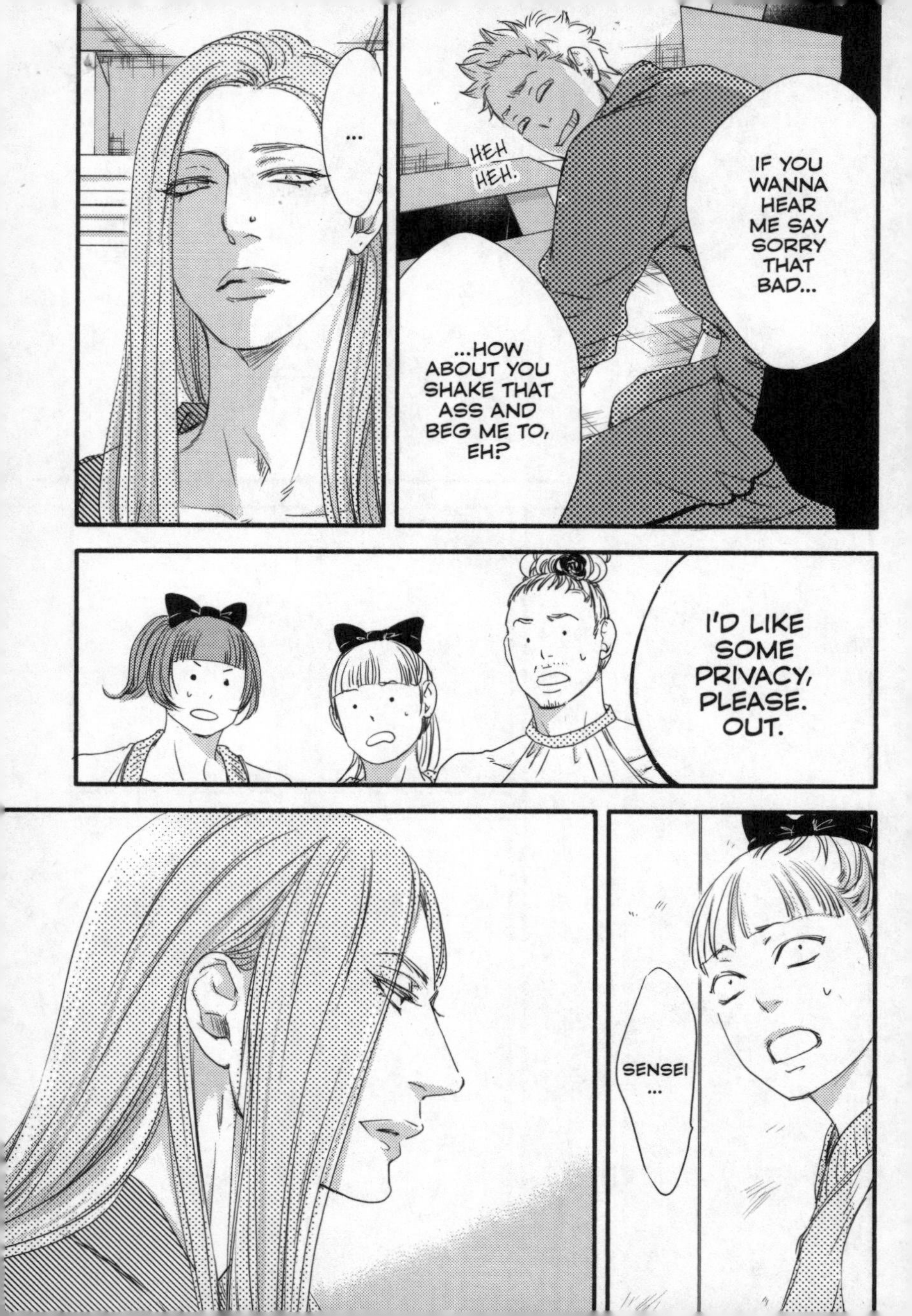
IF YOU WANNA HEAR ME SAY SORRY THAT BAD...
HEH HEH.
...HOW ABOUT YOU SHAKE THAT ASS AND BEG ME TO, EH?
...
I'D LIKE SOME PRIVACY, PLEASE. OUT.
SENSEI ...

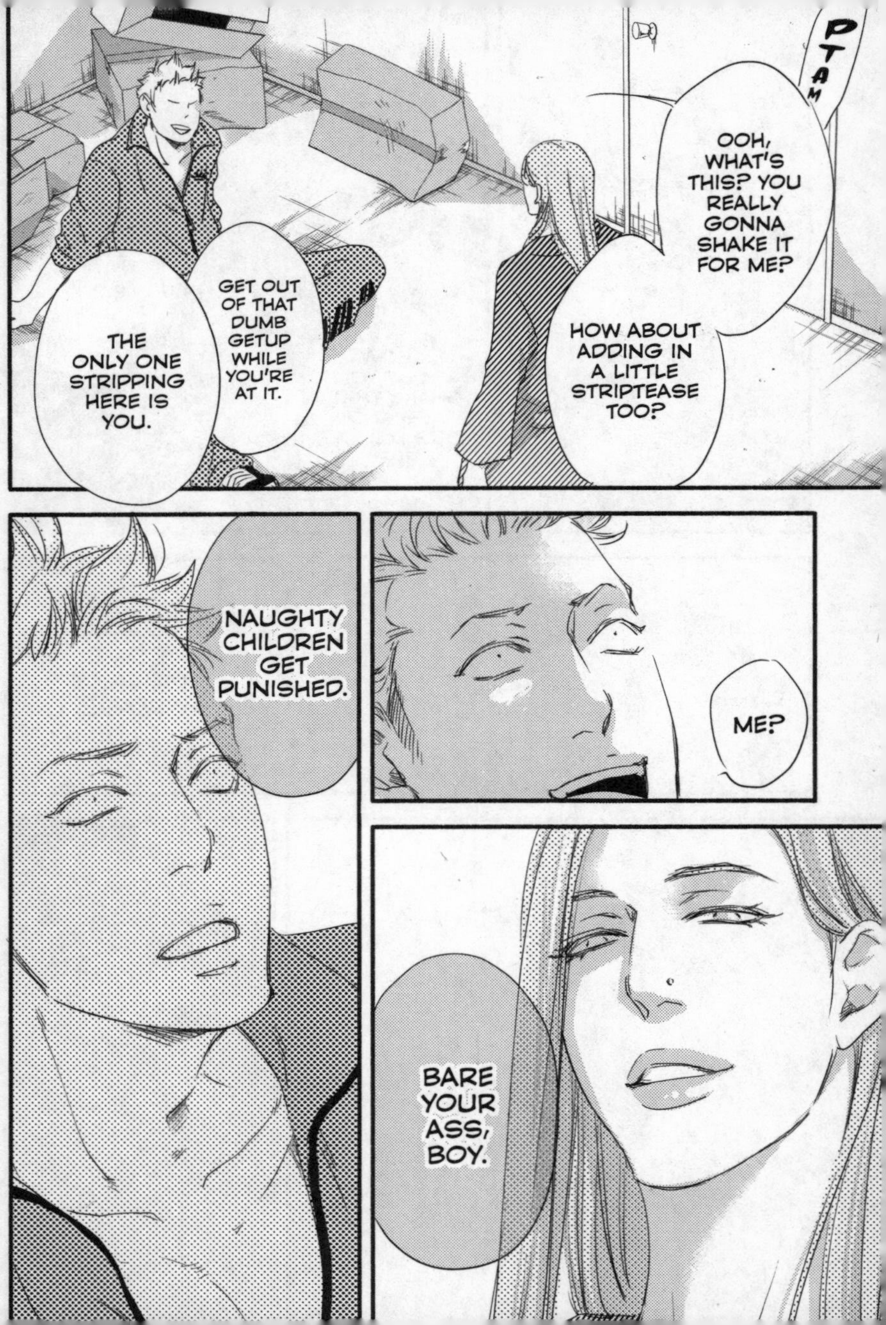
PTAM
OOH, WHAT'S THIS? YOU REALLY GONNA SHAKE IT FOR ME?
HOW ABOUT ADDING IN A LITTLE STRIPTEASE TOO?
GET OUT OF THAT DUMB GETUP WHILE YOU'RE AT IT.
THE ONLY ONE STRIPPING HERE IS YOU.
ME?
BARE YOUR ASS, BOY.
NAUGHTY CHILDREN GET PUNISHED.

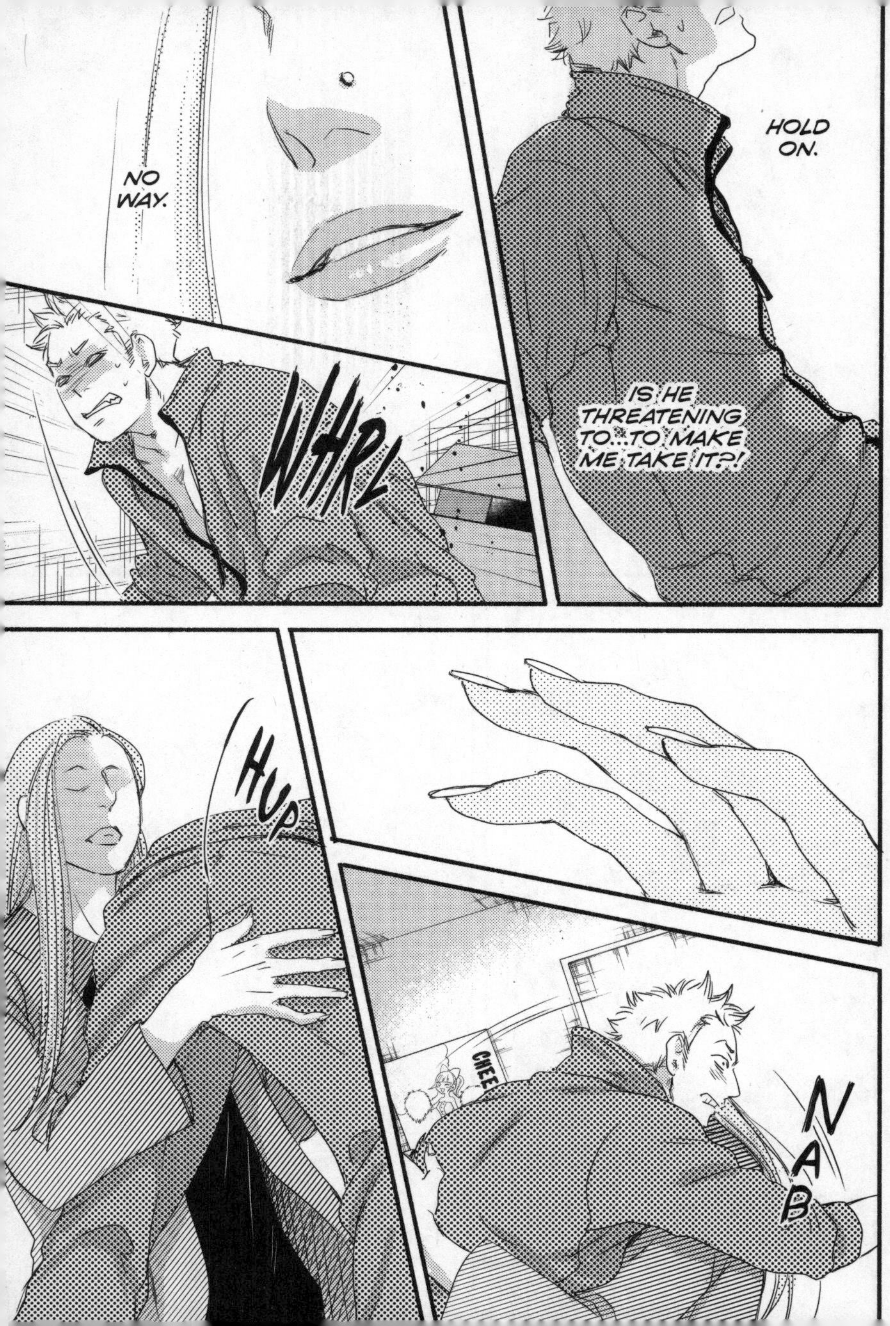
HOLD ON.
IS HE THREATENING TO...TO MAKE ME TAKE IT?!
NO WAY.
WHRL
CHEE
NAB
HUP

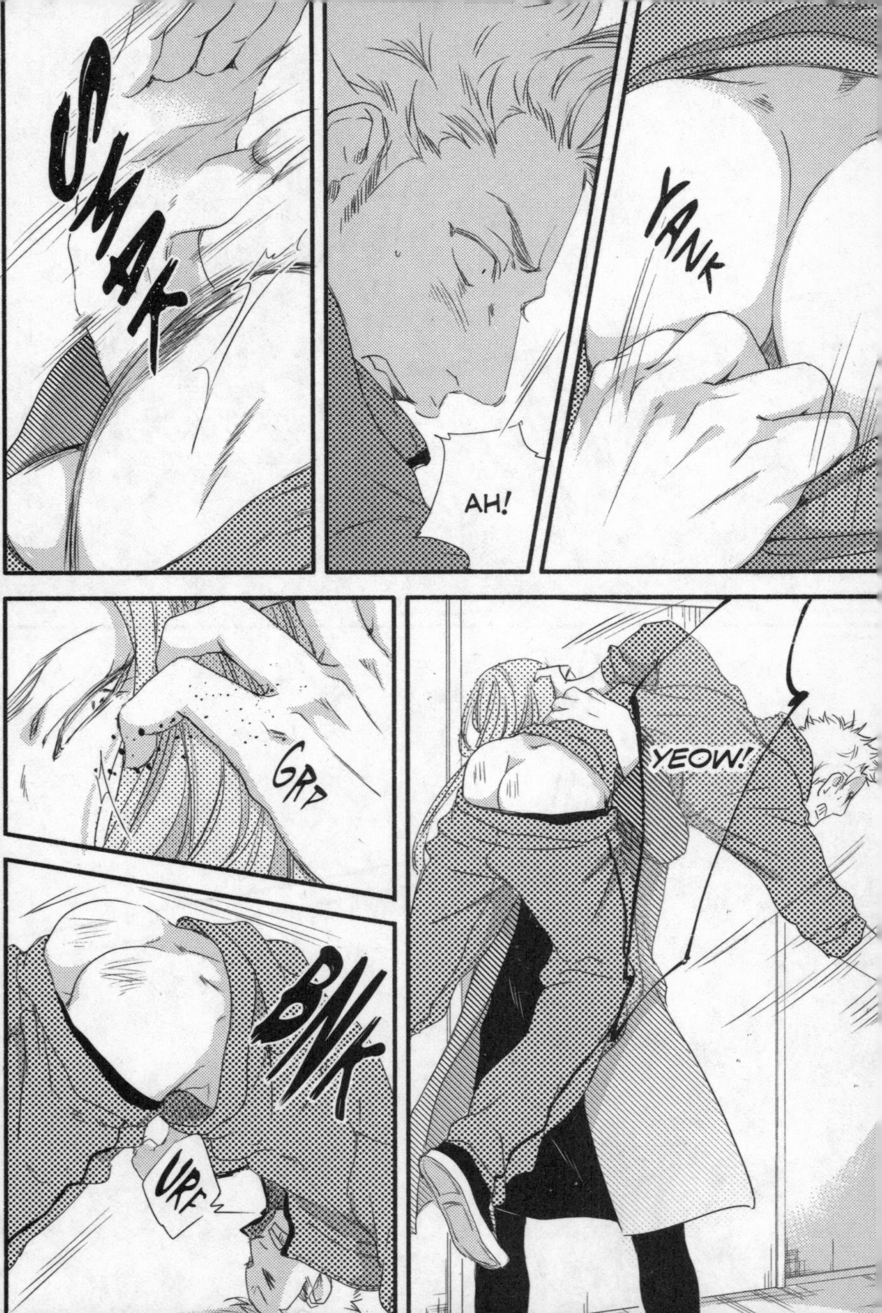
YANK
AH!
SMAK
YEOW!
GRP
BNK
URF

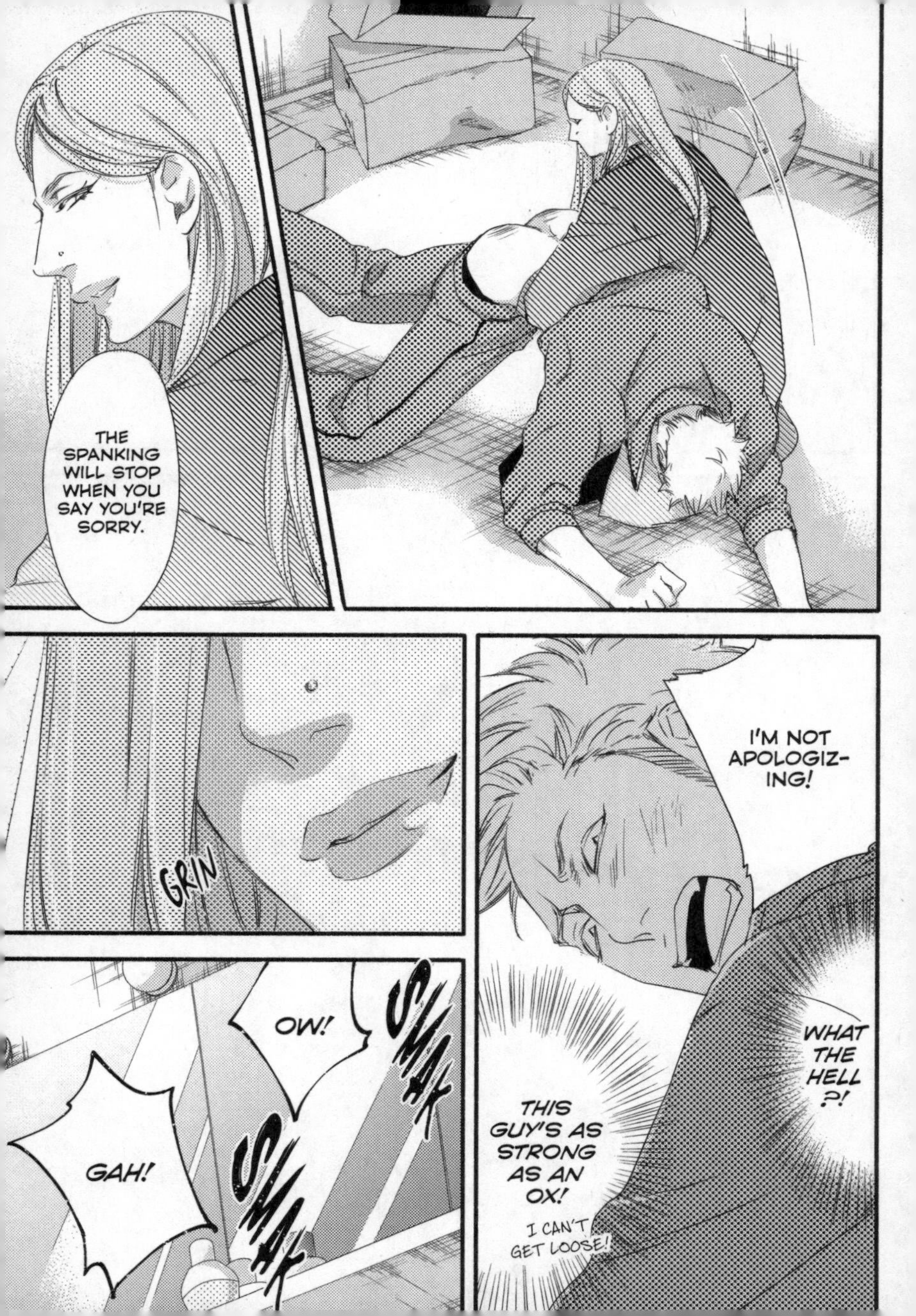
THE SPANKING WILL STOP WHEN YOU SAY YOU'RE SORRY.
I'M NOT APOLOGIZ-ING!
WHAT THE HELL ?!
THIS GUY'S AS STRONG AS AN OX!
I CAN'T GET LOOSE!
GRIN
OW!
SMAK
GAH!
SMAK
SMAK

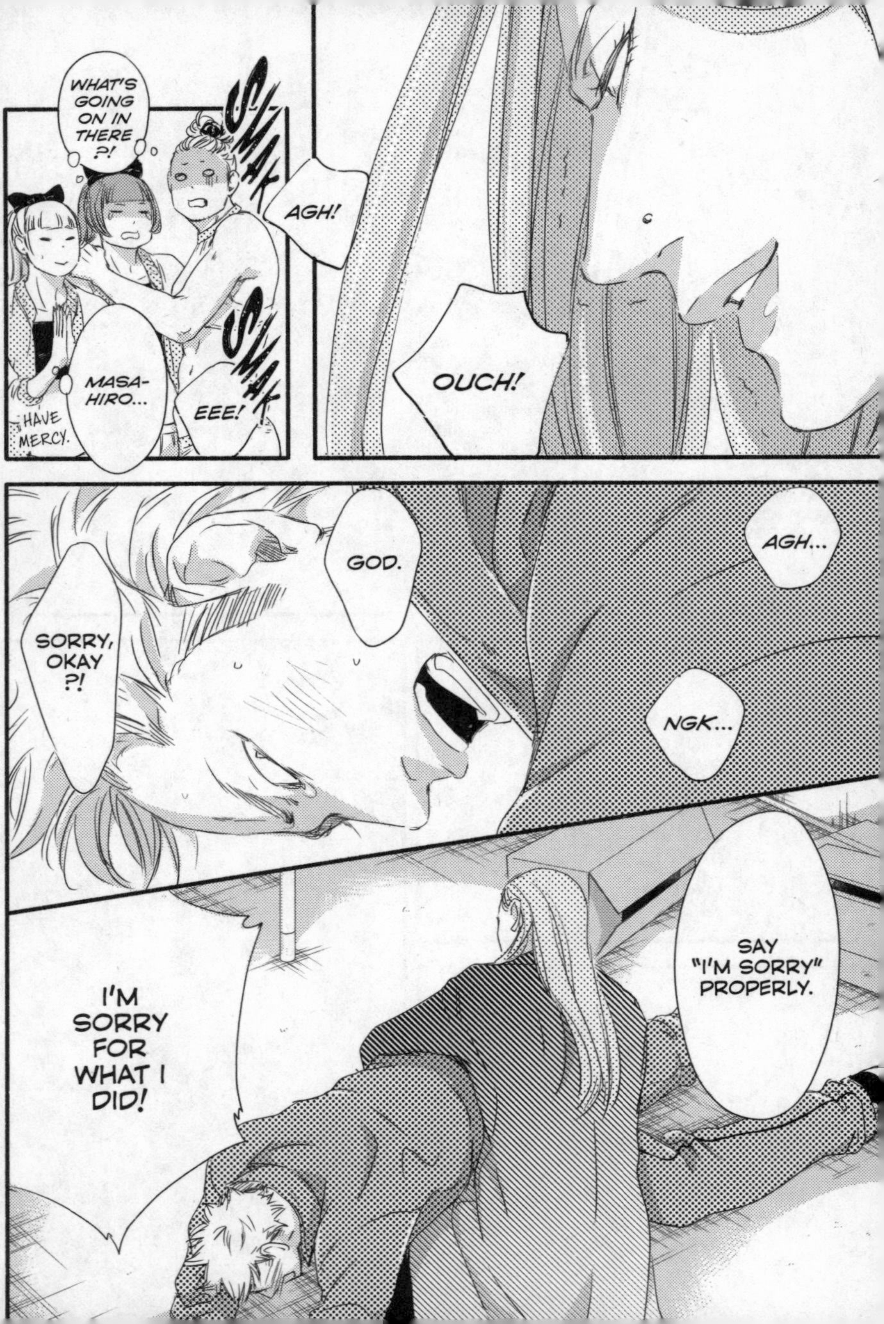
AGH!
OUCH!
WHAT'S GOING ON IN THERE?!
SMAK
SMAK
MASA-HIRO...
EEE!
HAVE MERCY.
AGH...
GOD.
NGK...
SORRY, OKAY?!
SAY "I'M SORRY" PROPERLY.
I'M SORRY FOR WHAT I DID!

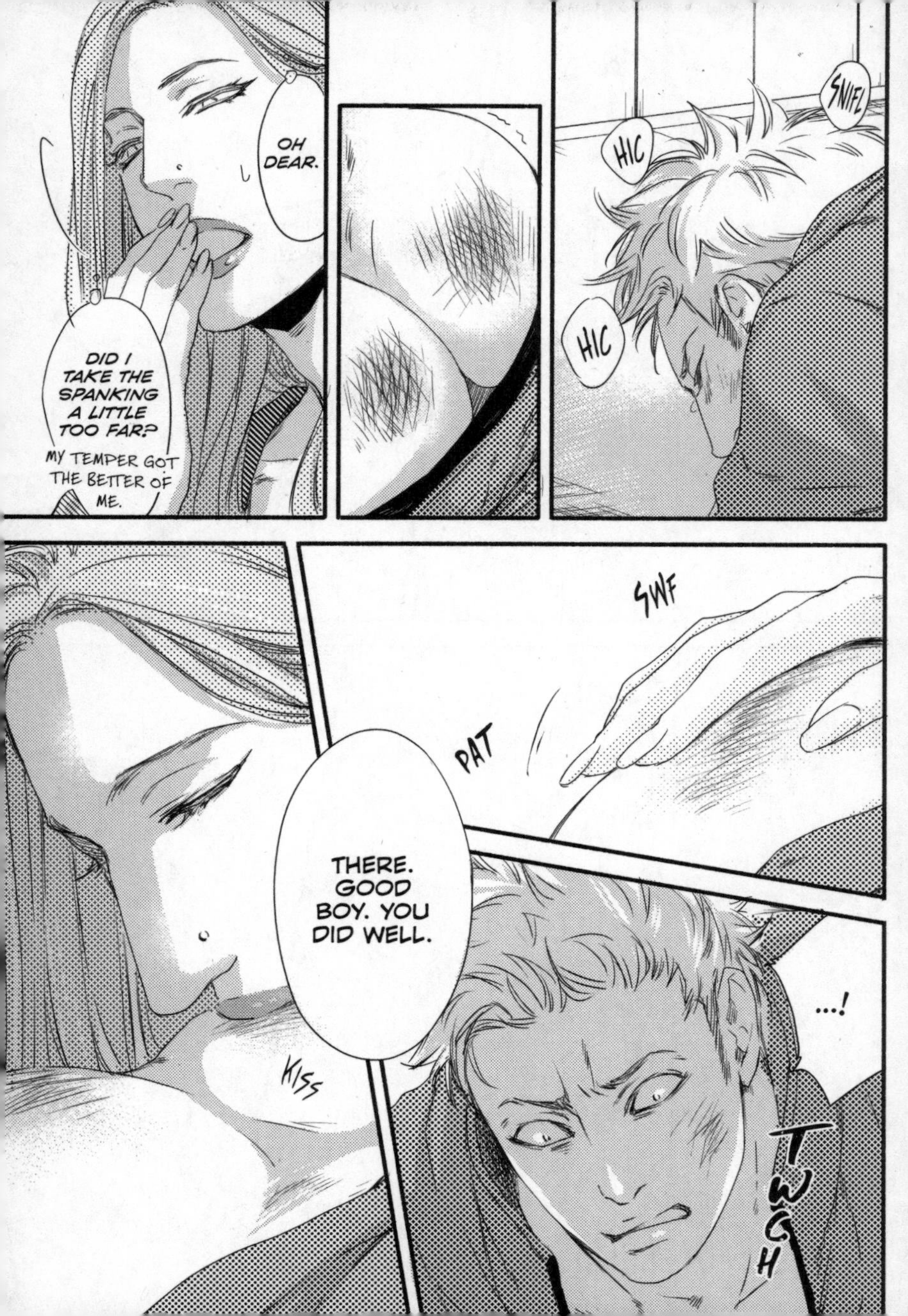
SNIFL
HIC
HIC
OH DEAR.
DID I TAKE THE SPANKING A LITTLE TOO FAR?
MY TEMPER GOT THE BETTER OF ME.
SWF
PAT
...!
TWGH
THERE. GOOD BOY. YOU DID WELL.
KISS

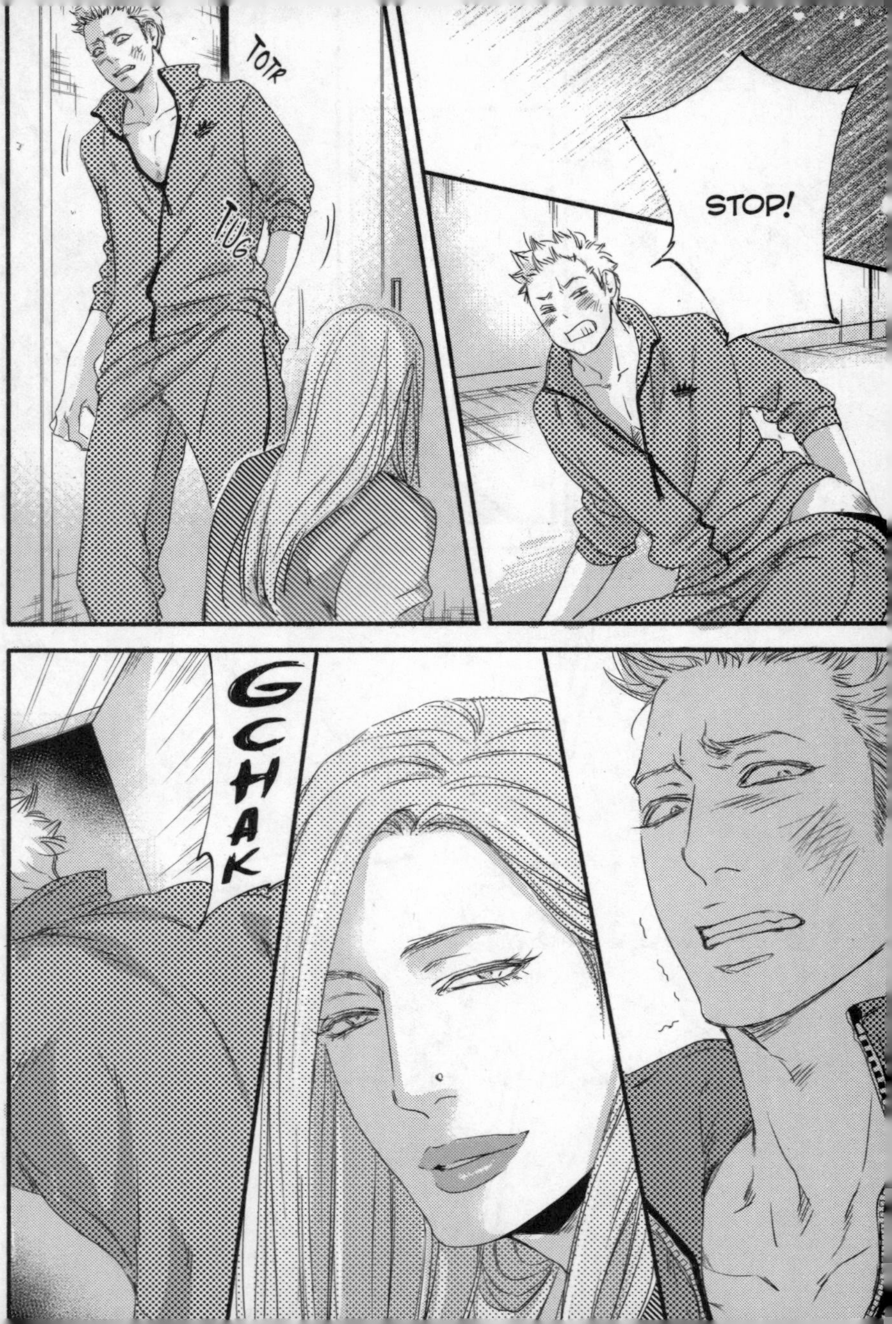
STOP!
TOTR
TUG
GCHAK

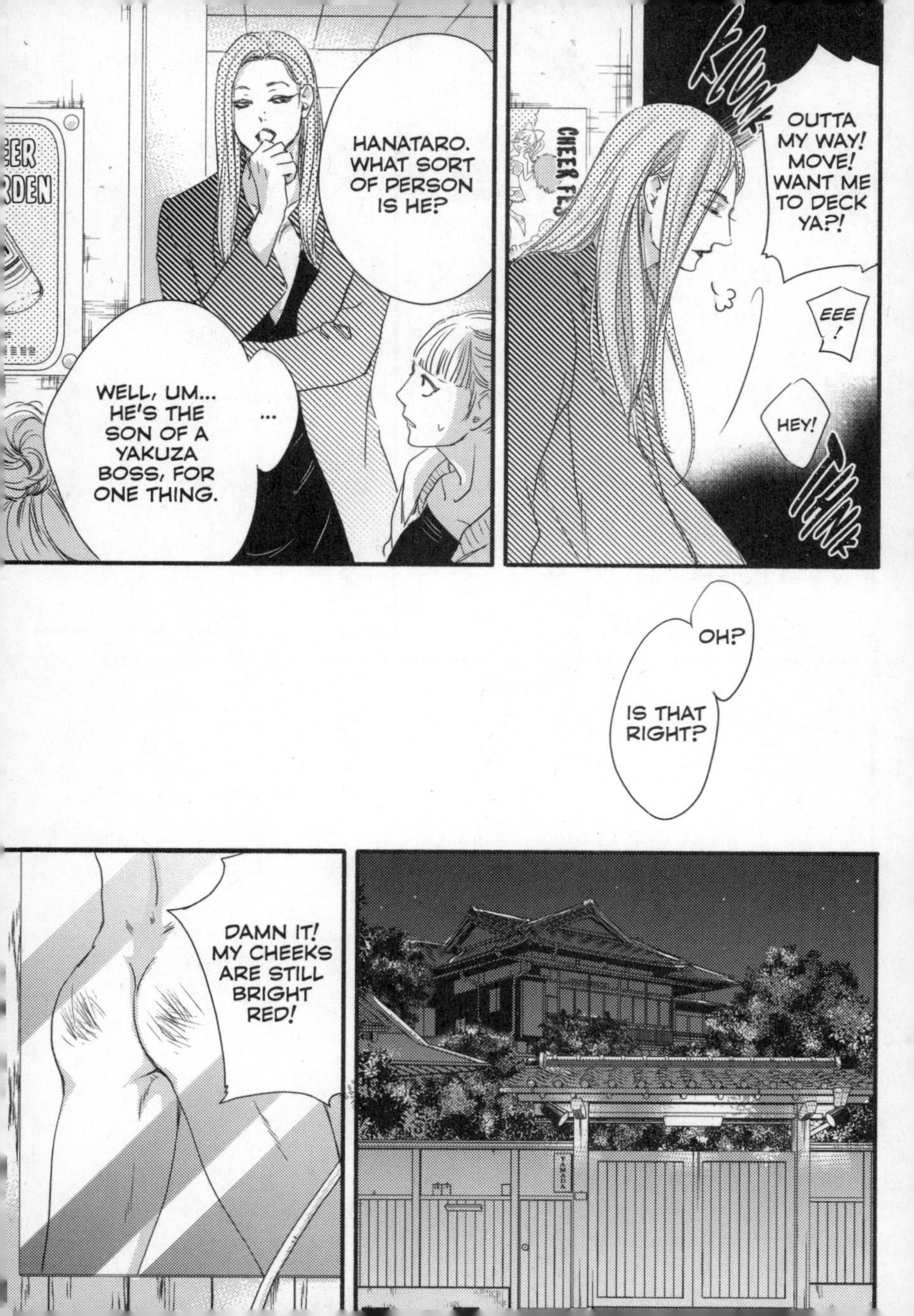
KLUNK
OUTTA MY WAY! MOVE! WANT ME TO DECK YA?!
EEE!
HEY!
THUNK
HANATARO. WHAT SORT OF PERSON IS HE?
WELL, UM... HE'S THE SON OF A YAKUZA BOSS, FOR ONE THING.
...
OH?
IS THAT RIGHT?
DAMN IT! MY CHEEKS ARE STILL BRIGHT RED!

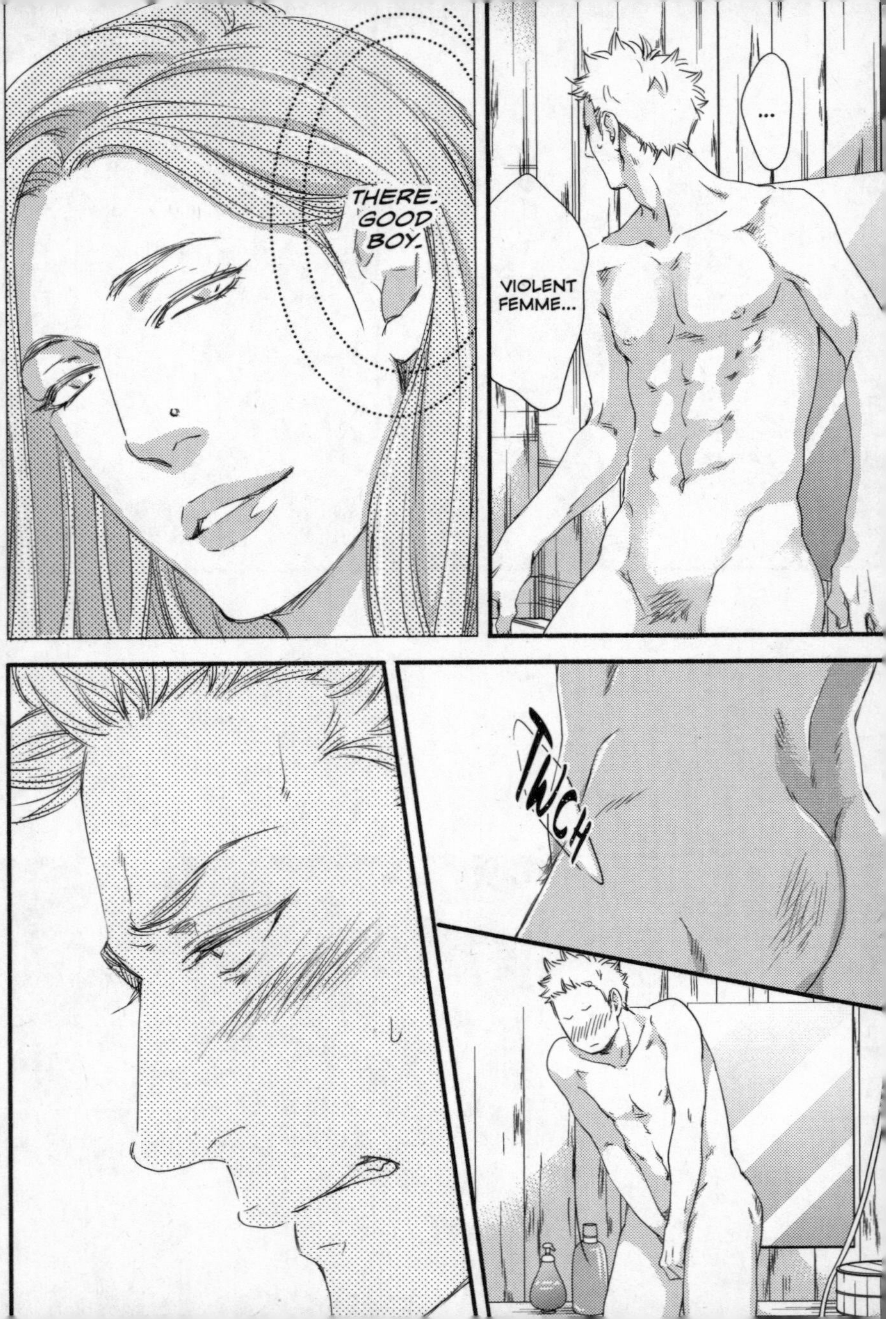
...
VIOLENT FEMME...
THERE. GOOD BOY.
TWCH

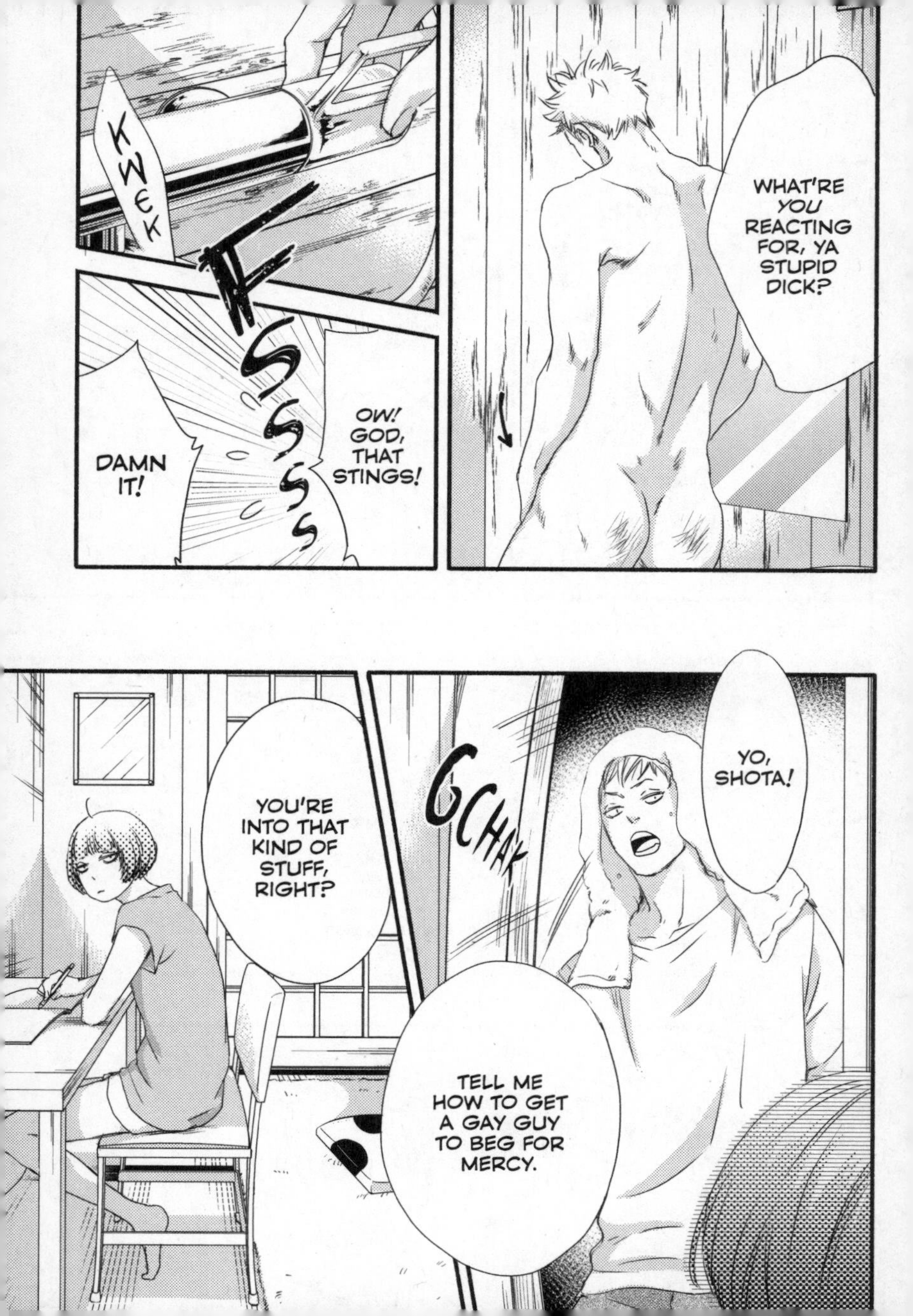
WHAT'RE YOU REACTING FOR, YA STUPID DICK?
KWEK
TSSSS
OW! GOD, THAT STINGS!
DAMN IT!
GCHAK
YO, SHOTA!
YOU'RE INTO THAT KIND OF STUFF, RIGHT?
TELL ME HOW TO GET A GAY GUY TO BEG FOR MERCY.

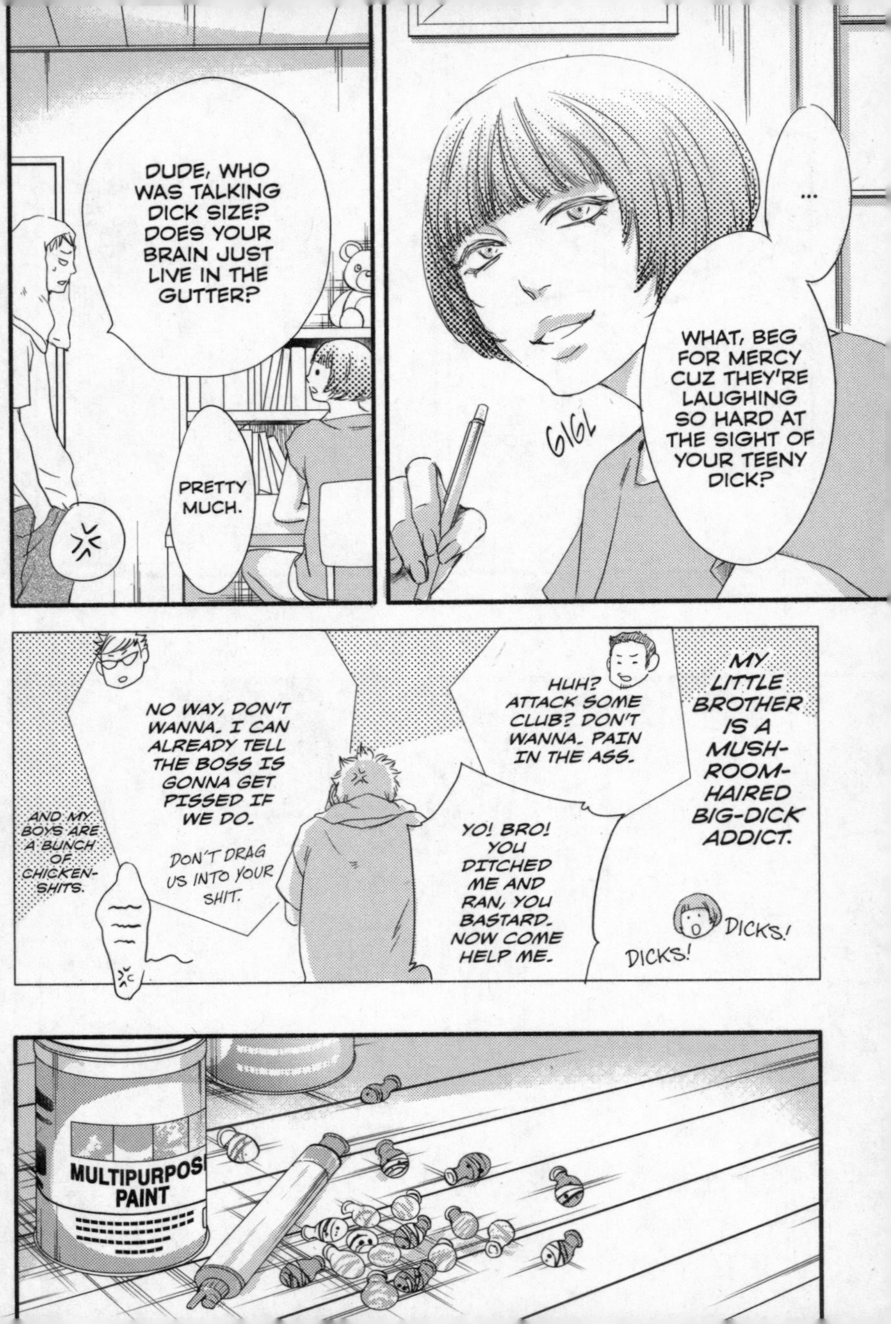
...
WHAT, BEG FOR MERCY CUZ THEY'RE LAUGHING SO HARD AT THE SIGHT OF YOUR TEENY DICK?
GIGL
DUDE, WHO WAS TALKING DICK SIZE? DOES YOUR BRAIN JUST LIVE IN THE GUTTER?
PRETTY MUCH.
MY LITTLE BROTHER IS A MUSH-ROOM-HAIRED BIG-DICK ADDICT.
HUH? ATTACK SOME CLUB? DON'T WANNA. PAIN IN THE ASS.
DICKS!
DICKS!
YO! BRO! YOU DITCHED ME AND RAN, YOU BASTARD. NOW COME HELP ME.
NO WAY, DON'T WANNA. I CAN ALREADY TELL THE BOSS IS GONNA GET PISSED IF WE DO.
DON'T DRAG US INTO YOUR SHIT.
AND MY BOYS ARE A BUNCH OF CHICKEN-SHITS.
MULTIPURPOS
PAINT

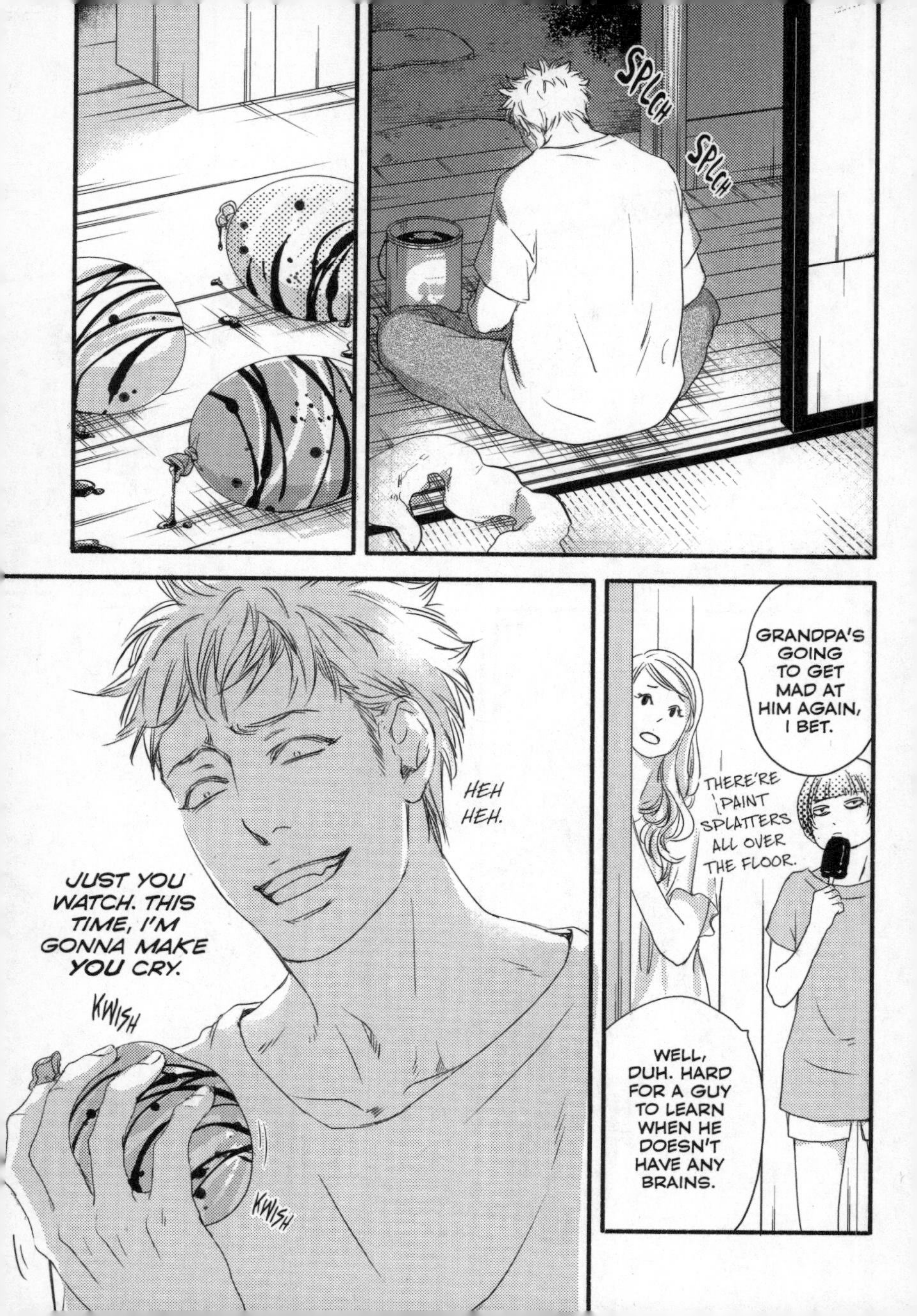
SPLCH
SPLCH
GRANDPA'S GOING TO GET MAD AT HIM AGAIN, I BET.
THERE'RE PAINT SPLATTERS ALL OVER THE FLOOR.
WELL, DUH. HARD FOR A GUY TO LEARN WHEN HE DOESN'T HAVE ANY BRAINS.
HEH HEH.
JUST YOU WATCH. THIS TIME, I'M GONNA MAKE YOU CRY.
KWISH
KWISH

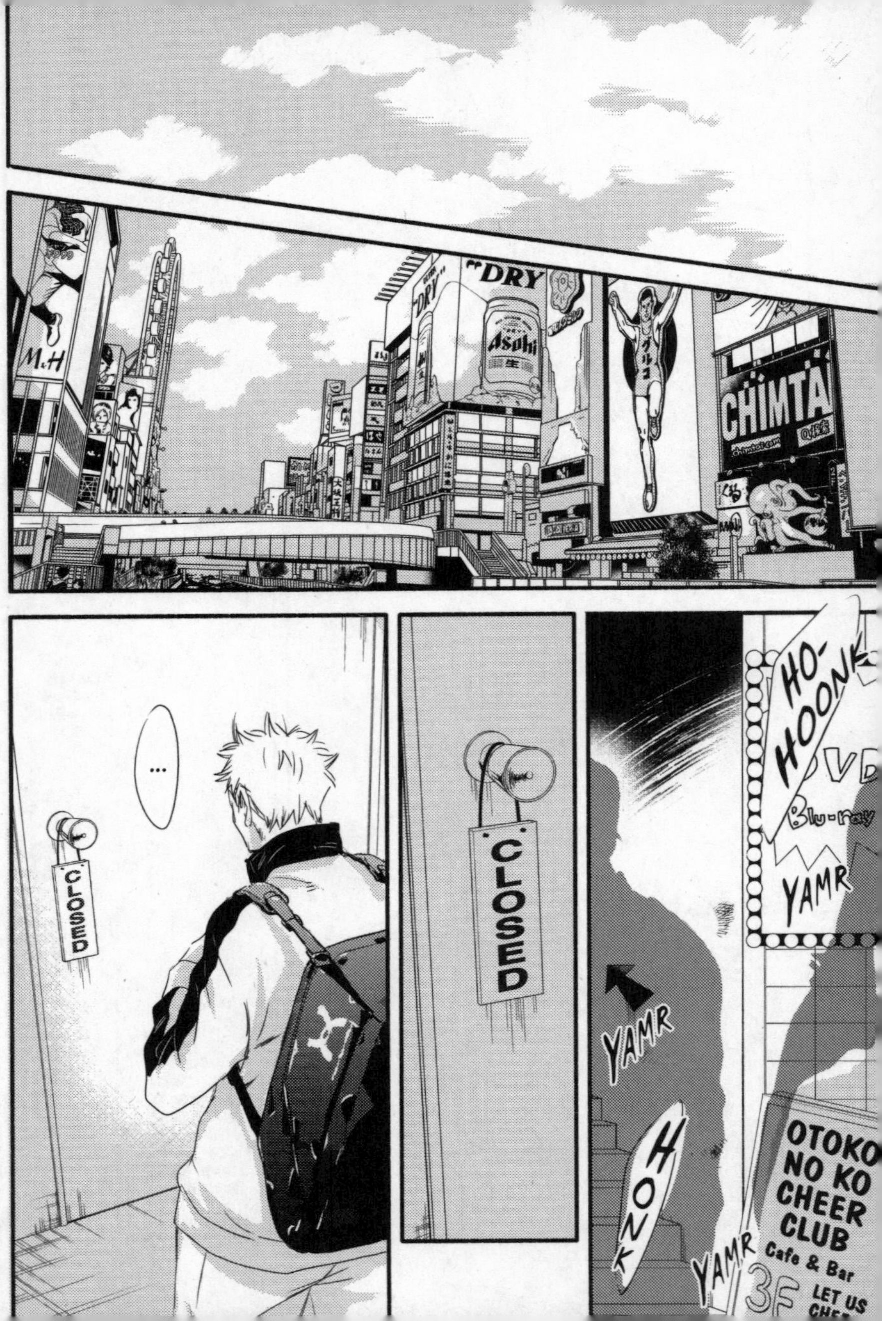
"DRY
DRY
Asahi
CHIMTA
HO-HOONK
Blu-ray
YAMR
YAMR
HONK
YAMR
OTOKO NO KO CHEER CLUB
Cafe & Bar
3F
LET US
CLOSED
...
CLOSED

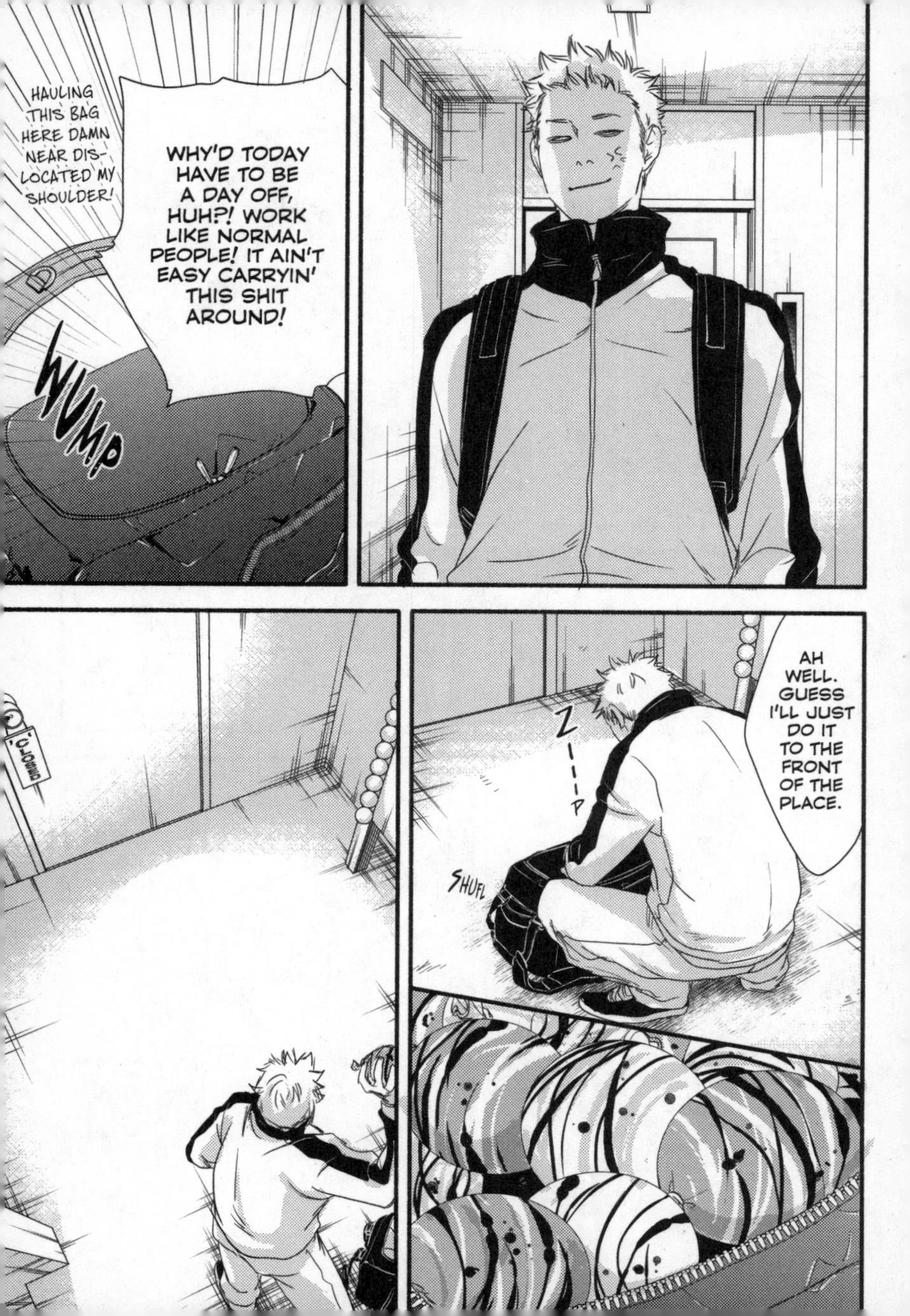
WHY'D TODAY HAVE TO BE A DAY OFF, HUH?! WORK LIKE NORMAL PEOPLE! IT AIN'T EASY CARRYIN' THIS SHIT AROUND!
HAULING THIS BAG HERE DAMN NEAR DIS-LOCATED MY SHOULDER!
WUMP
AH WELL. GUESS I'LL JUST DO IT TO THE FRONT OF THE PLACE.
ZIIIP
SHUFL

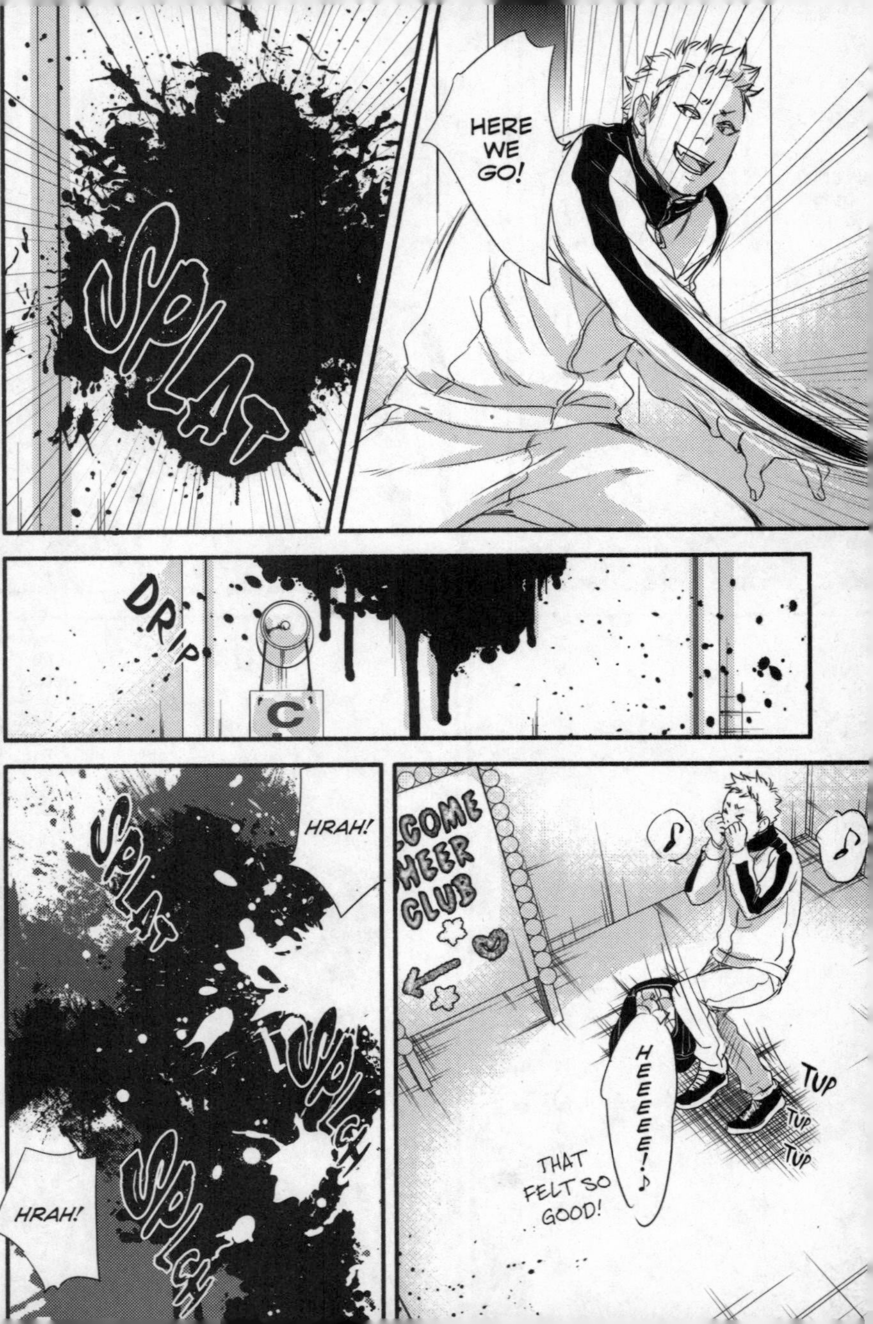
HERE WE GO!
SPLAT
DRIP
C
COME
HEER
CLUB
HEEEEE!♪
THAT FELT SO GOOD!
TUP
TUP
TUP
HRAH!
SPLAT
SPLACH
SPLCH
HRAH!

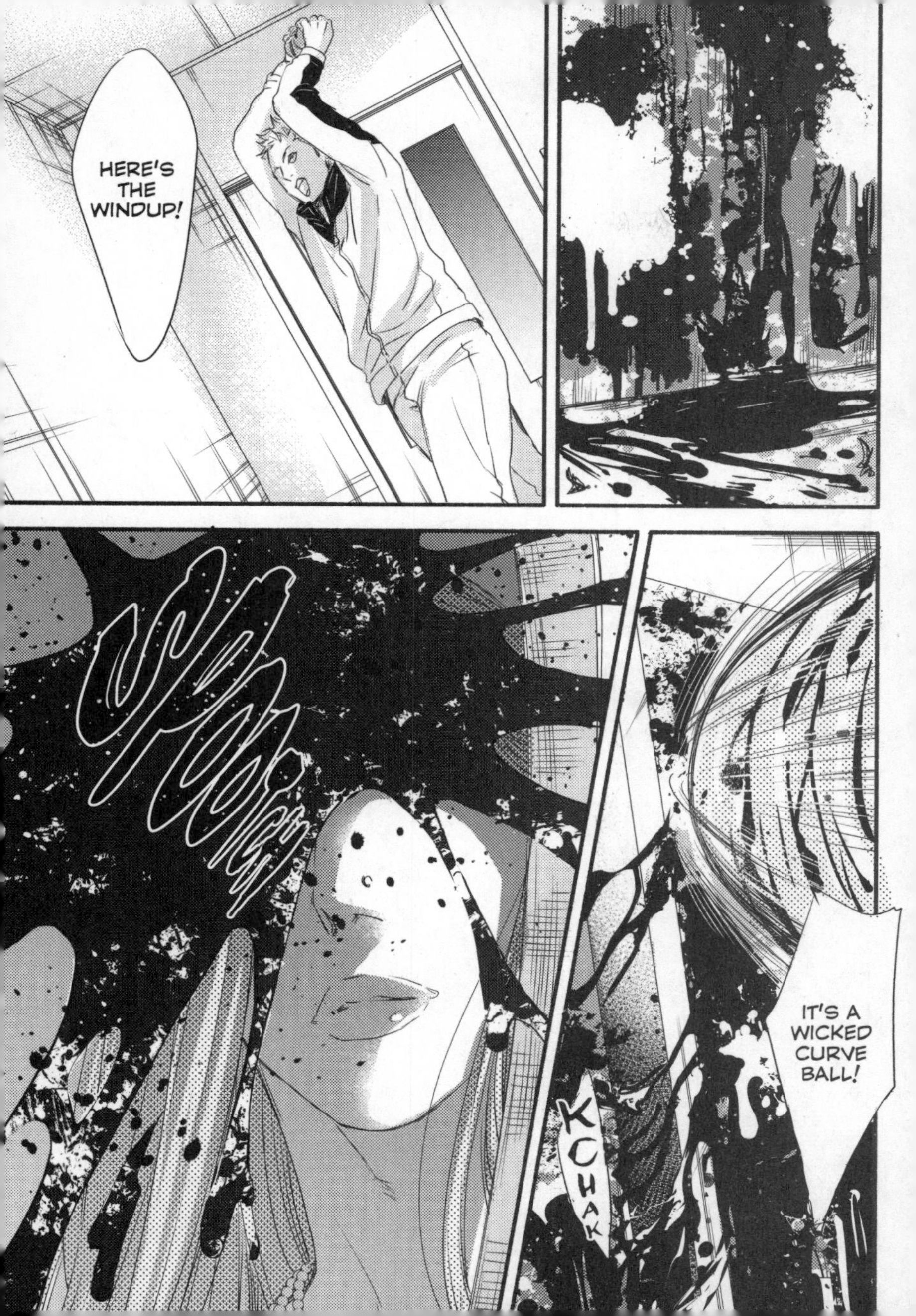
HERE'S THE WINDUP!
IT'S A WICKED CURVE BALL!
KCHAK

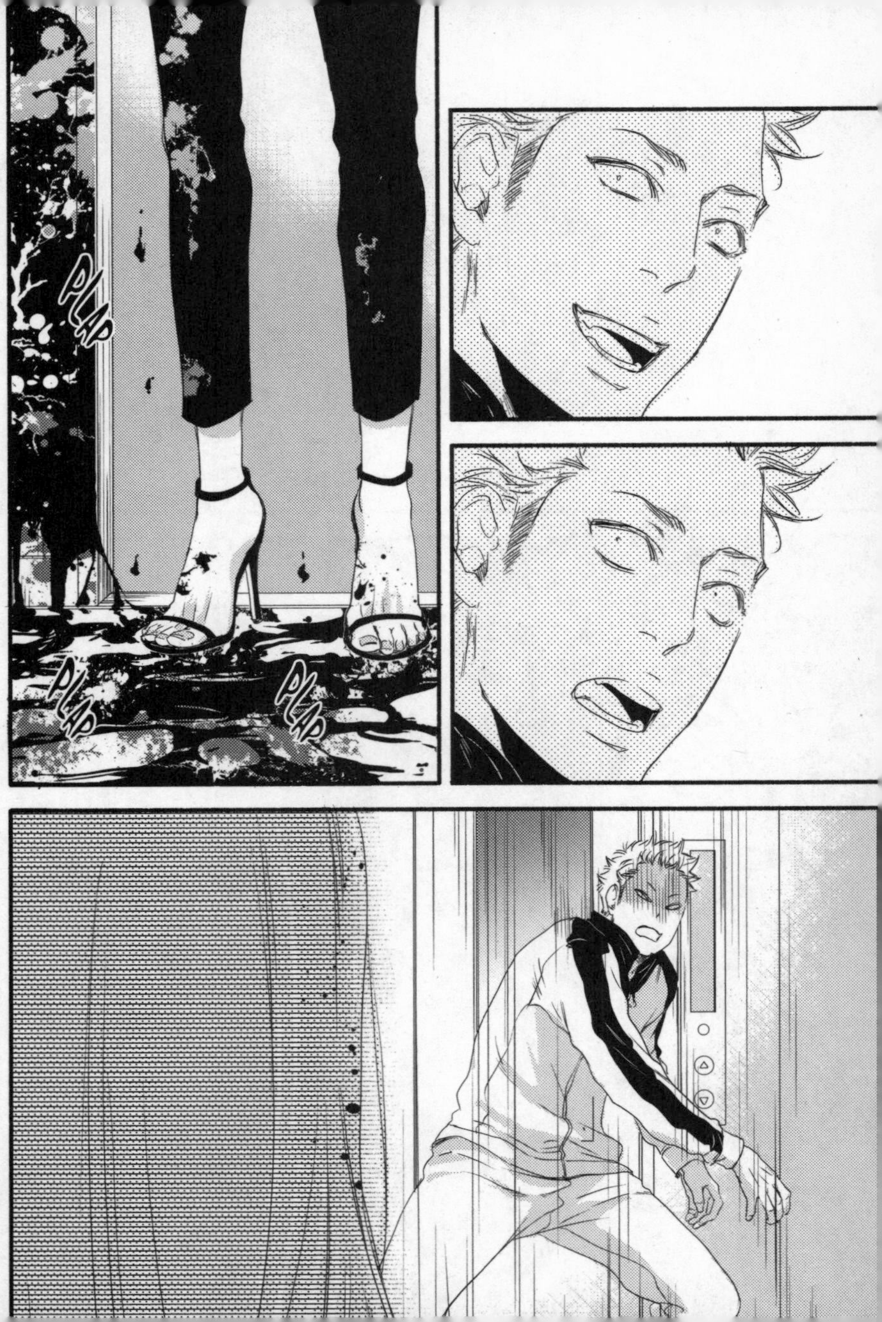
PLAP
PLAP
PLAP

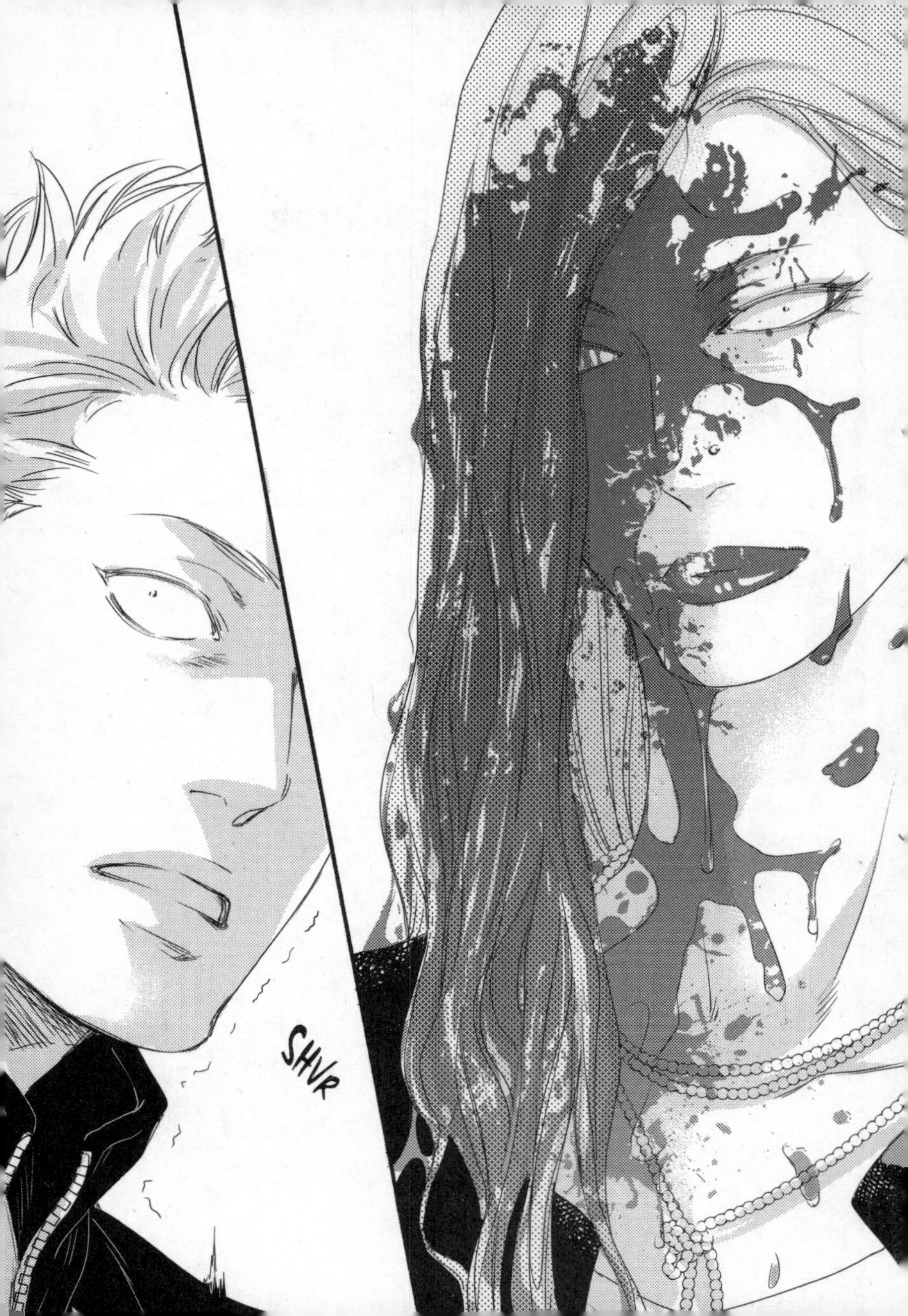
SHVR

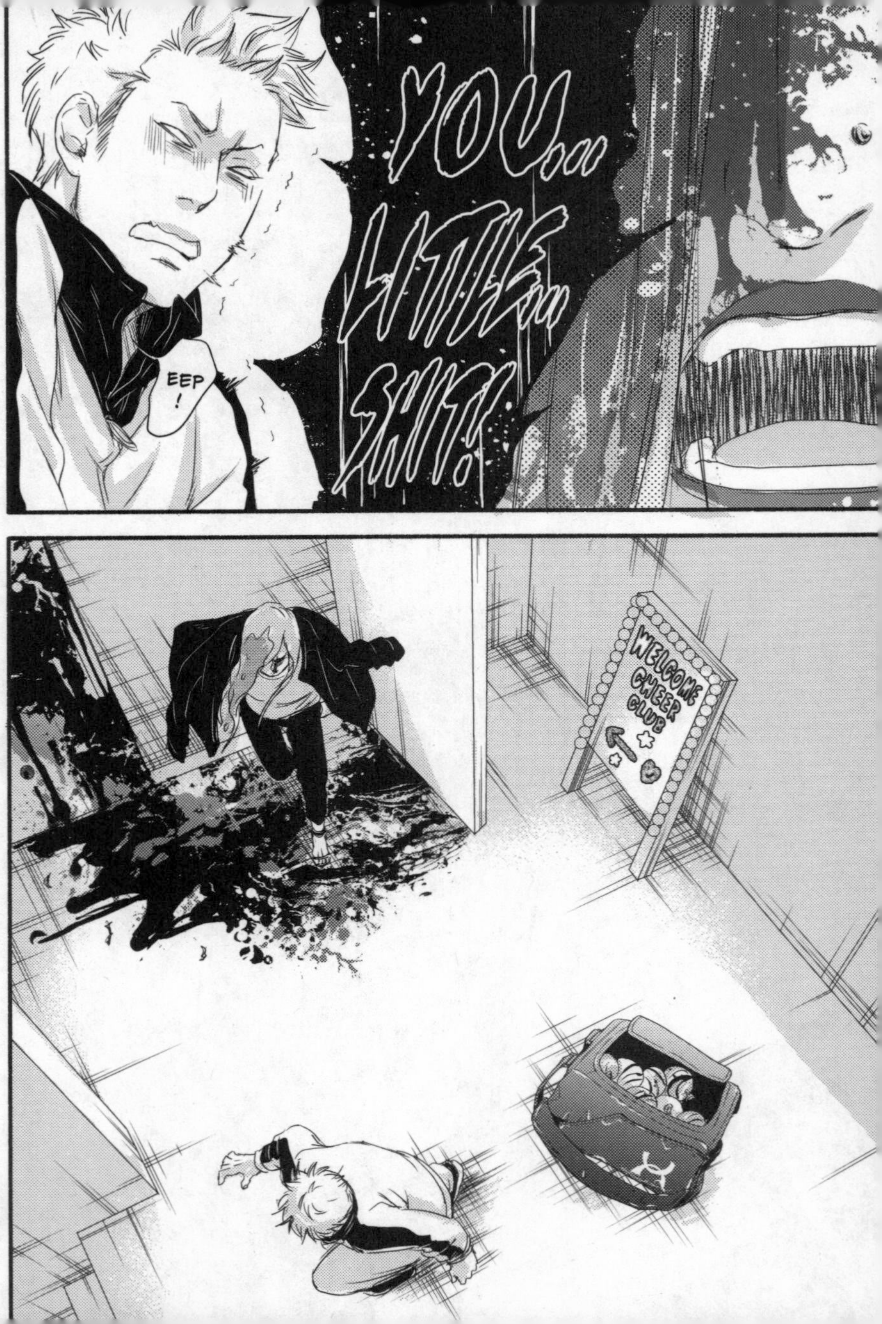
YOU... LITTLE... SHIT!!
EEP!
WELCOME CHEER CLUB

Chapter 2

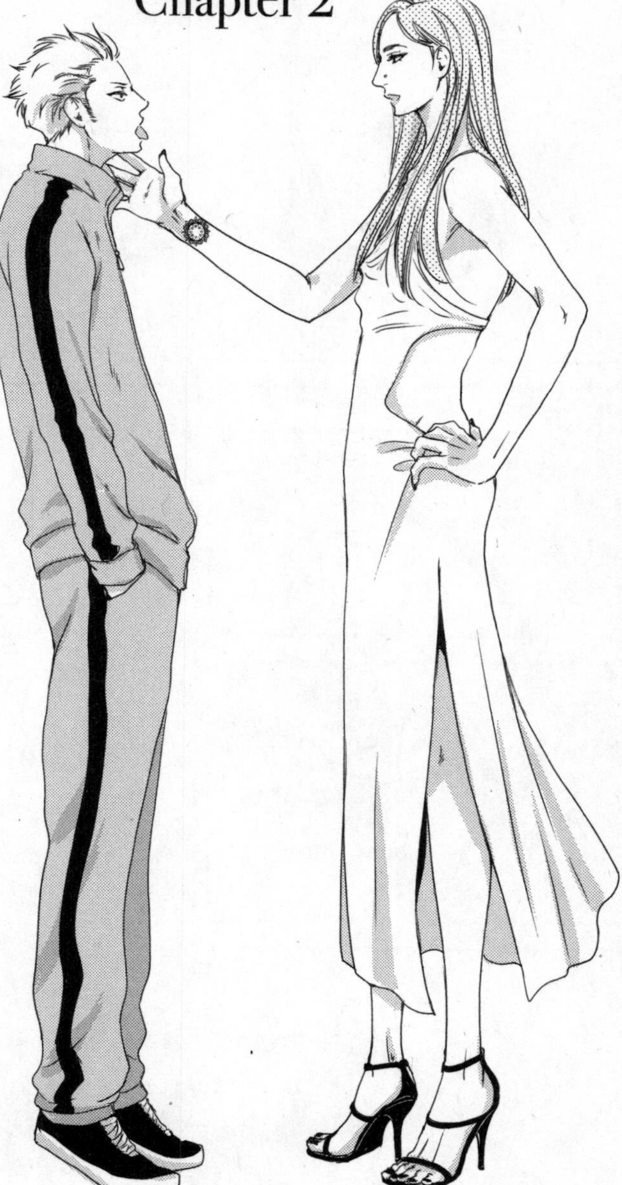

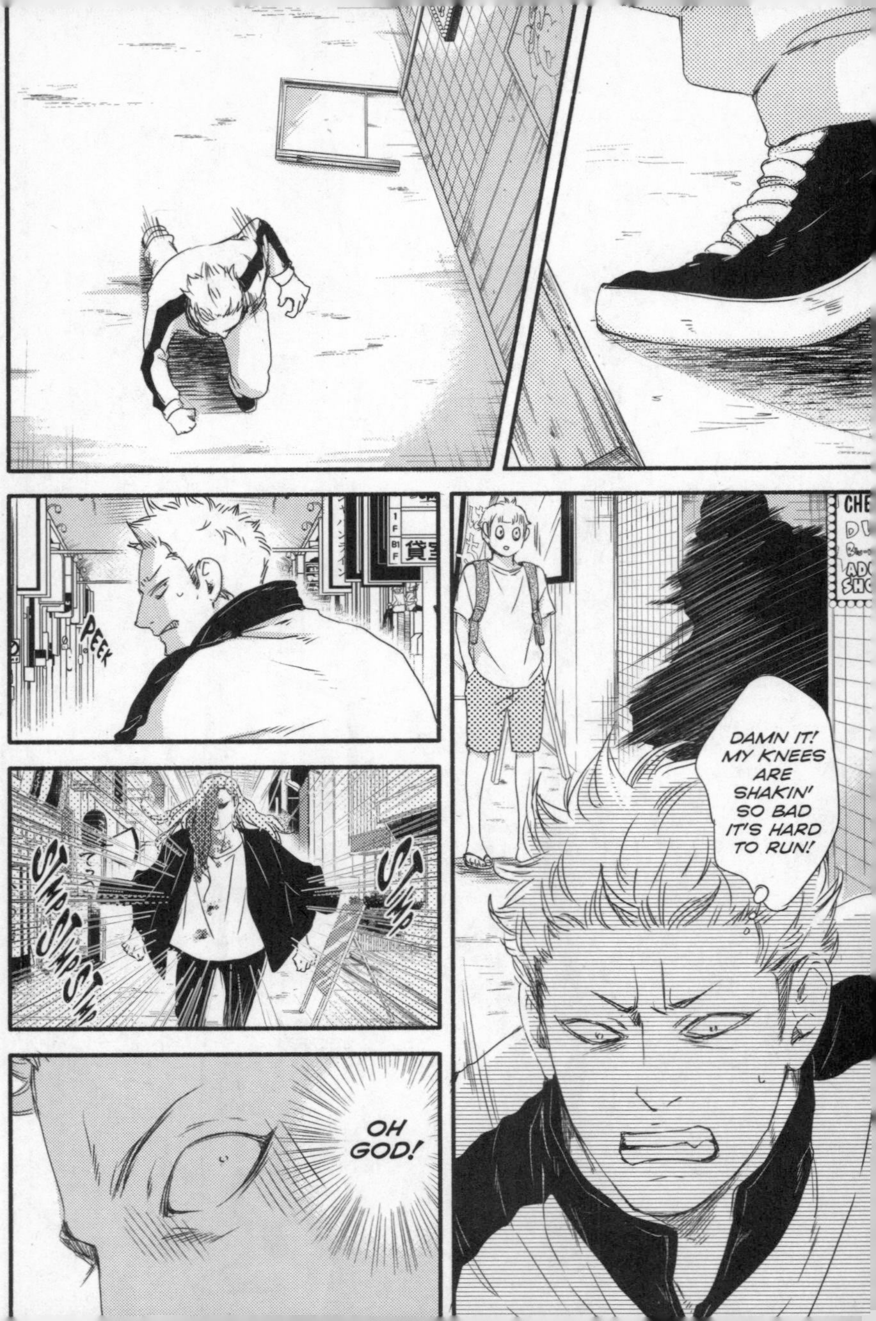
DAMN IT! MY KNEES ARE SHAKIN' SO BAD IT'S HARD TO RUN!
1F
B1F
貸室
PEEK
STMP
STMP STMP STMP
OH GOD!

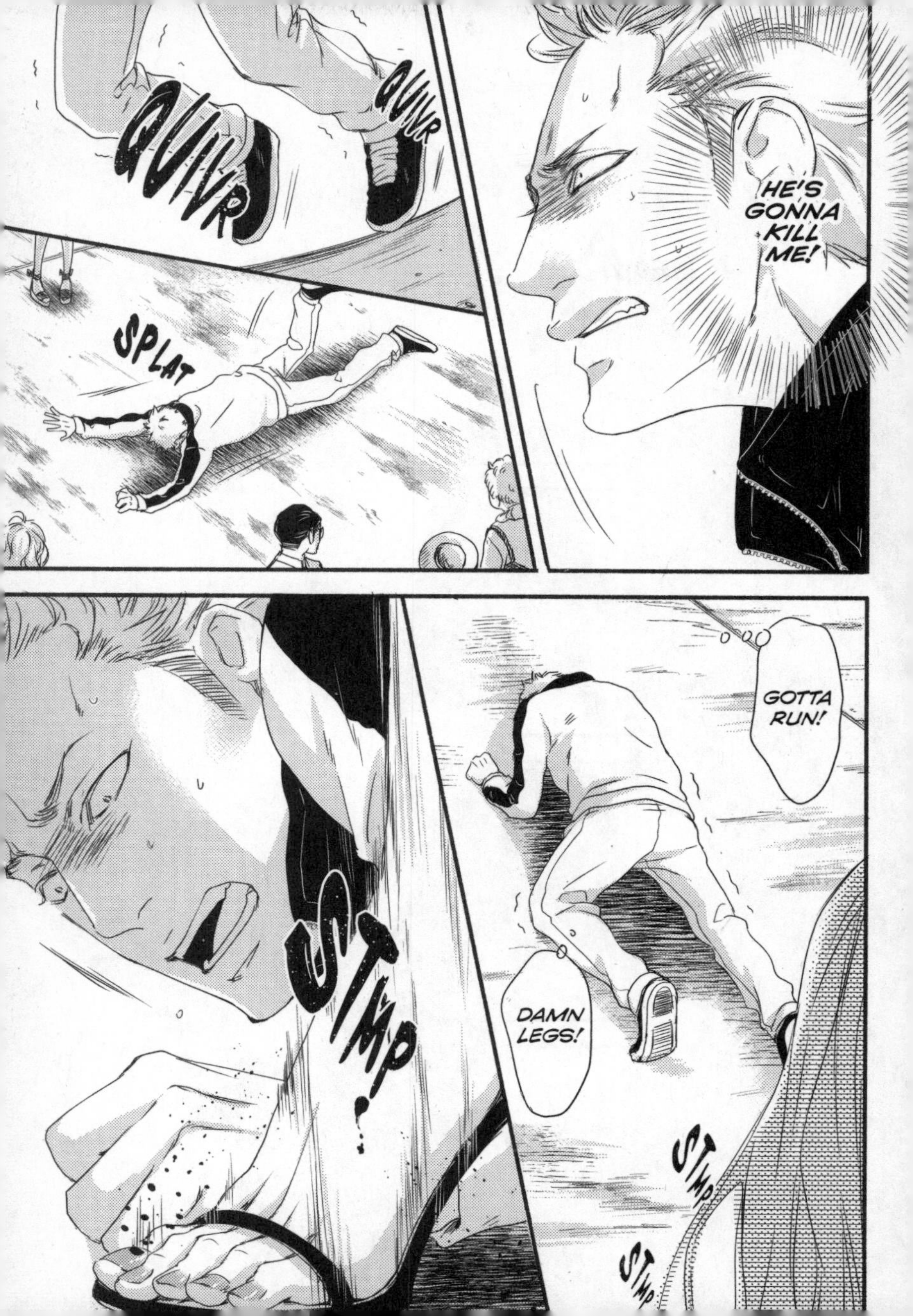
HE'S GONNA KILL ME!
QUIVR
QUIVR
SPLAT
GOTTA RUN!
DAMN LEGS!
STMP
STMP
STMP!

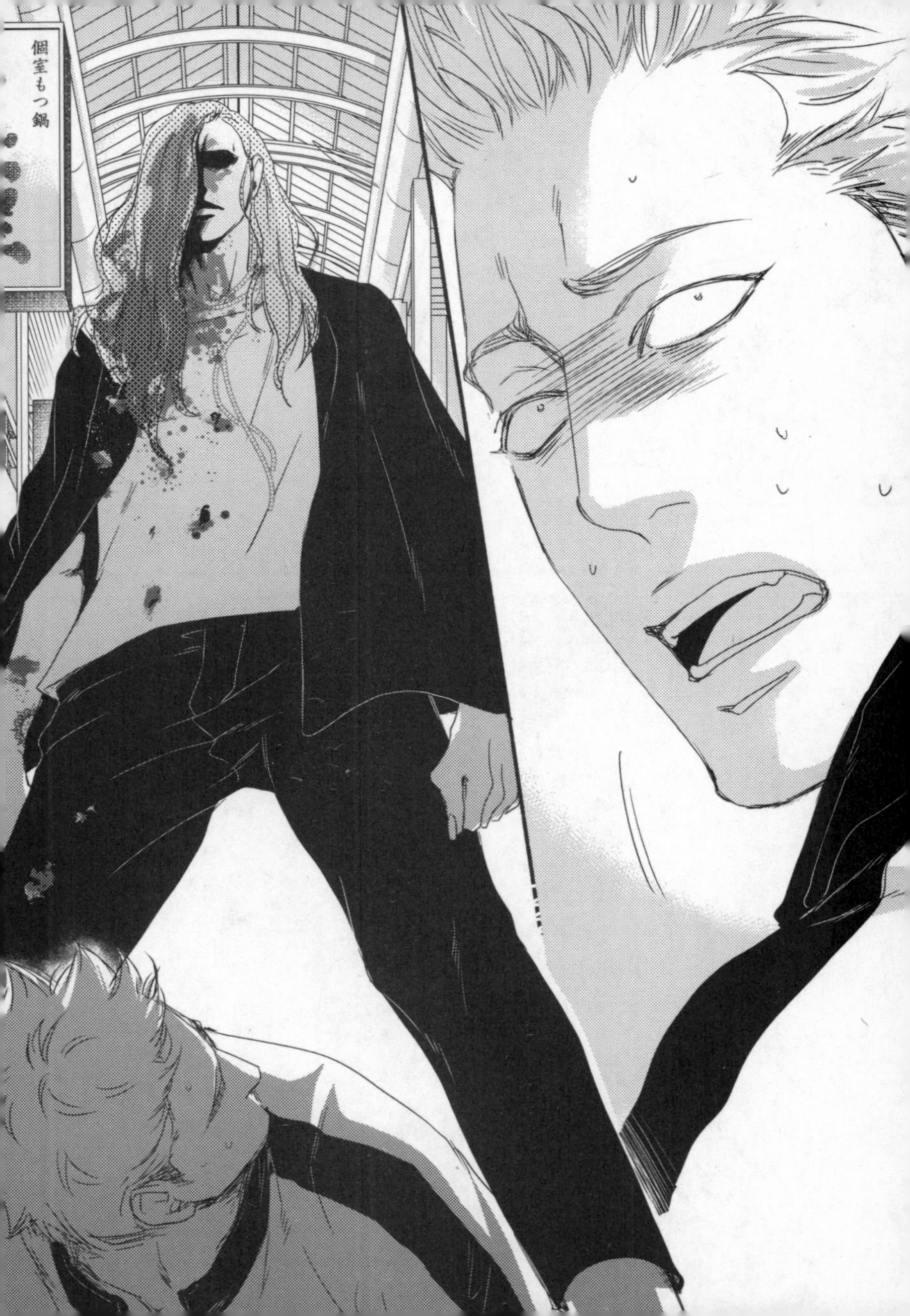
個室もつ鍋

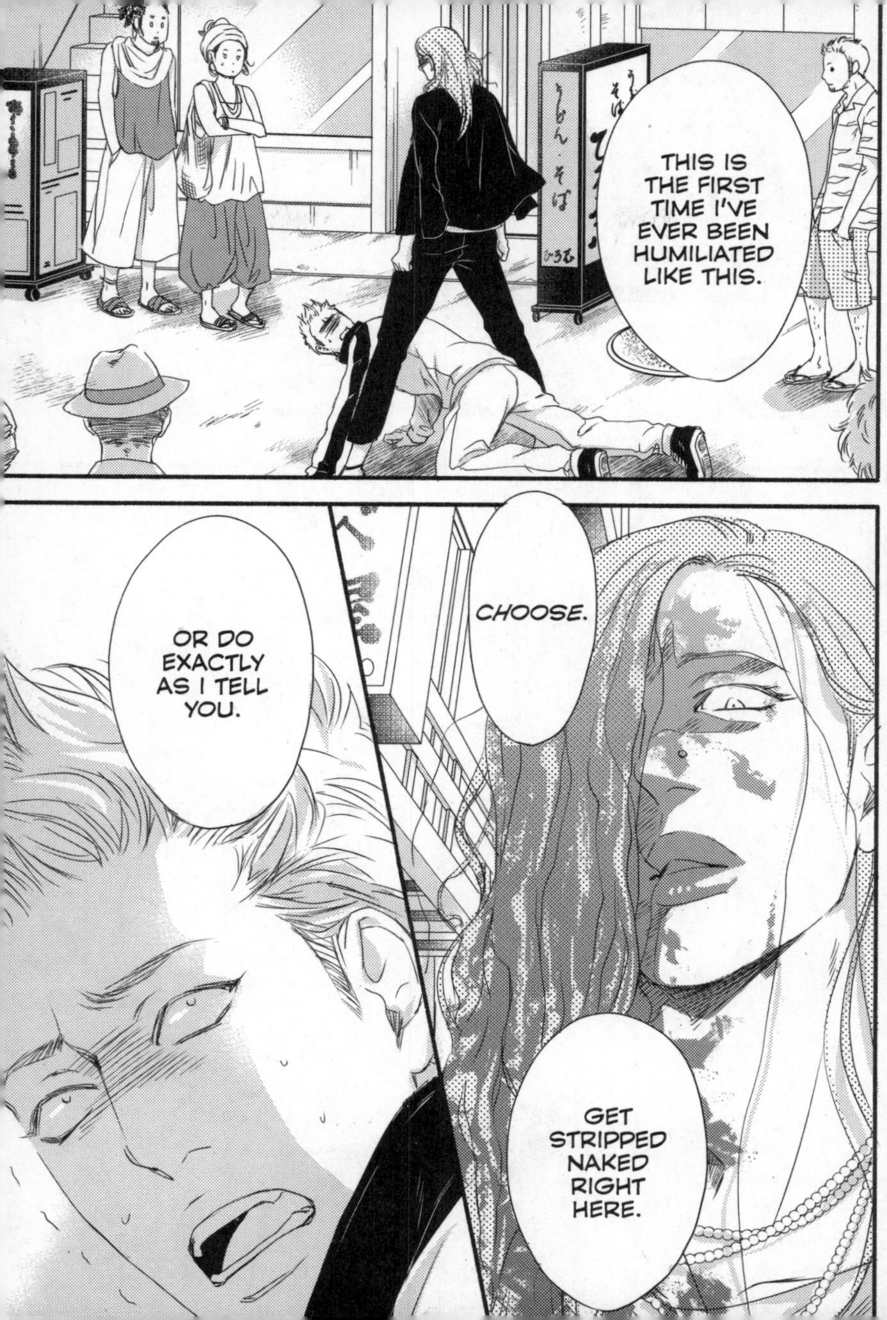
THIS IS THE FIRST TIME I'VE EVER BEEN HUMILIATED LIKE THIS.
CHOOSE.
GET STRIPPED NAKED RIGHT HERE.
OR DO EXACTLY AS I TELL YOU.

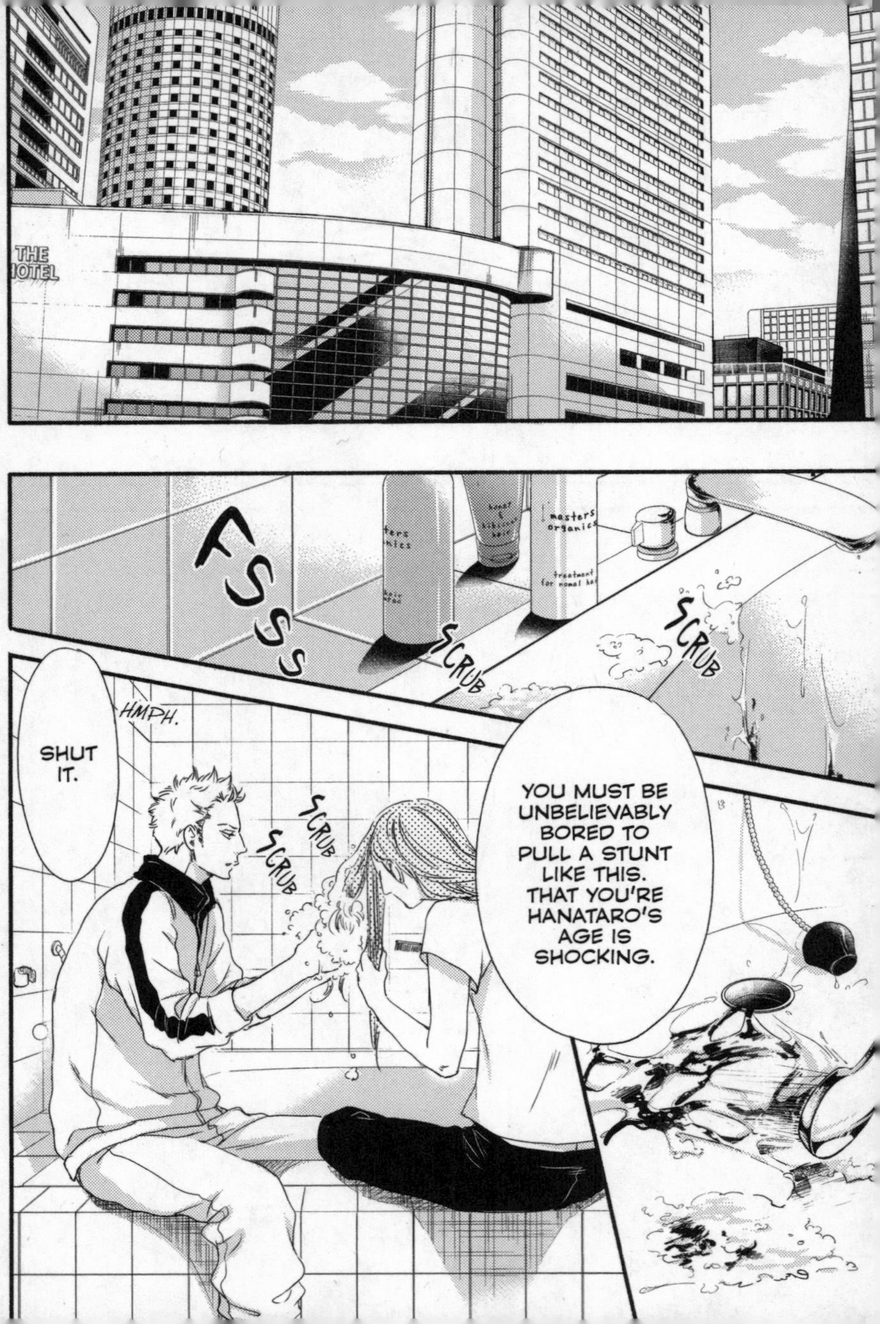
THE HOTEL
FSSS
SCRUB
SCRUB
masters organics
YOU MUST BE UNBELIEVABLY BORED TO PULL A STUNT LIKE THIS. THAT YOU'RE HANATARO'S AGE IS SHOCKING.
HMPH.
SHUT IT.
SCRUB
SCRUB

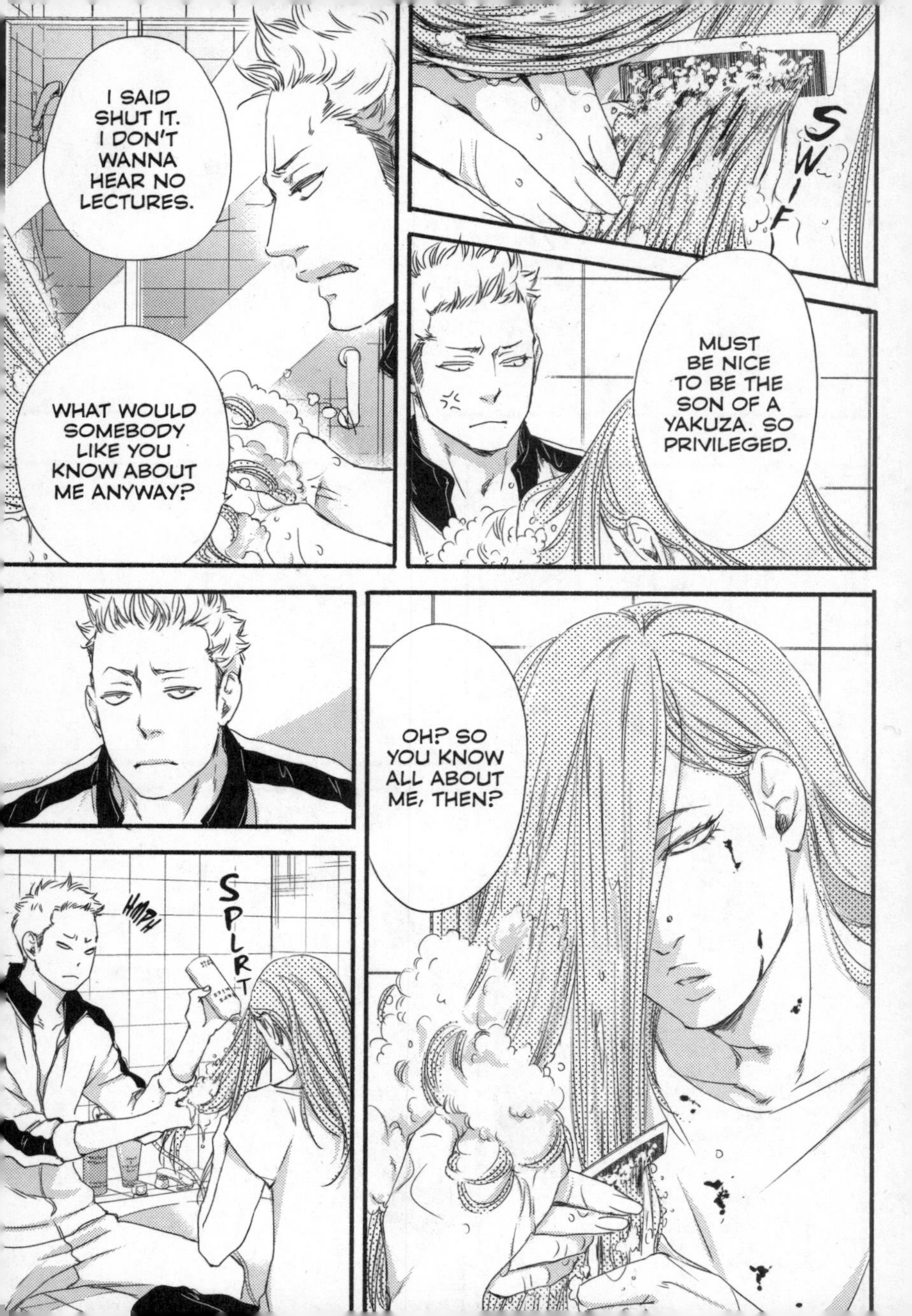
SWIF
MUST BE NICE TO BE THE SON OF A YAKUZA. SO PRIVILEGED.
I SAID SHUT IT. I DON'T WANNA HEAR NO LECTURES.
WHAT WOULD SOMEBODY LIKE YOU KNOW ABOUT ME ANYWAY?
OH? SO YOU KNOW ALL ABOUT ME, THEN?
HMPH
SPLRT

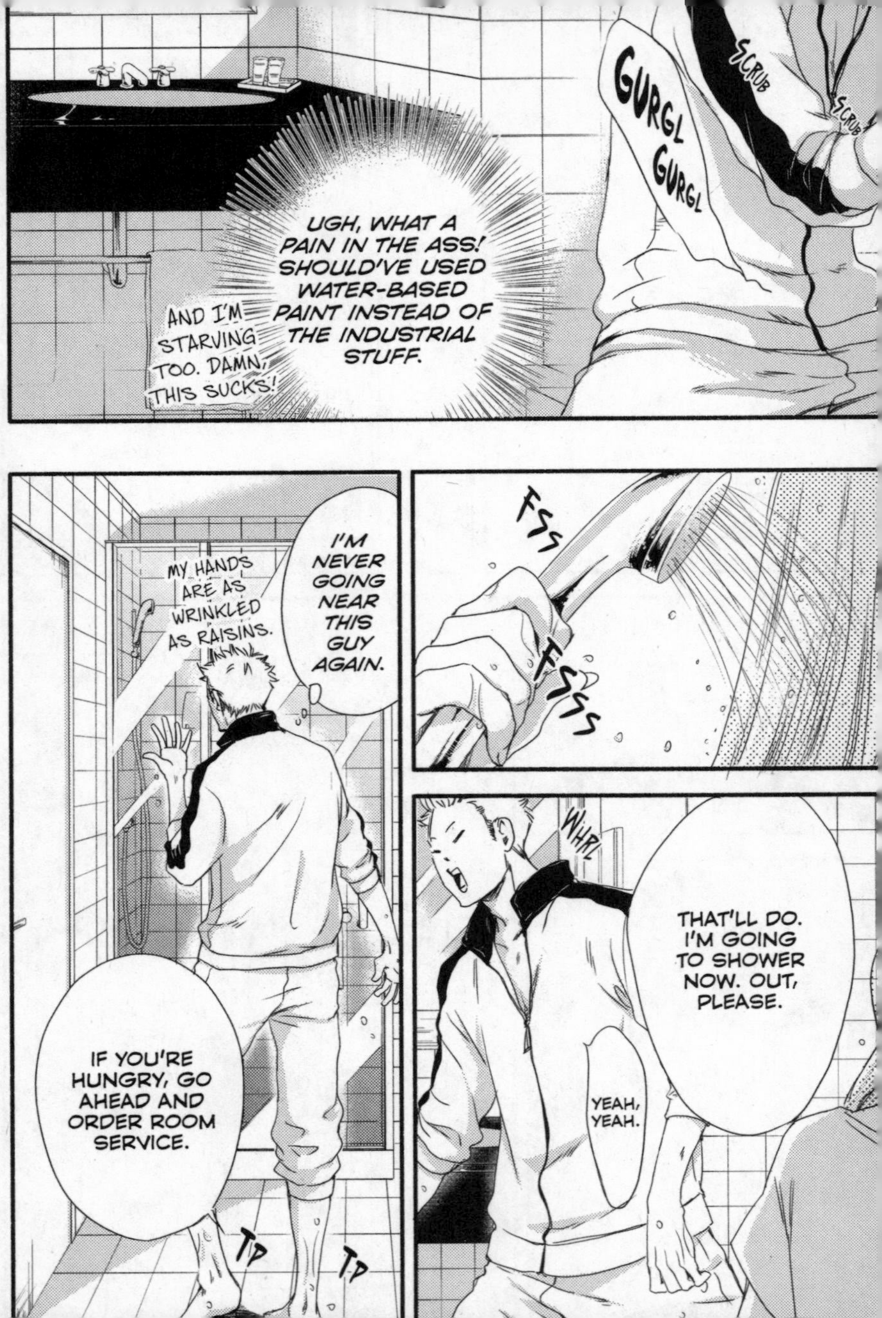
SCRUB
SCRUB
GURGL
GURGL
UGH, WHAT A PAIN IN THE ASS! SHOULD'VE USED WATER-BASED PAINT INSTEAD OF THE INDUSTRIAL STUFF.
AND I'M STARVING TOO. DAMN, THIS SUCKS!
FSS
FSSS
WHRL
THAT'LL DO. I'M GOING TO SHOWER NOW. OUT, PLEASE.
YEAH, YEAH.
I'M NEVER GOING NEAR THIS GUY AGAIN.
MY HANDS ARE AS WRINKLED AS RAISINS.
IF YOU'RE HUNGRY, GO AHEAD AND ORDER ROOM SERVICE.
TP
TP

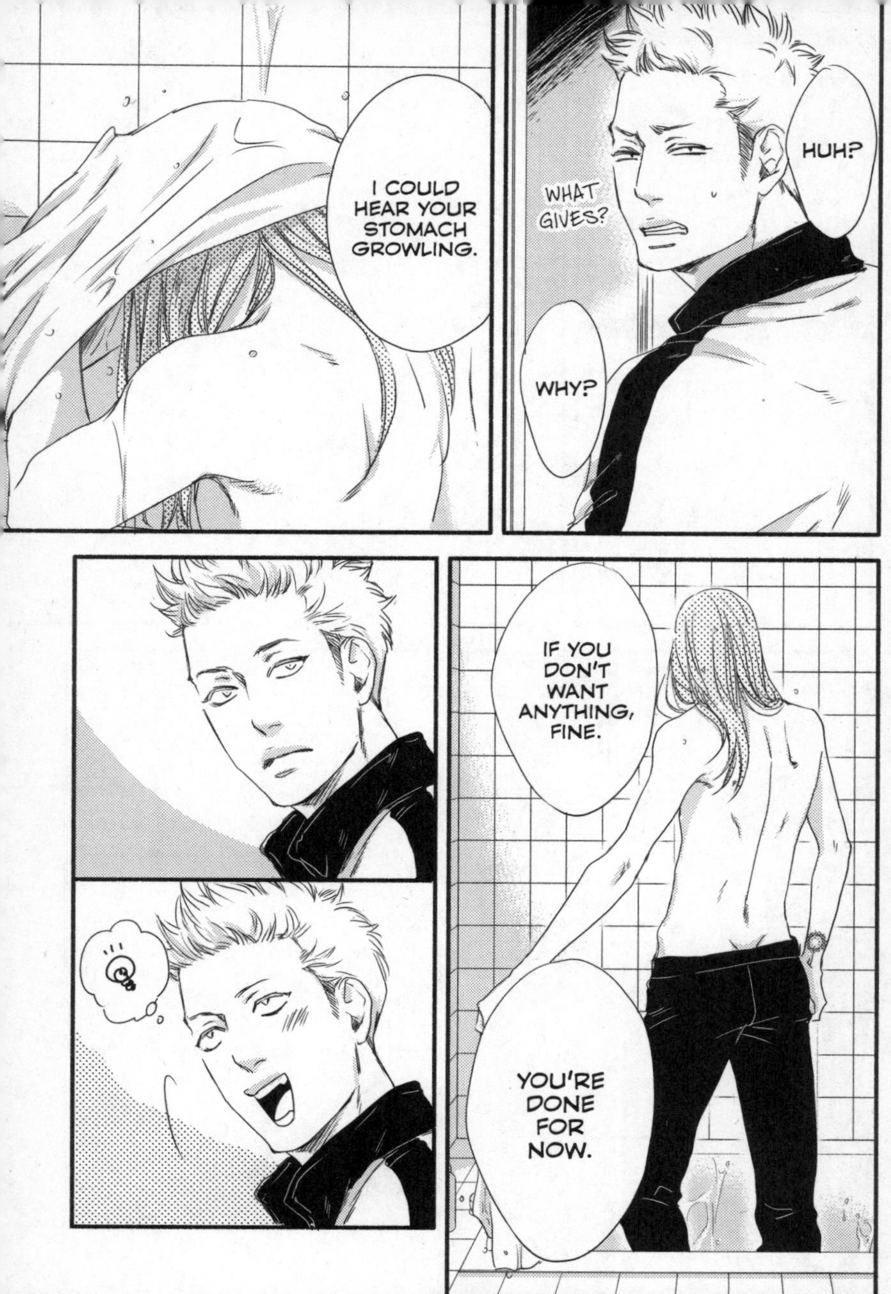
HUH?
WHAT GIVES?
WHY?
I COULD HEAR YOUR STOMACH GROWLING.
IF YOU DON'T WANT ANYTHING, FINE.
YOU'RE DONE FOR NOW.

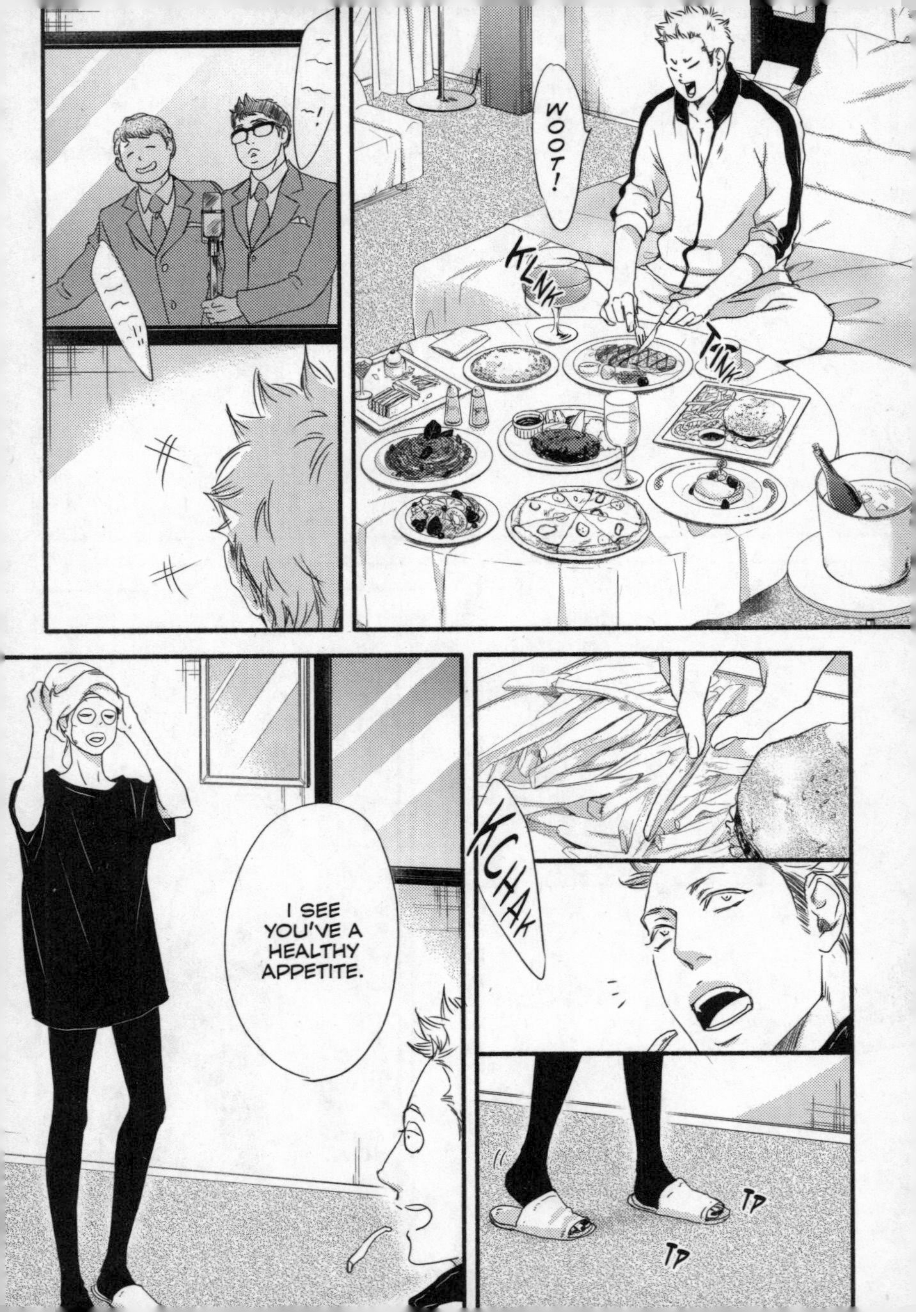
WOOT!
KLNK
TINK
~~~~!
~~~!!
KCHAK
TP
TP
I SEE YOU'VE A HEALTHY APPETITE.

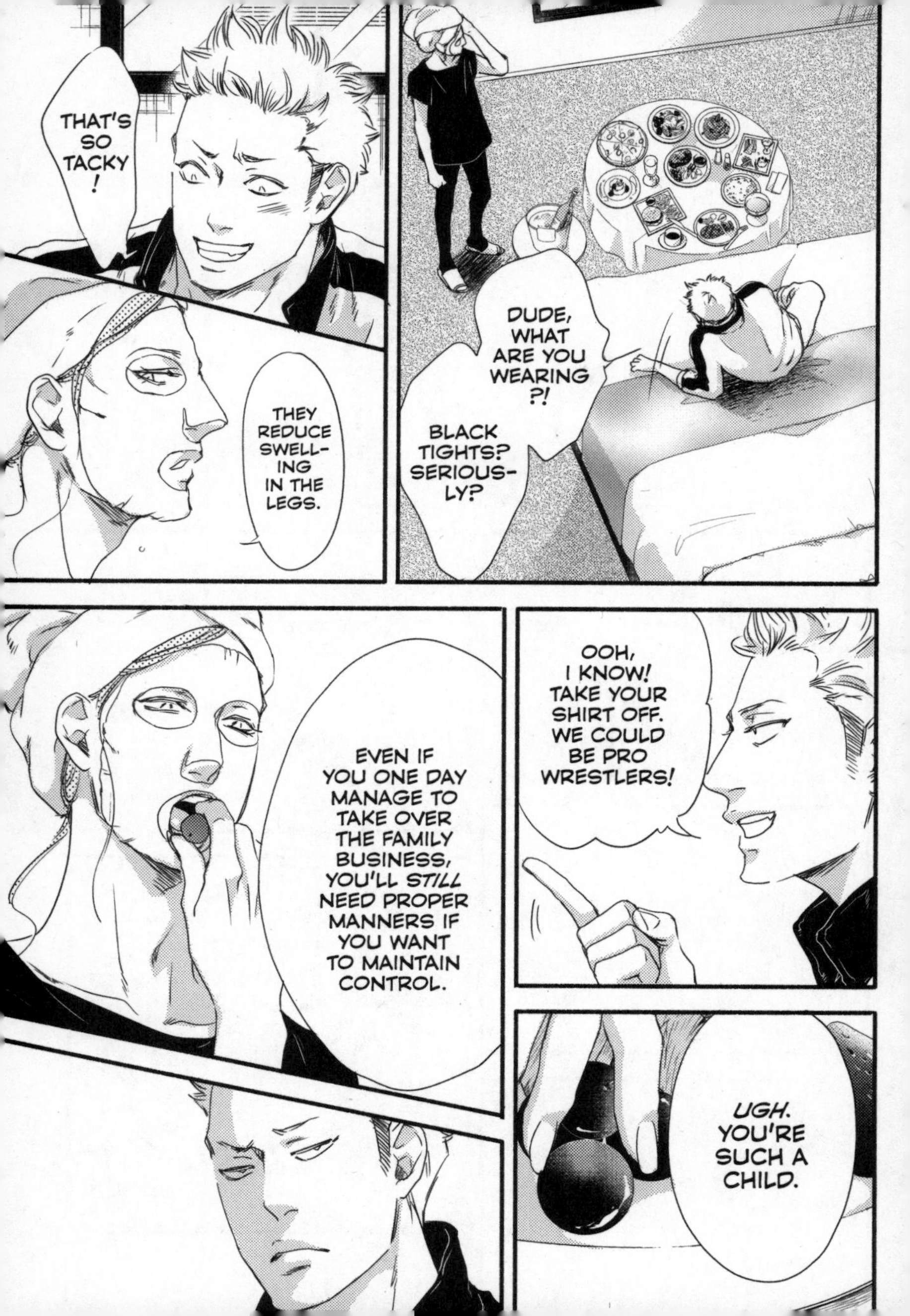
DUDE, WHAT ARE YOU WEARING?!
BLACK TIGHTS? SERIOUSLY?
THAT'S SO TACKY!
THEY REDUCE SWELLING IN THE LEGS.
OOH, I KNOW! TAKE YOUR SHIRT OFF. WE COULD BE PRO WRESTLERS!
UGH. YOU'RE SUCH A CHILD.
EVEN IF YOU ONE DAY MANAGE TO TAKE OVER THE FAMILY BUSINESS, YOU'LL *STILL* NEED PROPER MANNERS IF YOU WANT TO MAINTAIN CONTROL.

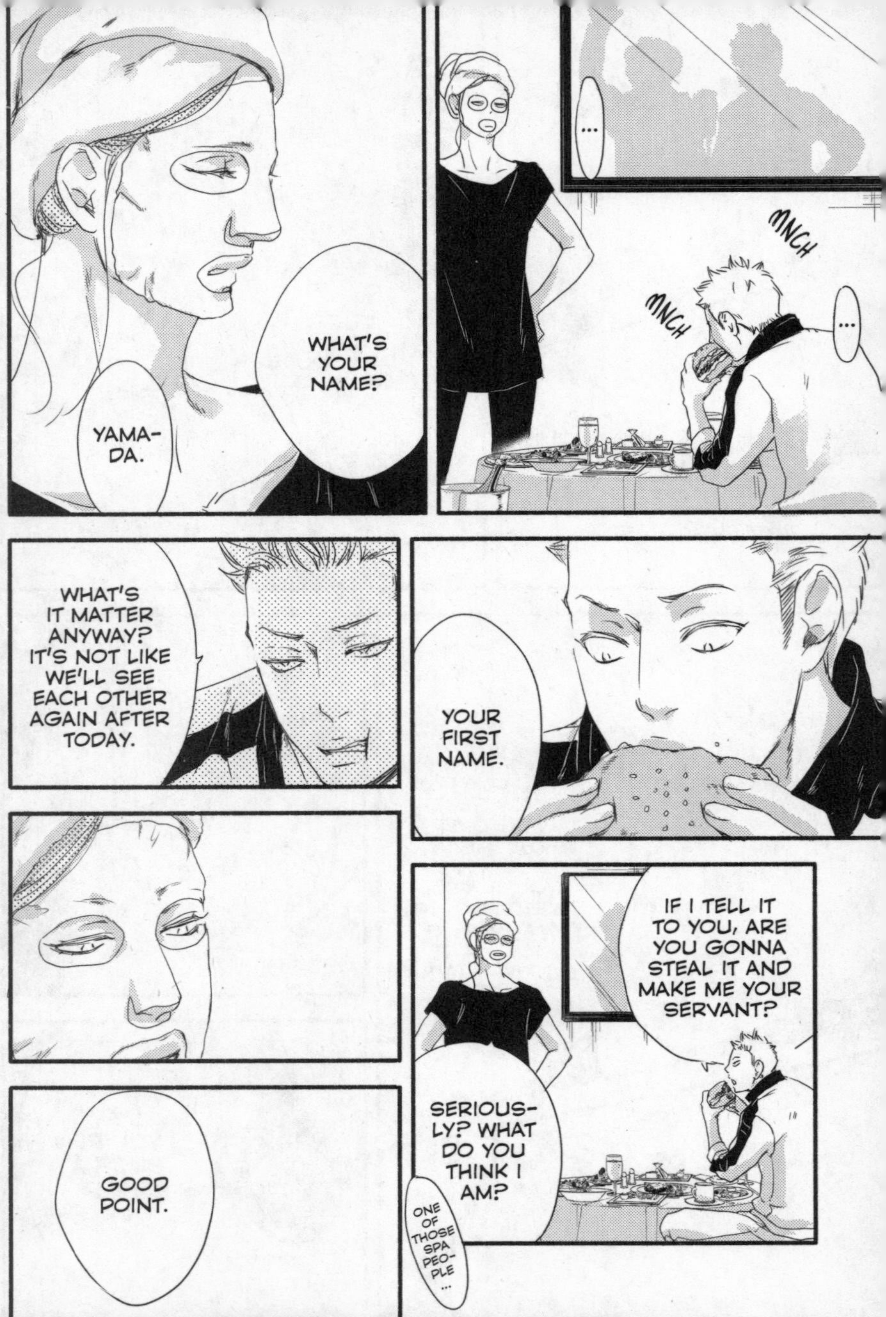
...
MNCH
MNCH
...
WHAT'S YOUR NAME?
YAMA-DA.
YOUR FIRST NAME.
WHAT'S IT MATTER ANYWAY? IT'S NOT LIKE WE'LL SEE EACH OTHER AGAIN AFTER TODAY.
GOOD POINT.
IF I TELL IT TO YOU, ARE YOU GONNA STEAL IT AND MAKE ME YOUR SERVANT?
SERIOUS-LY? WHAT DO YOU THINK I AM?
ONE OF THOSE SPA PEO-PLE...

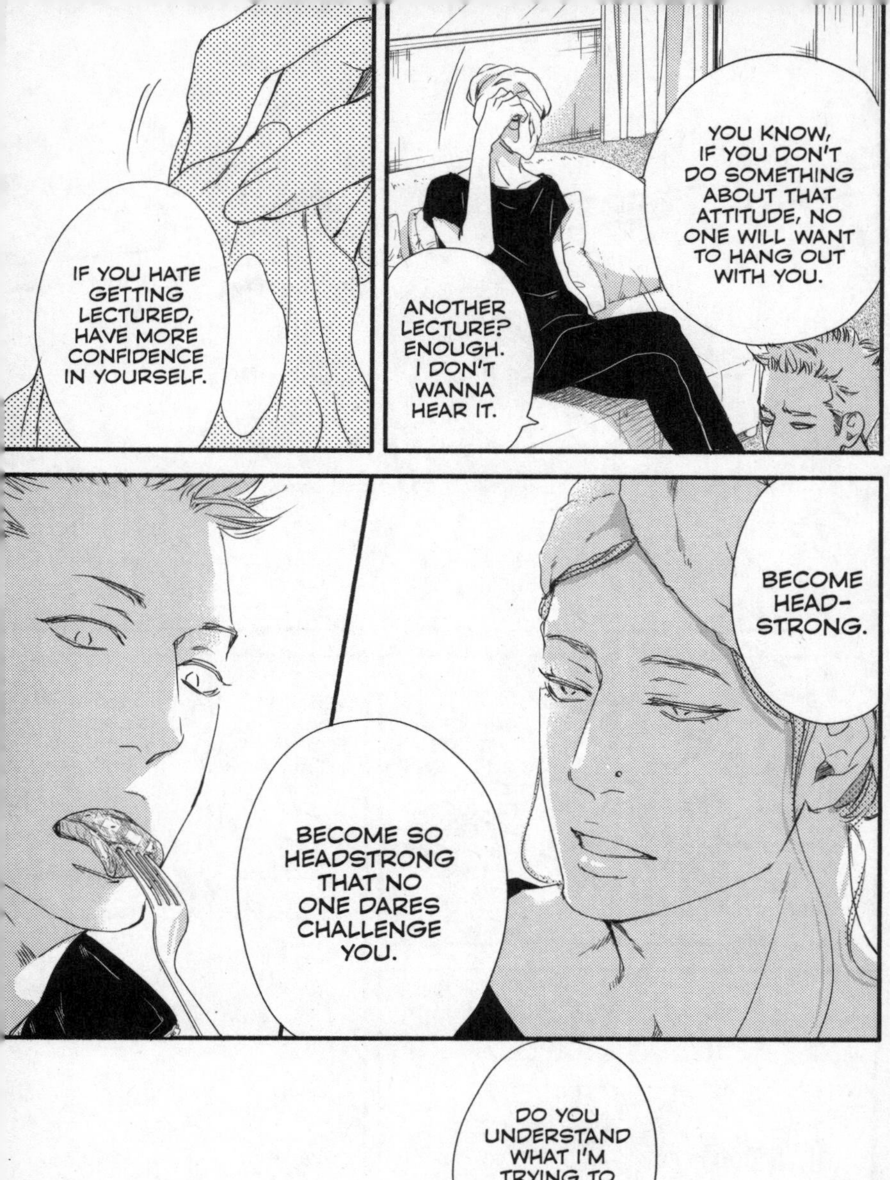
YOU KNOW, IF YOU DON'T DO SOMETHING ABOUT THAT ATTITUDE, NO ONE WILL WANT TO HANG OUT WITH YOU.
ANOTHER LECTURE? ENOUGH. I DON'T WANNA HEAR IT.
IF YOU HATE GETTING LECTURED, HAVE MORE CONFIDENCE IN YOURSELF.
BECOME HEAD-STRONG.
BECOME SO HEADSTRONG THAT NO ONE DARES CHALLENGE YOU.
DO YOU UNDERSTAND WHAT I'M TRYING TO TELL YOU?

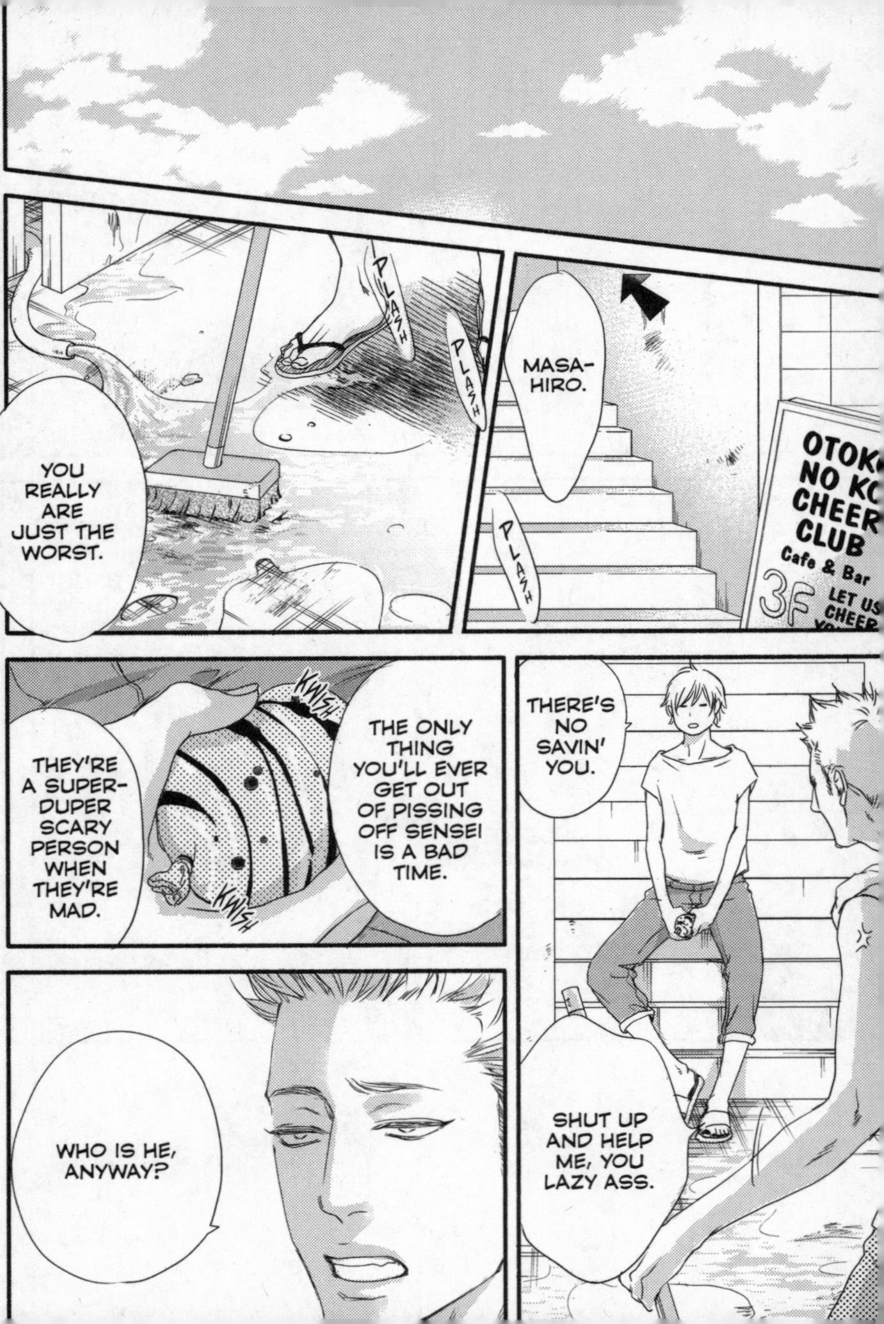
MASA-HIRO.
PLASH
OTOK
NO K
CHEER
CLUB
Cafe & Bar
3F
LET US
CHEER
PLASH
PLASH
YOU REALLY ARE JUST THE WORST.
THERE'S NO SAVIN' YOU.
SHUT UP AND HELP ME, YOU LAZY ASS.
KWISH
THE ONLY THING YOU'LL EVER GET OUT OF PISSING OFF SENSEI IS A BAD TIME.
THEY'RE A SUPER-DUPER SCARY PERSON WHEN THEY'RE MAD.
KWISH
WHO IS HE, ANYWAY?

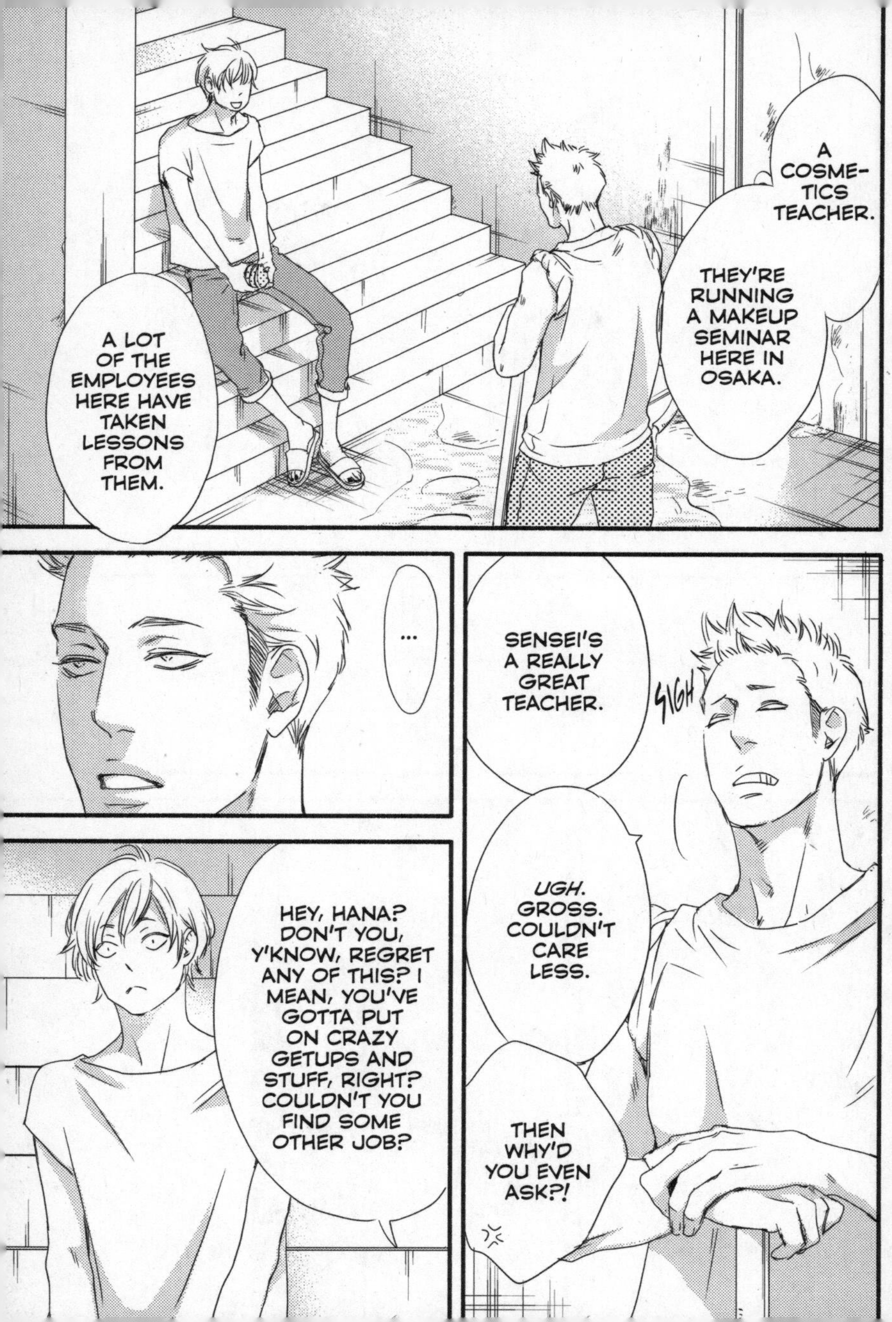
A COSME-TICS TEACHER.
THEY'RE RUNNING A MAKEUP SEMINAR HERE IN OSAKA.
A LOT OF THE EMPLOYEES HERE HAVE TAKEN LESSONS FROM THEM.
SENSEI'S A REALLY GREAT TEACHER.
SIGH
UGH. GROSS. COULDN'T CARE LESS.
THEN WHY'D YOU EVEN ASK?!
...
HEY, HANA? DON'T YOU, Y'KNOW, REGRET ANY OF THIS? I MEAN, YOU'VE GOTTA PUT ON CRAZY GETUPS AND STUFF, RIGHT? COULDN'T YOU FIND SOME OTHER JOB?

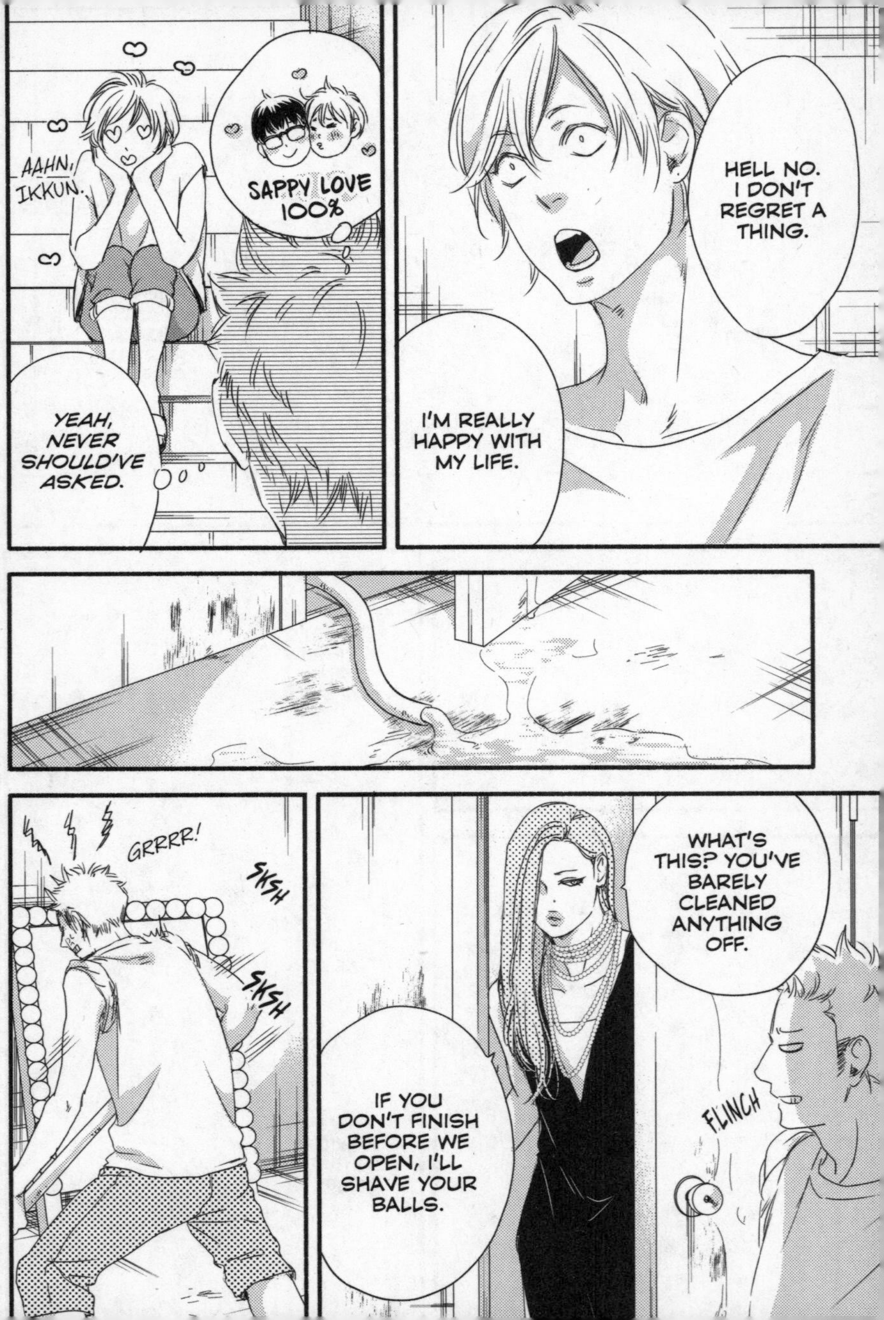
HELL NO. I DON'T REGRET A THING.
I'M REALLY HAPPY WITH MY LIFE.
SAPPY LOVE 100%
AAHN, IKKUN.
YEAH, NEVER SHOULD'VE ASKED.
WHAT'S THIS? YOU'VE BARELY CLEANED ANYTHING OFF.
IF YOU DON'T FINISH BEFORE WE OPEN, I'LL SHAVE YOUR BALLS.
FLINCH
GRRRR!
SKSH
SKSH

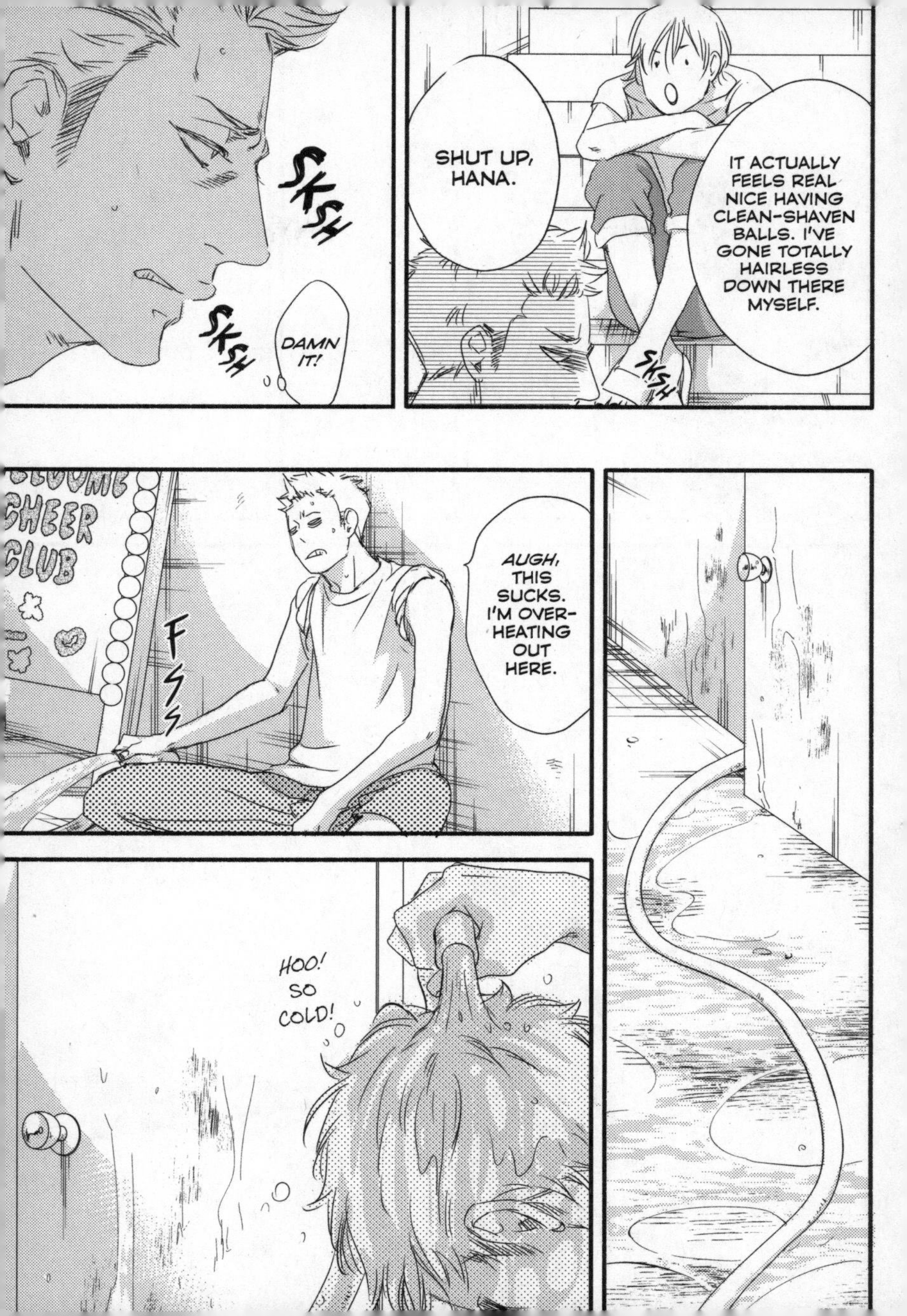
IT ACTUALLY FEELS REAL NICE HAVING CLEAN-SHAVEN BALLS. I'VE GONE TOTALLY HAIRLESS DOWN THERE MYSELF.
SHUT UP, HANA.
SKSH
SKSH
SKSH
DAMN IT!
AUGH, THIS SUCKS. I'M OVER-HEATING OUT HERE.
FSS
CHEER CLUB
HOO! SO COLD!

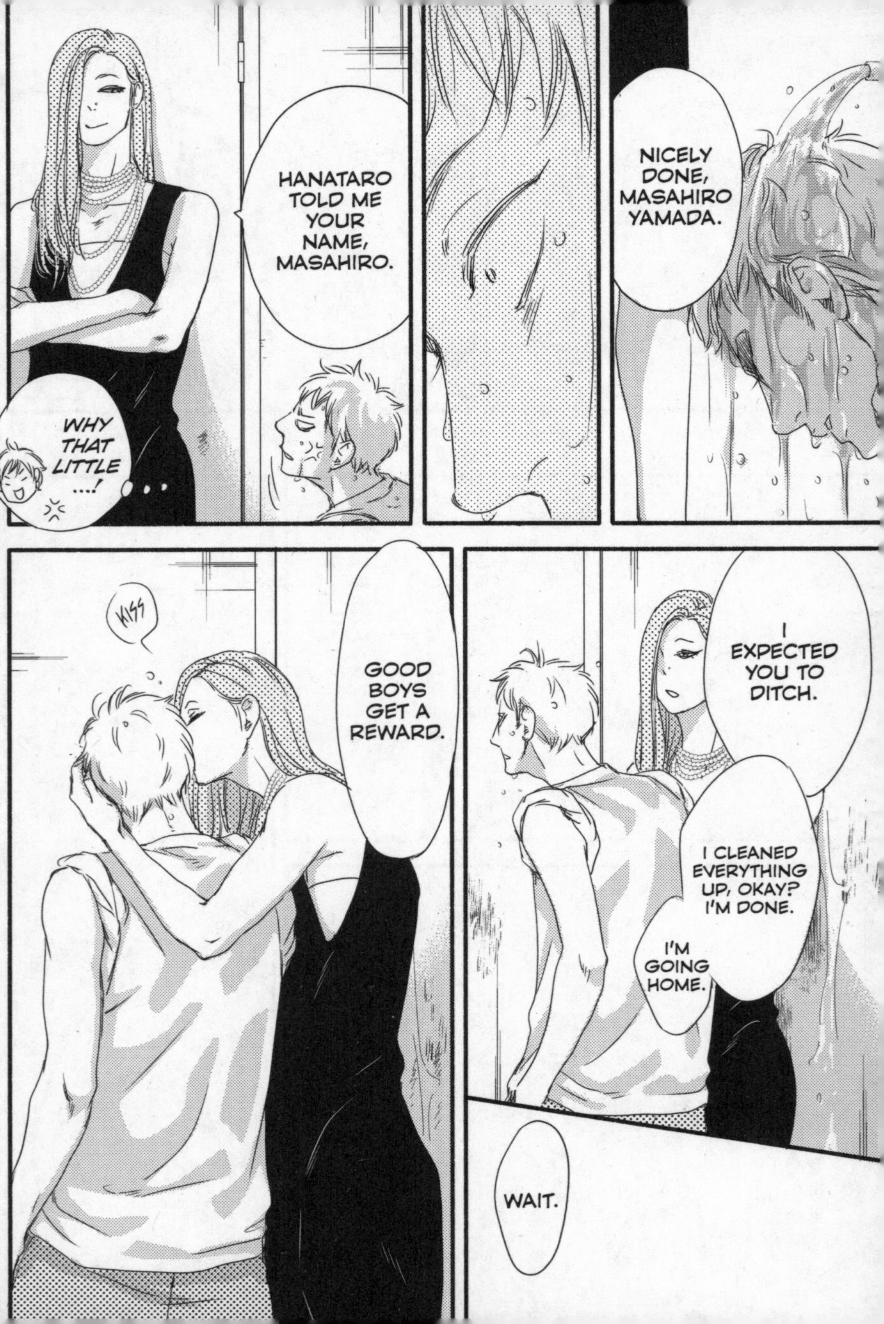
NICELY DONE, MASAHIRO YAMADA.
HANATARO TOLD ME YOUR NAME, MASAHIRO.
WHY THAT LITTLE ...!
I EXPECTED YOU TO DITCH.
I CLEANED EVERYTHING UP, OKAY? I'M DONE.
I'M GOING HOME.
WAIT.
GOOD BOYS GET A REWARD.
KISS

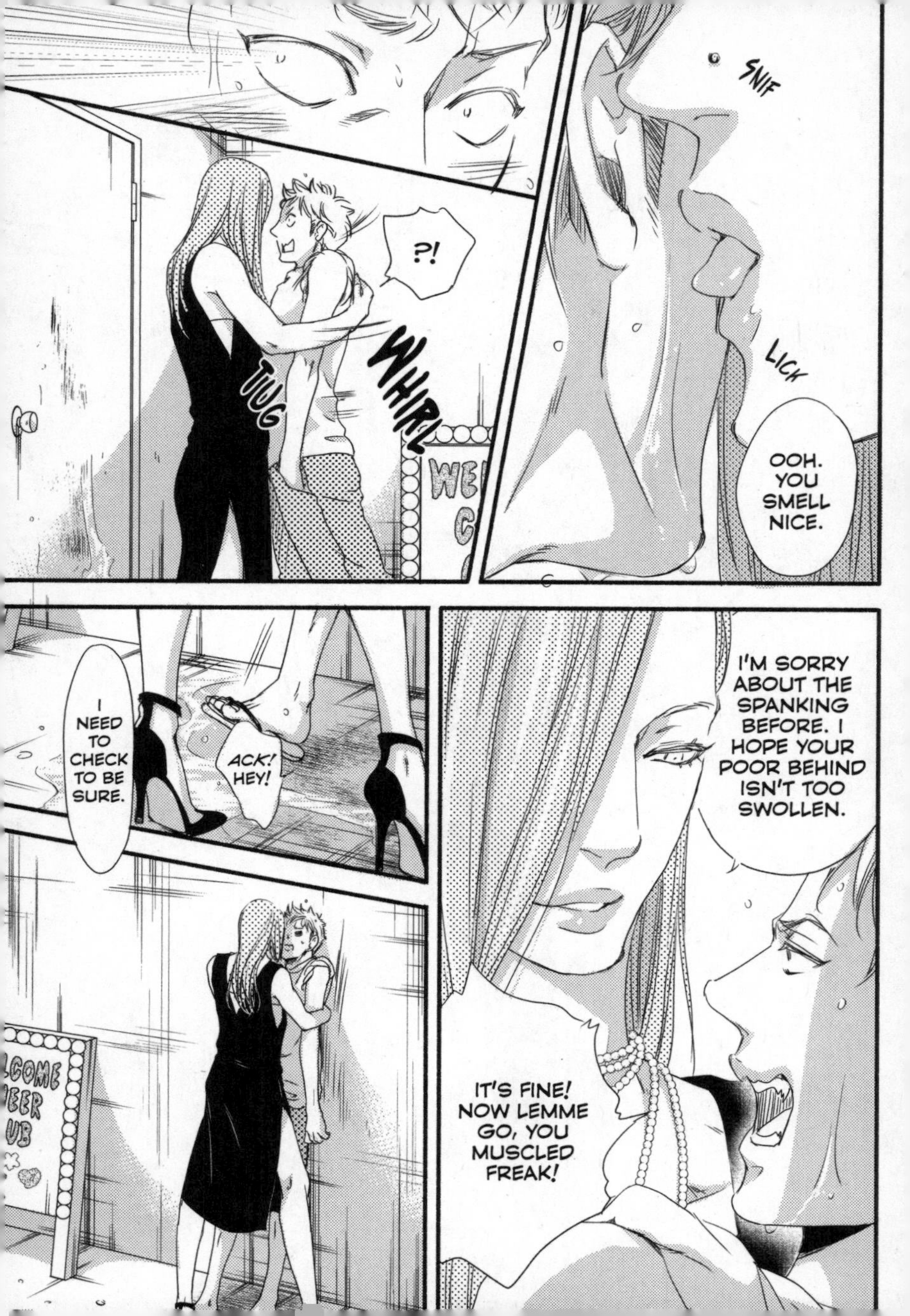
SNIF
LICK
OOH. YOU SMELL NICE.
?!
WHIRL
TUG
I'M SORRY ABOUT THE SPANKING BEFORE. I HOPE YOUR POOR BEHIND ISN'T TOO SWOLLEN.
IT'S FINE! NOW LEMME GO, YOU MUSCLED FREAK!
ACK! HEY!
I NEED TO CHECK TO BE SURE.

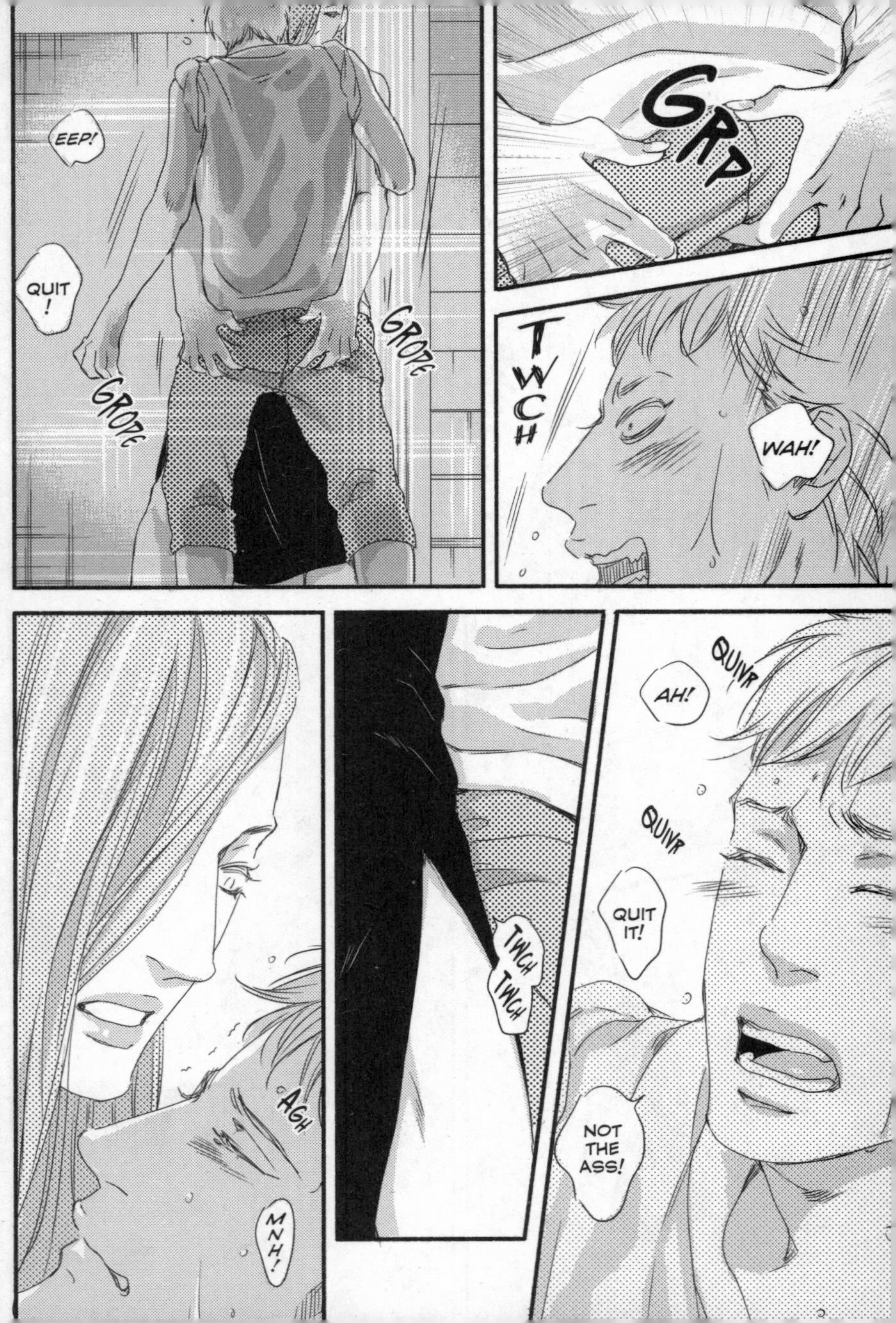
GRP
TWCH
WAH!
EEP!
QUIT!
GROPE
GROPE
QUIVR
AH!
QUIVR
QUIT IT!
NOT THE ASS!
TWCH TWCH
AGH
MNH!

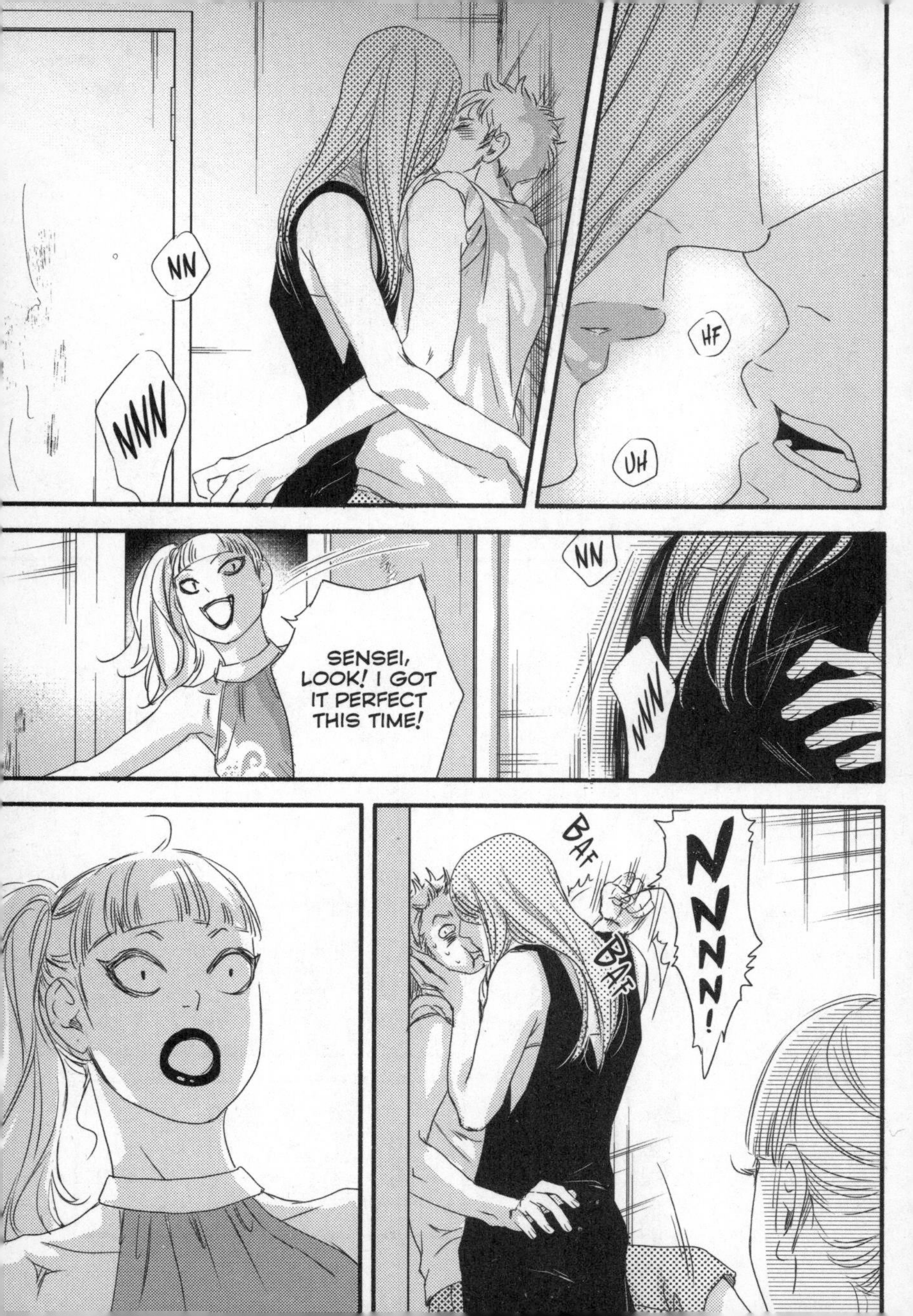
HF
UH
NN
NNN
NN
NNN
SENSEI, LOOK! I GOT IT PERFECT THIS TIME!
NNNN!
BAF
BAF

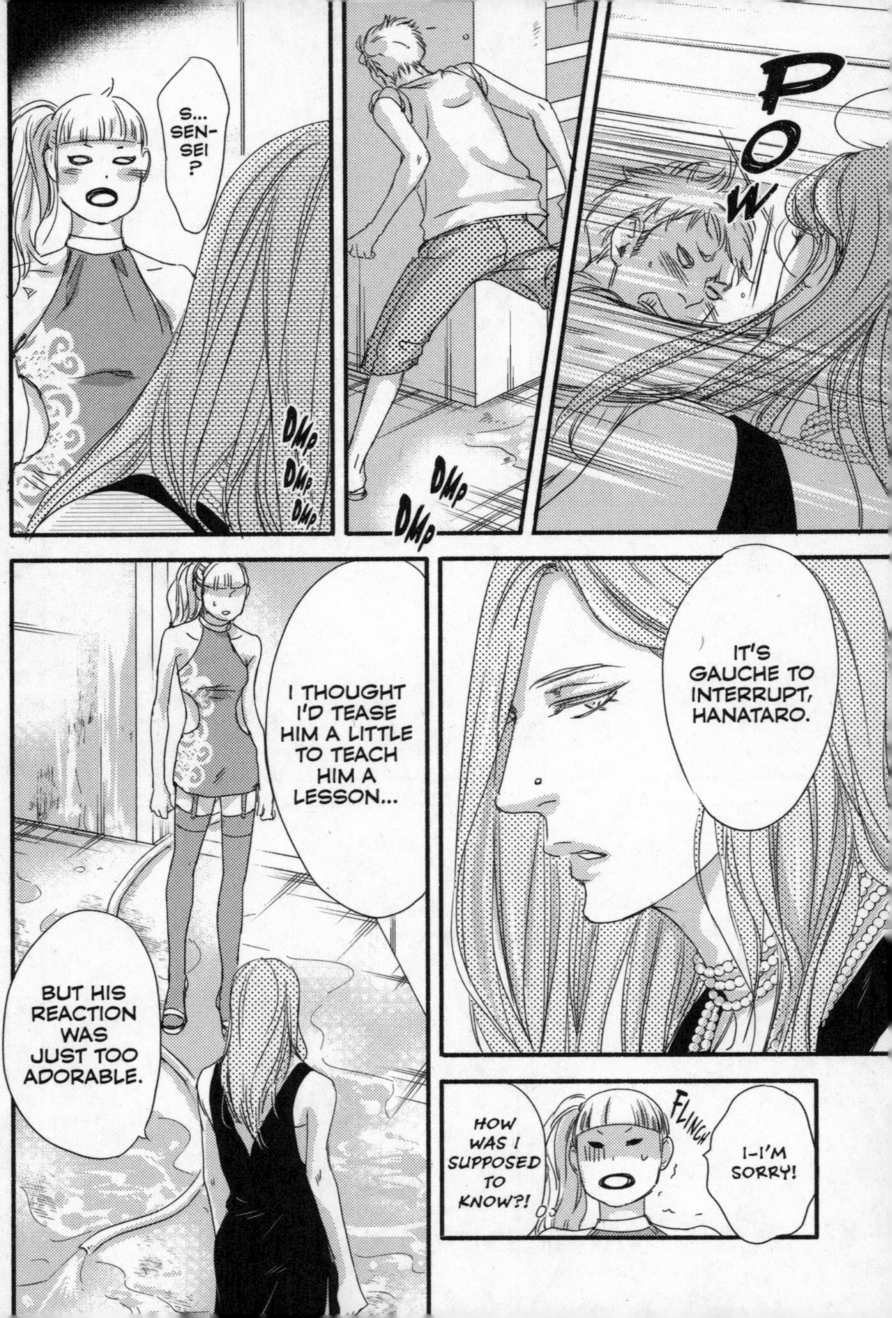
POW
DMP
DMP
S... SEN-SEI?
DMP
DMP
DMP
IT'S GAUCHE TO INTERRUPT, HANATARO.
I-I'M SORRY!
FLINCH
HOW WAS I SUPPOSED TO KNOW?!
I THOUGHT I'D TEASE HIM A LITTLE TO TEACH HIM A LESSON...
BUT HIS REACTION WAS JUST TOO ADORABLE.

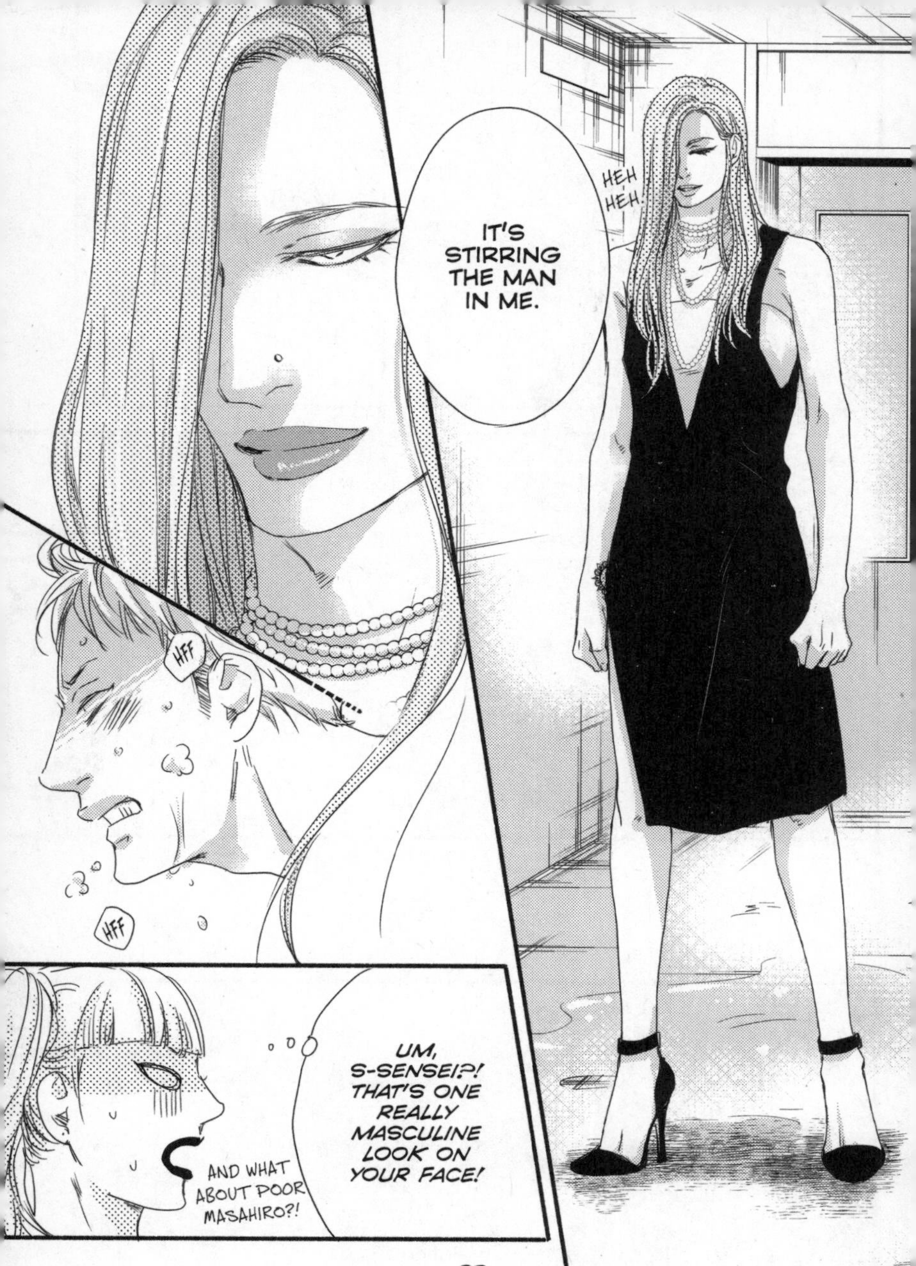
HEH HEH.
IT'S STIRRING THE MAN IN ME.
HFF
HFF
UM, S-SENSEI?! THAT'S ONE REALLY MASCULINE LOOK ON YOUR FACE!
AND WHAT ABOUT POOR MASAHIRO?!

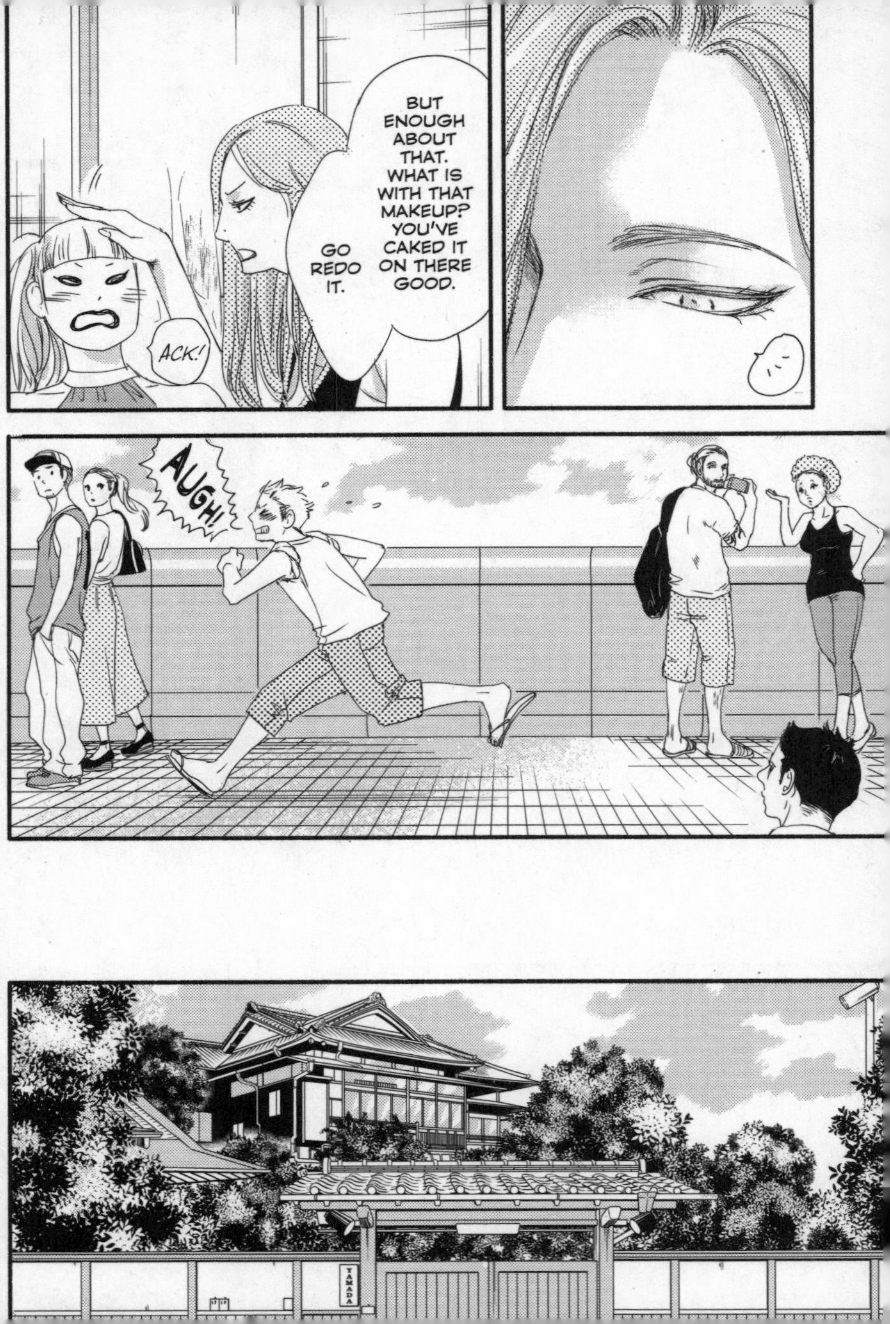
BUT ENOUGH ABOUT THAT. WHAT IS WITH THAT MAKEUP? YOU'VE CAKED IT ON THERE GOOD.
GO REDO IT.
ACK!
AUGH!
YAMADA

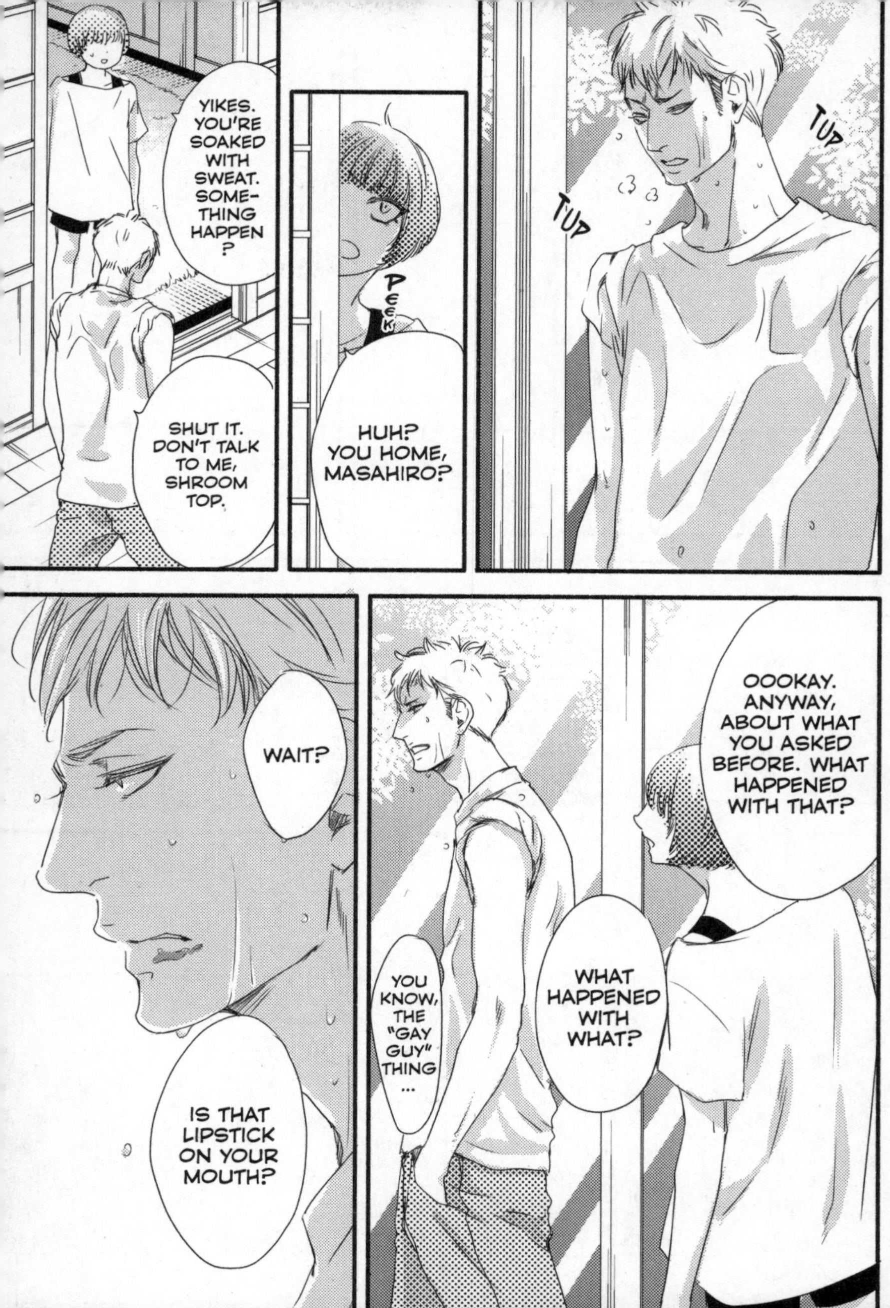
TUP
TUP
PEEK
HUH? YOU HOME, MASAHIRO?
YIKES. YOU'RE SOAKED WITH SWEAT. SOME-THING HAPPEN?
SHUT IT. DON'T TALK TO ME, SHROOM TOP.
OOOKAY. ANYWAY, ABOUT WHAT YOU ASKED BEFORE. WHAT HAPPENED WITH THAT?
WHAT HAPPENED WITH WHAT?
YOU KNOW, THE "GAY GUY" THING...
WAIT?
IS THAT LIPSTICK ON YOUR MOUTH?

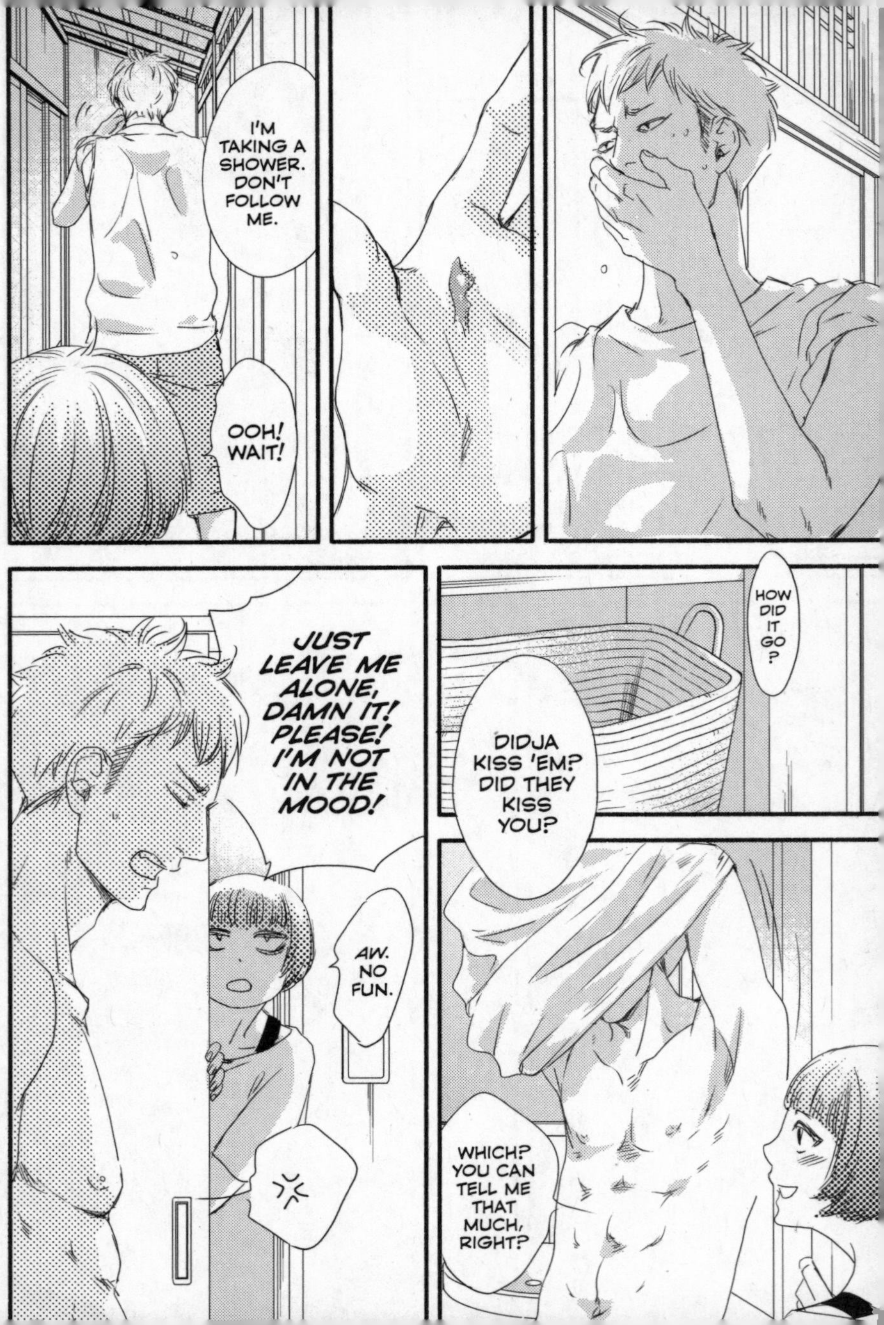
I'M TAKING A SHOWER. DON'T FOLLOW ME.
OOH! WAIT!
HOW DID IT GO?
DIDJA KISS 'EM? DID THEY KISS YOU?
WHICH? YOU CAN TELL ME THAT MUCH, RIGHT?
JUST LEAVE ME ALONE, DAMN IT! PLEASE! I'M NOT IN THE MOOD!
AW. NO FUN.

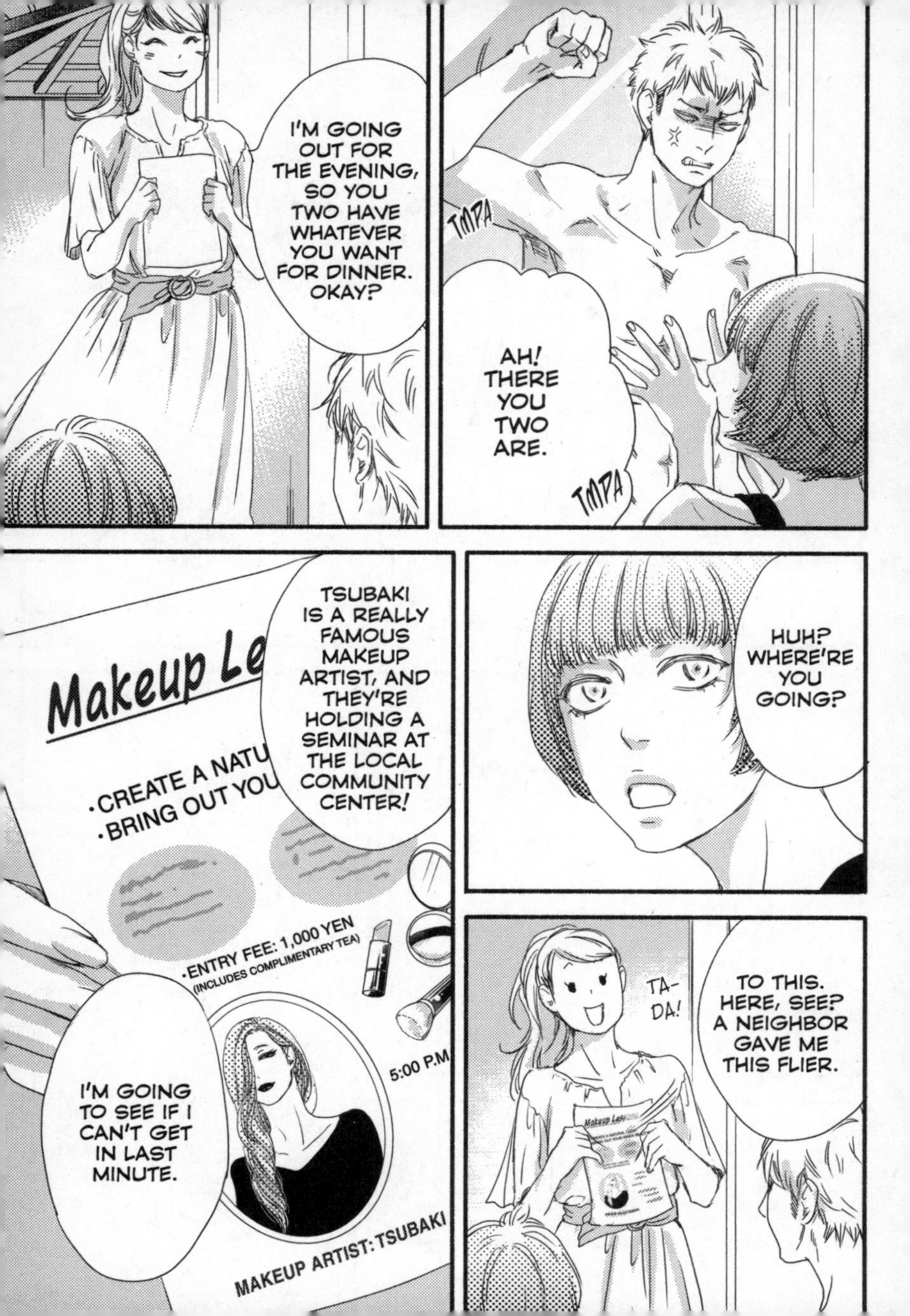
TMPA
AH! THERE YOU TWO ARE.
TMPA
I'M GOING OUT FOR THE EVENING, SO YOU TWO HAVE WHATEVER YOU WANT FOR DINNER. OKAY?
HUH? WHERE'RE YOU GOING?
TA-DA!
TO THIS. HERE, SEE? A NEIGHBOR GAVE ME THIS FLIER.
TSUBAKI IS A REALLY FAMOUS MAKEUP ARTIST, AND THEY'RE HOLDING A SEMINAR AT THE LOCAL COMMUNITY CENTER!
Makeup Le
·CREATE A NATU
·BRING OUT YOU
·ENTRY FEE: 1,000 YEN
(INCLUDES COMPLIMENTARY TEA)
5:00 P.M
MAKEUP ARTIST: TSUBAKI
I'M GOING TO SEE IF I CAN'T GET IN LAST MINUTE.

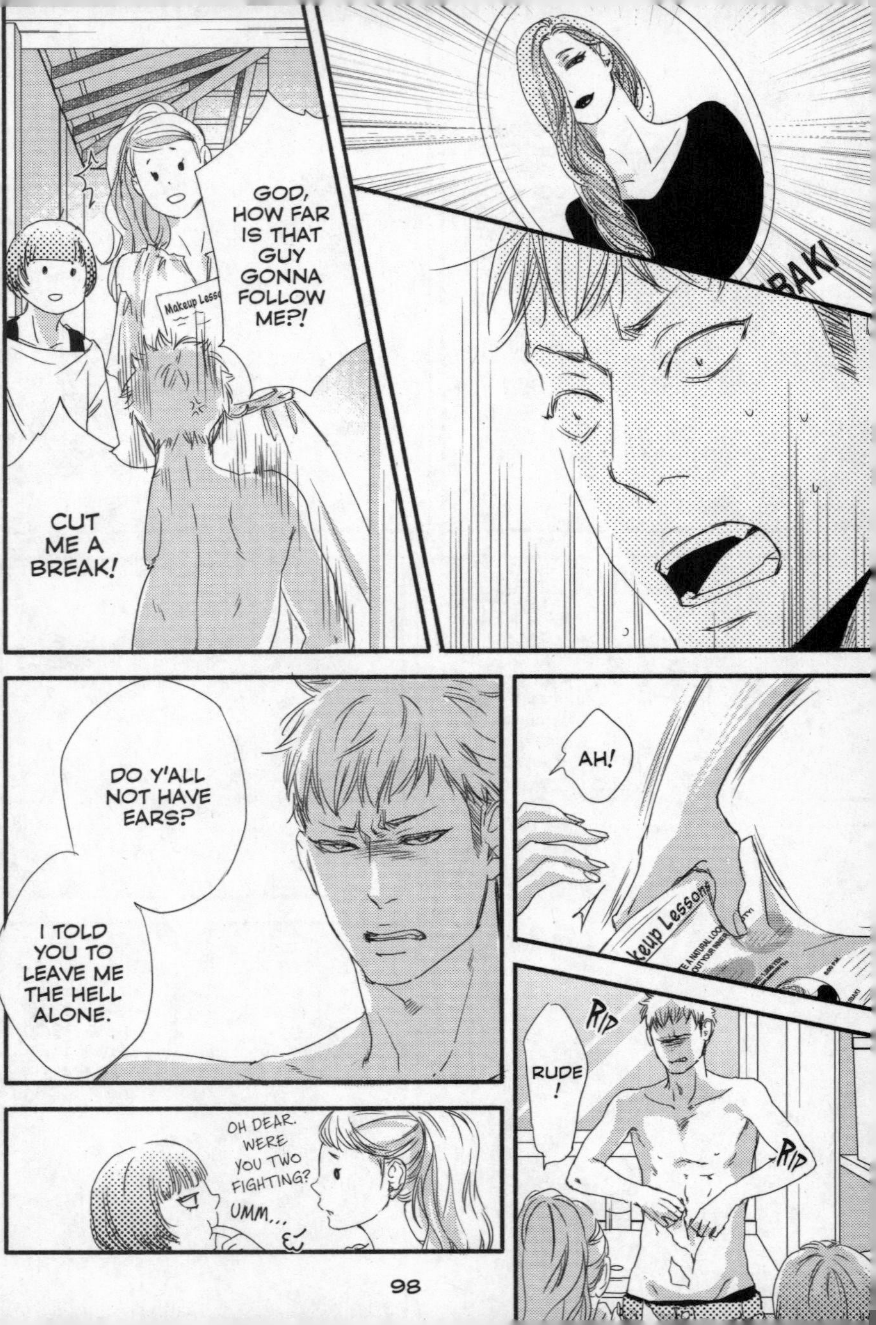
BAKI
GOD, HOW FAR IS THAT GUY GONNA FOLLOW ME?!
CUT ME A BREAK!
AH!
Makeup Lessons
DO Y'ALL NOT HAVE EARS?
I TOLD YOU TO LEAVE ME THE HELL ALONE.
RIP
RUDE!
RIP
OH DEAR. WERE YOU TWO FIGHTING?
UMM...

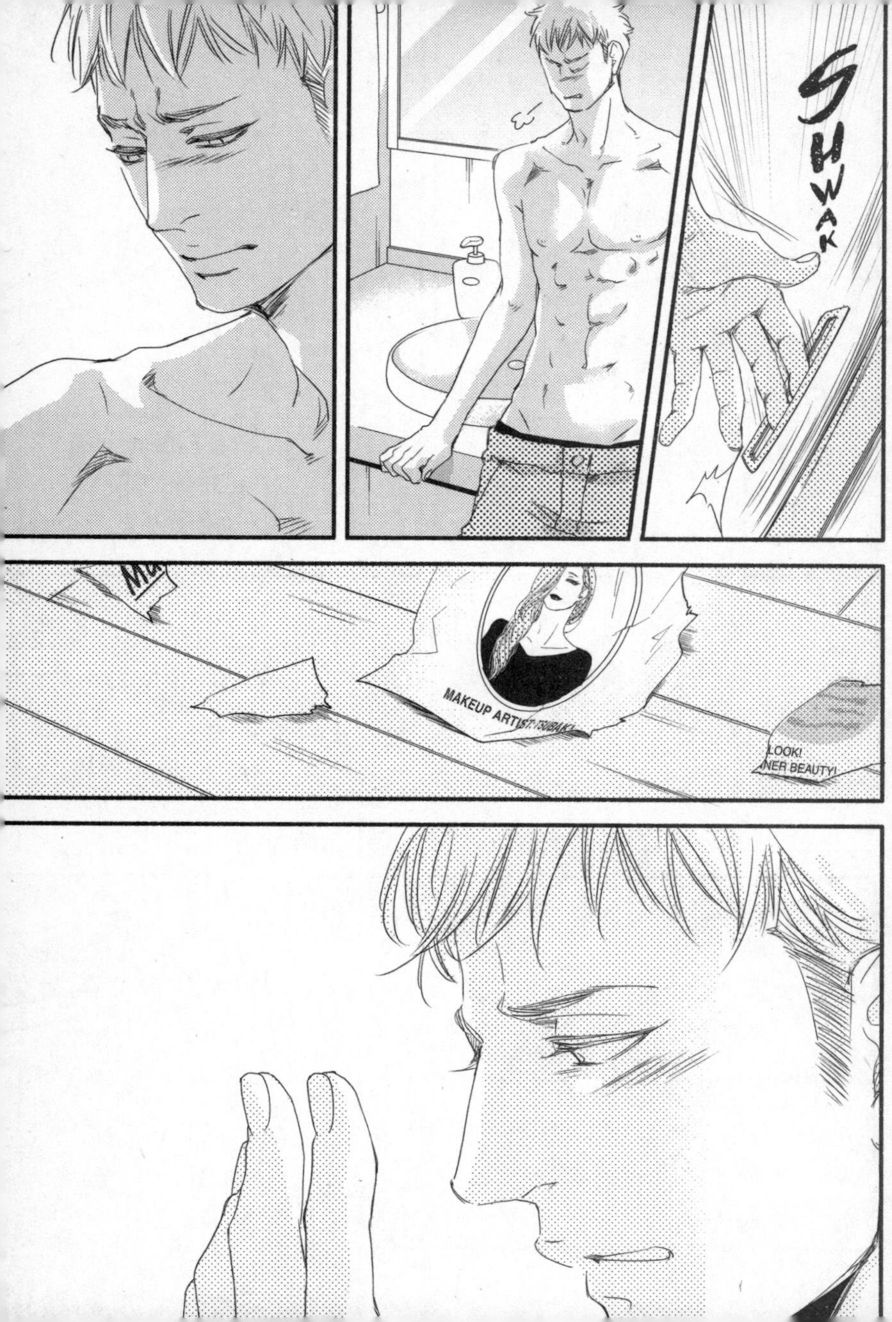
SHWAK
LOOK!
NER BEAUTY!
MAKEUP ARTIST: TSUBAKI
Ma

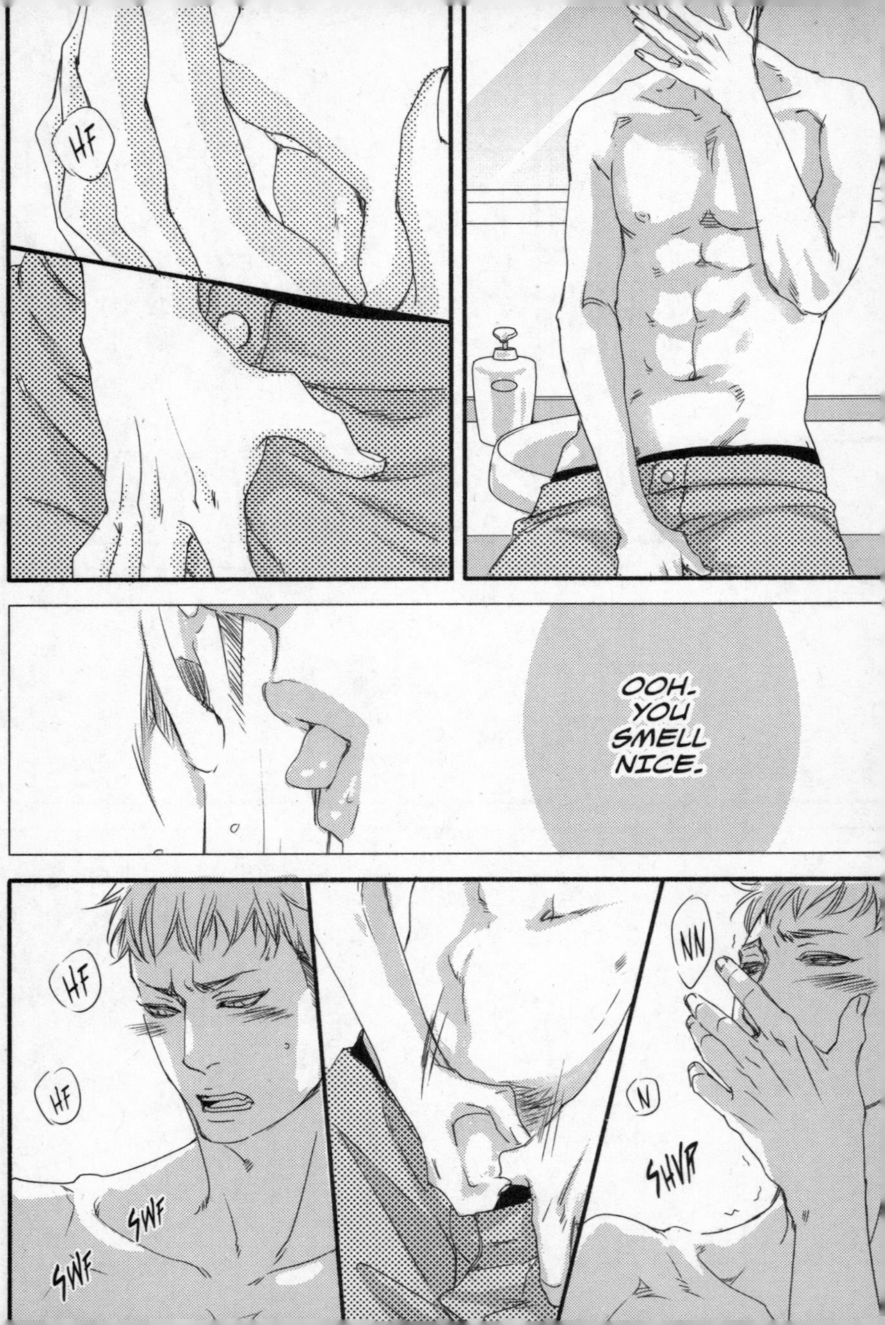
HF
OOH. YOU SMELL NICE.
NN
N
SHVR
HF
HF
SWF
SWF

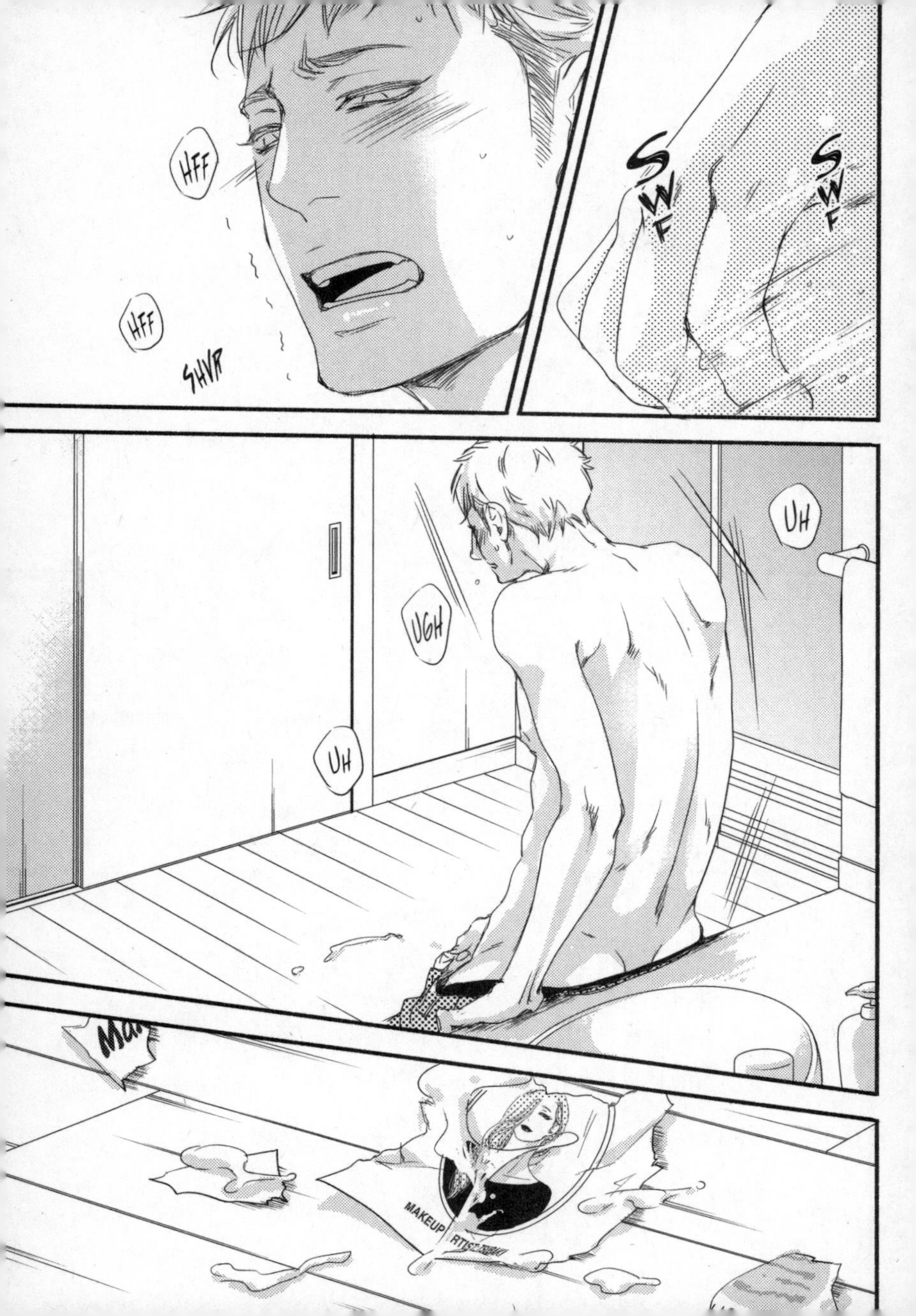
SWF
SWF
HFF
HFF
SHVR
UH
UGH
UH
Ma
MAKEUP

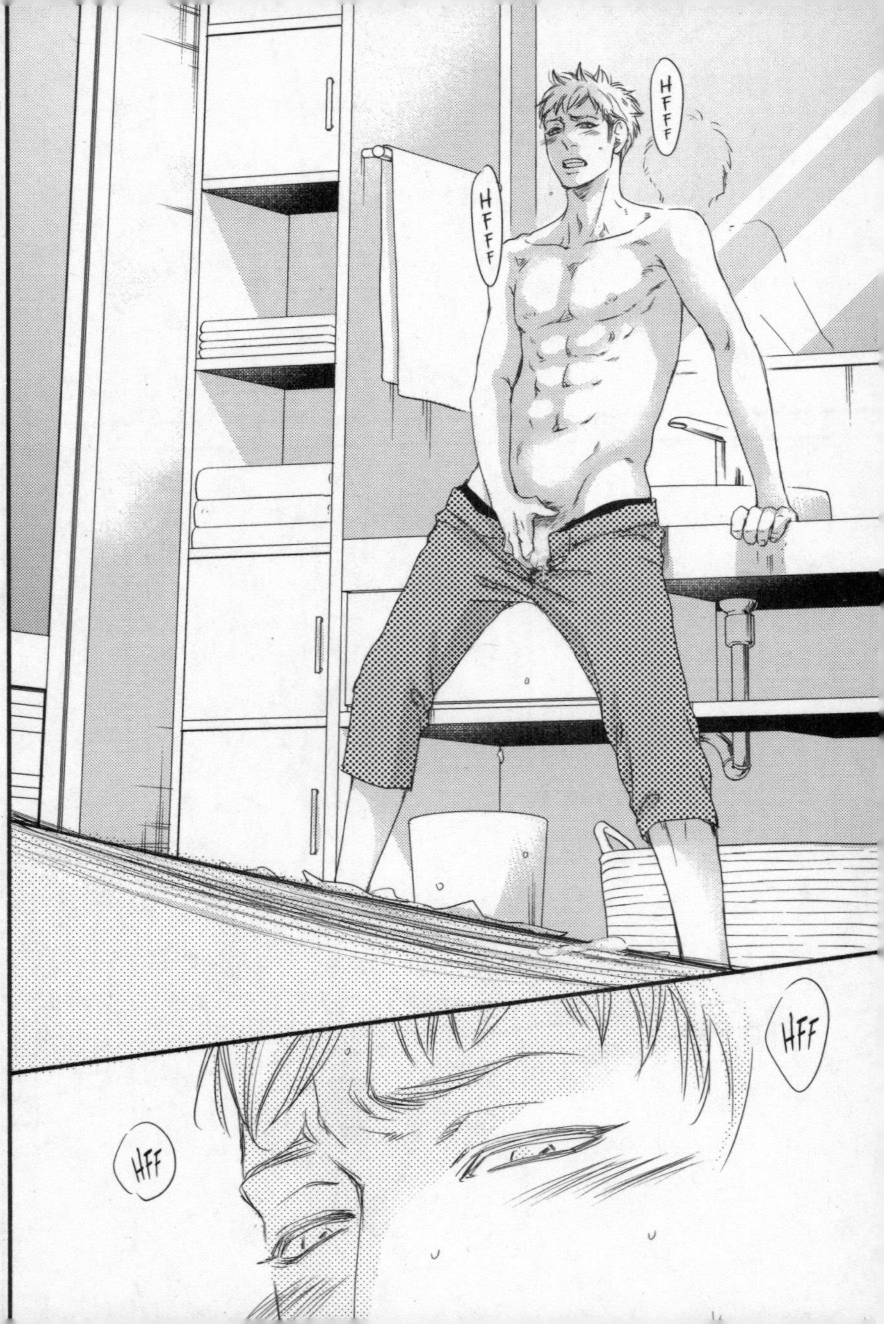
HFFF
HFFF
HFF
HFF

Chapter 3

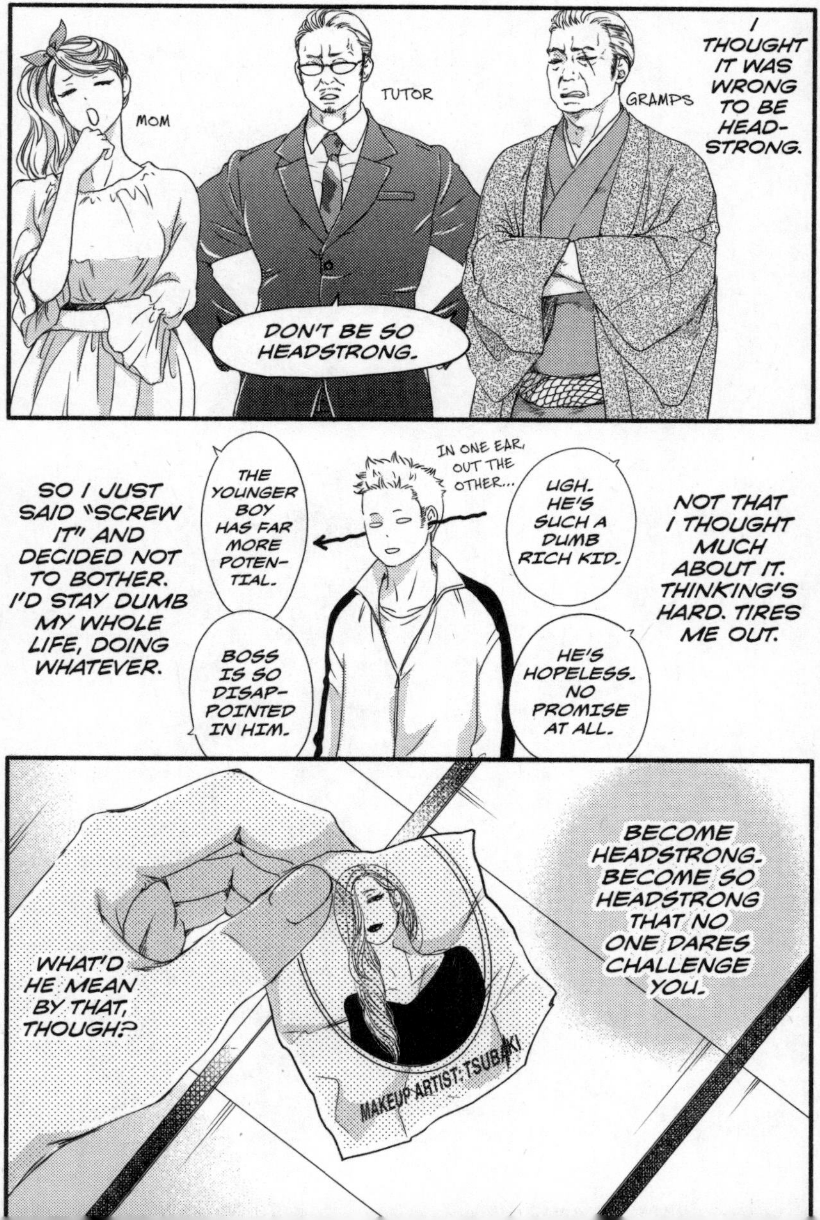
I THOUGHT IT WAS WRONG TO BE HEAD-STRONG.
GRAMPS
TUTOR
DON'T BE SO HEADSTRONG.
MOM
NOT THAT I THOUGHT MUCH ABOUT IT. THINKING'S HARD. TIRES ME OUT.
UGH. HE'S SUCH A DUMB RICH KID.
HE'S HOPELESS. NO PROMISE AT ALL.
IN ONE EAR, OUT THE OTHER...
THE YOUNGER BOY HAS FAR MORE POTEN-TIAL.
BOSS IS SO DISAP-POINTED IN HIM.
SO I JUST SAID "SCREW IT" AND DECIDED NOT TO BOTHER. I'D STAY DUMB MY WHOLE LIFE, DOING WHATEVER.
BECOME HEADSTRONG. BECOME SO HEADSTRONG THAT NO ONE DARES CHALLENGE YOU.
MAKEUP ARTIST: TSUBAKI
WHAT'D HE MEAN BY THAT, THOUGH?

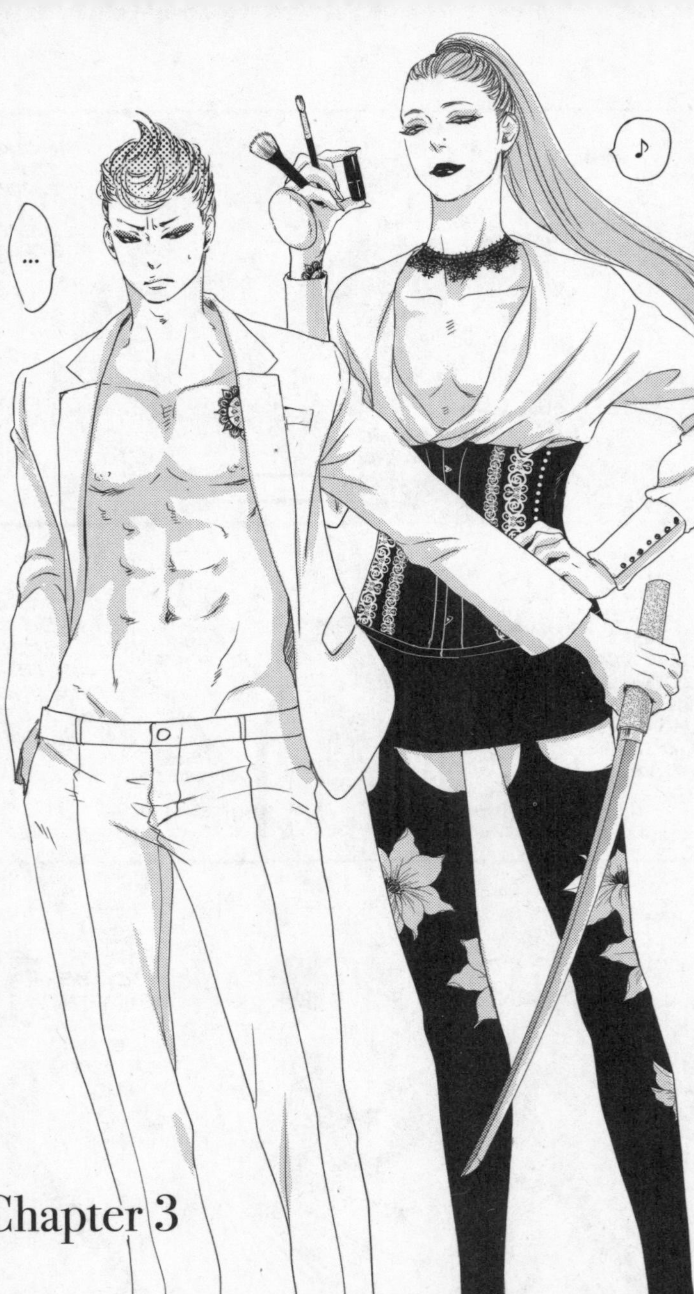
♪
...

Chapter 3

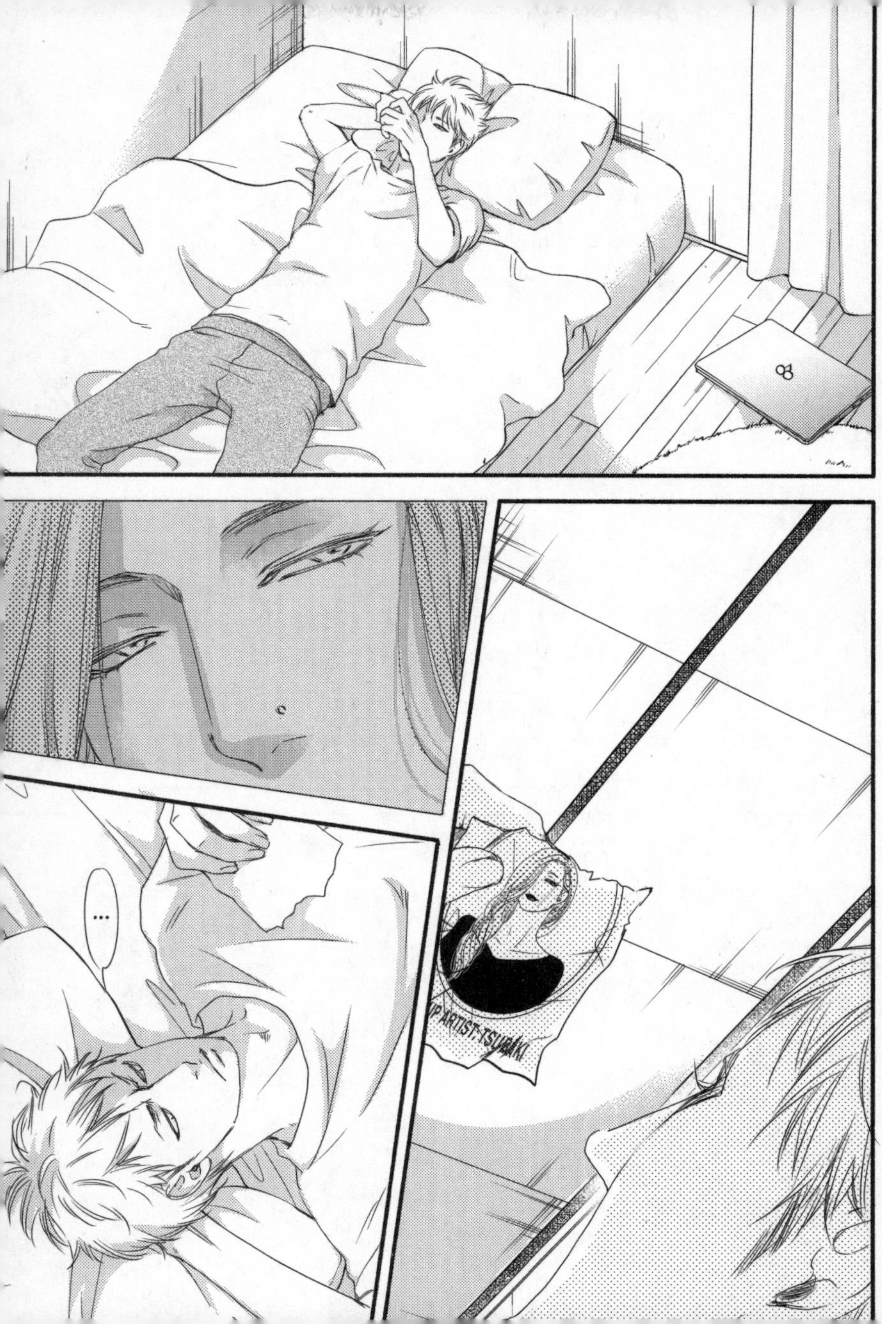
P ARTIST: TSUBAKI
...

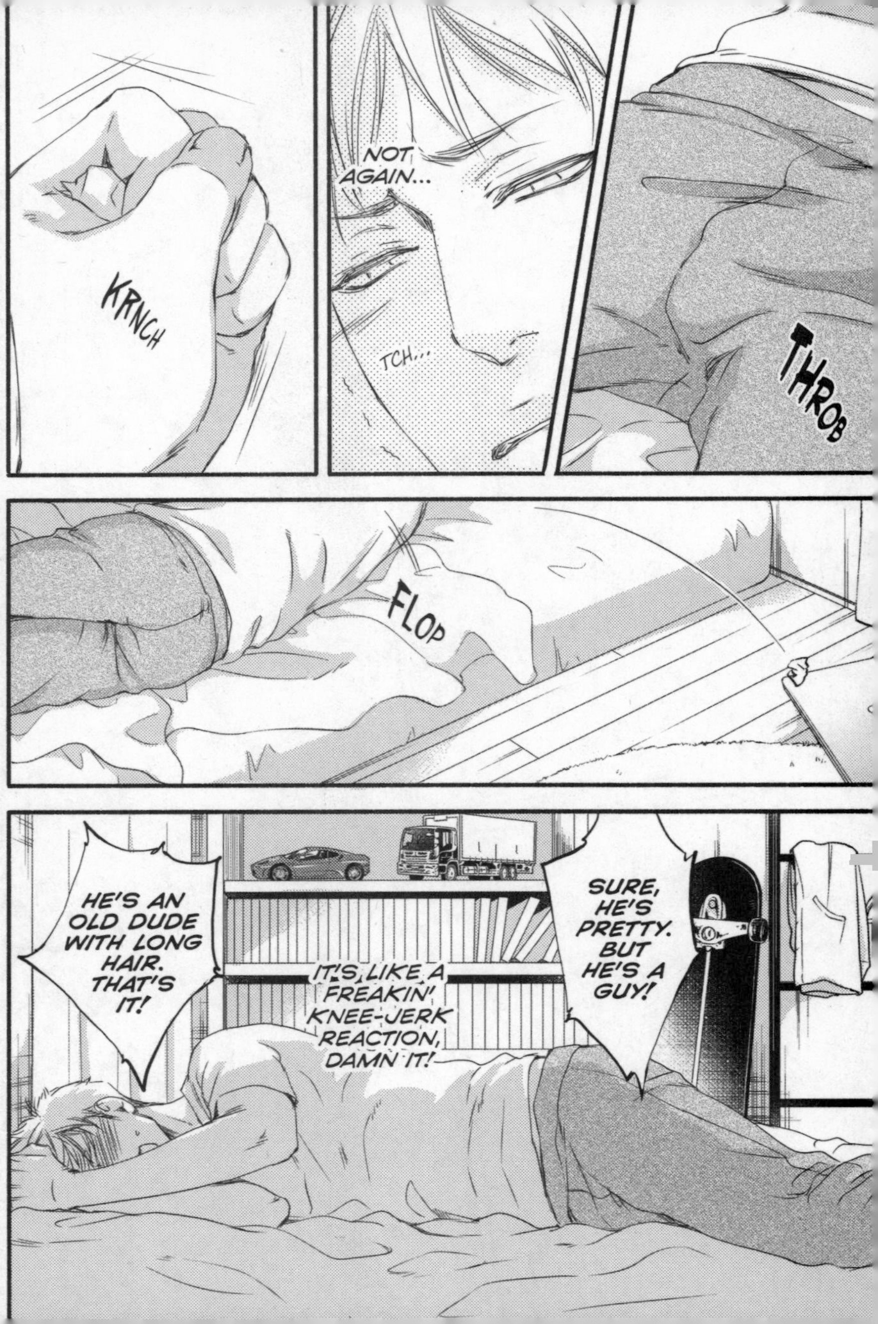
THROB
NOT AGAIN...
TCH...
KRNCH
FLOP
SURE, HE'S PRETTY. BUT HE'S A GUY!
IT'S LIKE A FREAKIN' KNEE-JERK REACTION, DAMN IT!
HE'S AN OLD DUDE WITH LONG HAIR. THAT'S IT!

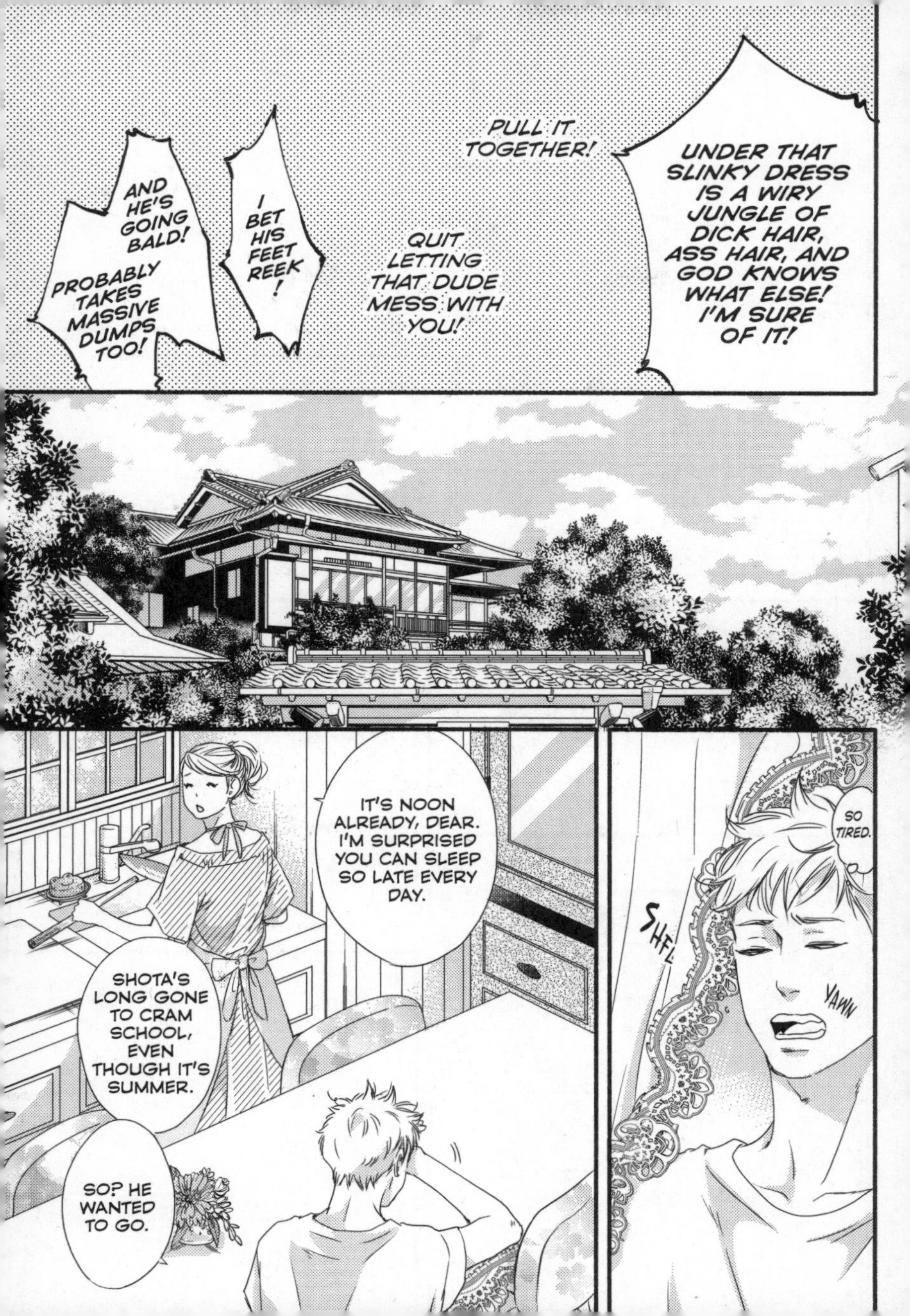
UNDER THAT SLINKY DRESS IS A WIRY JUNGLE OF DICK HAIR, ASS HAIR, AND GOD KNOWS WHAT ELSE! I'M SURE OF IT!
PULL IT TOGETHER!
QUIT LETTING THAT DUDE MESS WITH YOU!
I BET HIS FEET REEK!
AND HE'S GOING BALD!
PROBABLY TAKES MASSIVE DUMPS TOO!
SO TIRED.
SHFL
YAWN
IT'S NOON ALREADY, DEAR. I'M SURPRISED YOU CAN SLEEP SO LATE EVERY DAY.
SHOTA'S LONG GONE TO CRAM SCHOOL, EVEN THOUGH IT'S SUMMER.
SO? HE WANTED TO GO.

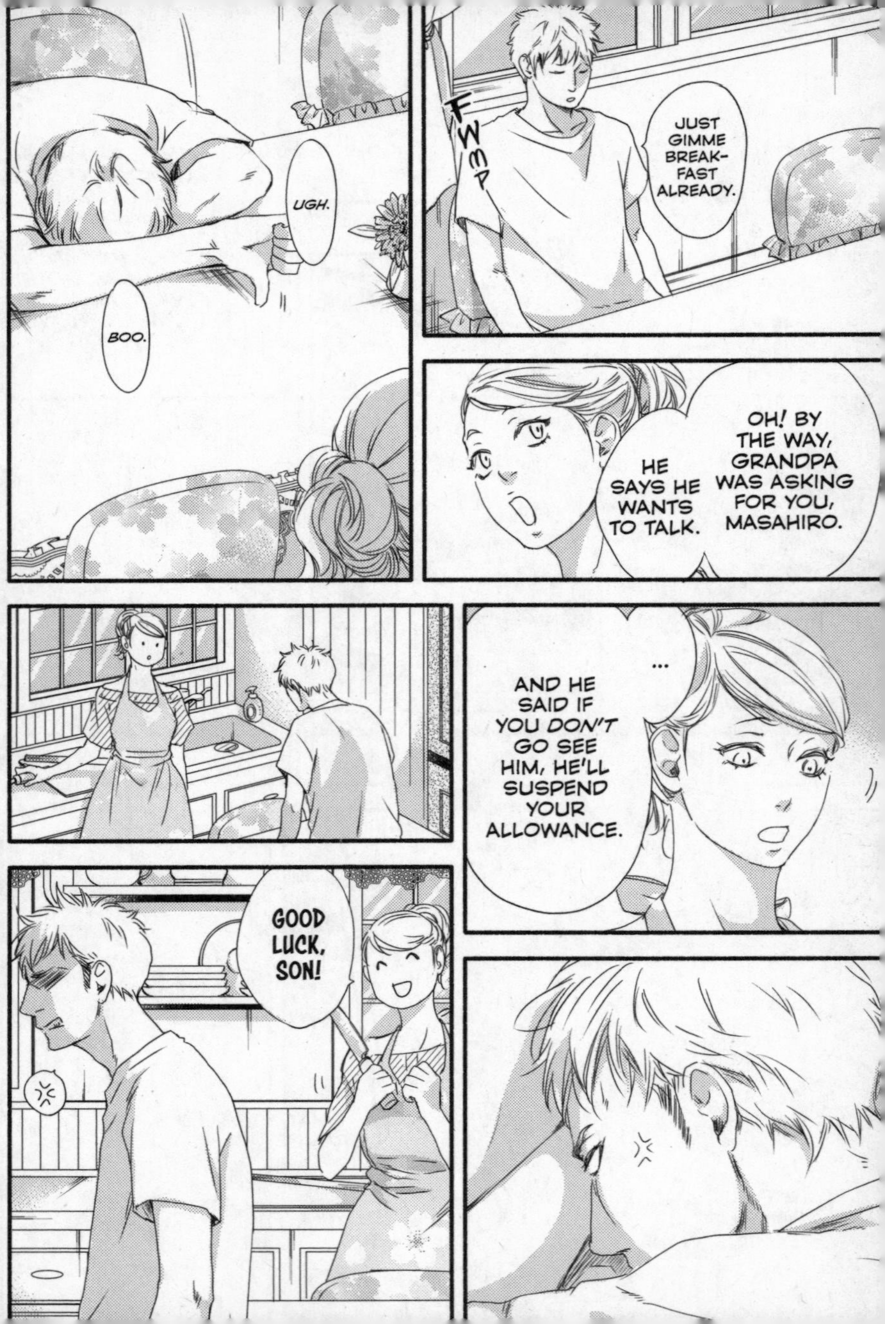
FWMP
JUST GIMME BREAK-FAST ALREADY.
OH! BY THE WAY, GRANDPA WAS ASKING FOR YOU, MASAHIRO.
HE SAYS HE WANTS TO TALK.
UGH.
BOO.
...
AND HE SAID IF YOU *DON'T* GO SEE HIM, HE'LL SUSPEND YOUR ALLOWANCE.
GOOD LUCK, SON!

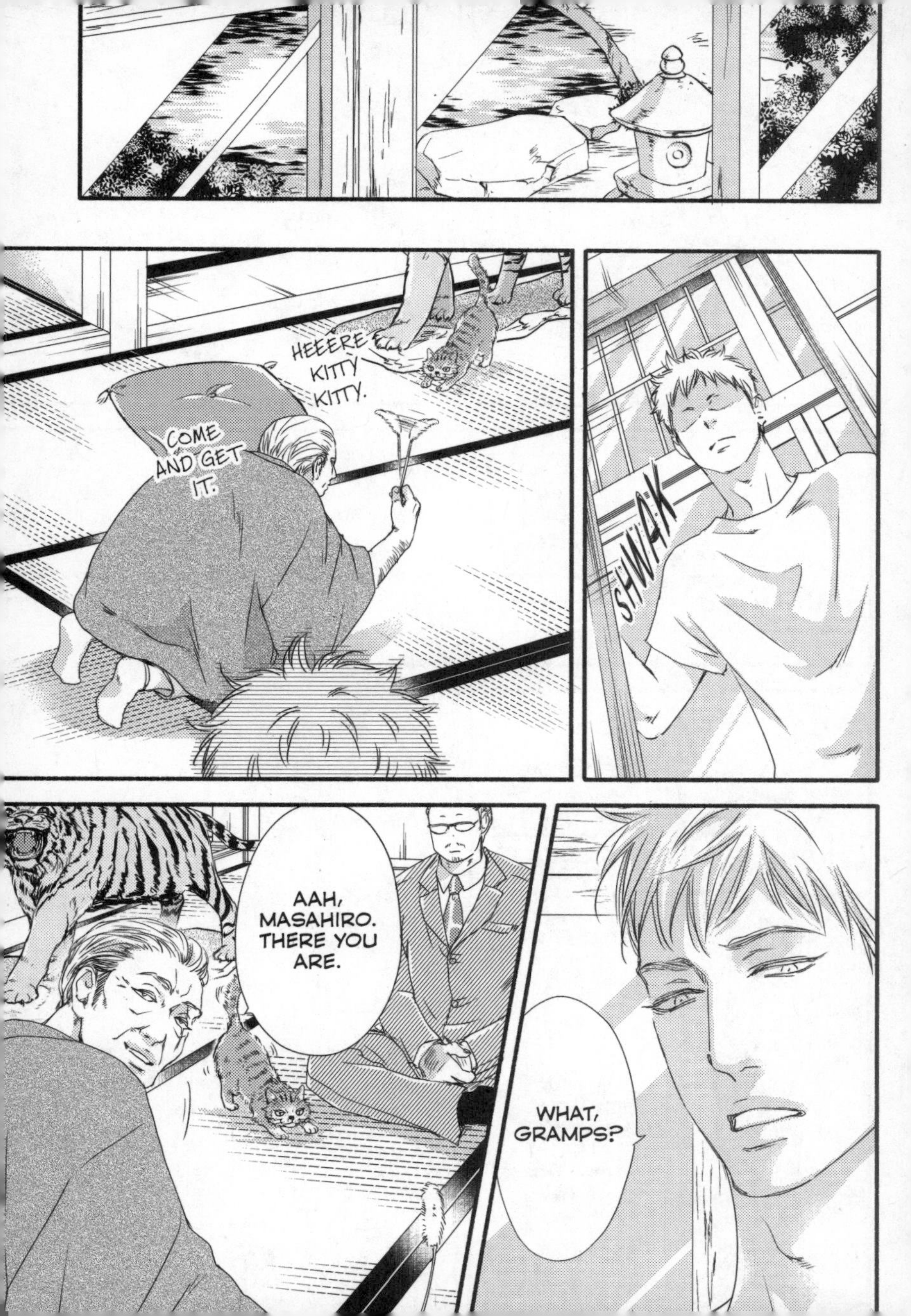
SHWAK
HEEERE KITTY KITTY.
COME AND GET IT.
WHAT, GRAMPS?
AAH, MASAHIRO. THERE YOU ARE.

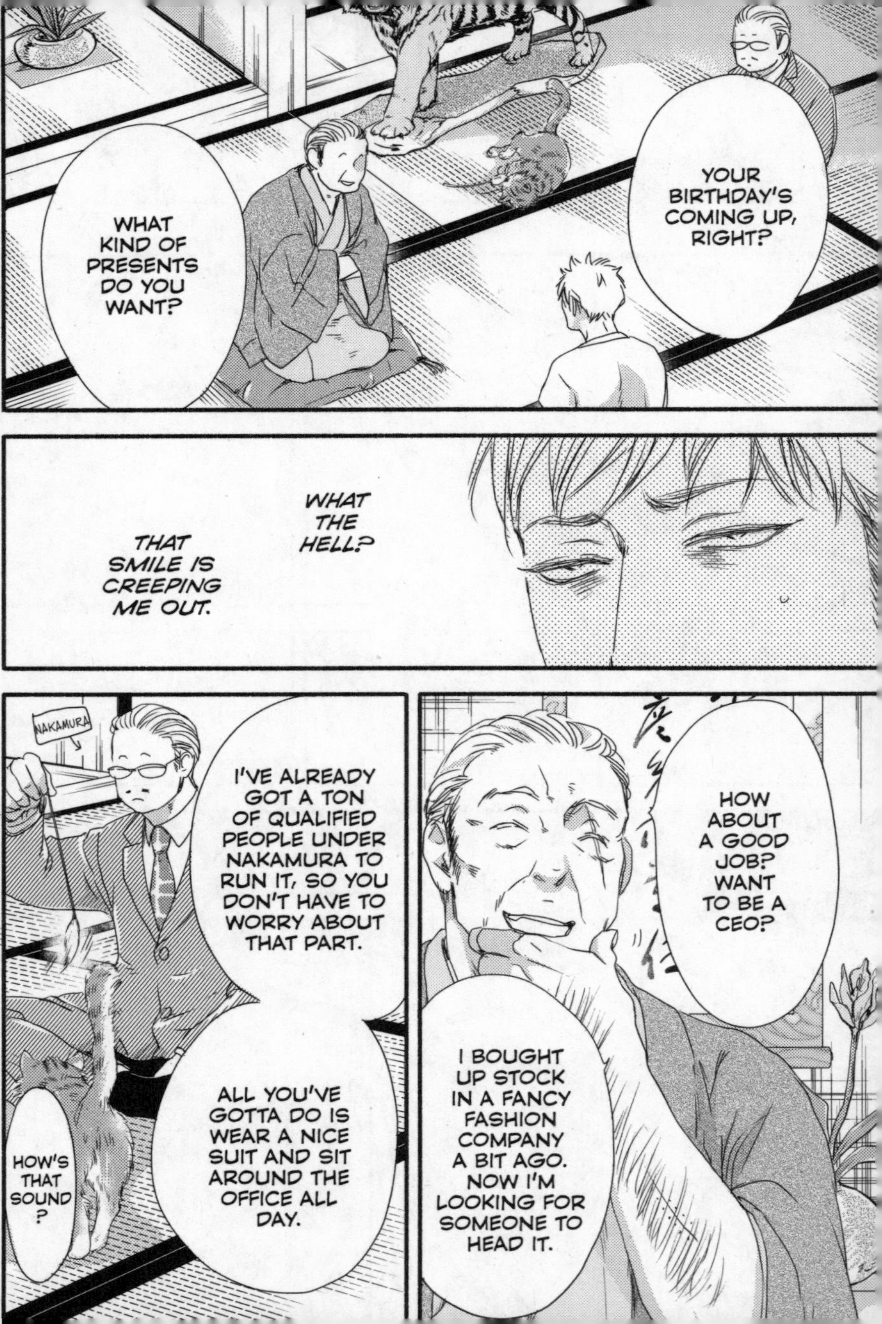
YOUR BIRTHDAY'S COMING UP, RIGHT?
WHAT KIND OF PRESENTS DO YOU WANT?
WHAT THE HELL?
THAT SMILE IS CREEPING ME OUT.
HOW ABOUT A GOOD JOB? WANT TO BE A CEO?
I BOUGHT UP STOCK IN A FANCY FASHION COMPANY A BIT AGO. NOW I'M LOOKING FOR SOMEONE TO HEAD IT.
NAKAMURA
I'VE ALREADY GOT A TON OF QUALIFIED PEOPLE UNDER NAKAMURA TO RUN IT, SO YOU DON'T HAVE TO WORRY ABOUT THAT PART.
ALL YOU'VE GOTTA DO IS WEAR A NICE SUIT AND SIT AROUND THE OFFICE ALL DAY.
HOW'S THAT SOUND?

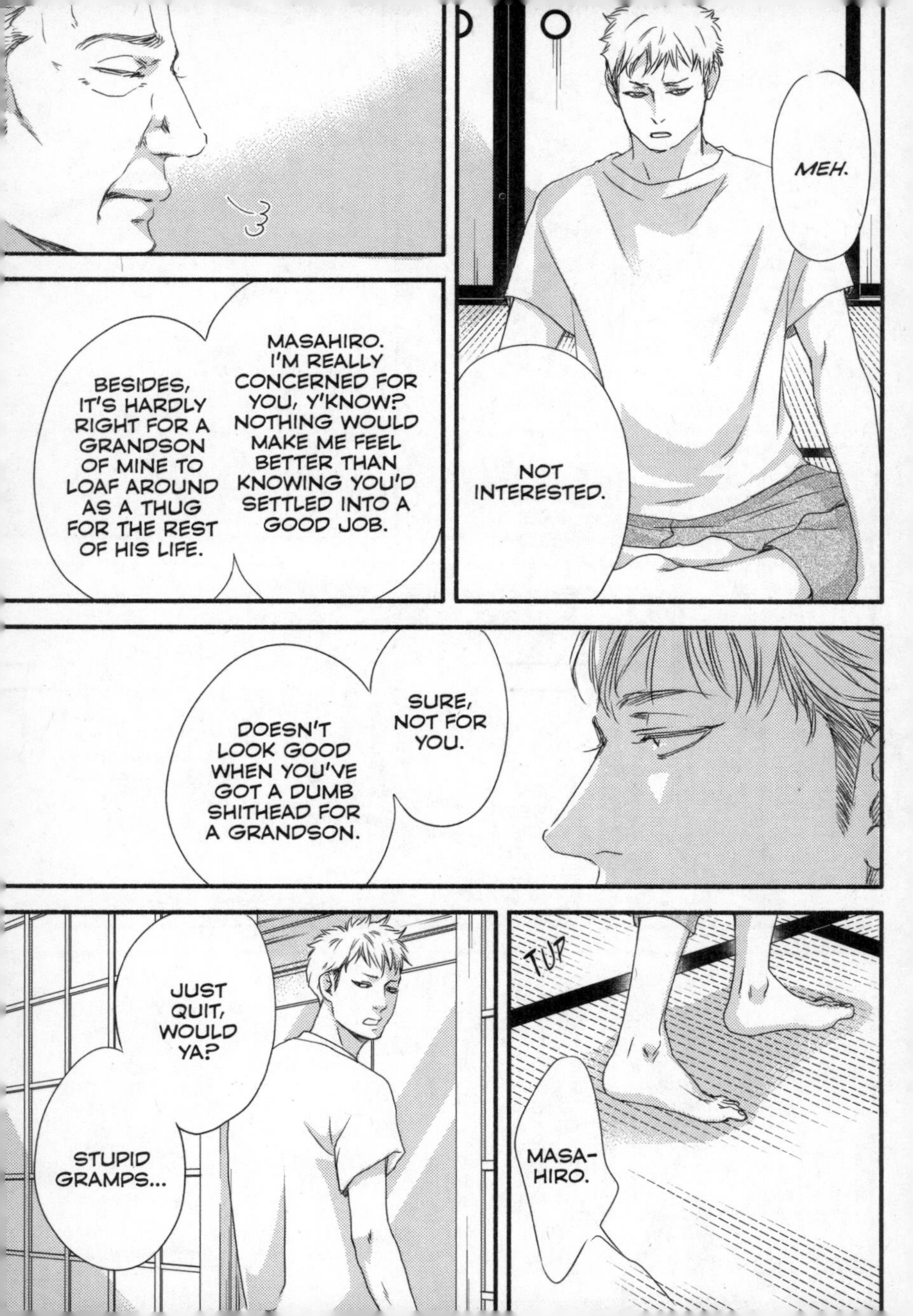
MEH.
NOT INTERESTED.
MASAHIRO. I'M REALLY CONCERNED FOR YOU, Y'KNOW? NOTHING WOULD MAKE ME FEEL BETTER THAN KNOWING YOU'D SETTLED INTO A GOOD JOB.
BESIDES, IT'S HARDLY RIGHT FOR A GRANDSON OF MINE TO LOAF AROUND AS A THUG FOR THE REST OF HIS LIFE.
SURE, NOT FOR YOU.
DOESN'T LOOK GOOD WHEN YOU'VE GOT A DUMB SHITHEAD FOR A GRANDSON.
TUP
MASA-HIRO.
JUST QUIT, WOULD YA?
STUPID GRAMPS...

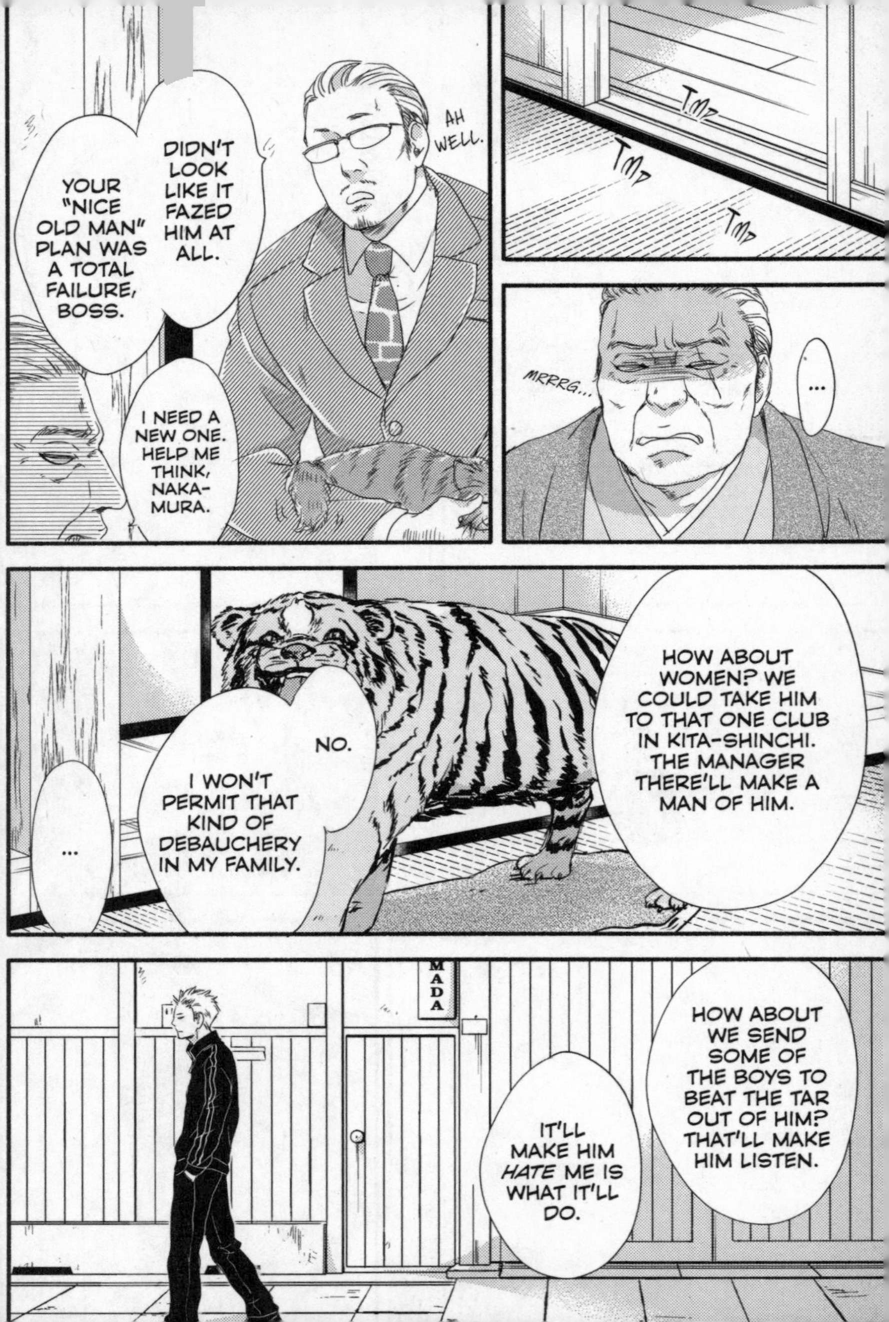
TMP
TMP
TMP
MRRRG...
...
AH WELL.
DIDN'T LOOK LIKE IT FAZED HIM AT ALL.
YOUR "NICE OLD MAN" PLAN WAS A TOTAL FAILURE, BOSS.
I NEED A NEW ONE. HELP ME THINK, NAKAMURA.
HOW ABOUT WOMEN? WE COULD TAKE HIM TO THAT ONE CLUB IN KITA-SHINCHI. THE MANAGER THERE'LL MAKE A MAN OF HIM.
NO.
I WON'T PERMIT THAT KIND OF DEBAUCHERY IN MY FAMILY.
...
MADA
HOW ABOUT WE SEND SOME OF THE BOYS TO BEAT THE TAR OUT OF HIM? THAT'LL MAKE HIM LISTEN.
IT'LL MAKE HIM *HATE* ME IS WHAT IT'LL DO.

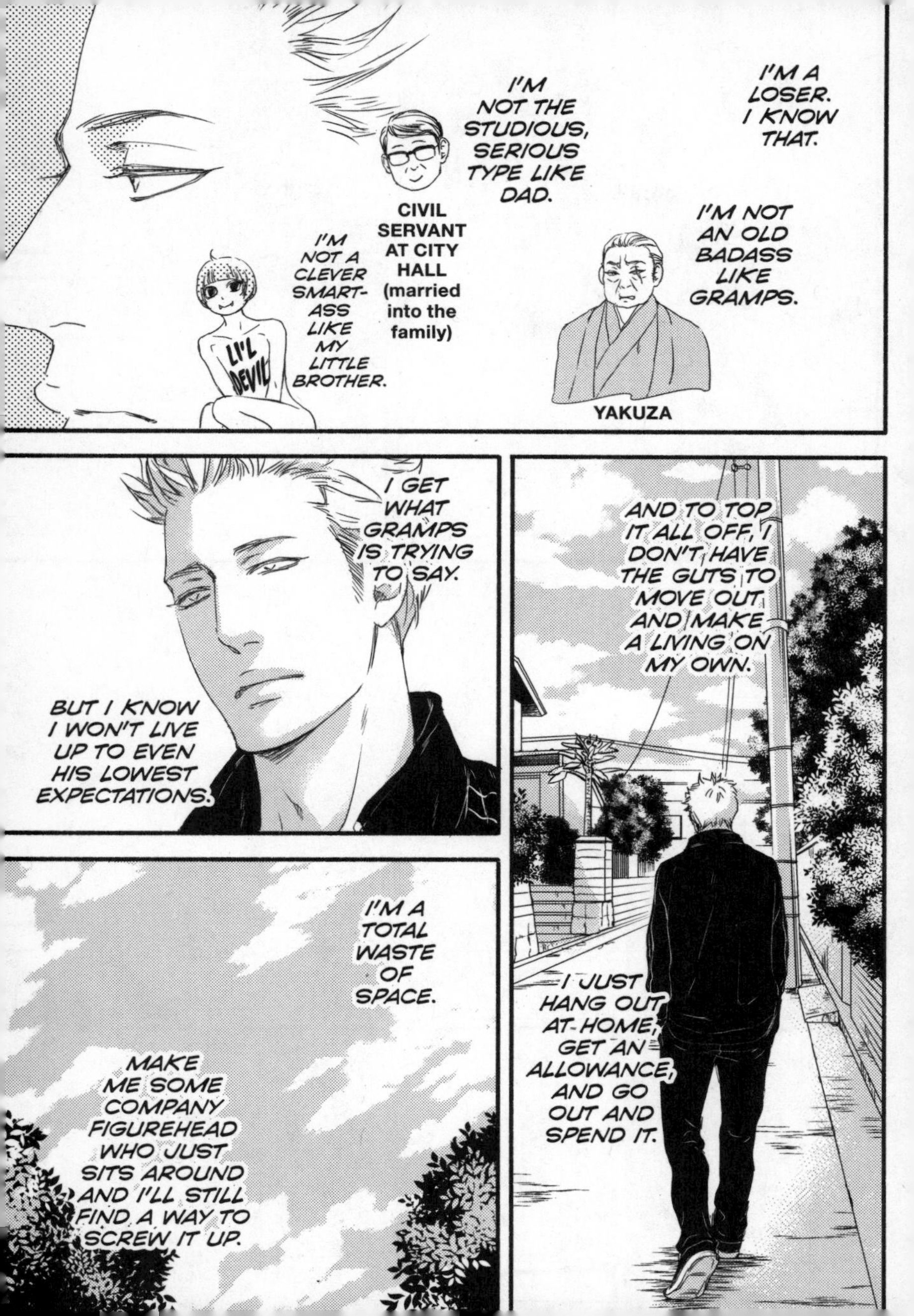
I'M A LOSER. I KNOW THAT.
I'M NOT AN OLD BADASS LIKE GRAMPS.
YAKUZA
I'M NOT THE STUDIOUS, SERIOUS TYPE LIKE DAD.
CIVIL SERVANT AT CITY HALL (married into the family)
I'M NOT A CLEVER SMART-ASS LIKE MY LITTLE BROTHER.
LI'L DEVIL
AND TO TOP IT ALL OFF, I DON'T HAVE THE GUTS TO MOVE OUT AND MAKE A LIVING ON MY OWN.
I JUST HANG OUT AT HOME, GET AN ALLOWANCE, AND GO OUT AND SPEND IT.
I GET WHAT GRAMPS IS TRYING TO SAY.
BUT I KNOW I WON'T LIVE UP TO EVEN HIS LOWEST EXPECTATIONS.
I'M A TOTAL WASTE OF SPACE.
MAKE ME SOME COMPANY FIGUREHEAD WHO JUST SITS AROUND AND I'LL STILL FIND A WAY TO SCREW IT UP.

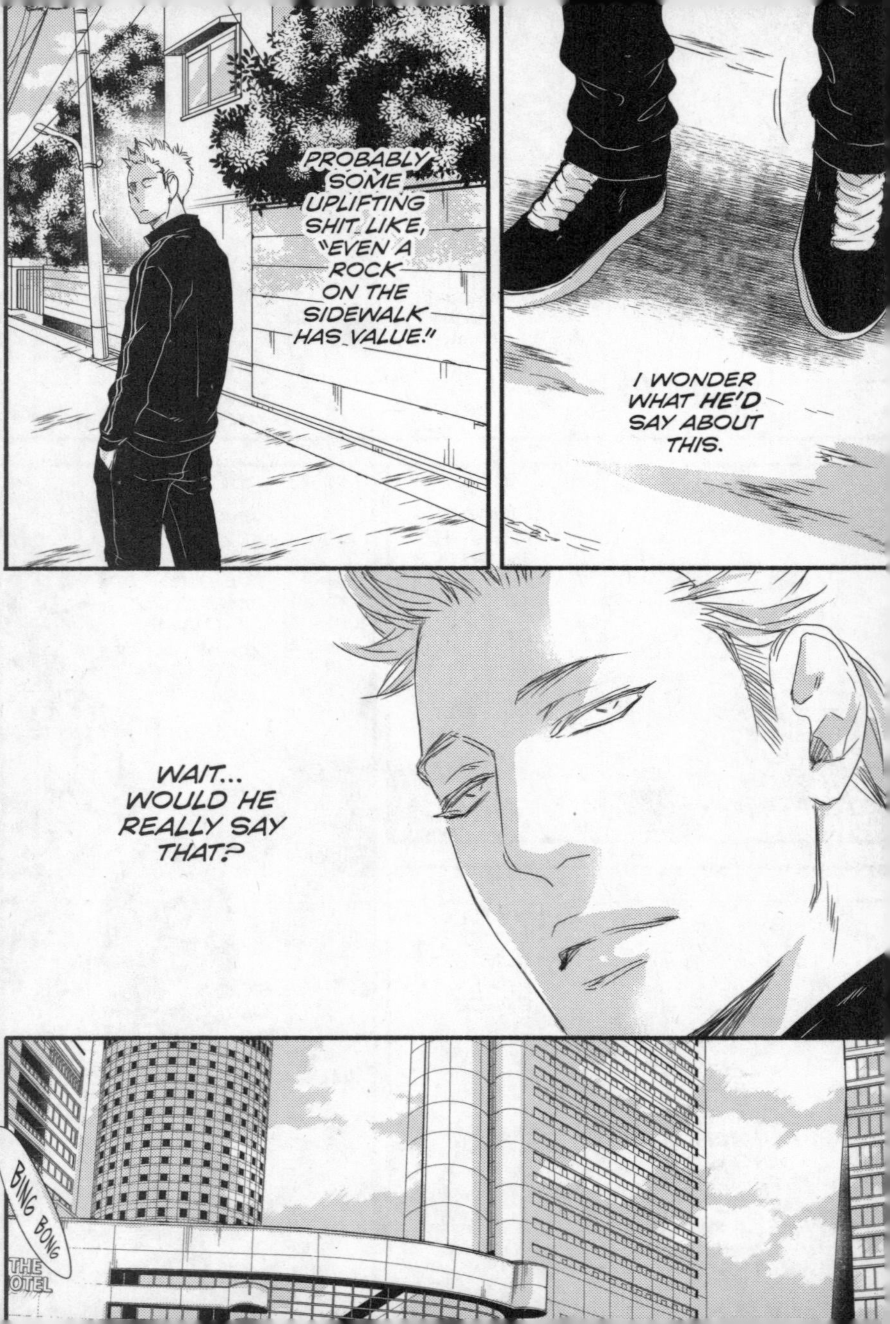
I WONDER WHAT HE'D SAY ABOUT THIS.
PROBABLY SOME UPLIFTING SHIT LIKE, "EVEN A ROCK ON THE SIDEWALK HAS VALUE!"
WAIT... WOULD HE REALLY SAY THAT?
BING BONG
THE
OTEL

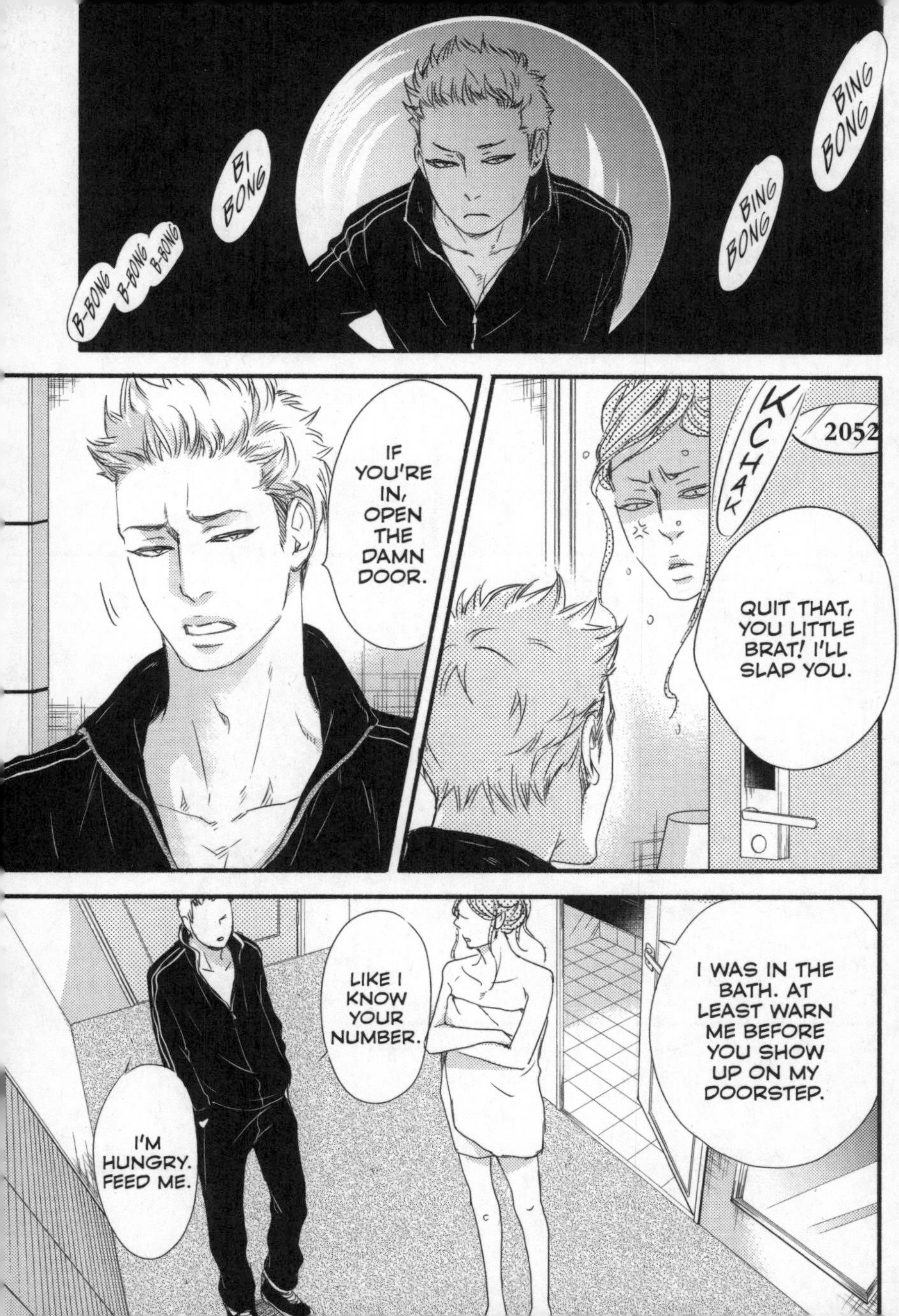
BING BONG
BING BONG
BI BONG
B-BONG B-BONG B-BONG
KCHAK
2052
QUIT THAT, YOU LITTLE BRAT! I'LL SLAP YOU.
IF YOU'RE IN, OPEN THE DAMN DOOR.
I WAS IN THE BATH. AT LEAST WARN ME BEFORE YOU SHOW UP ON MY DOORSTEP.
LIKE I KNOW YOUR NUMBER.
I'M HUNGRY. FEED ME.

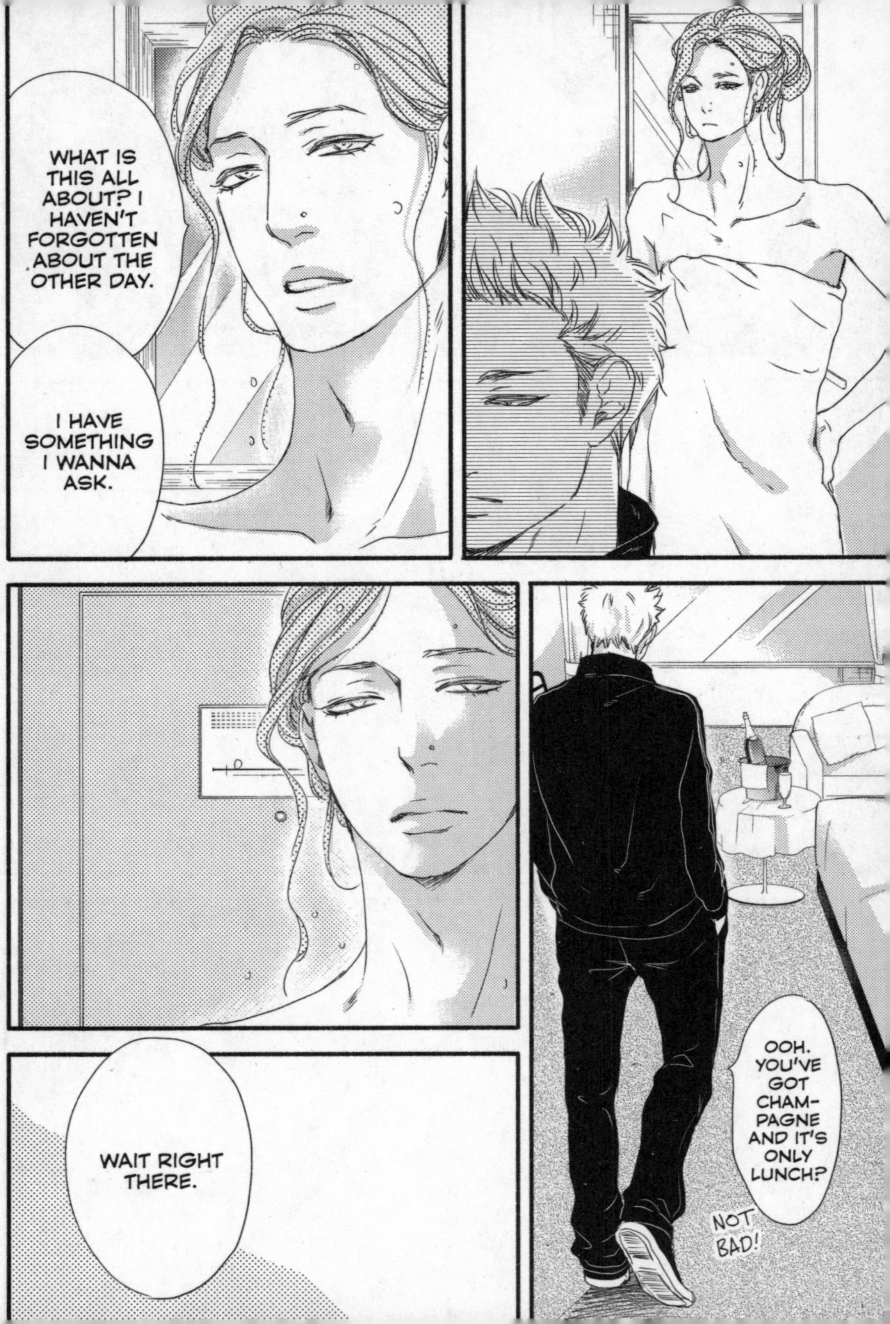
WHAT IS THIS ALL ABOUT? I HAVEN'T FORGOTTEN ABOUT THE OTHER DAY.
I HAVE SOMETHING I WANNA ASK.
OOH. YOU'VE GOT CHAM-PAGNE AND IT'S ONLY LUNCH?
NOT BAD!
WAIT RIGHT THERE.

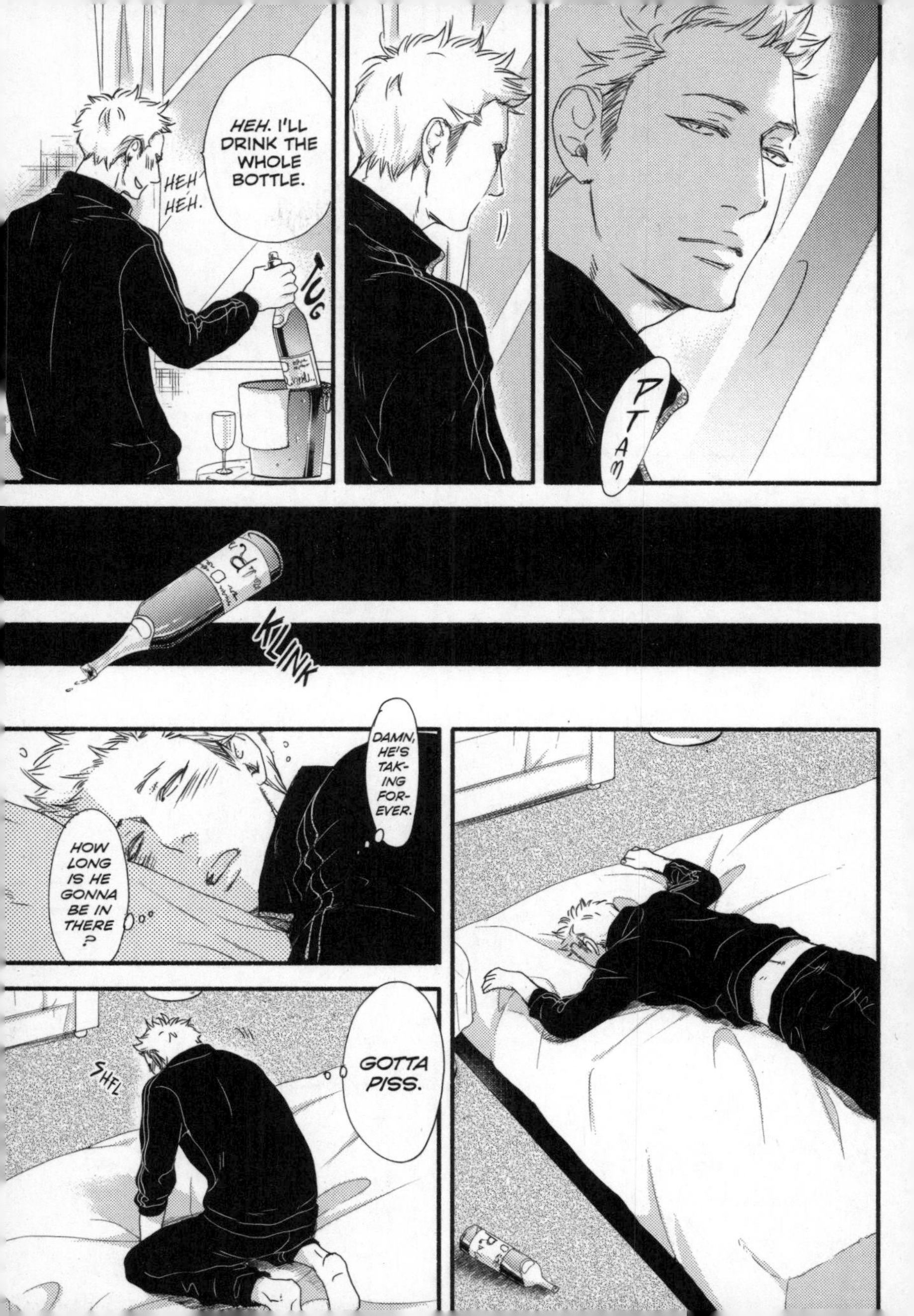
PTAM
HEH. I'LL DRINK THE WHOLE BOTTLE.
HEH HEH.
TUG
KLINK
DAMN, HE'S TAKING FOREVER.
HOW LONG IS HE GONNA BE IN THERE?
GOTTA PISS.
SHFL

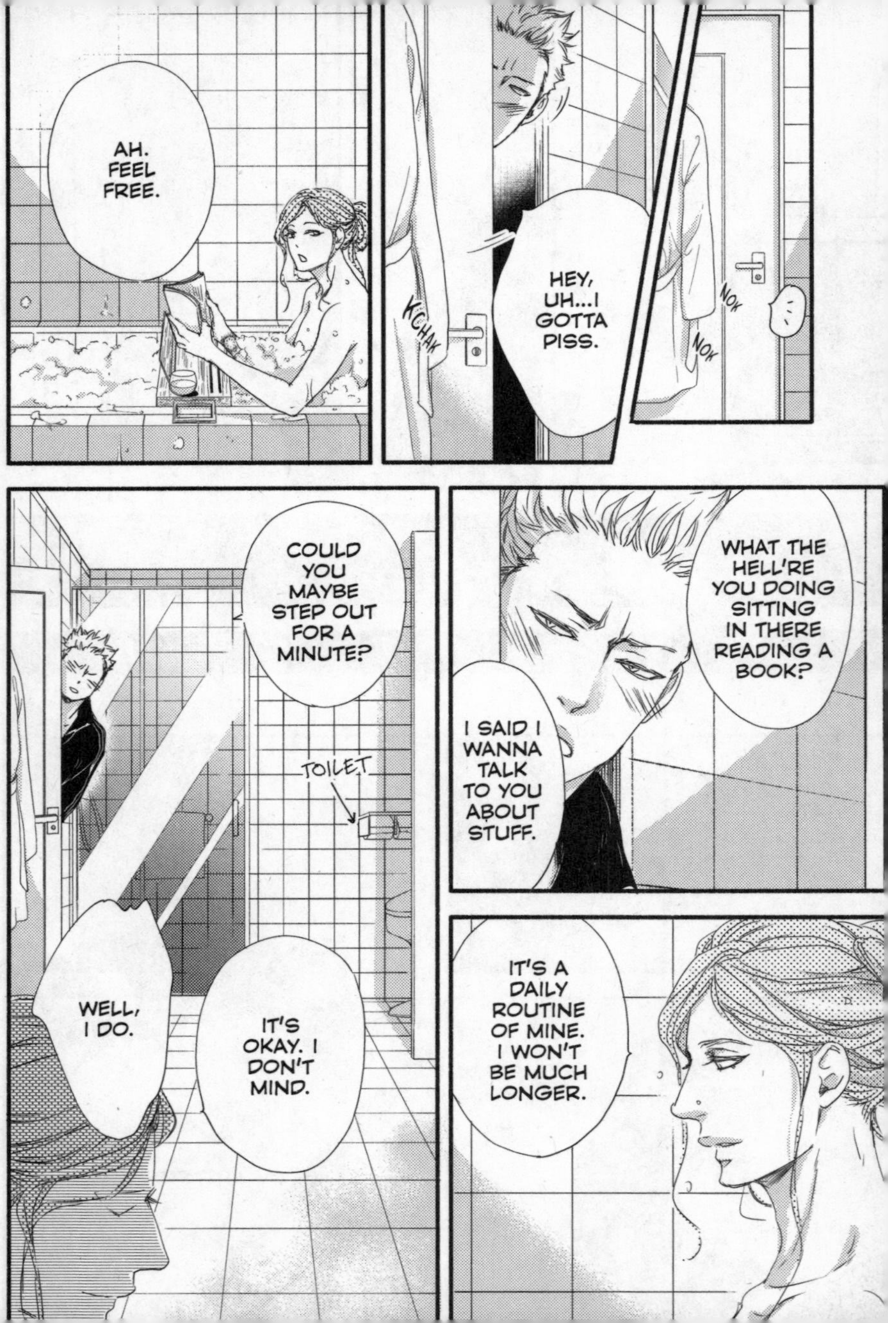
NOK
NOK
...
KCHAK
HEY, UH...I GOTTA PISS.
AH. FEEL FREE.
WHAT THE HELL'RE YOU DOING SITTING IN THERE READING A BOOK?
I SAID I WANNA TALK TO YOU ABOUT STUFF.
IT'S A DAILY ROUTINE OF MINE. I WON'T BE MUCH LONGER.
COULD YOU MAYBE STEP OUT FOR A MINUTE?
TOILET
IT'S OKAY. I DON'T MIND.
WELL, I DO.

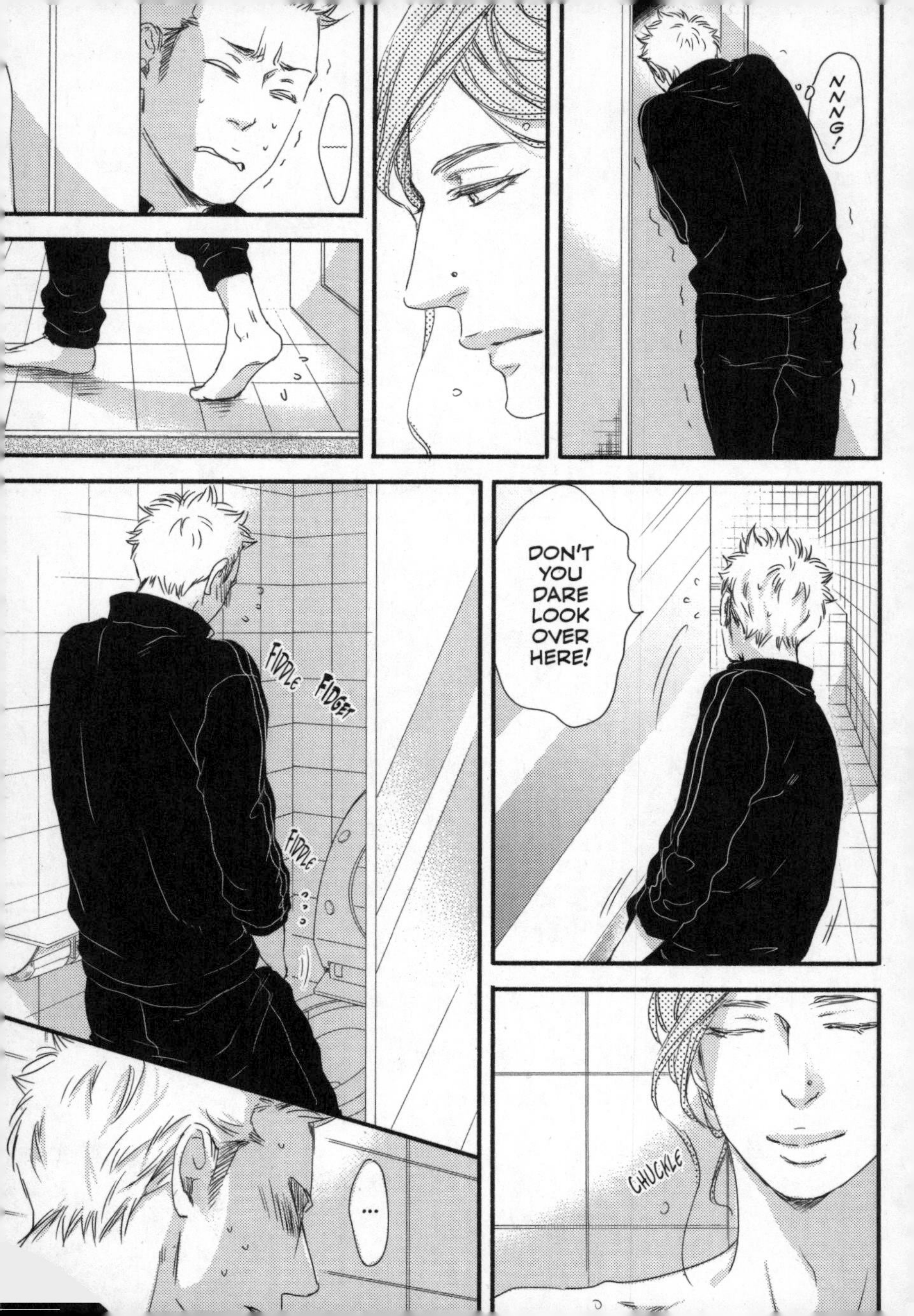
NNNG!
DON'T YOU DARE LOOK OVER HERE!
CHUCKLE
FIDDLE
FIDGET
FIDDLE
...

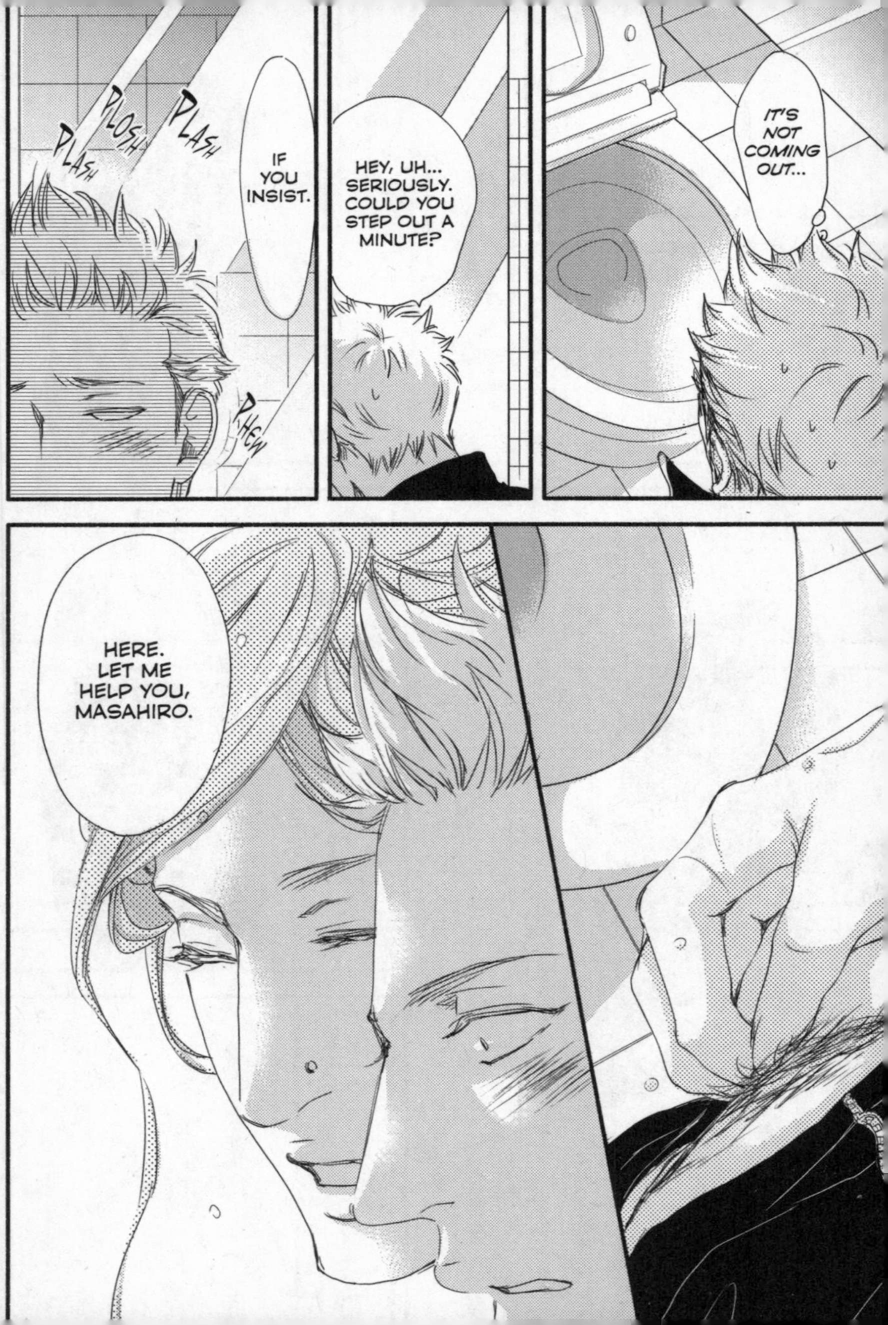
IT'S NOT COMING OUT...
HEY, UH... SERIOUSLY. COULD YOU STEP OUT A MINUTE?
IF YOU INSIST.
PLASH
PLOSH
PLASH
P-HEW
HERE. LET ME HELP YOU, MASAHIRO.

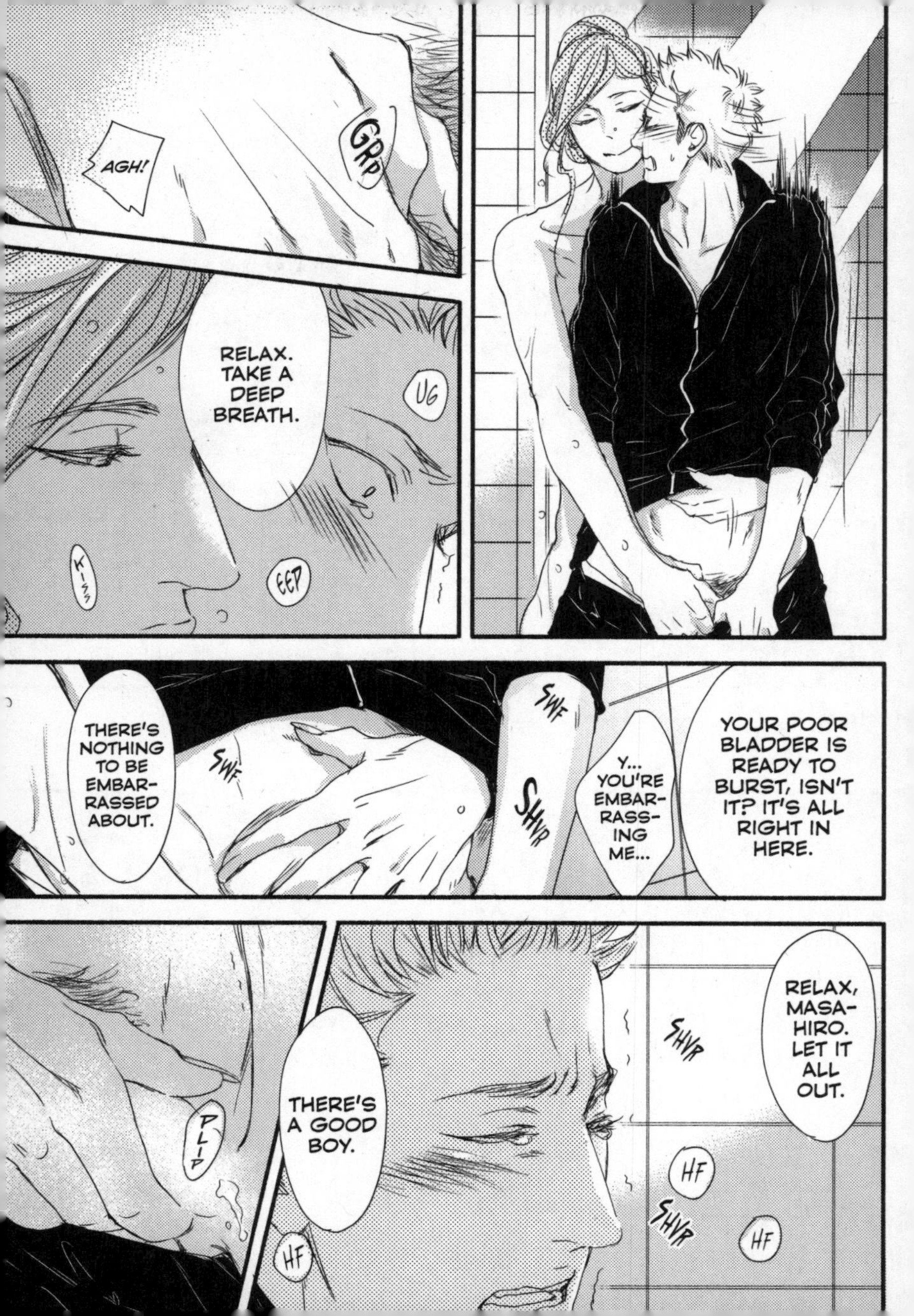
GRP
AGH!
UG
RELAX. TAKE A DEEP BREATH.
EEP
KISS
YOUR POOR BLADDER IS READY TO BURST, ISN'T IT? IT'S ALL RIGHT IN HERE.
Y... YOU'RE EMBAR-RASS-ING ME...
SWF
SHVR
SWF
THERE'S NOTHING TO BE EMBAR-RASSED ABOUT.
RELAX, MASA-HIRO. LET IT ALL OUT.
SHVR
HF
SHVR
HF
THERE'S A GOOD BOY.
HF
PLIP

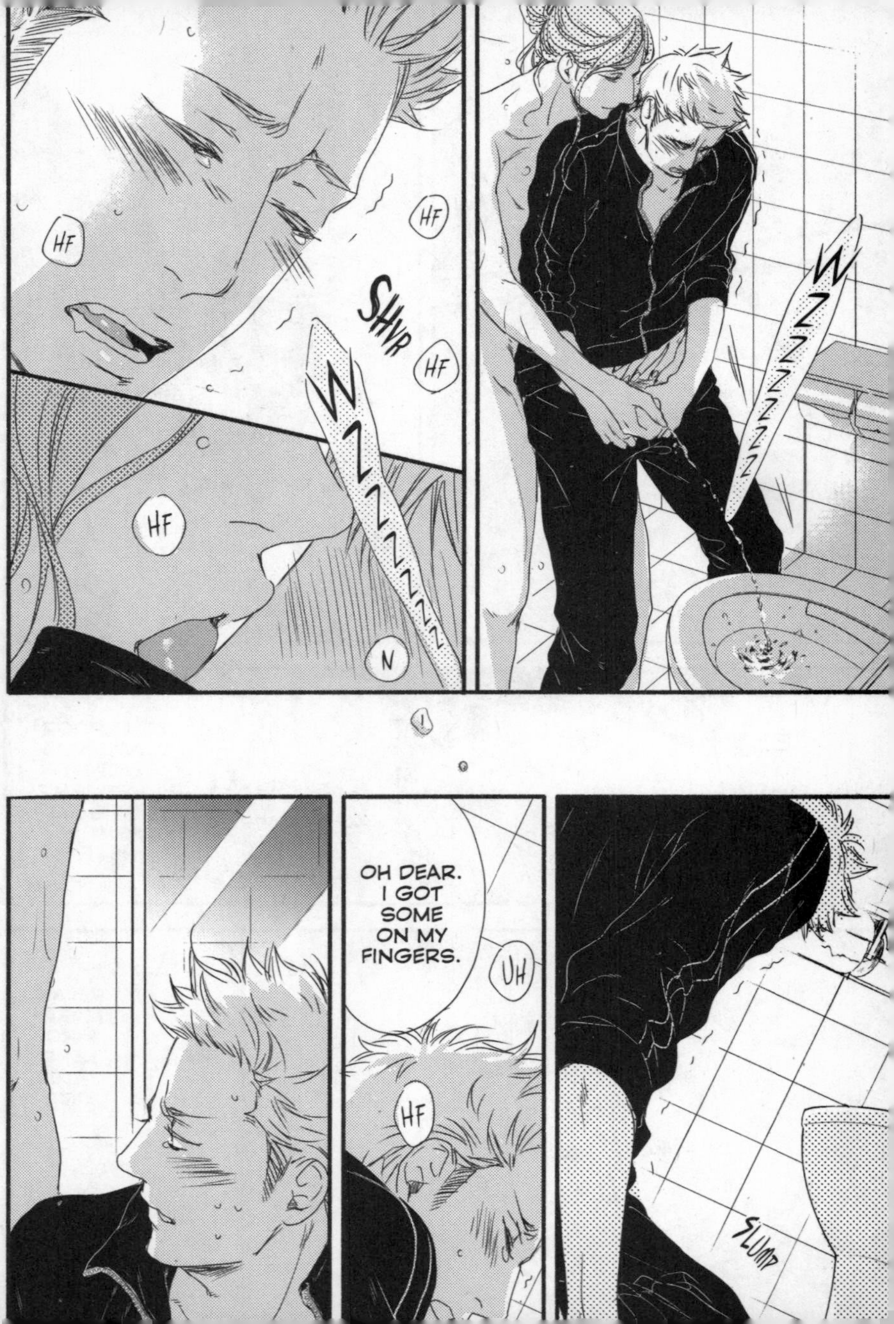
WZZZZZZZZ
HF
SHVR
HF
HF
WZZZZZZZZ
HF
N
SLUMP
OH DEAR. I GOT SOME ON MY FINGERS.
UH
HF

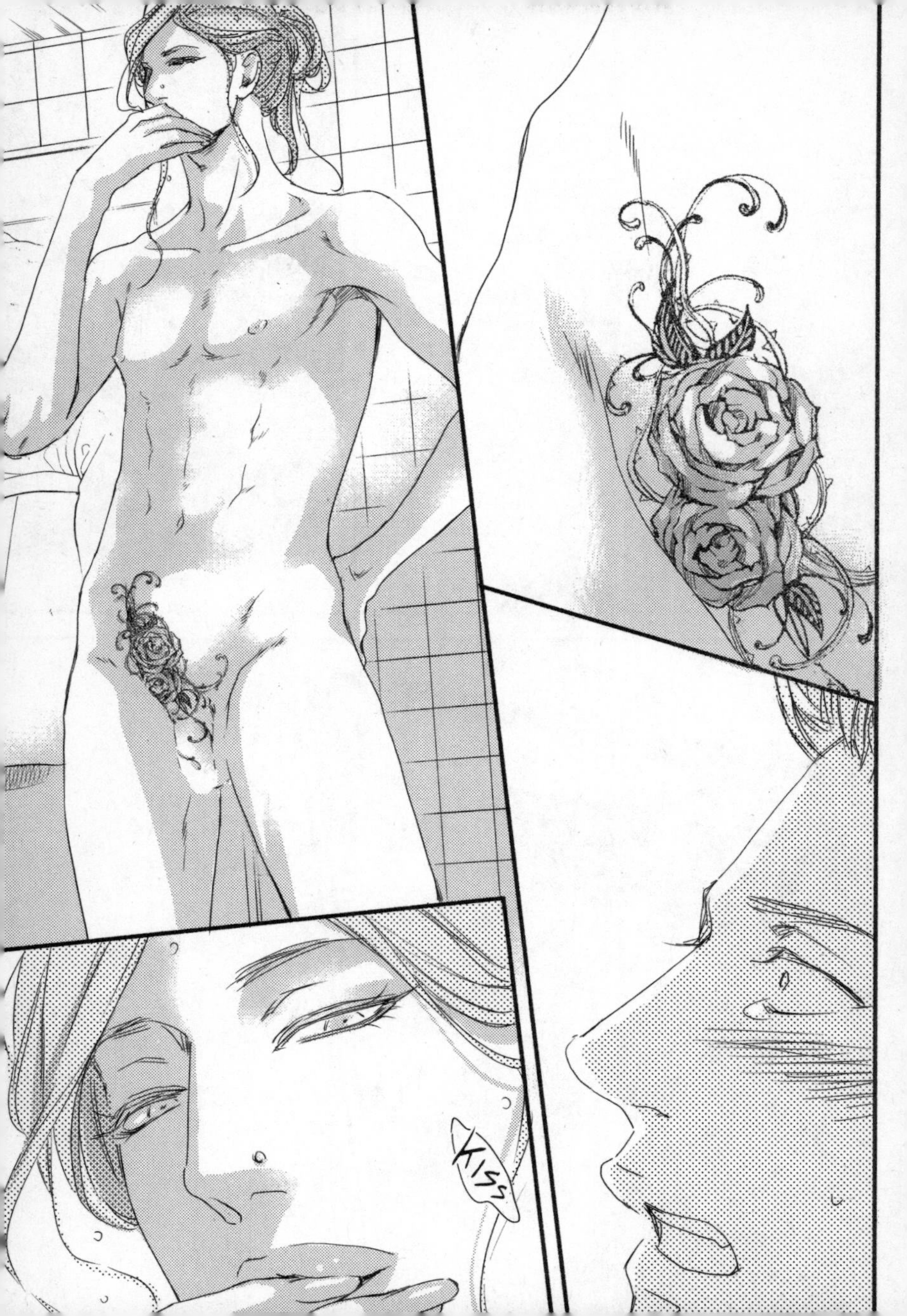
KISS

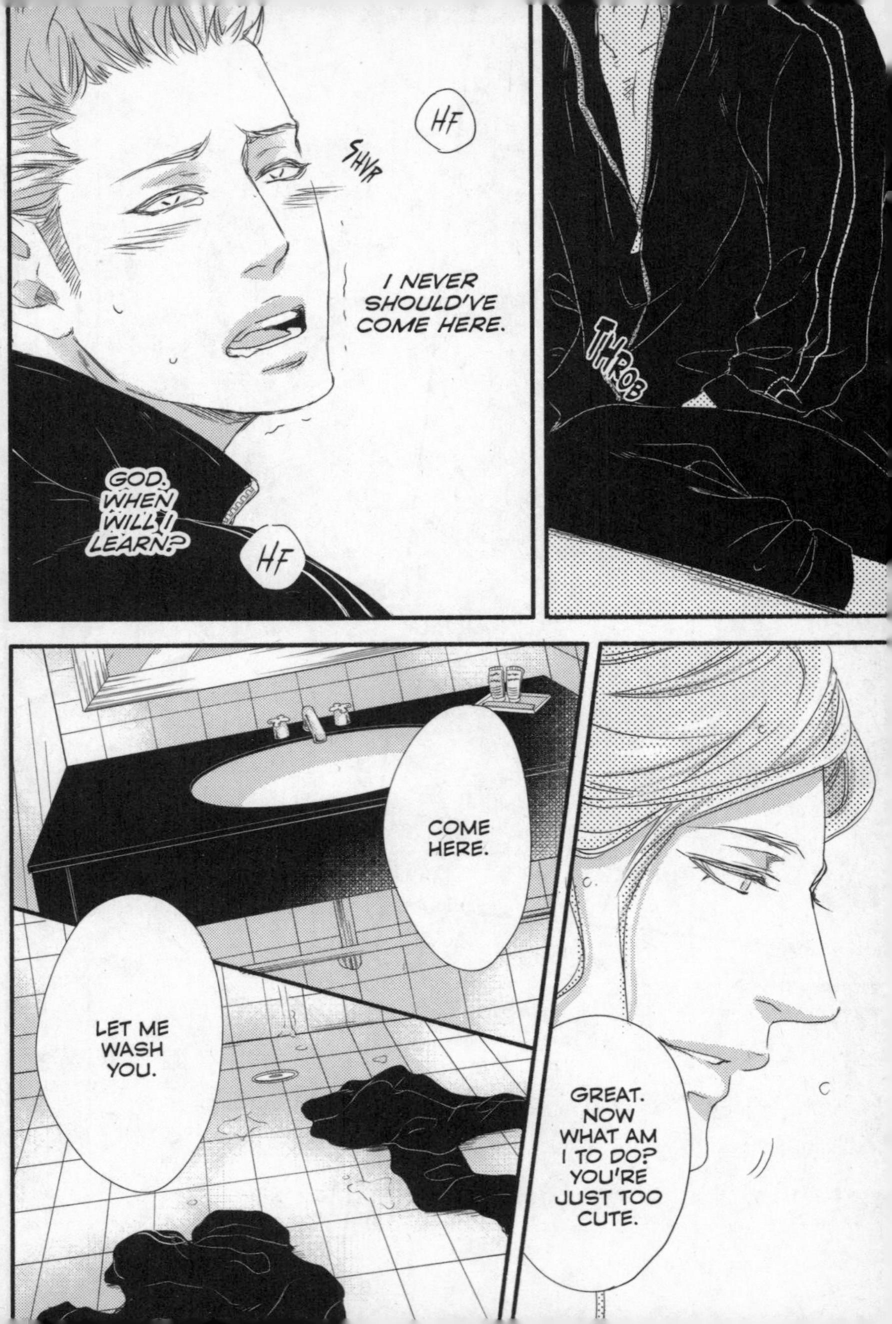
THROB
HF
SHVR
I NEVER SHOULD'VE COME HERE.
HF
GOD. WHEN WILL I LEARN?
GREAT. NOW WHAT AM I TO DO? YOU'RE JUST TOO CUTE.
COME HERE.
LET ME WASH YOU.

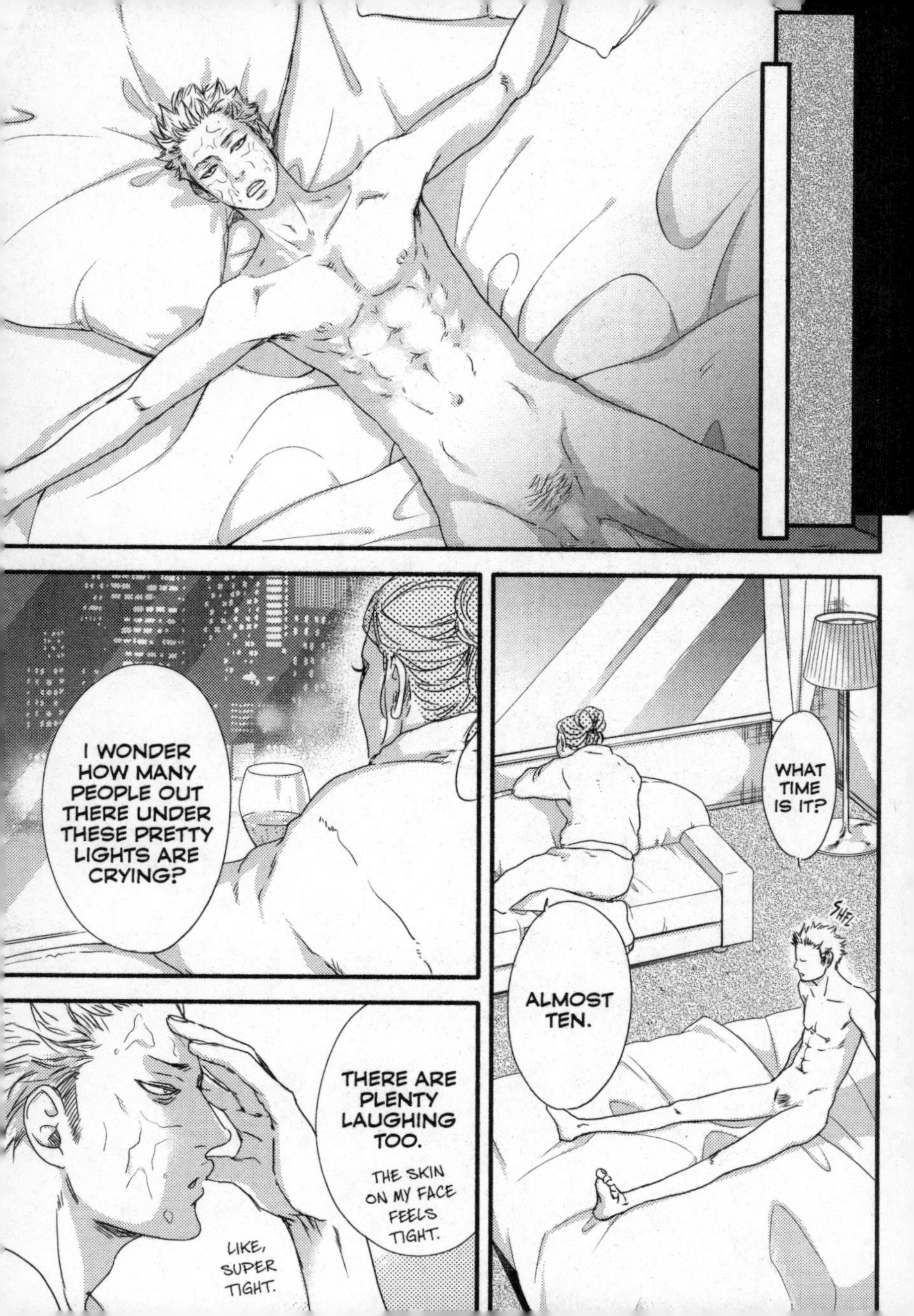
WHAT TIME IS IT?
SHFL
ALMOST TEN.
I WONDER HOW MANY PEOPLE OUT THERE UNDER THESE PRETTY LIGHTS ARE CRYING?
THERE ARE PLENTY LAUGHING TOO.
THE SKIN ON MY FACE FEELS TIGHT.
LIKE, SUPER TIGHT.

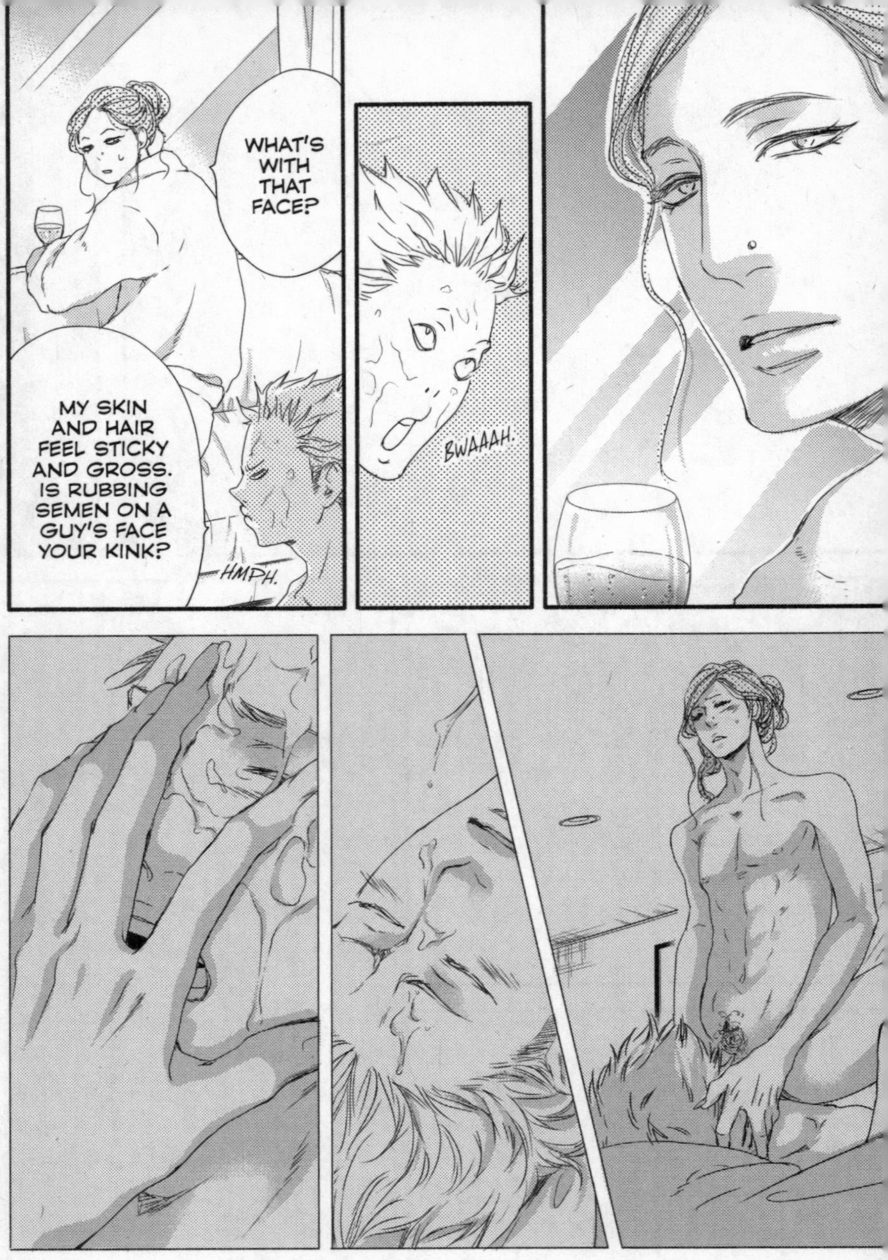
BWAAAH.
WHAT'S WITH THAT FACE?
MY SKIN AND HAIR FEEL STICKY AND GROSS. IS RUBBING SEMEN ON A GUY'S FACE YOUR KINK?
HMPH.

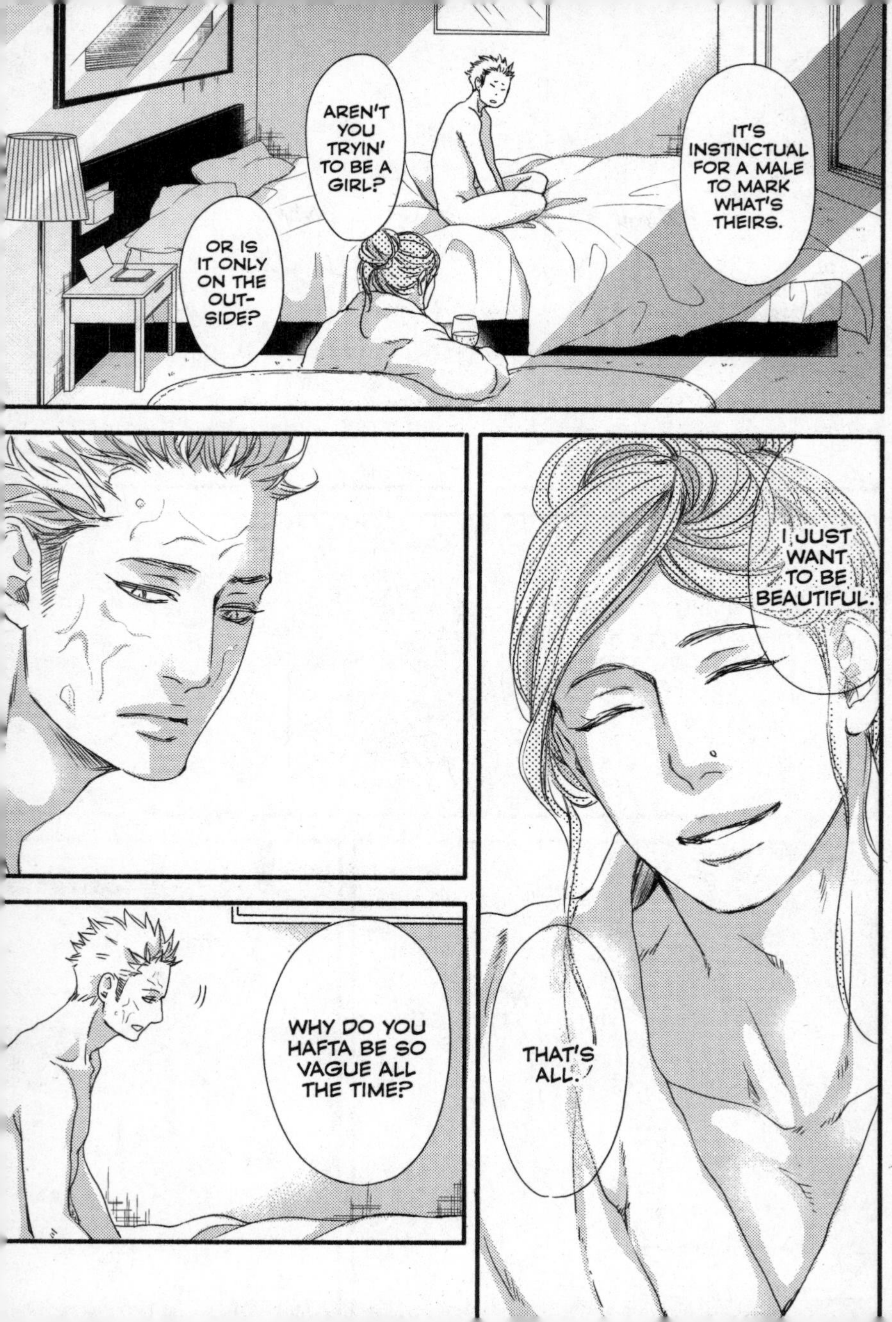
IT'S INSTINCTUAL FOR A MALE TO MARK WHAT'S THEIRS.
AREN'T YOU TRYIN' TO BE A GIRL?
OR IS IT ONLY ON THE OUT-SIDE?
I JUST WANT TO BE BEAUTIFUL.
THAT'S ALL.
WHY DO YOU HAFTA BE SO VAGUE ALL THE TIME?

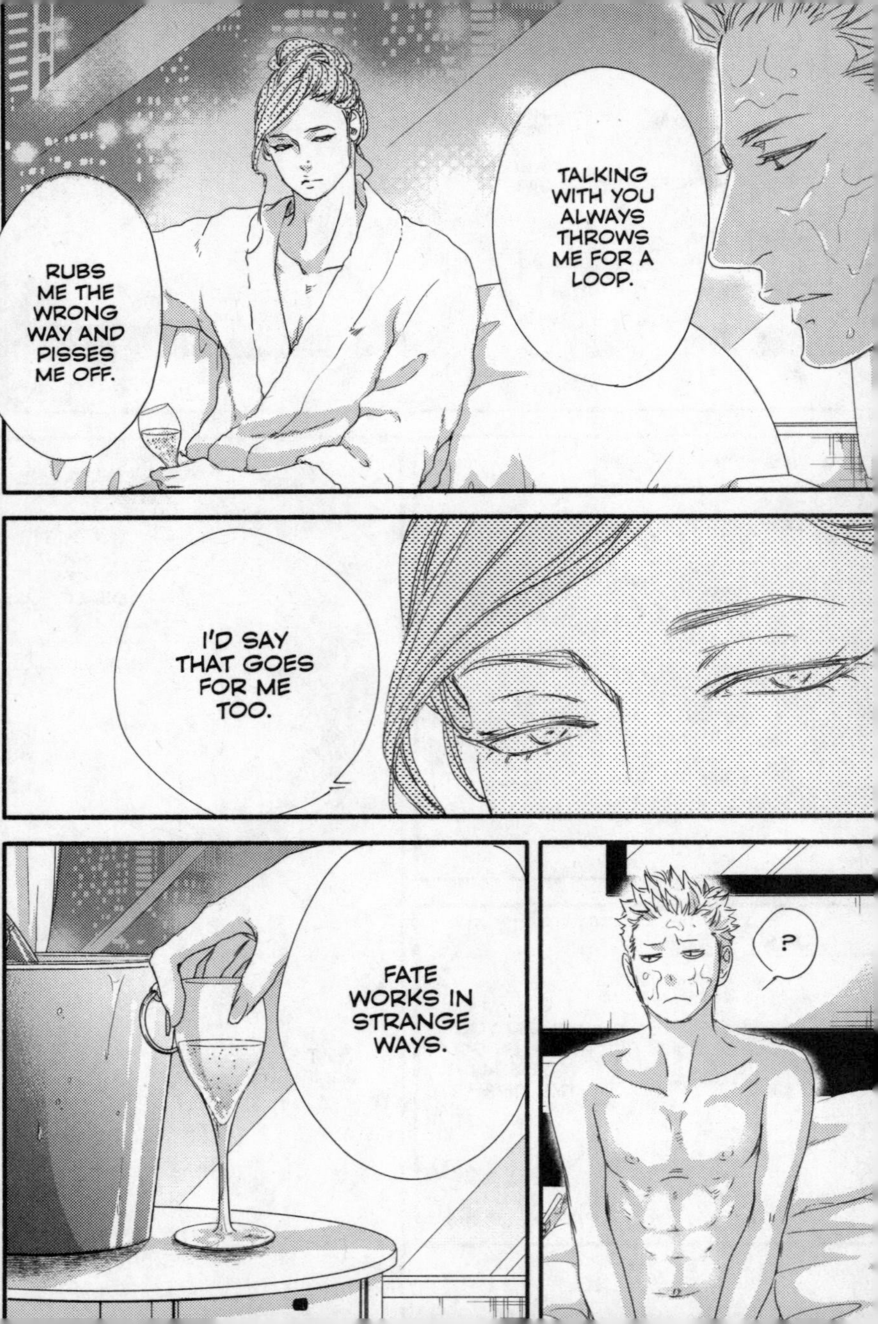
TALKING WITH YOU ALWAYS THROWS ME FOR A LOOP.
RUBS ME THE WRONG WAY AND PISSES ME OFF.
I'D SAY THAT GOES FOR ME TOO.
?
FATE WORKS IN STRANGE WAYS.

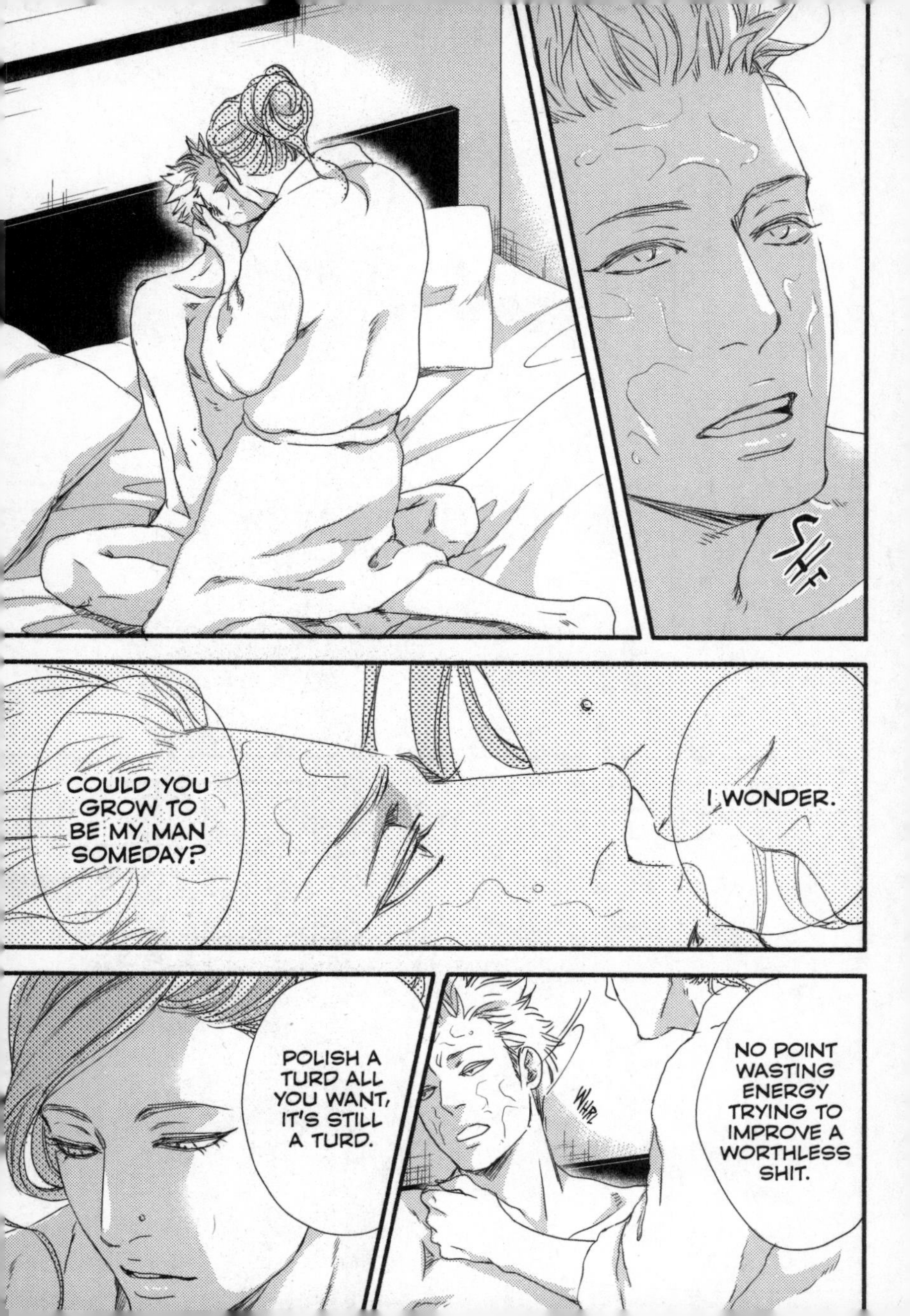
SHF
I WONDER.
COULD YOU GROW TO BE MY MAN SOMEDAY?
NO POINT WASTING ENERGY TRYING TO IMPROVE A WORTHLESS SHIT.
WHRL
POLISH A TURD ALL YOU WANT, IT'S STILL A TURD.

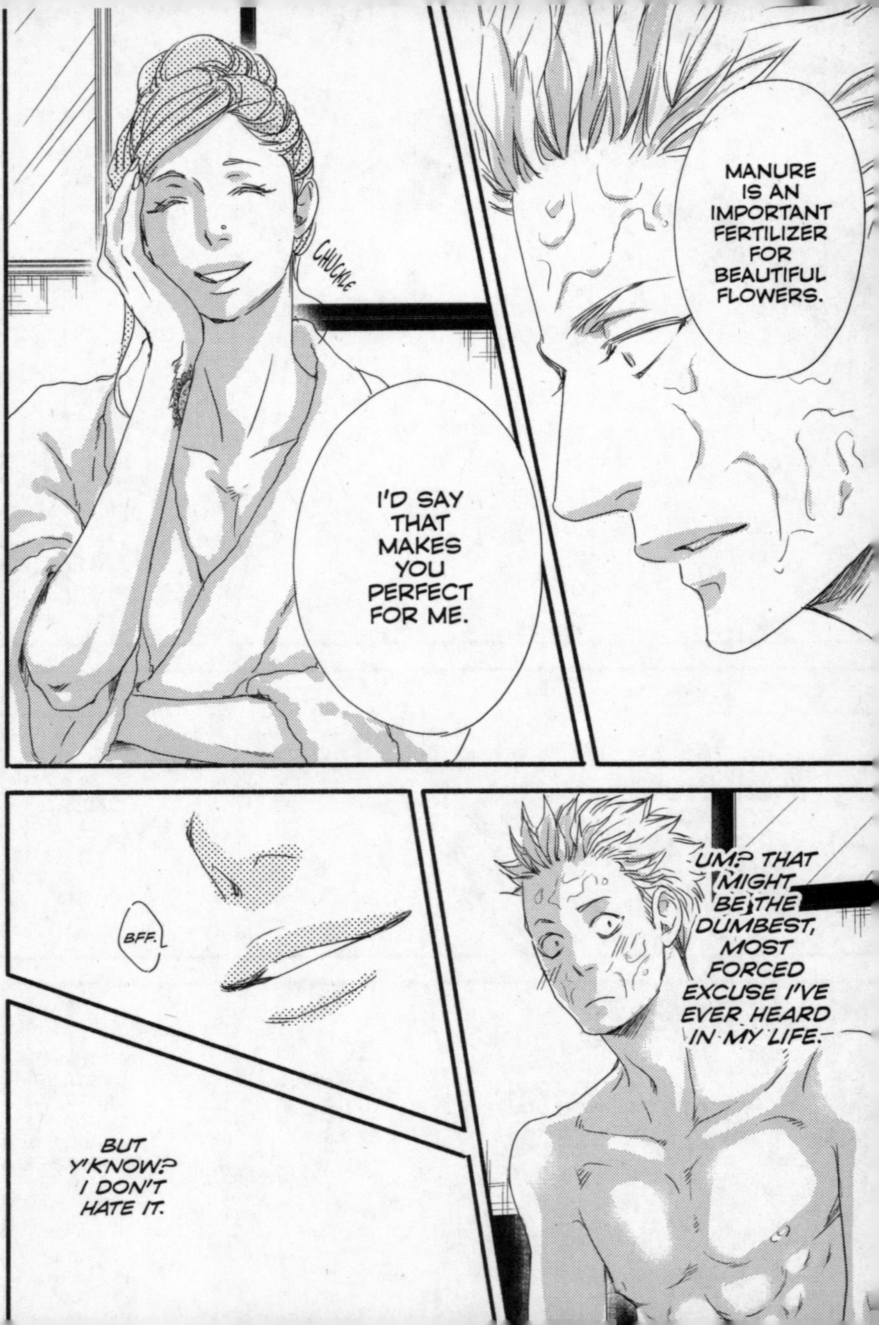
MANURE IS AN IMPORTANT FERTILIZER FOR BEAUTIFUL FLOWERS.
CHUCKLE
I'D SAY THAT MAKES YOU PERFECT FOR ME.
UM? THAT MIGHT BE THE DUMBEST, MOST FORCED EXCUSE I'VE EVER HEARD IN MY LIFE.
BFF.
BUT Y'KNOW? I DON'T HATE IT.

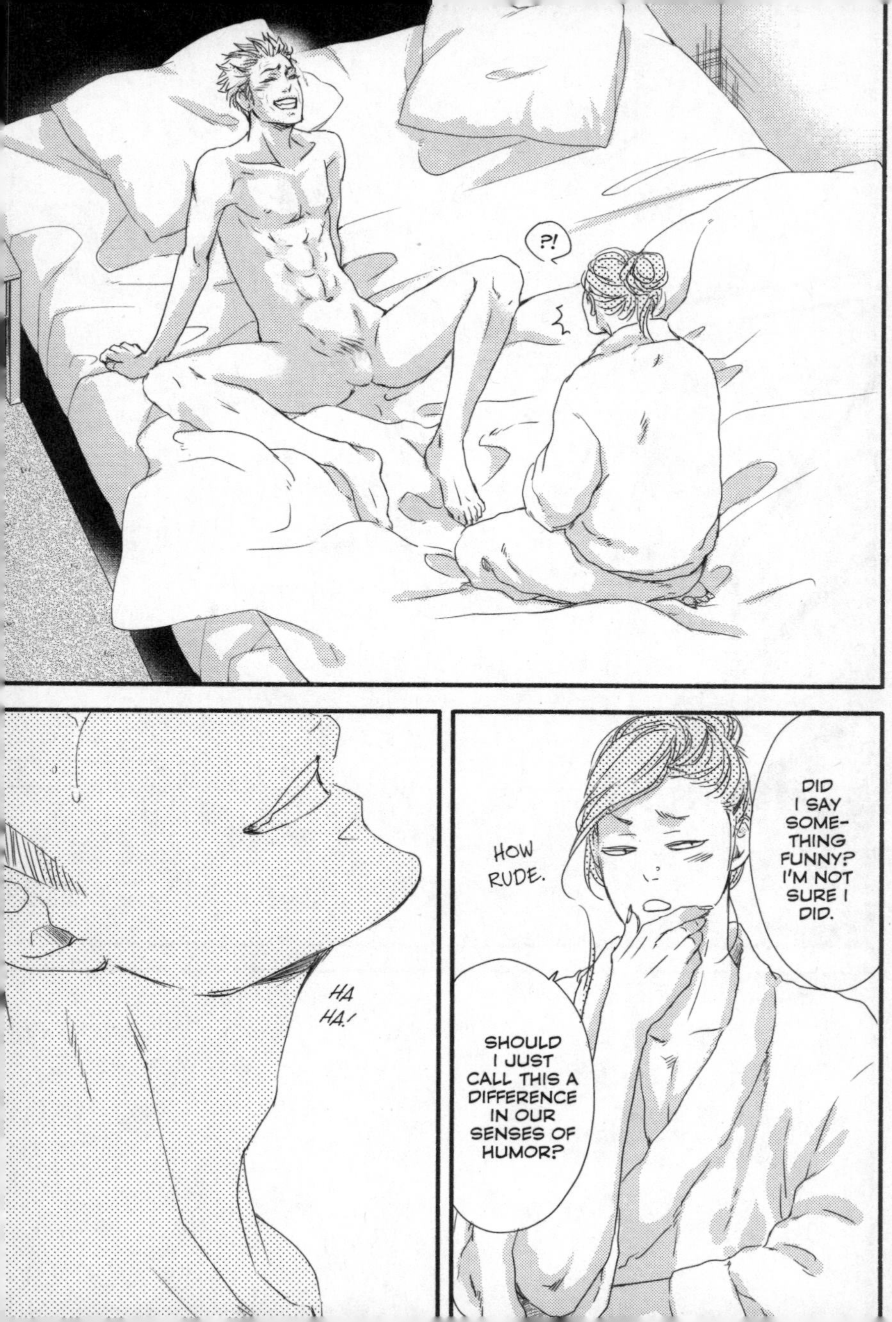
?!
DID I SAY SOME-THING FUNNY? I'M NOT SURE I DID.
HOW RUDE.
SHOULD I JUST CALL THIS A DIFFERENCE IN OUR SENSES OF HUMOR?
HA HA!

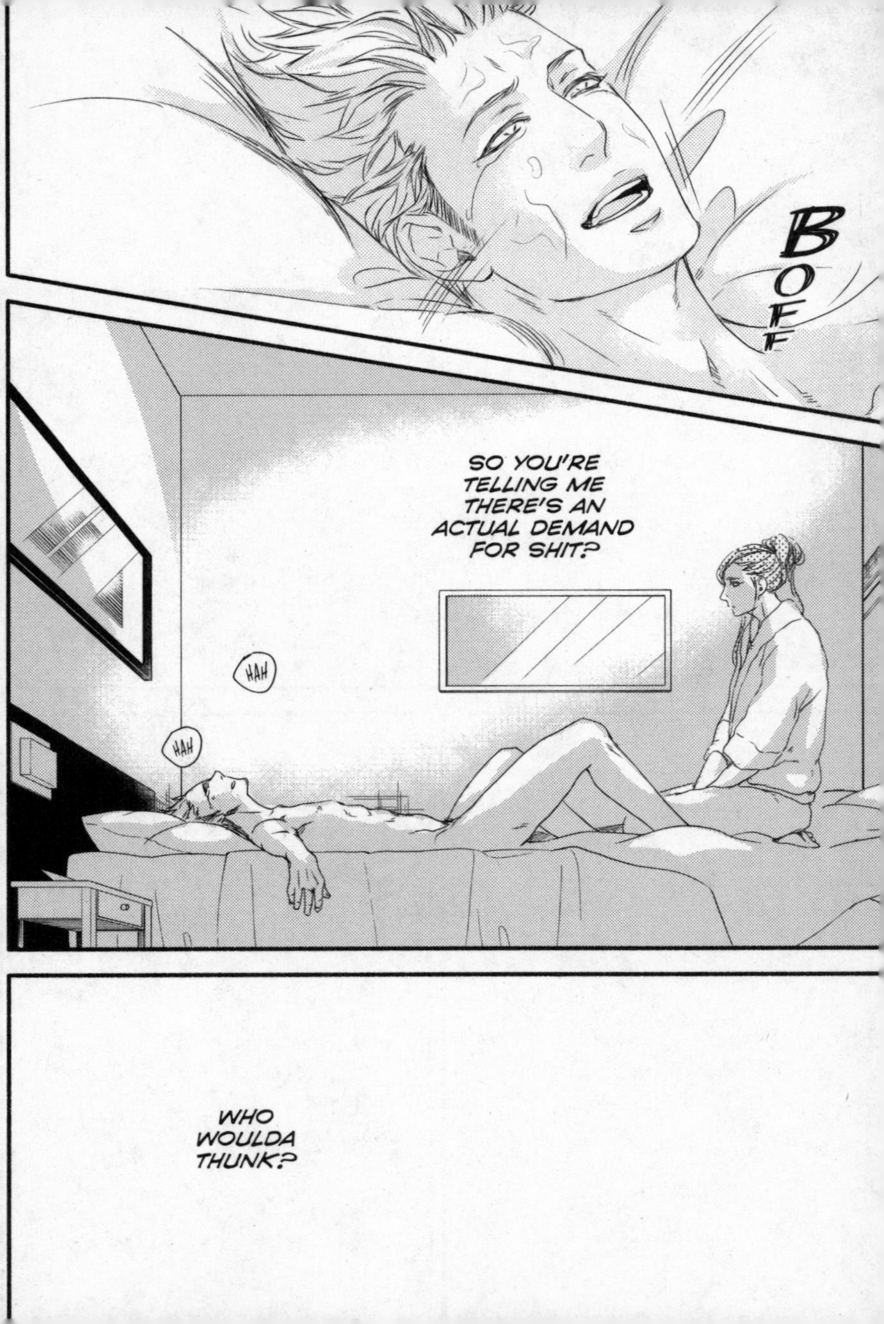
BOFF
SO YOU'RE TELLING ME THERE'S AN ACTUAL DEMAND FOR SHIT?
HAH
HAH
WHO WOULDA THUNK?

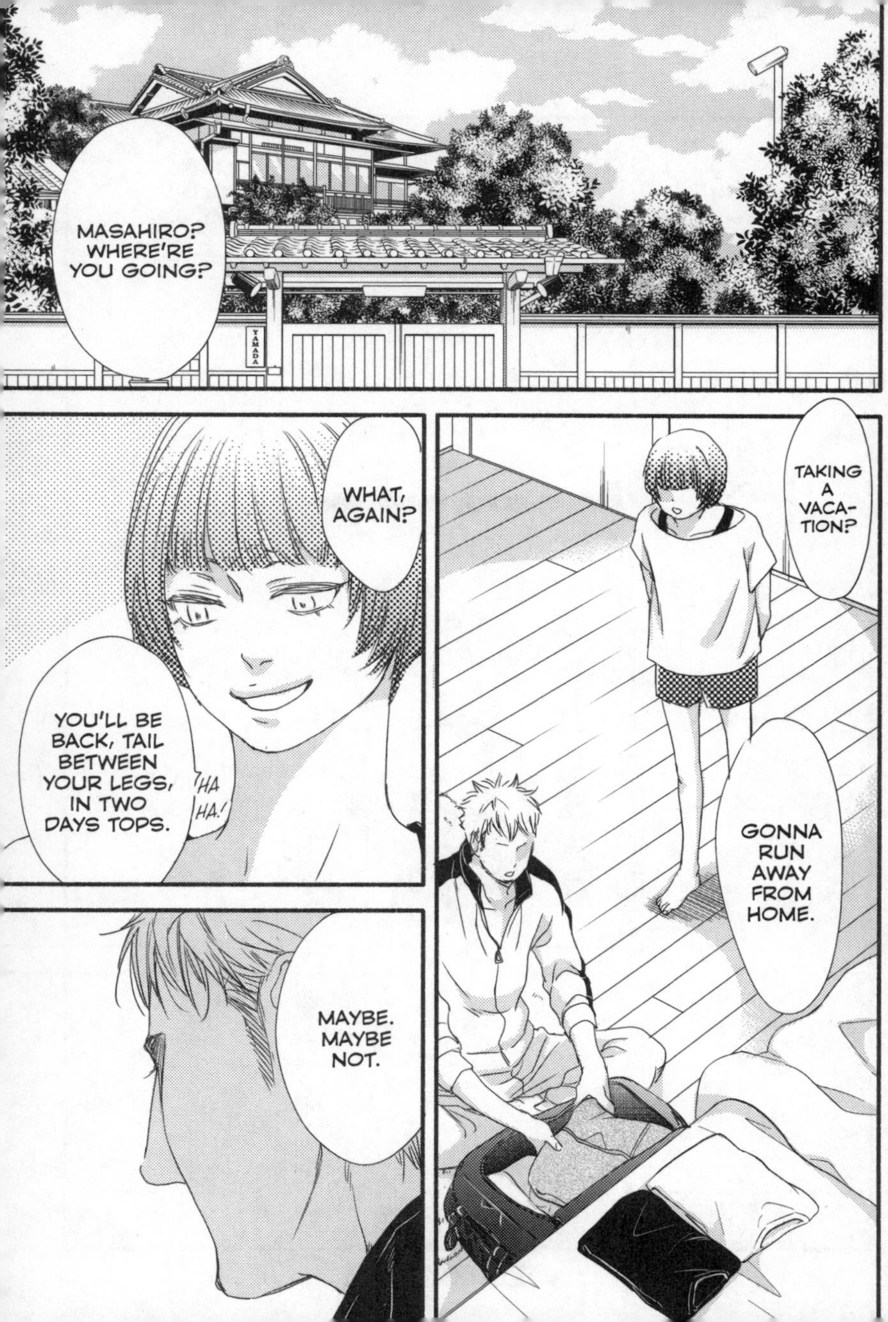
MASAHIRO? WHERE'RE YOU GOING?
YAMADA
TAKING A VACATION?
GONNA RUN AWAY FROM HOME.
WHAT, AGAIN?
YOU'LL BE BACK, TAIL BETWEEN YOUR LEGS, IN TWO DAYS TOPS.
HA HA!
MAYBE. MAYBE NOT.

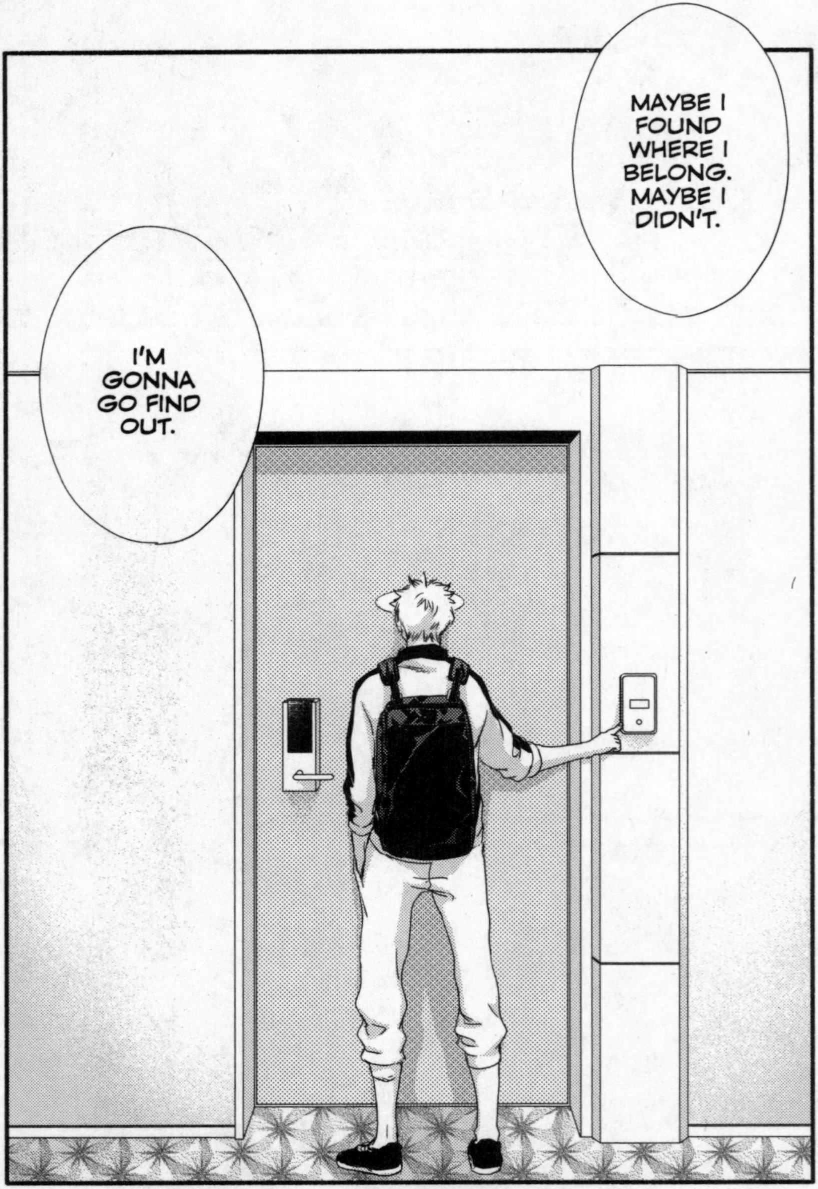
MAYBE I FOUND WHERE I BELONG. MAYBE I DIDN'T.
I'M GONNA GO FIND OUT.

to be continued

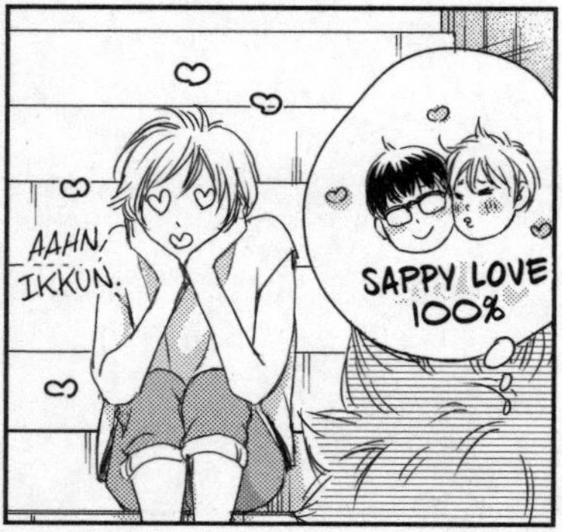
SAPPY LOVE 100%
AAHN, IKKUN.

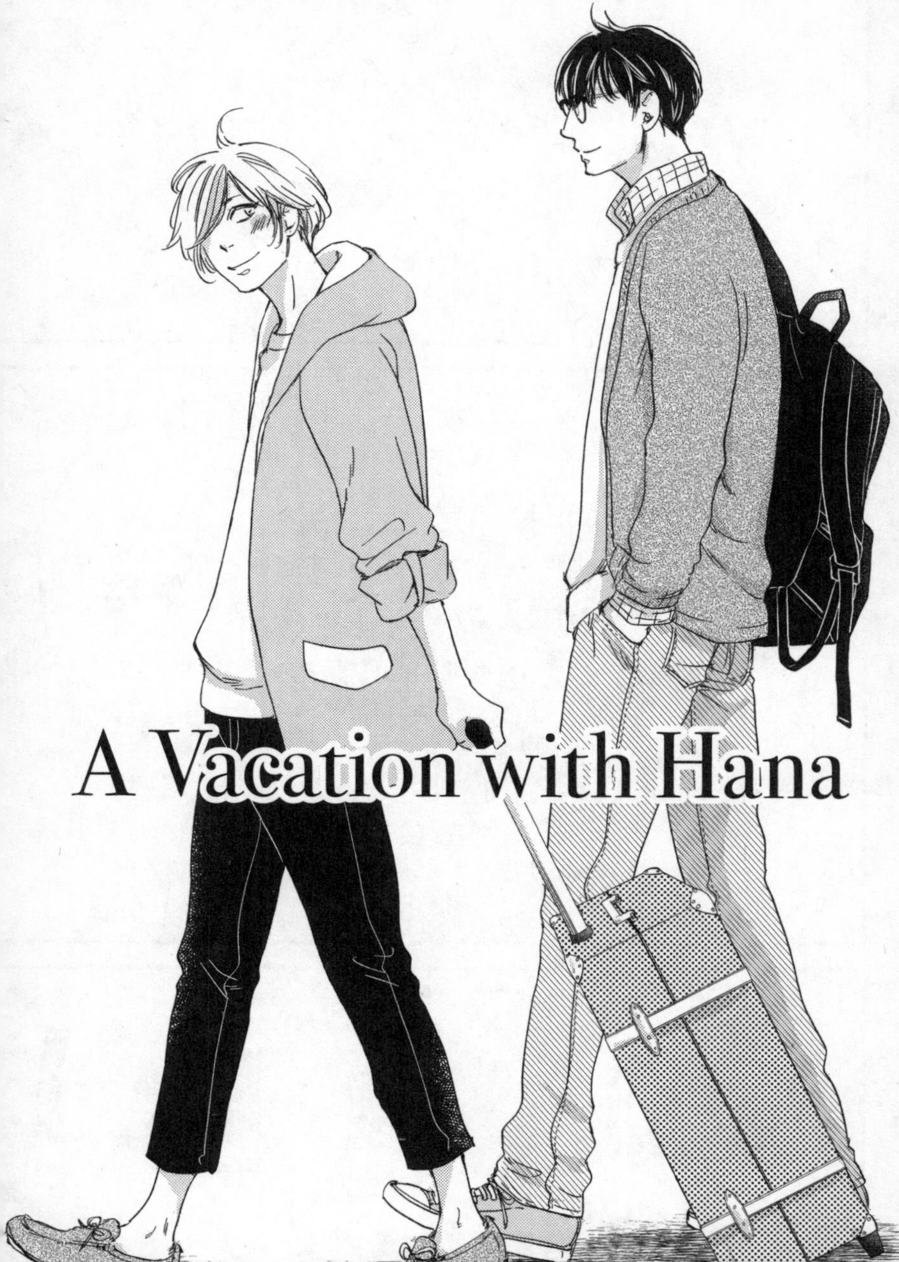
A Vacation with Hana

KANSAI

TOP PICKS! 2017 ISSUE

HOT SPRINGS 3 INNS

THE COZIEST, MOST RELAX...
INNS FOR YOUR TRIP WITH...
YOU SPECIAL SOMEON...

IKKUUUN... I WANNA MAKE OUT.

SURE. IN A MINUTE.

HOT SPRINGS MAPS THE BEST HOTELS

INCLUDES COUPON! 300 YEN

PRIVATE BATHS DATE SPOTS

I ALMOST HAVE THE BEST, MOST EFFICIENT SCHEDULE PUT TOGETHER.

YUKEMURI WALKING COURSE

AM 8:00 - DEPART
9:30 ~
10:30 ~ } STRO...
11:35 ~ } LUN...
12:00 ~
13:30 ~

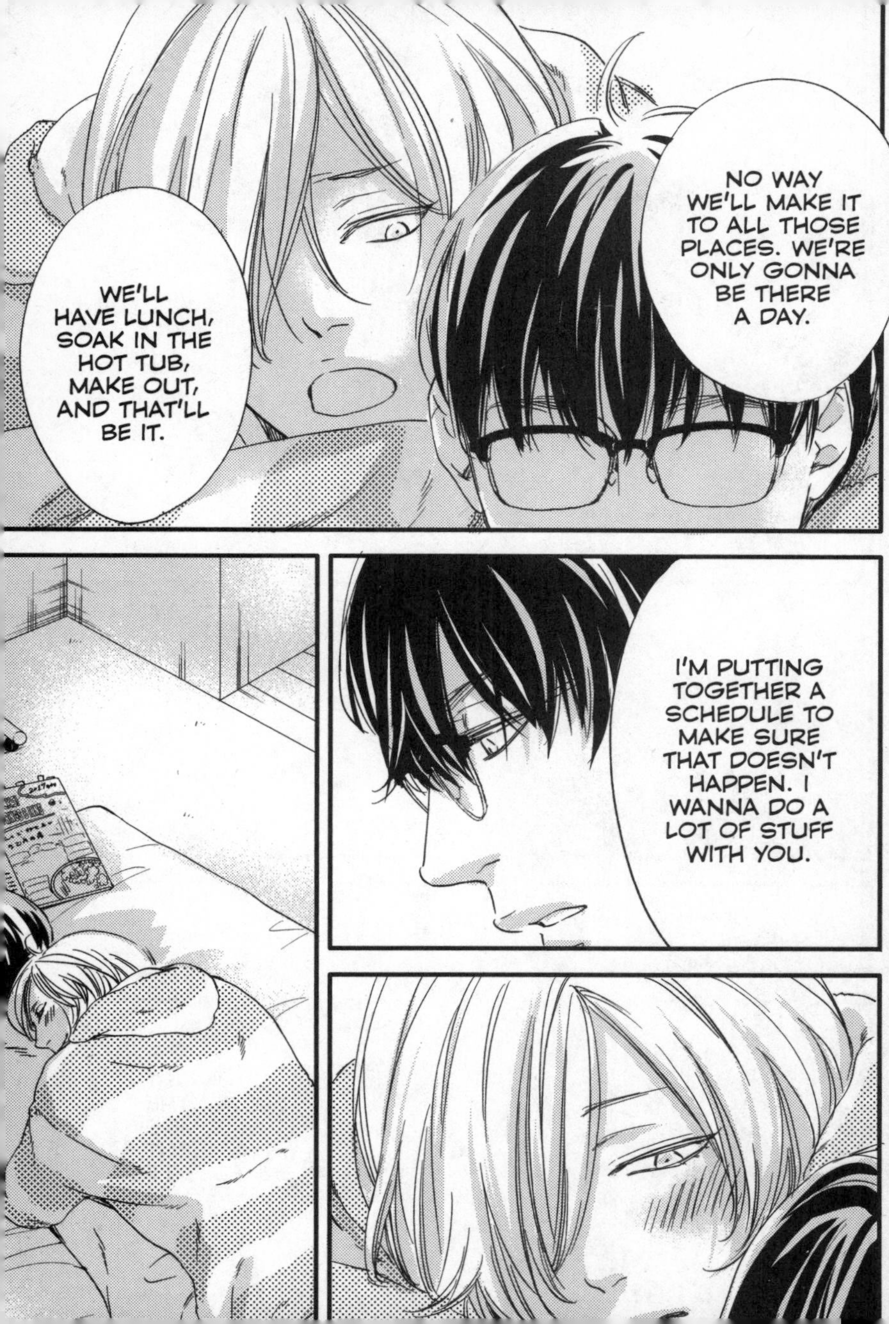
NO WAY WE'LL MAKE IT TO ALL THOSE PLACES. WE'RE ONLY GONNA BE THERE A DAY.
WE'LL HAVE LUNCH, SOAK IN THE HOT TUB, MAKE OUT, AND THAT'LL BE IT.
I'M PUTTING TOGETHER A SCHEDULE TO MAKE SURE THAT DOESN'T HAPPEN. I WANNA DO A LOT OF STUFF WITH YOU.

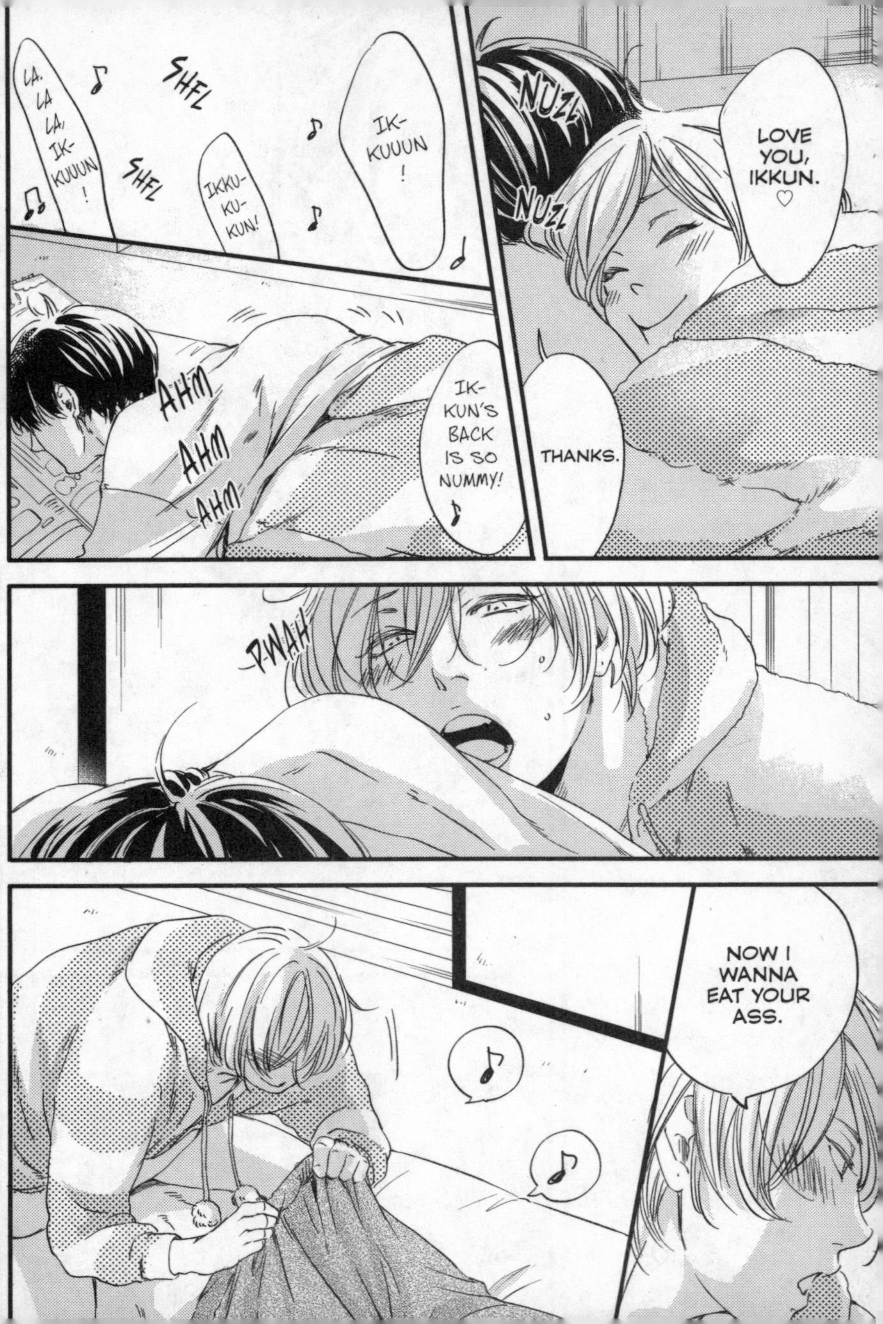
NUZL
NUZL
LOVE YOU, IKKUN. ♡
THANKS.
IK-KUUUN! ♪
IKKU-KU-KUN! ♪
SHFL
SHFL
LA. LA. LA. IK-KUUUN! ♪
AHM
AHM
AHM
IK-KUN'S BACK IS SO NUMMY! ♪
D-WAH
NOW I WANNA EAT YOUR ASS.
♪
♪

↑ THE IKKUN SONG

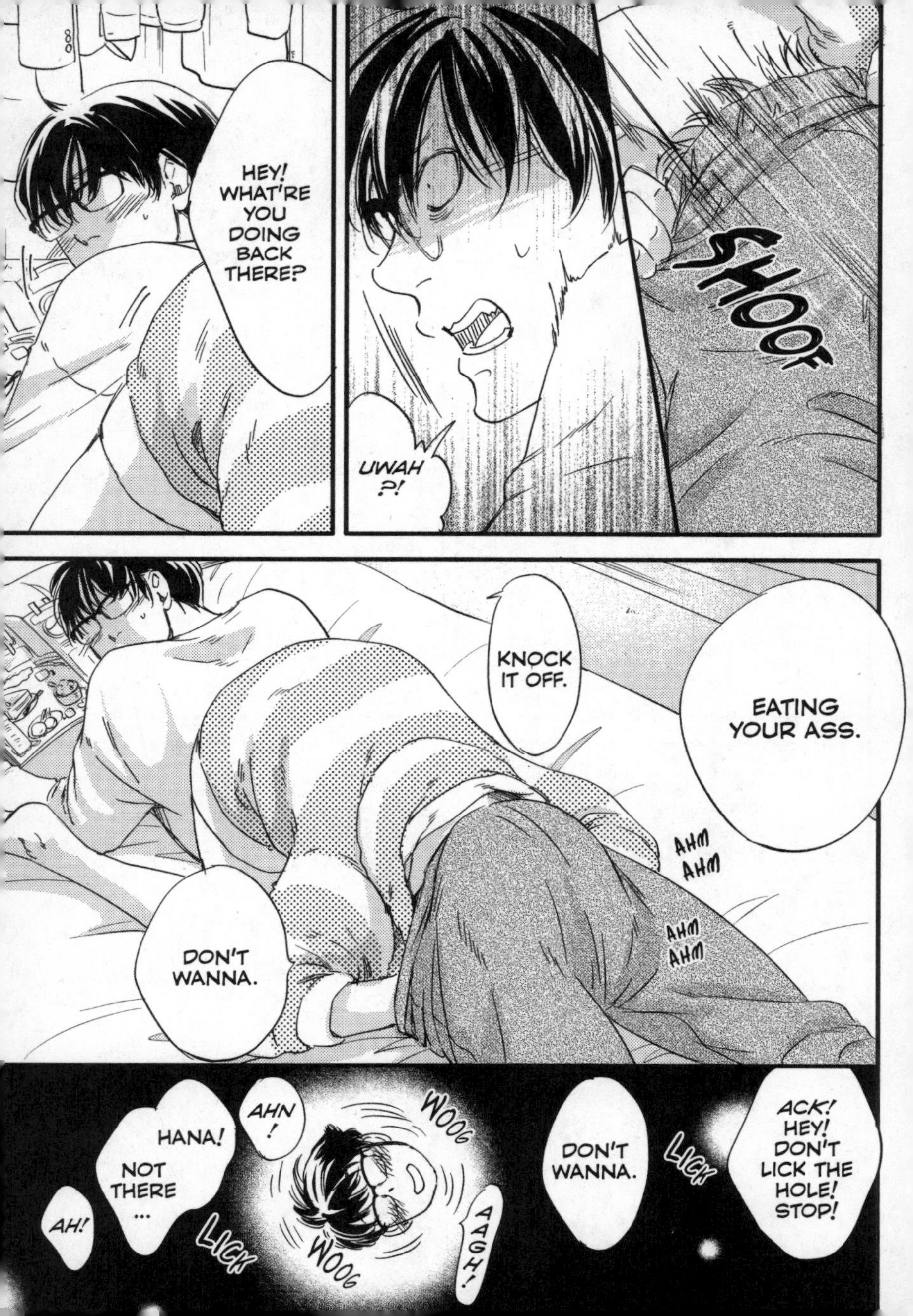
SHOOF
UWAH ?!
HEY! WHAT'RE YOU DOING BACK THERE?
EATING YOUR ASS.
KNOCK IT OFF.
AHM AHM
AHM AHM
DON'T WANNA.
ACK! HEY! DON'T LICK THE HOLE! STOP!
LICK
DON'T WANNA.
WOOG
AAGH!
AHN!
HANA! NOT THERE ...
LICK
WOOG
AH!

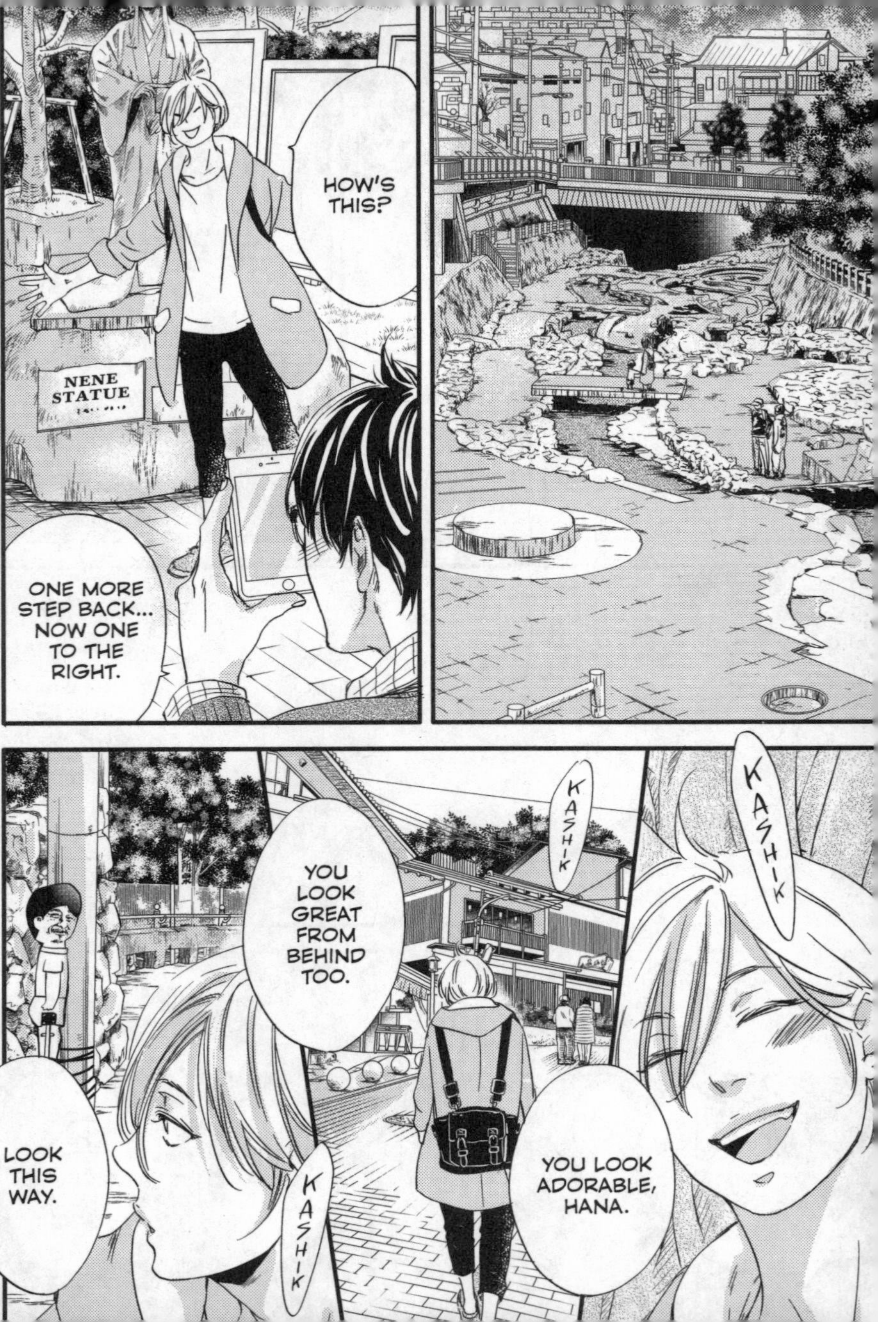
HOW'S THIS?
NENE STATUE
ONE MORE STEP BACK... NOW ONE TO THE RIGHT.
KASHIK
YOU LOOK ADORABLE, HANA.
KASHIK
YOU LOOK GREAT FROM BEHIND TOO.
KASHIK
LOOK THIS WAY.

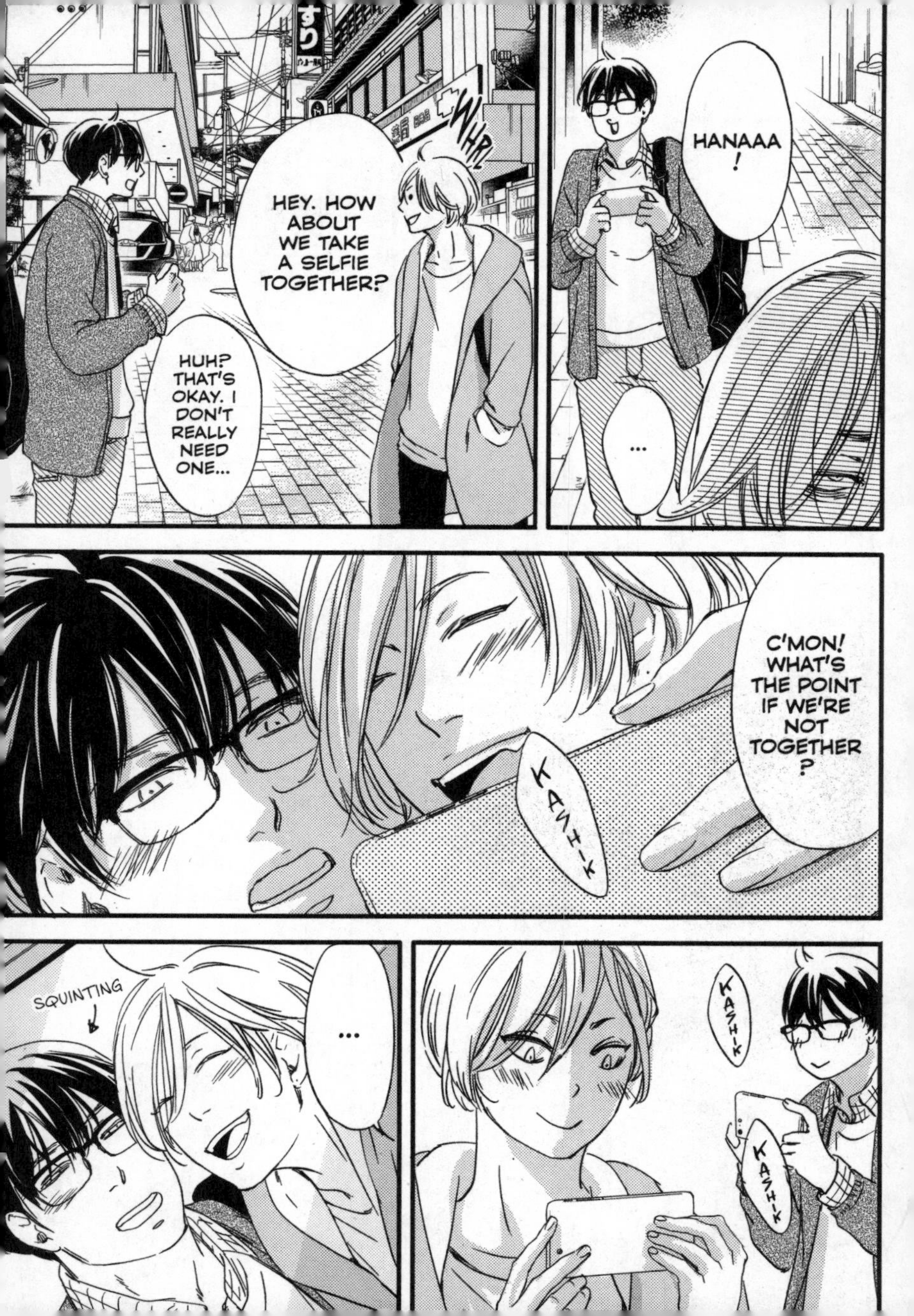
HANAAA!
...
WHR
HEY. HOW ABOUT WE TAKE A SELFIE TOGETHER?
HUH? THAT'S OKAY. I DON'T REALLY NEED ONE...
C'MON! WHAT'S THE POINT IF WE'RE NOT TOGETHER?
KASHIK
KASHIK
KASHIK
...
SQUINTING

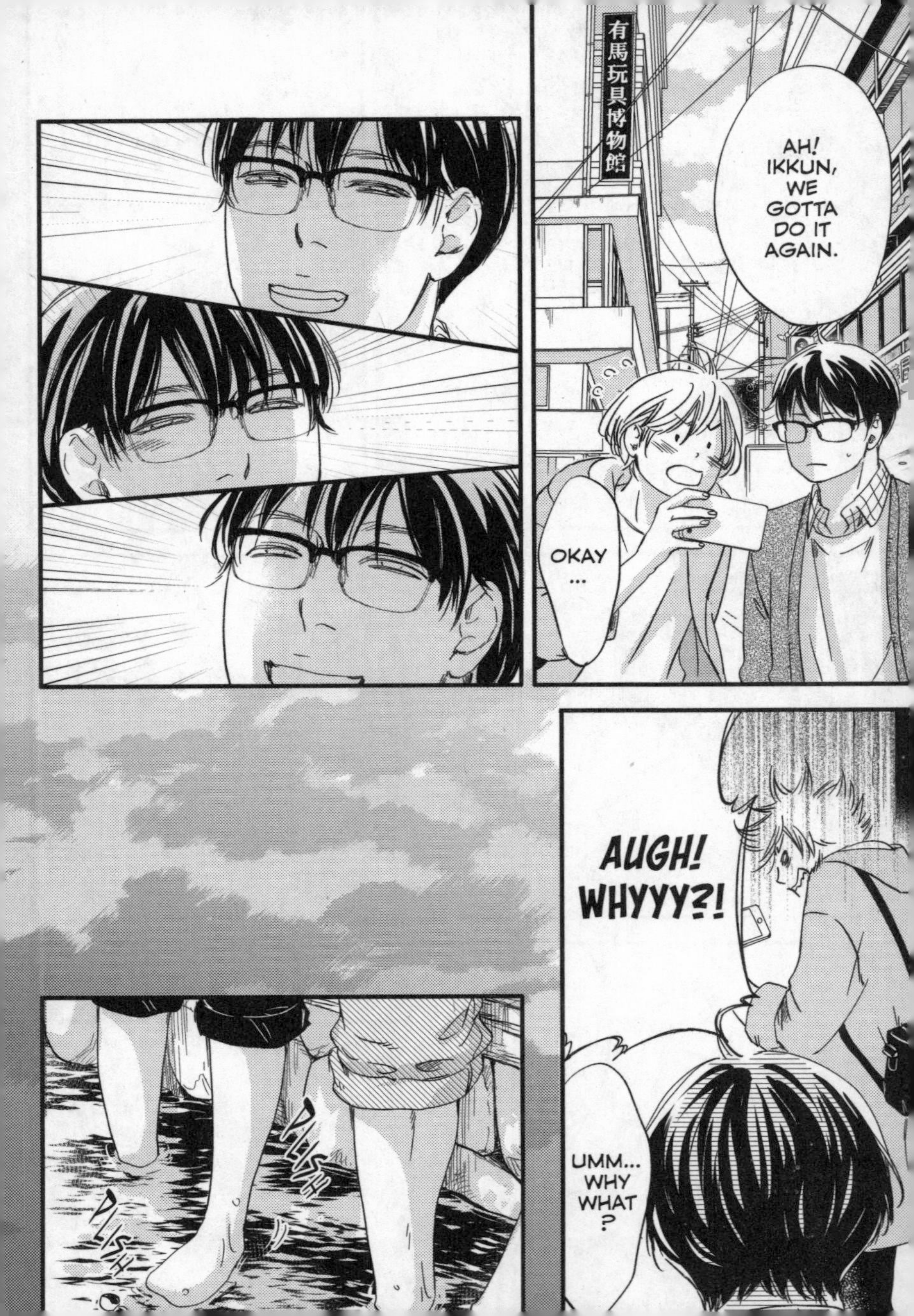
有馬玩具博物館
AH! IKKUN, WE GOTTA DO IT AGAIN.
OKAY ...
AUGH! WHYYY?!
UMM... WHY WHAT?
PLISH
PLISH

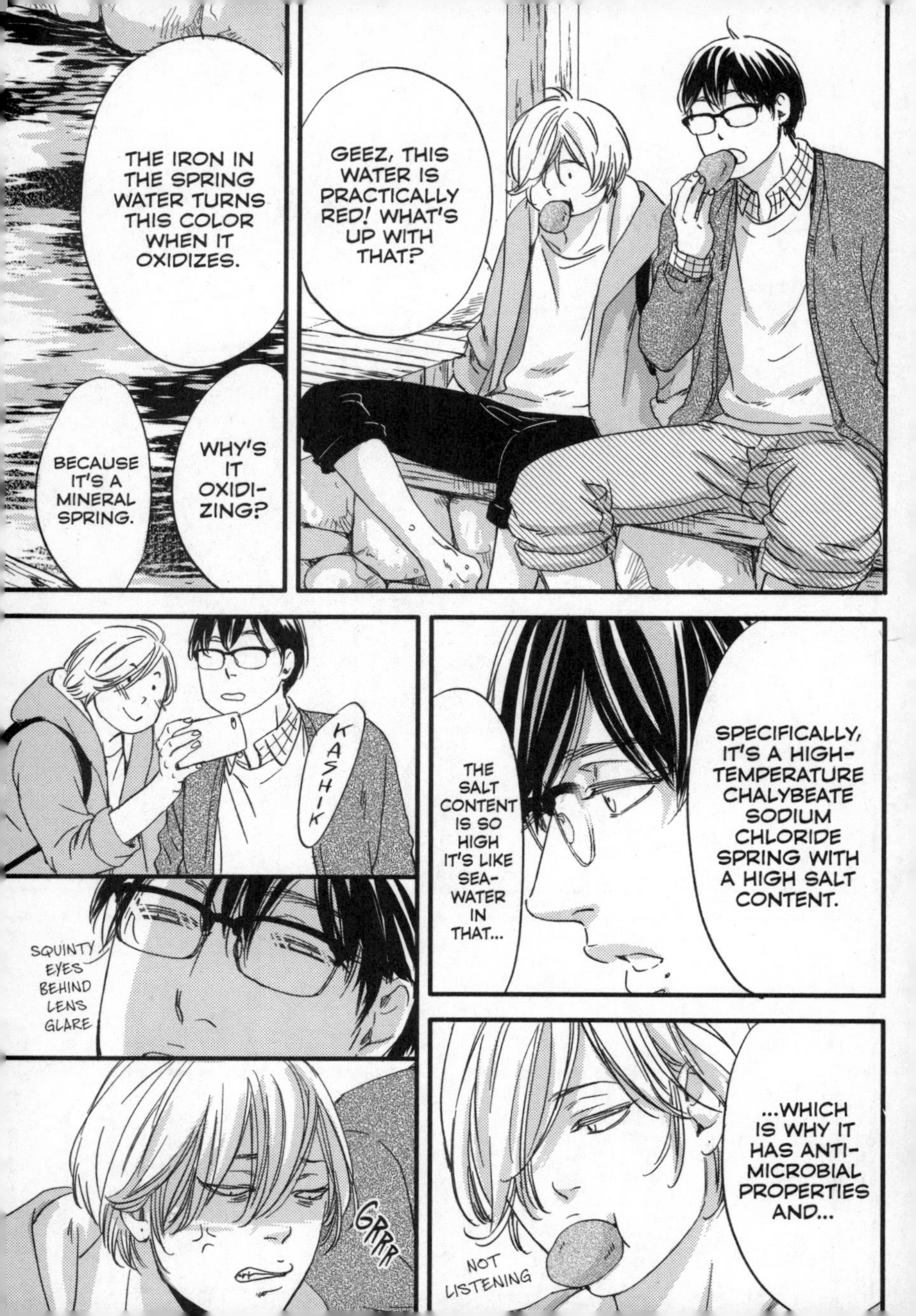
GEEZ, THIS WATER IS PRACTICALLY RED! WHAT'S UP WITH THAT?
THE IRON IN THE SPRING WATER TURNS THIS COLOR WHEN IT OXIDIZES.
WHY'S IT OXIDI-ZING?
BECAUSE IT'S A MINERAL SPRING.
SPECIFICALLY, IT'S A HIGH-TEMPERATURE CHALYBEATE SODIUM CHLORIDE SPRING WITH A HIGH SALT CONTENT.
THE SALT CONTENT IS SO HIGH IT'S LIKE SEA-WATER IN THAT...
KASHIK
SQUINTY EYES BEHIND LENS GLARE
...WHICH IS WHY IT HAS ANTI-MICROBIAL PROPERTIES AND...
NOT LISTENING
GRRR

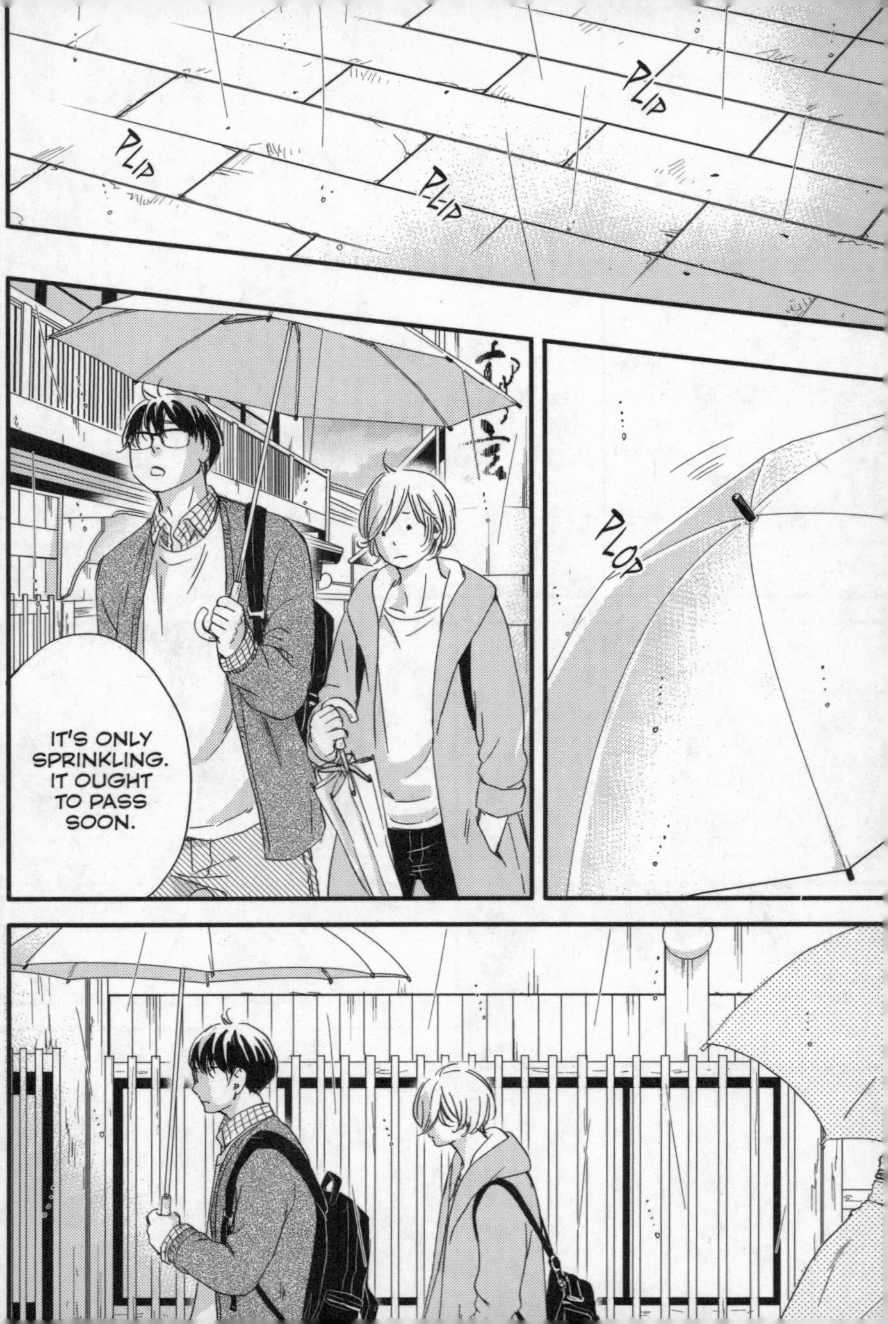
PLIP
PL-IP
PLIP
PLOP
IT'S ONLY SPRINKLING. IT OUGHT TO PASS SOON.

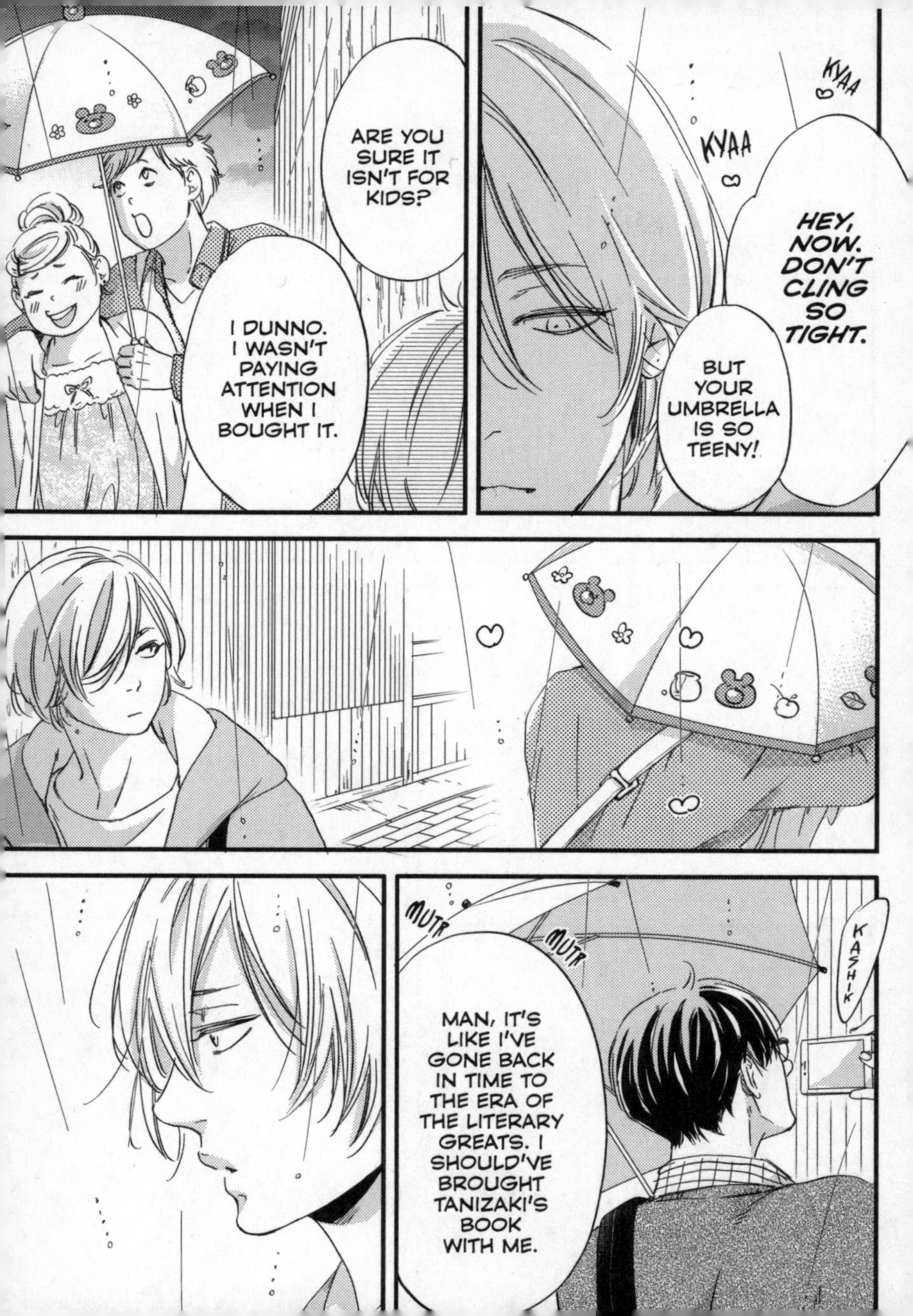
KYAA
KYAA
HEY, NOW. DON'T CLING SO TIGHT.
BUT YOUR UMBRELLA IS SO TEENY!
ARE YOU SURE IT ISN'T FOR KIDS?
I DUNNO. I WASN'T PAYING ATTENTION WHEN I BOUGHT IT.
KASHIK
MUTR
MUTR
MAN, IT'S LIKE I'VE GONE BACK IN TIME TO THE ERA OF THE LITERARY GREATS. I SHOULD'VE BROUGHT TANIZAKI'S BOOK WITH ME.

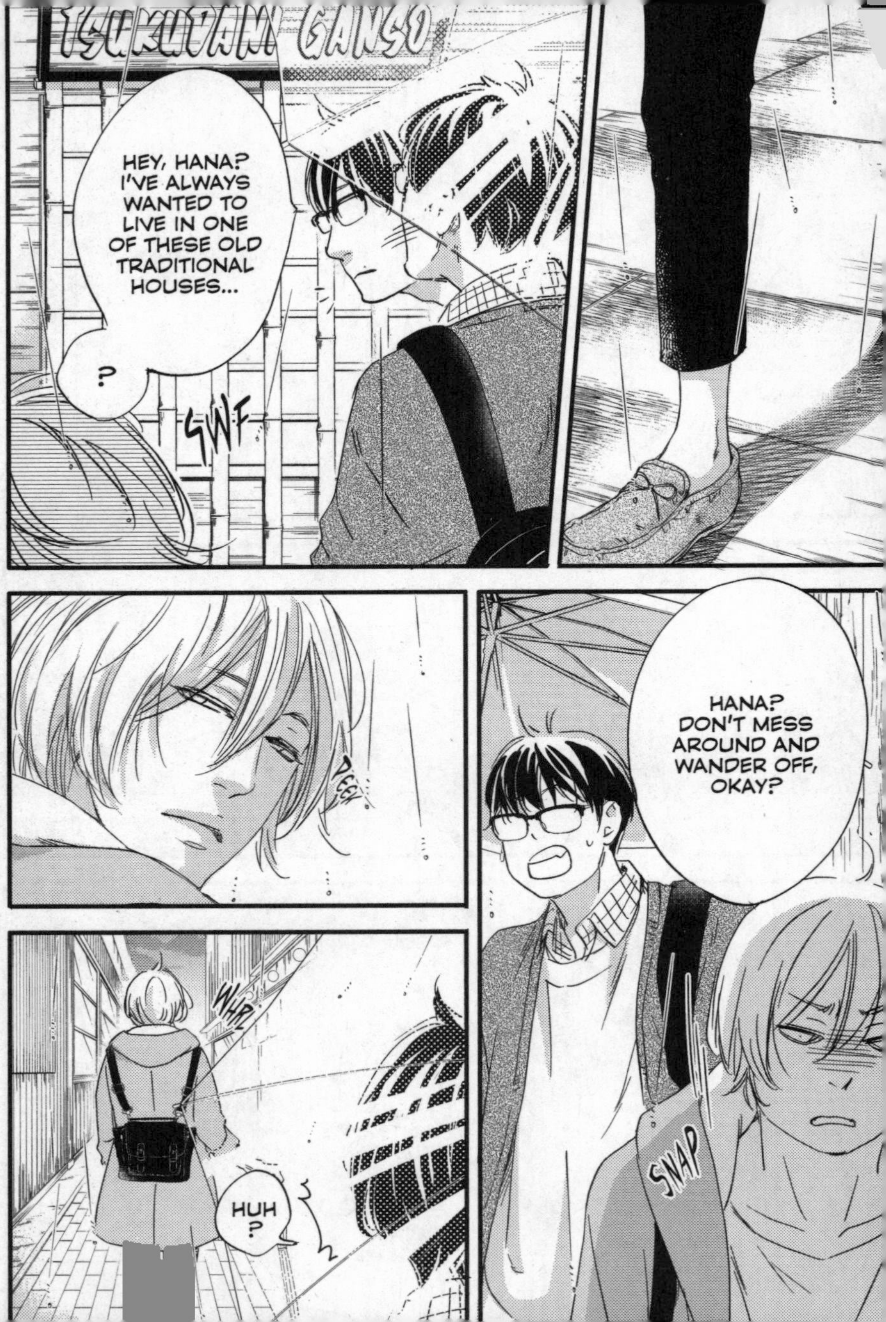
TSUKUDANI GANSO
HEY, HANA? I'VE ALWAYS WANTED TO LIVE IN ONE OF THESE OLD TRADITIONAL HOUSES...
?
SWF
HANA? DON'T MESS AROUND AND WANDER OFF, OKAY?
SNAP
PEEK
WHR
HUH?

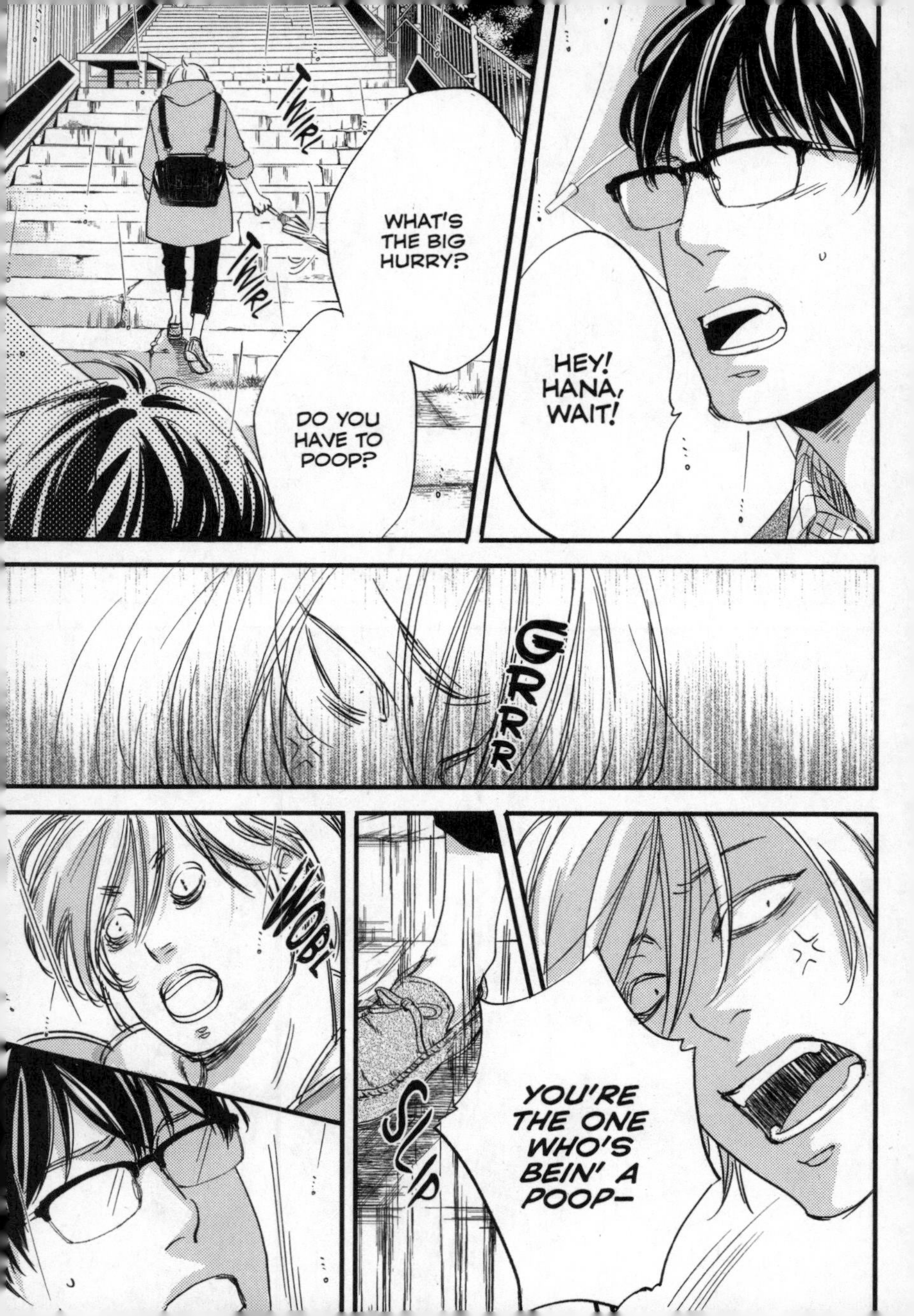
HEY! HANA, WAIT!
TWIRL
WHAT'S THE BIG HURRY?
TWIRL
DO YOU HAVE TO POOP?
GRRR
YOU'RE THE ONE WHO'S BEIN' A POOP—
SLIP
WOBL

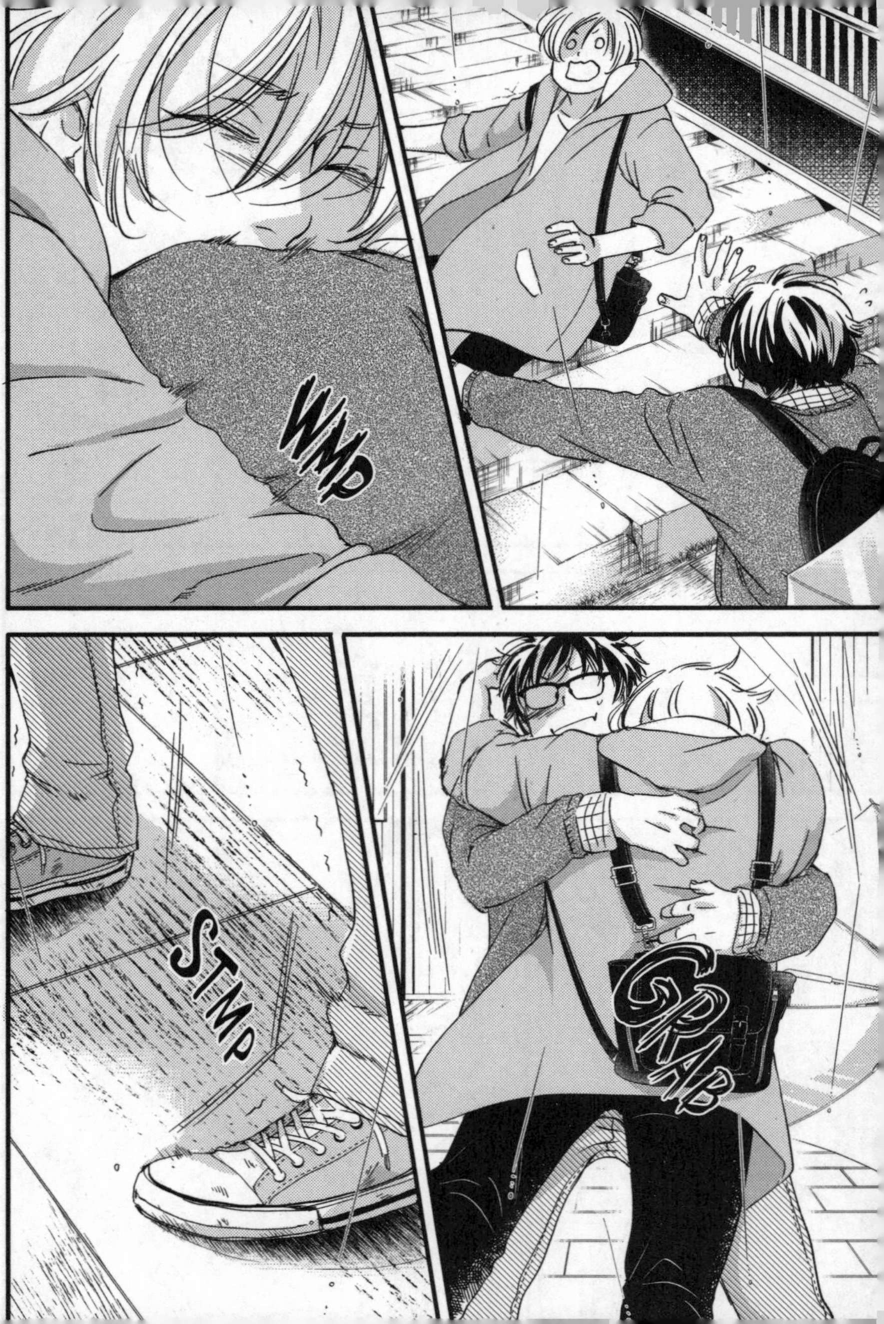
WMP
GRAB
STMP

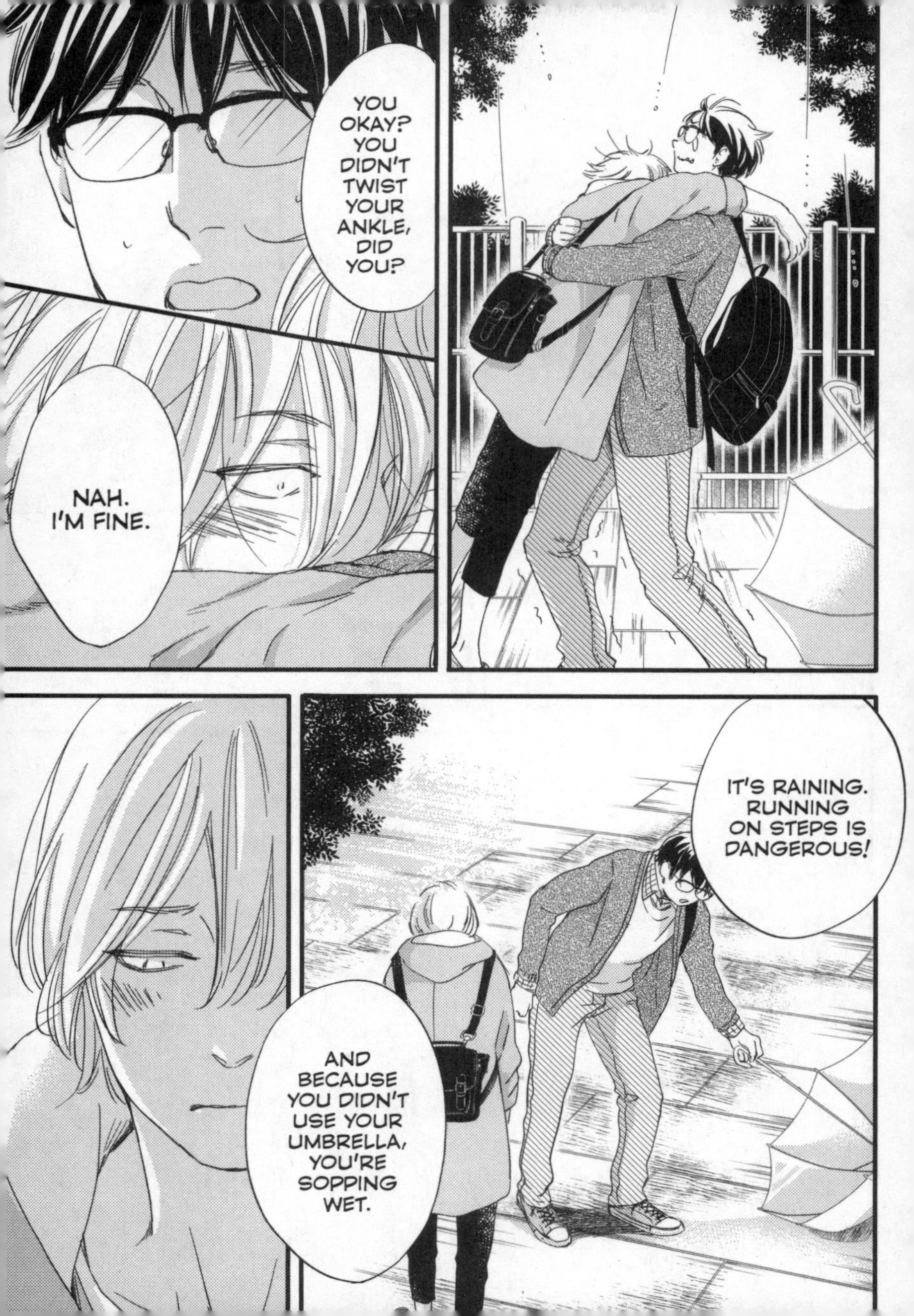
YOU OKAY? YOU DIDN'T TWIST YOUR ANKLE, DID YOU?
NAH. I'M FINE.
IT'S RAINING. RUNNING ON STEPS IS DANGEROUS!
AND BECAUSE YOU DIDN'T USE YOUR UMBRELLA, YOU'RE SOPPING WET.

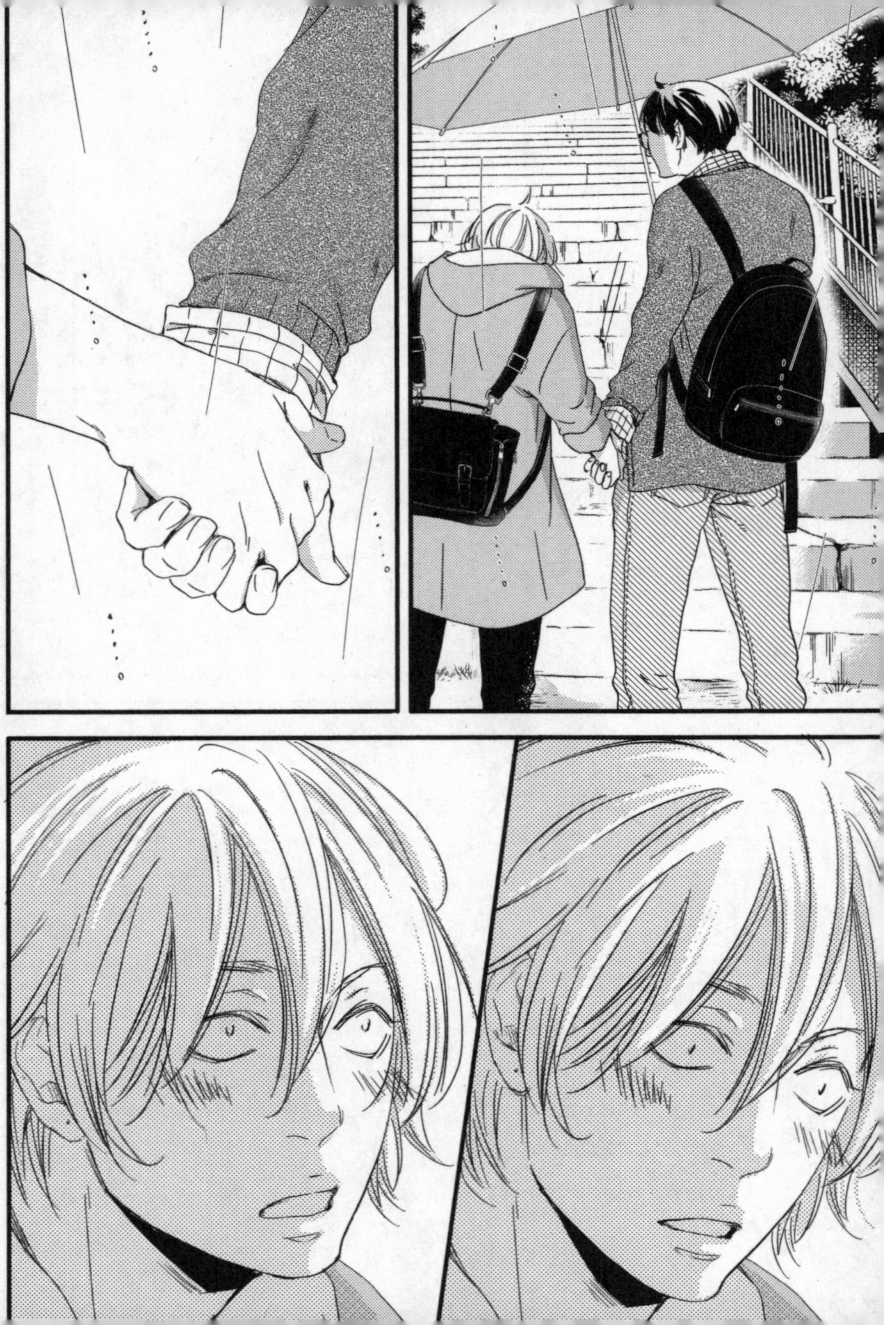

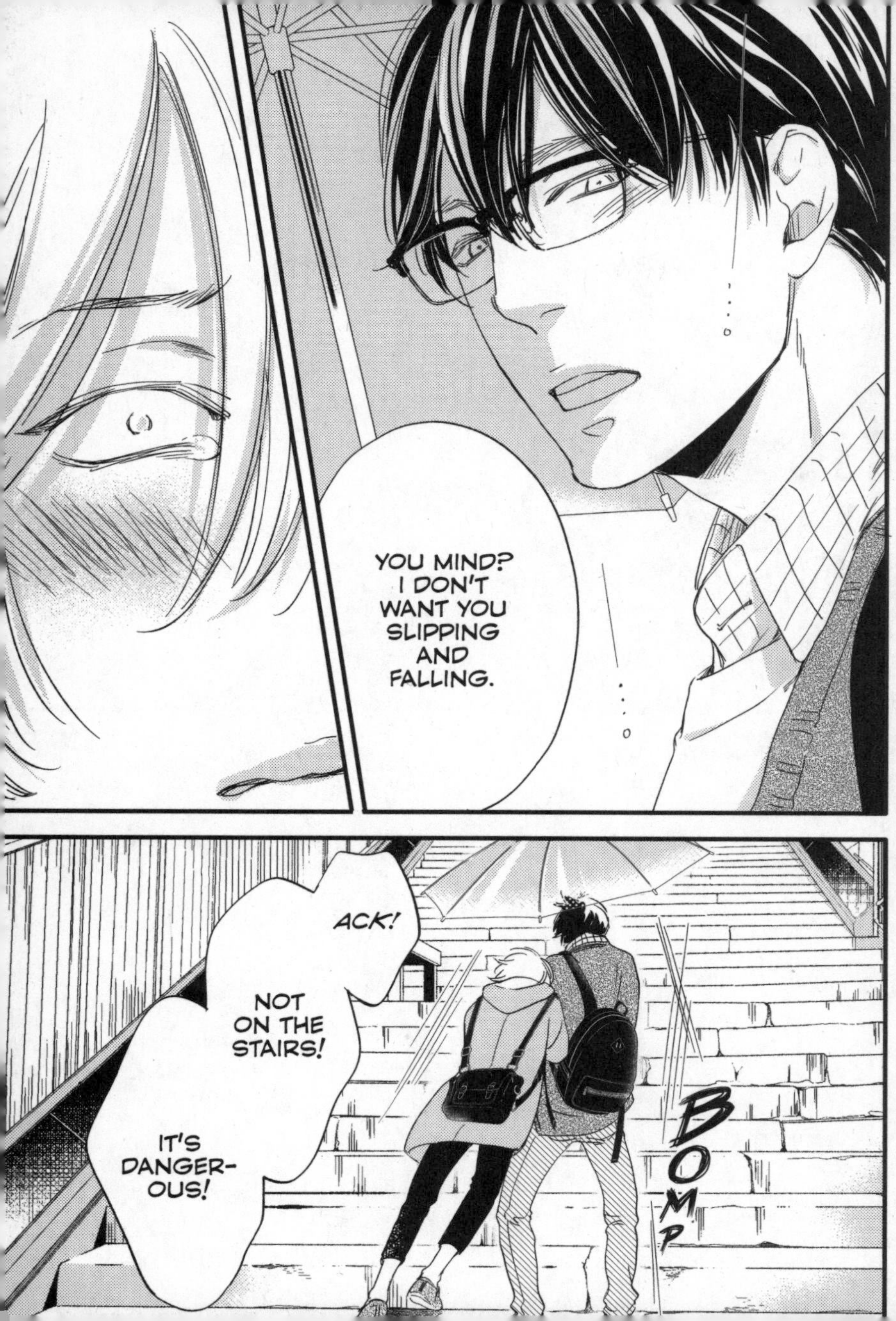
YOU MIND? I DON'T WANT YOU SLIPPING AND FALLING.
ACK!
NOT ON THE STAIRS!
IT'S DANGER-OUS!
BOMP

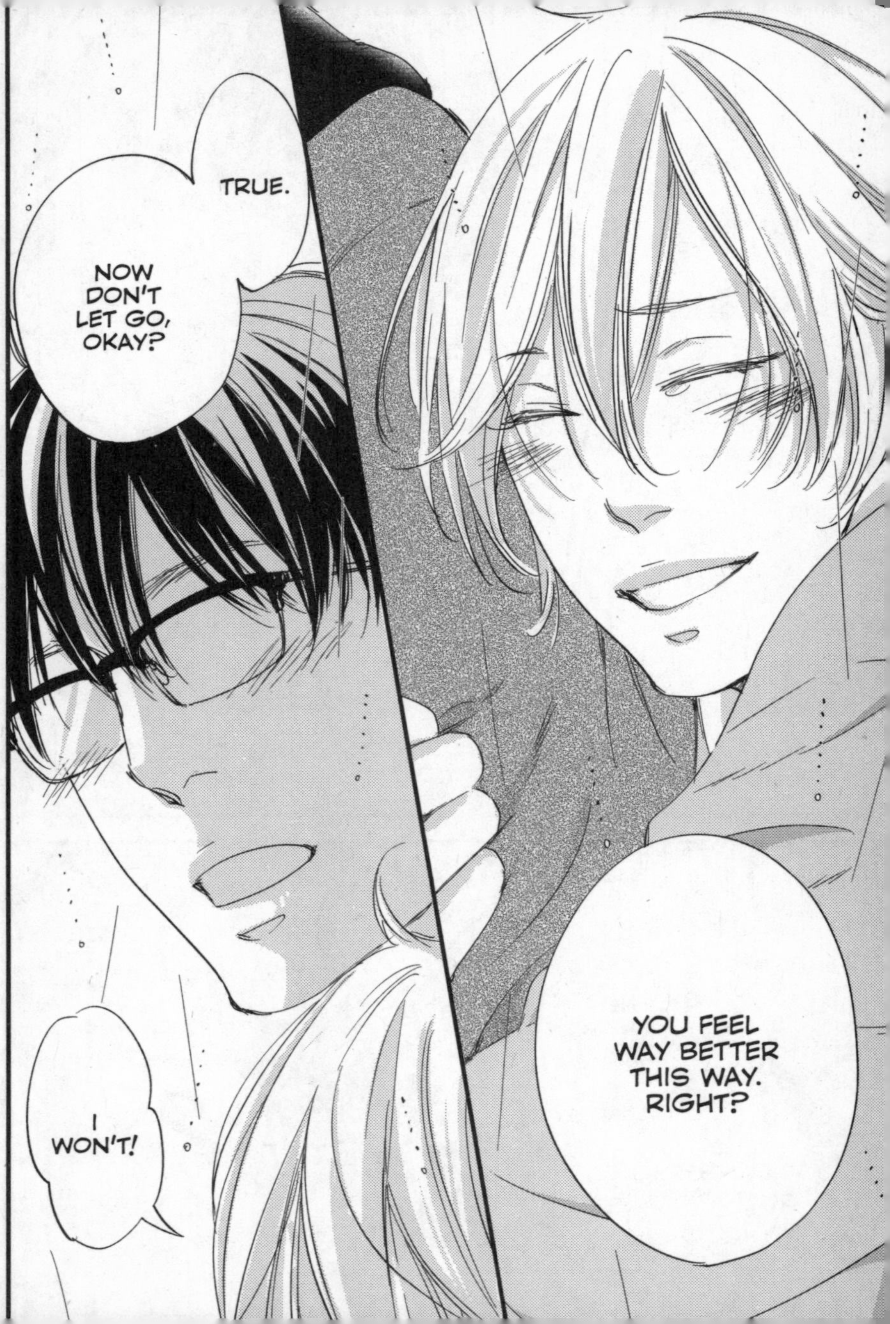
YOU FEEL WAY BETTER THIS WAY. RIGHT?
TRUE.
NOW DON'T LET GO, OKAY?
I WON'T!

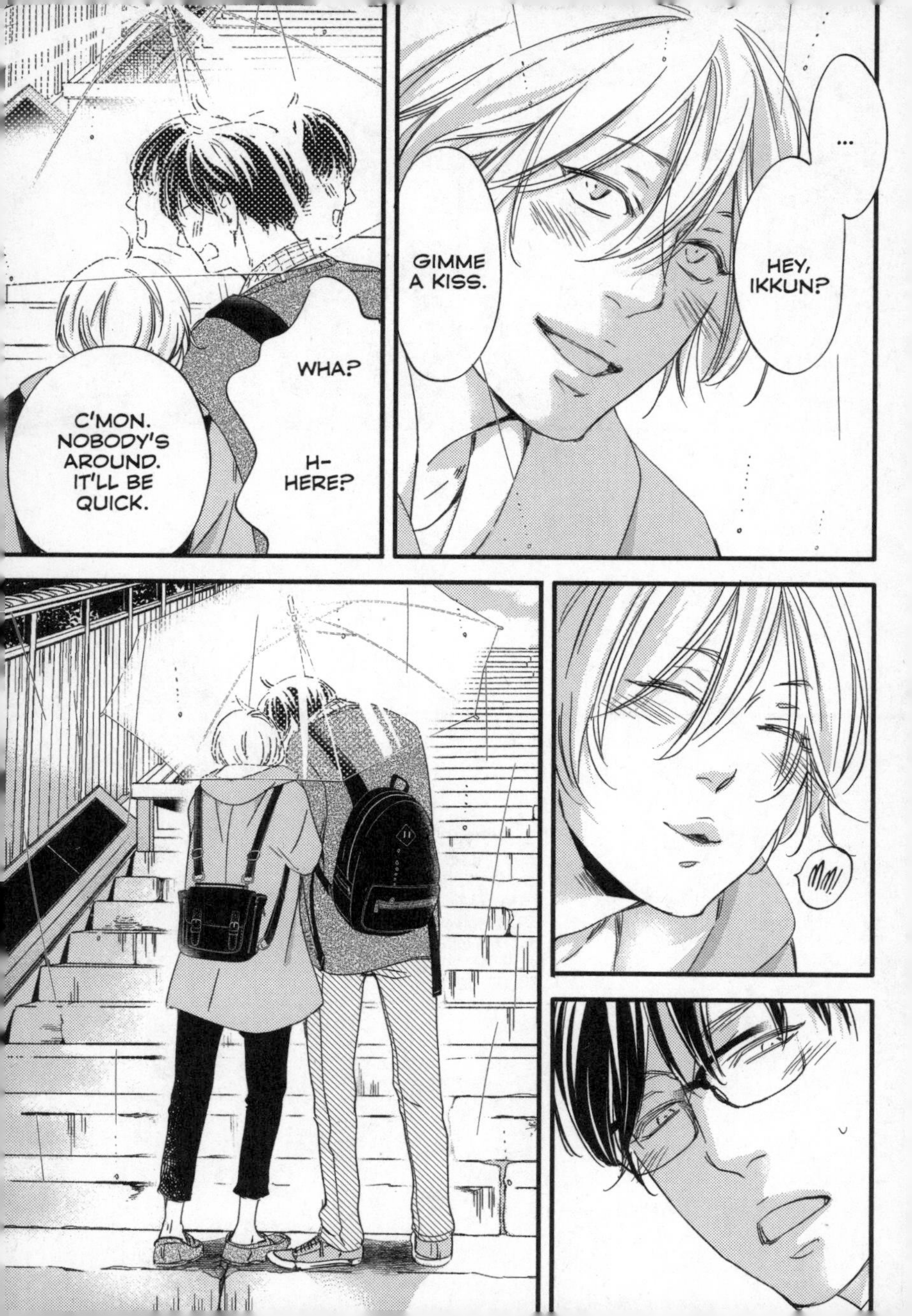
...
HEY, IKKUN?
GIMME A KISS.
WHA?
H-HERE?
C'MON. NOBODY'S AROUND. IT'LL BE QUICK.
MM!

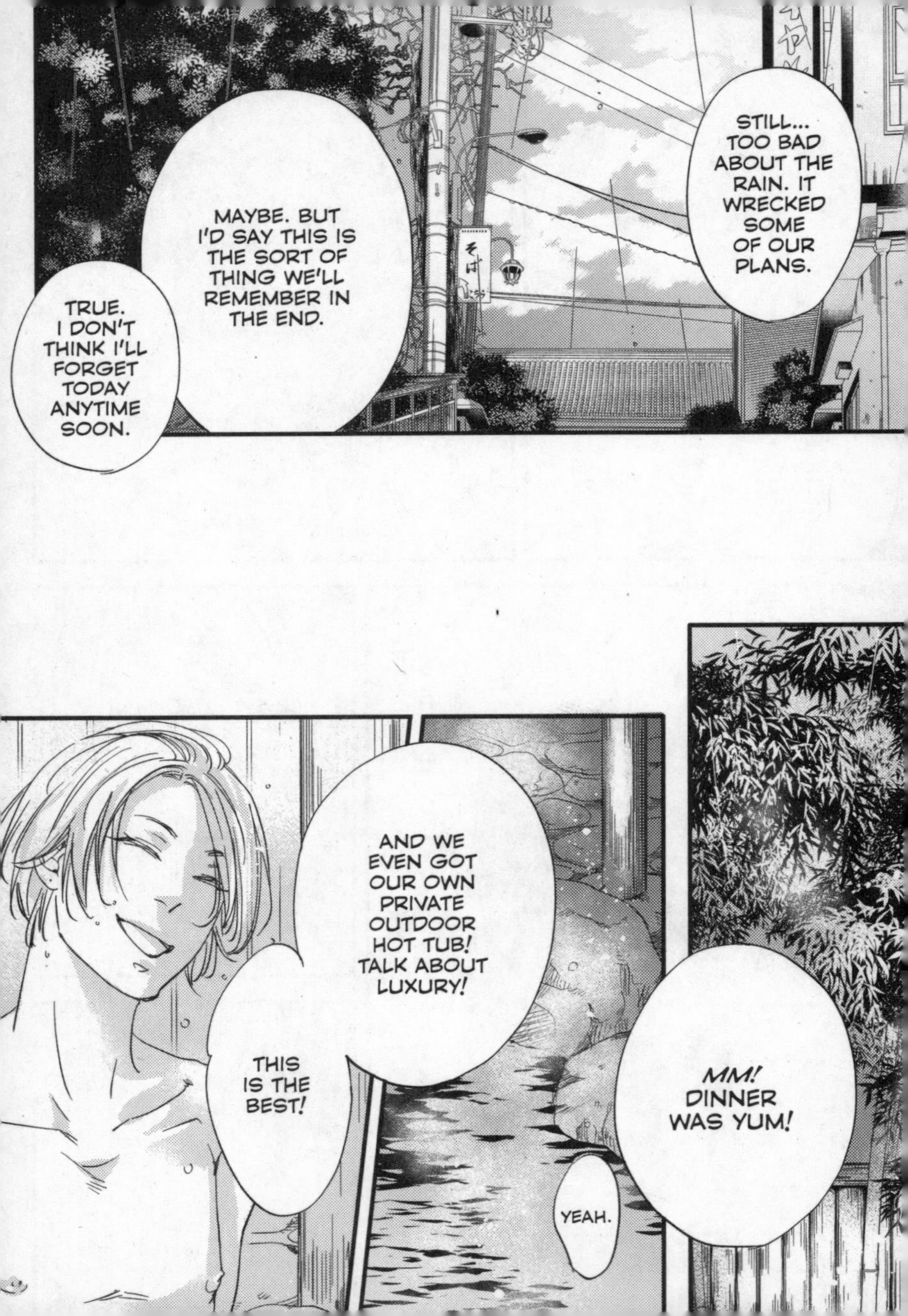
STILL... TOO BAD ABOUT THE RAIN. IT WRECKED SOME OF OUR PLANS.
そば
MAYBE. BUT I'D SAY THIS IS THE SORT OF THING WE'LL REMEMBER IN THE END.
TRUE. I DON'T THINK I'LL FORGET TODAY ANYTIME SOON.
MM! DINNER WAS YUM!
YEAH.
AND WE EVEN GOT OUR OWN PRIVATE OUTDOOR HOT TUB! TALK ABOUT LUXURY!
THIS IS THE BEST!

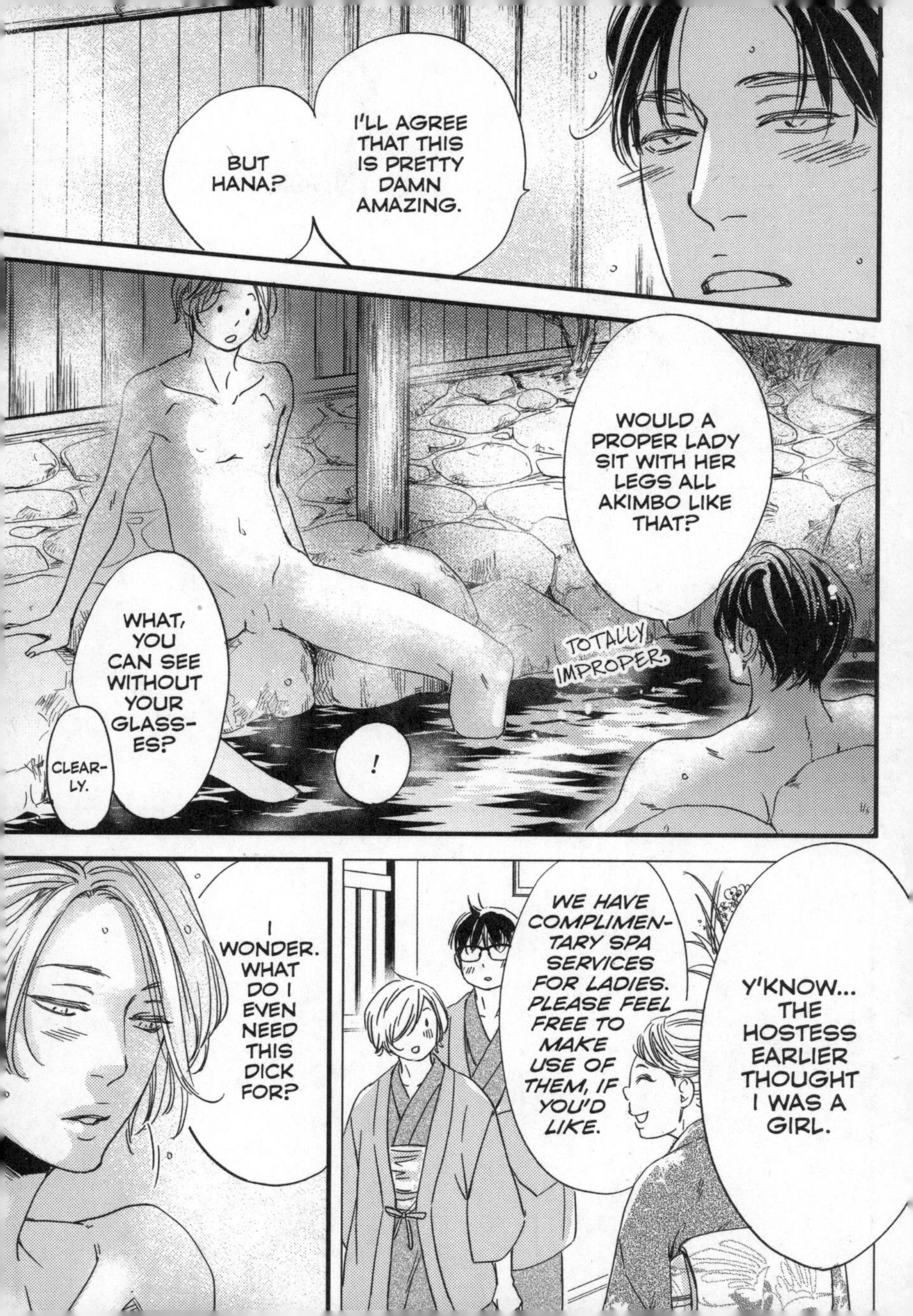
I'LL AGREE THAT THIS IS PRETTY DAMN AMAZING.
BUT HANA?
WOULD A PROPER LADY SIT WITH HER LEGS ALL AKIMBO LIKE THAT?
TOTALLY IMPROPER.
!
WHAT, YOU CAN SEE WITHOUT YOUR GLASS-ES?
CLEAR-LY.
Y'KNOW... THE HOSTESS EARLIER THOUGHT I WAS A GIRL.
WE HAVE COMPLIMEN-TARY SPA SERVICES FOR LADIES. PLEASE FEEL FREE TO MAKE USE OF THEM, IF YOU'D LIKE.
I WONDER. WHAT DO I EVEN NEED THIS DICK FOR?

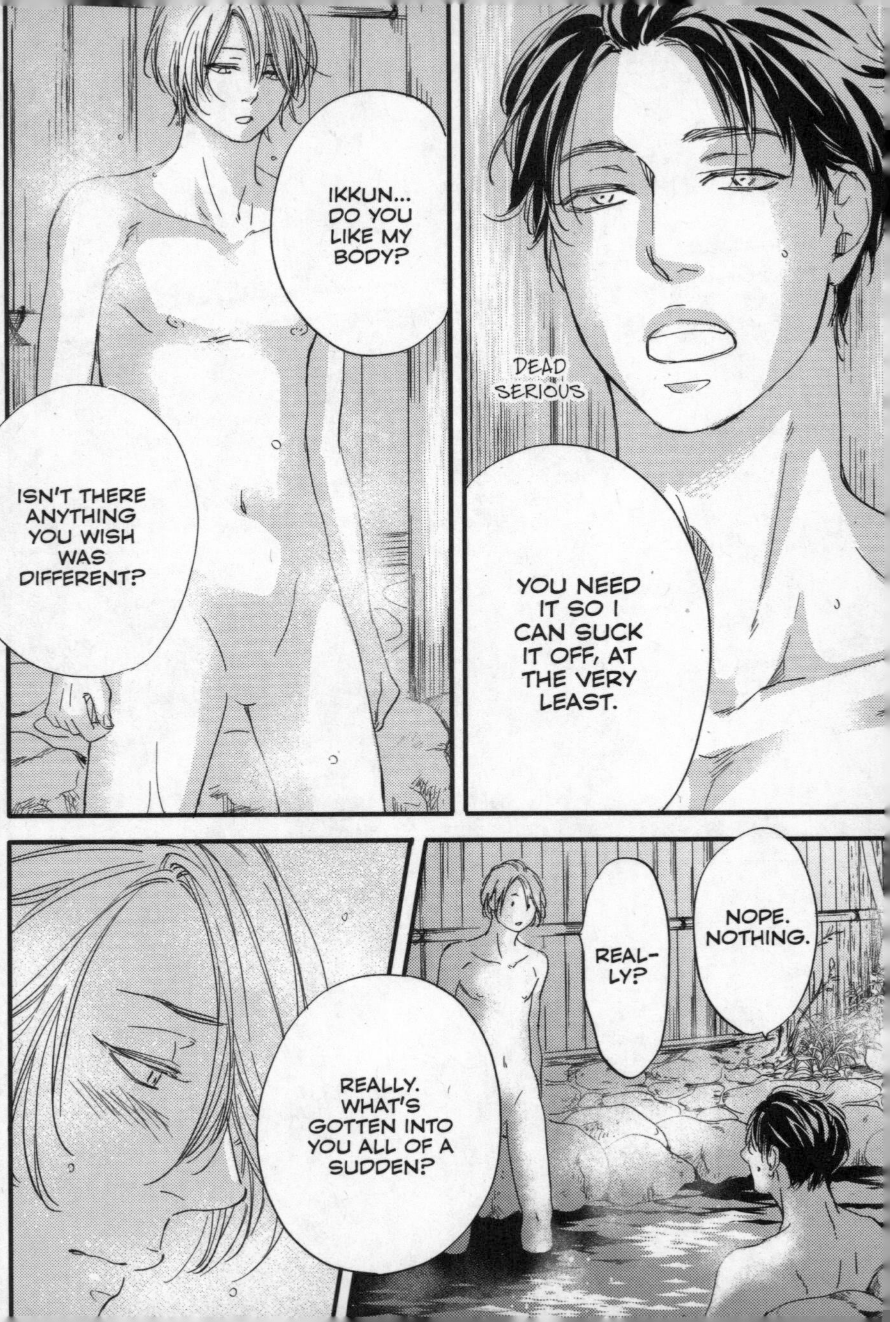
DEAD SERIOUS
YOU NEED IT SO I CAN SUCK IT OFF, AT THE VERY LEAST.
IKKUN... DO YOU LIKE MY BODY?
ISN'T THERE ANYTHING YOU WISH WAS DIFFERENT?
NOPE. NOTHING.
REAL-LY?
REALLY. WHAT'S GOTTEN INTO YOU ALL OF A SUDDEN?

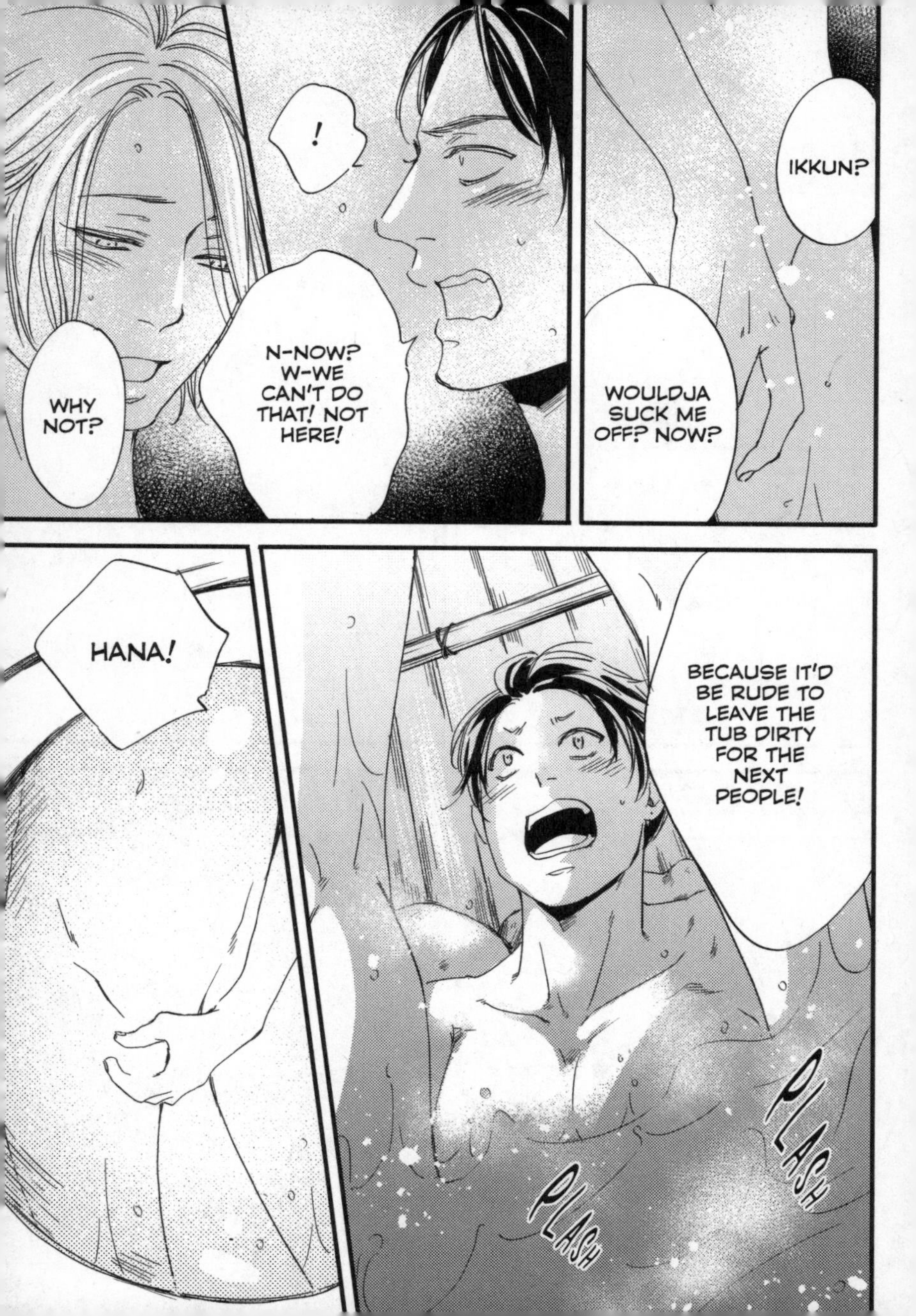
IKKUN?
WOULDJA SUCK ME OFF? NOW?
!
N-NOW? W-WE CAN'T DO THAT! NOT HERE!
WHY NOT?
BECAUSE IT'D BE RUDE TO LEAVE THE TUB DIRTY FOR THE NEXT PEOPLE!
PLASH
PLASH
HANA!

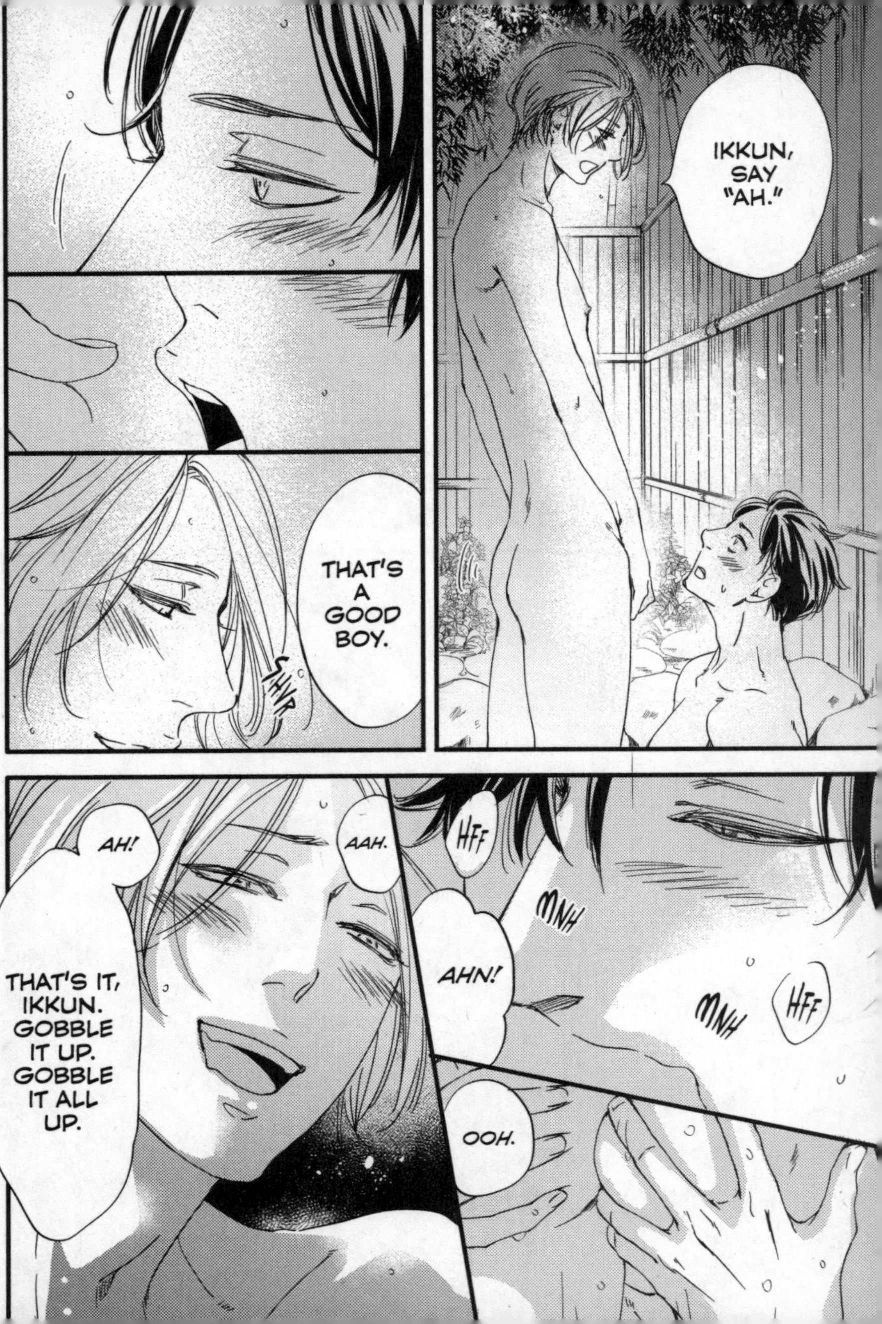
IKKUN, SAY "AH."
THAT'S A GOOD BOY.
SHVR
HFF
MNH
HFF
MNH
AHN!
AAH.
AH!
THAT'S IT, IKKUN. GOBBLE IT UP. GOBBLE IT ALL UP.
OOH.

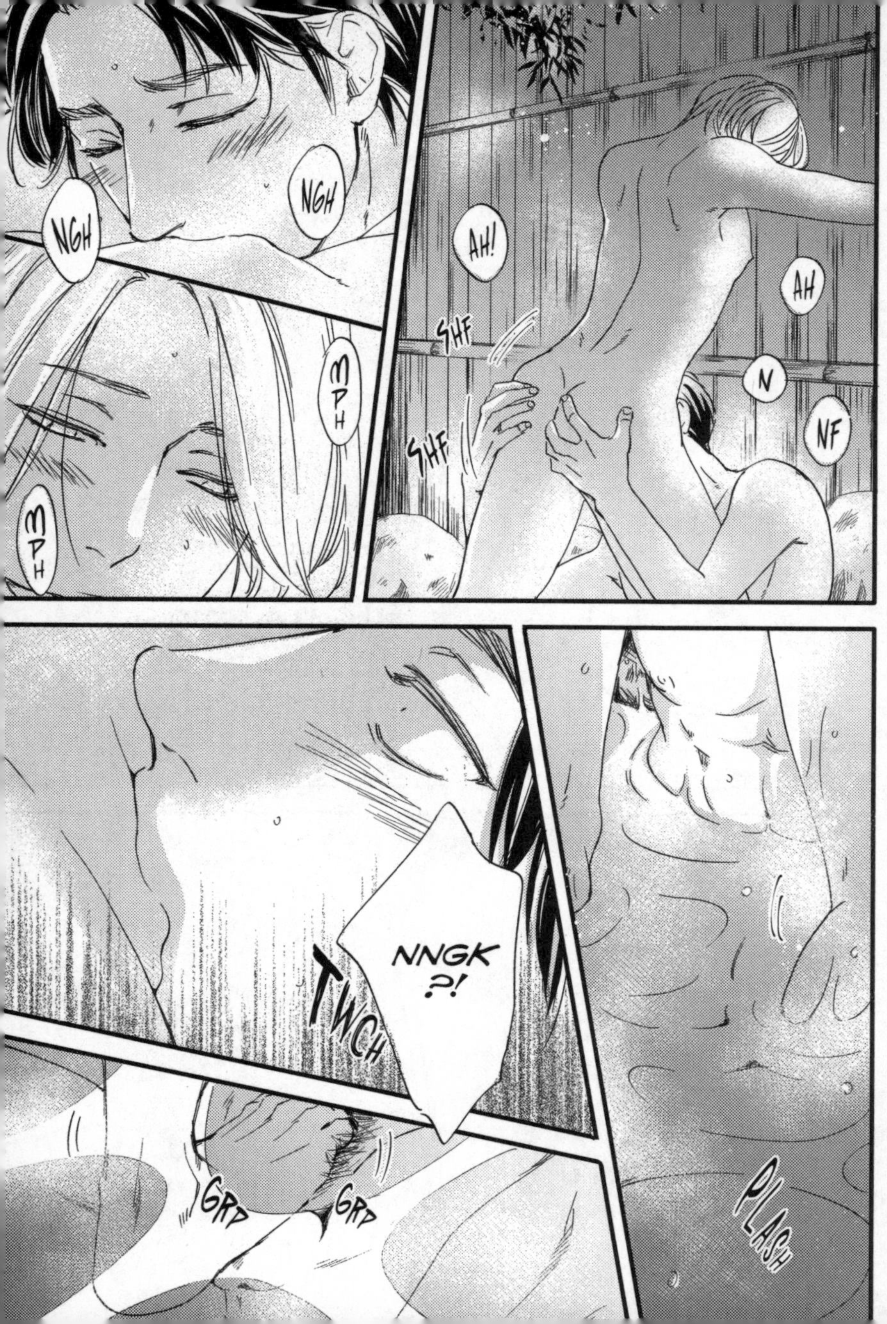
AH
AH!
SHF
N
NF
SHF
NGH
NGH
MPH
MPH
PLASH
NNGK ?!
TWCH
GRP
GRP

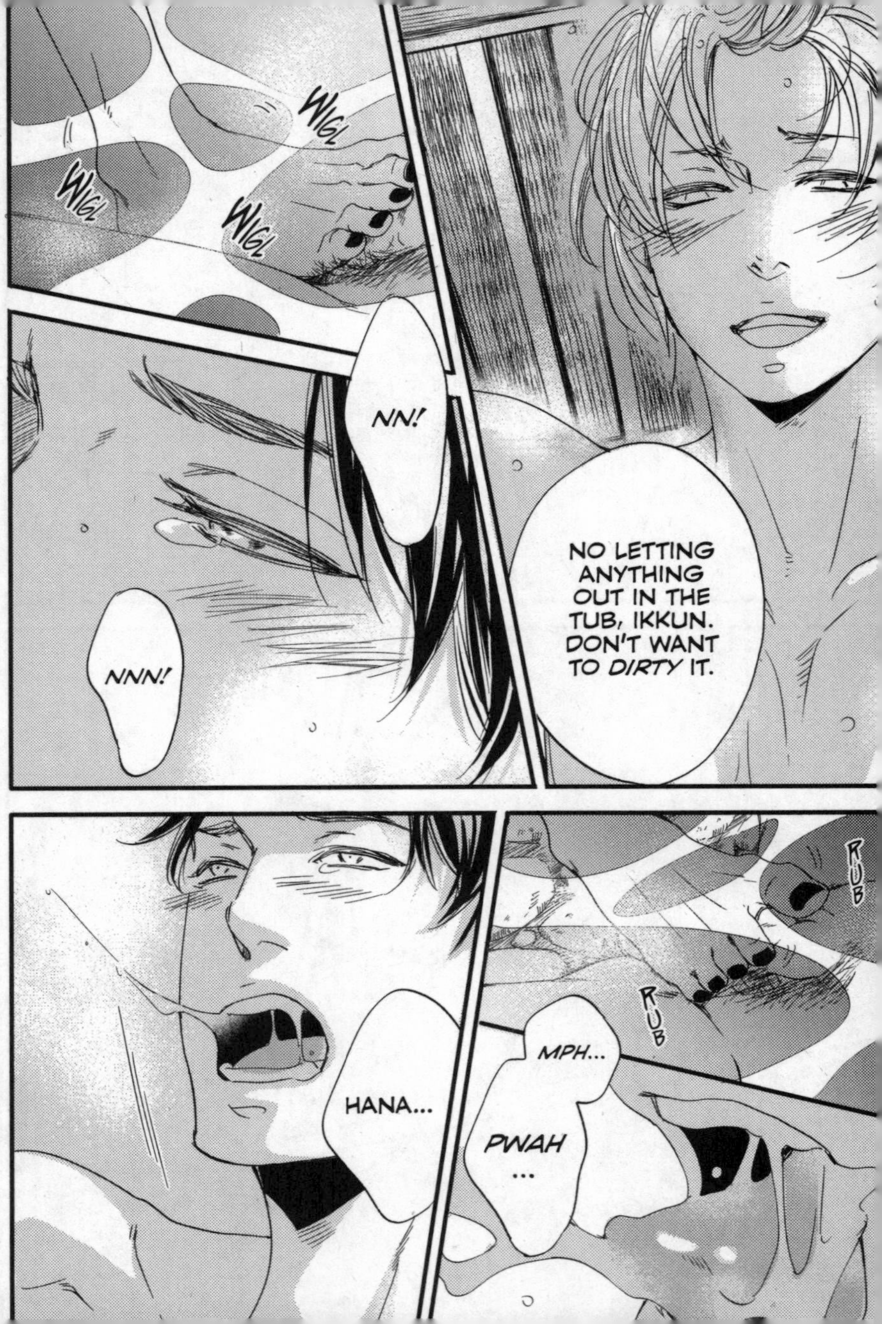
NO LETTING ANYTHING OUT IN THE TUB, IKKUN. DON'T WANT TO *DIRTY* IT.
WIGL
WIGL
WIGL
NN!
NNN!
RUB
RUB
MPH...
PWAH ...
HANA...

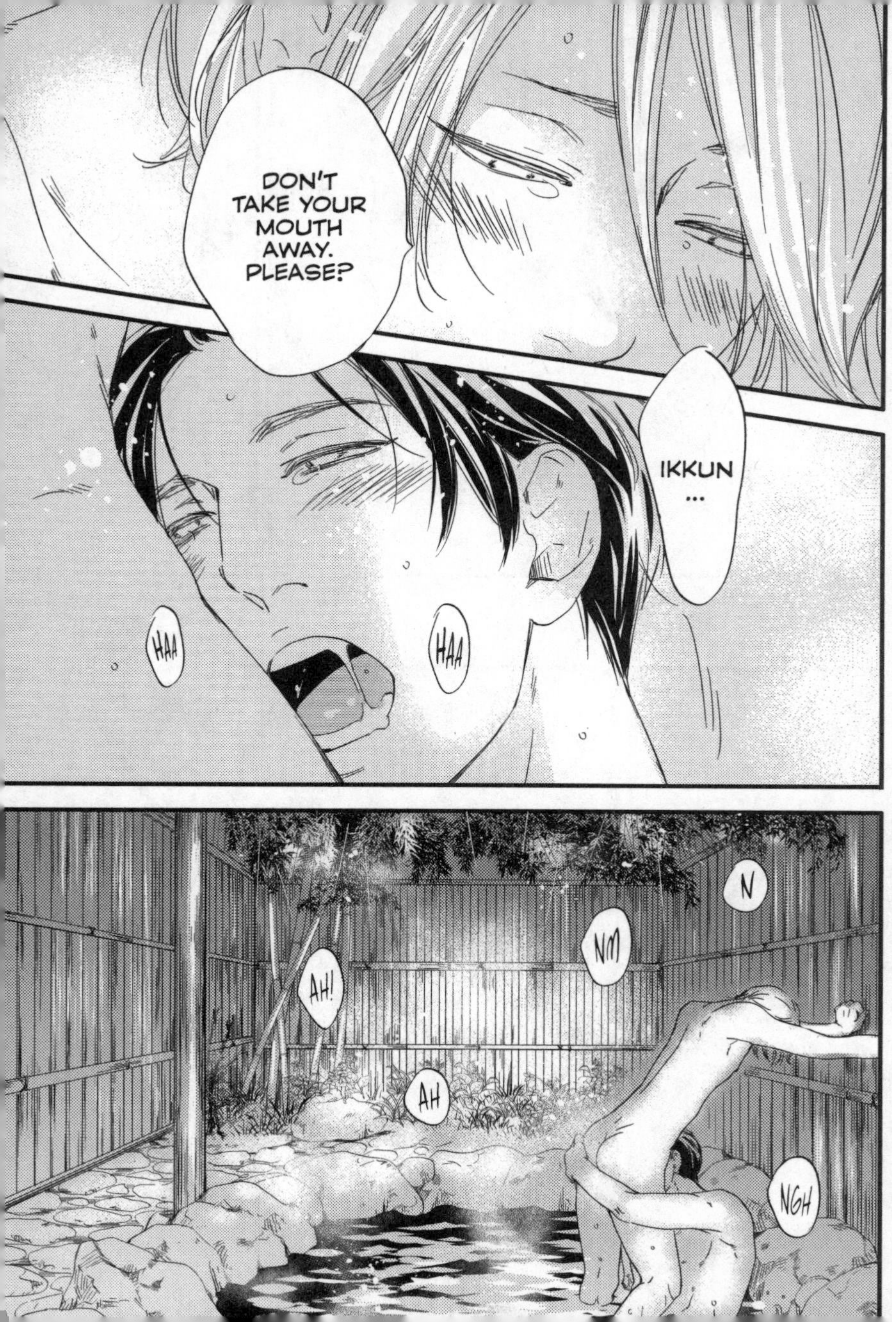
DON'T TAKE YOUR MOUTH AWAY. PLEASE?
IKKUN ...
HAA
HAA
N
NM
AH!
AH
NGH

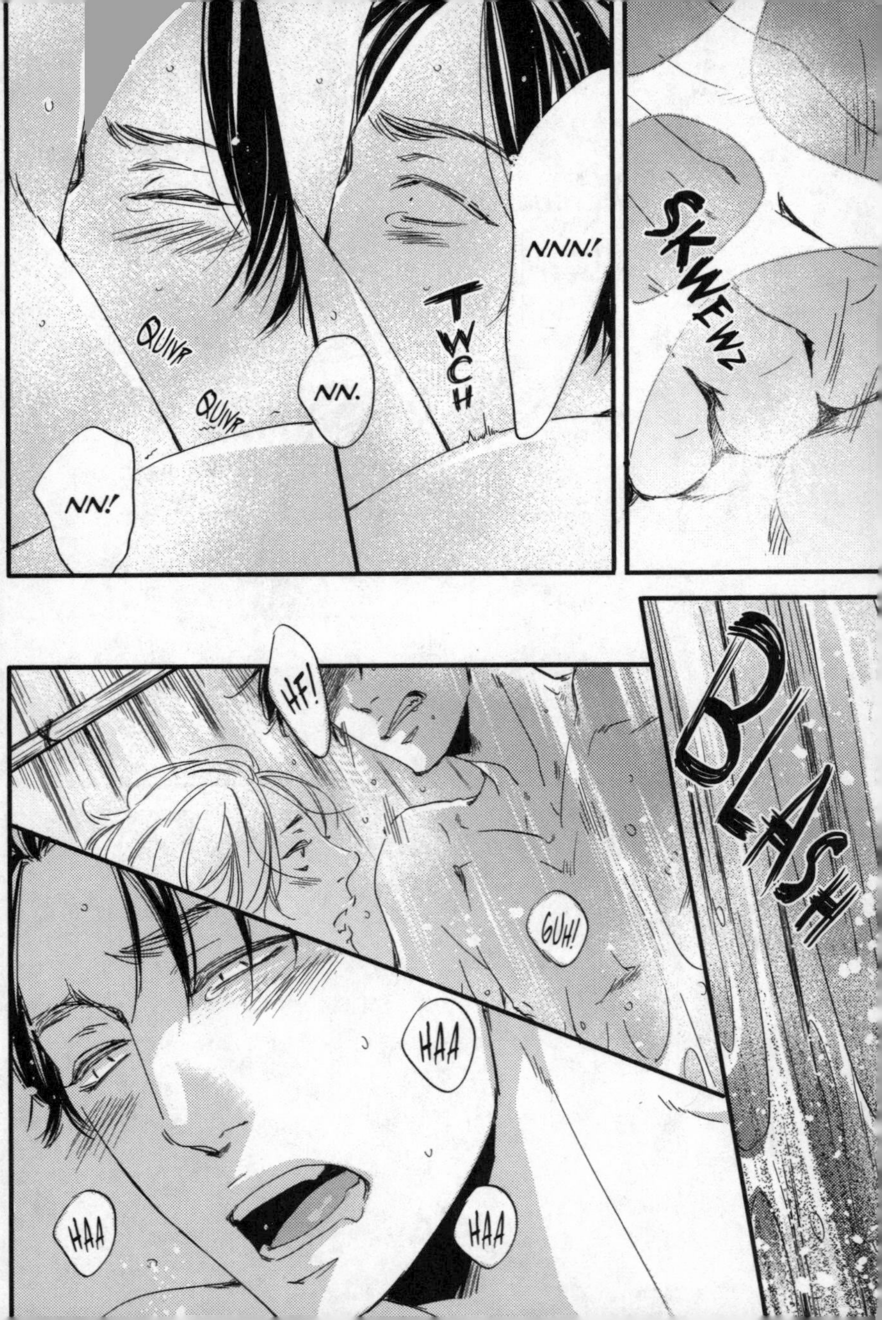
SKWEWZ
NNN!
TWCH
NN.
QUIVR
QUIVR
NN!
BLASH
HF!
GUH!
HAA
HAA
HAA

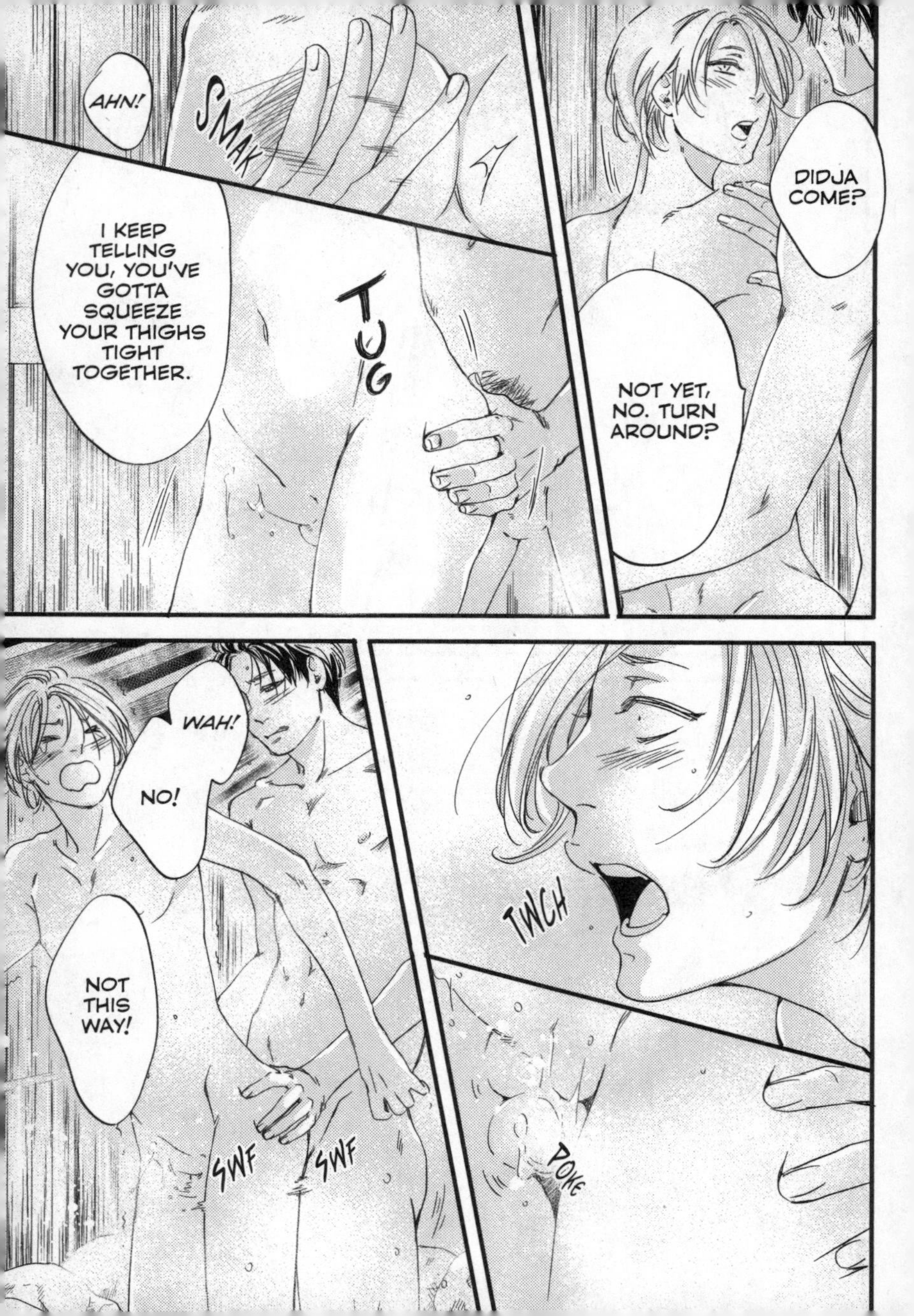
DIDJA COME?
NOT YET, NO. TURN AROUND?
AHN!
SMAK
I KEEP TELLING YOU, YOU'VE GOTTA SQUEEZE YOUR THIGHS TIGHT TOGETHER.
TUG
TWCH
POKE
WAH!
NO!
NOT THIS WAY!
SWF
SWF

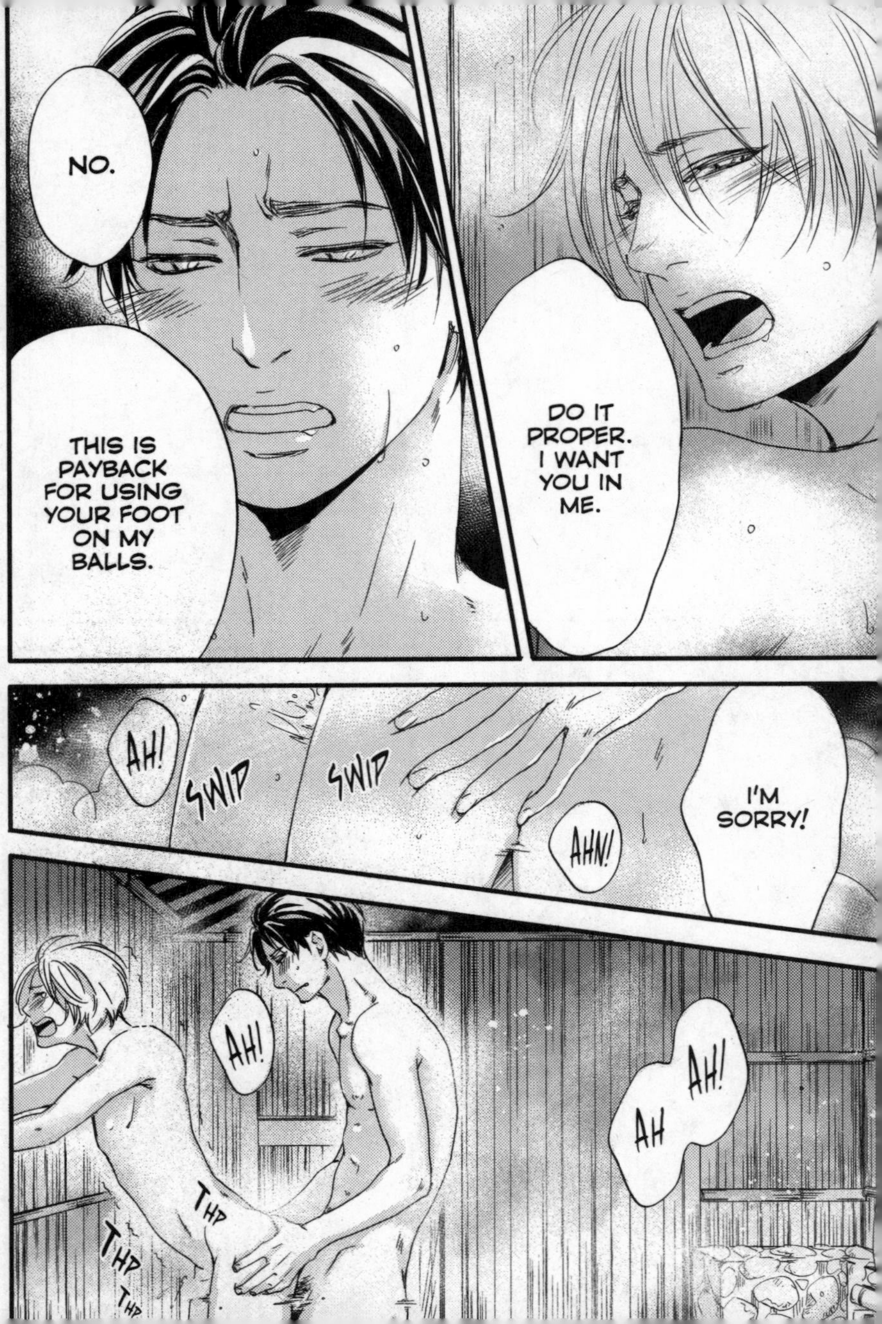
DO IT PROPER. I WANT YOU IN ME.
NO.
THIS IS PAYBACK FOR USING YOUR FOOT ON MY BALLS.
I'M SORRY!
AHN!
SWIP
SWIP
AH!
AH!
AH
AH!
THP
THP
THP

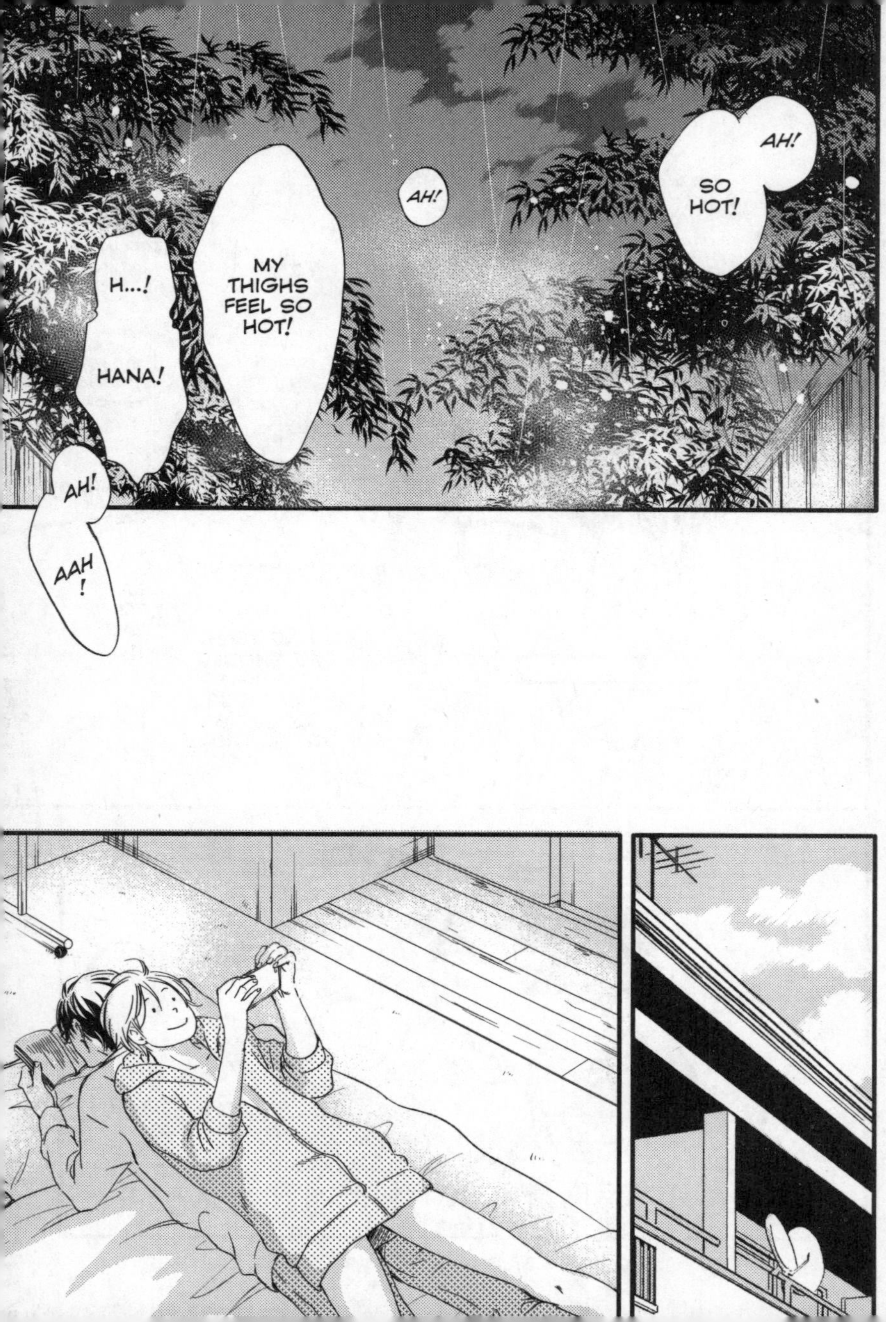
AH! SO HOT!
AH!
MY THIGHS FEEL SO HOT!
H...! HANA!
AH!
AAH!

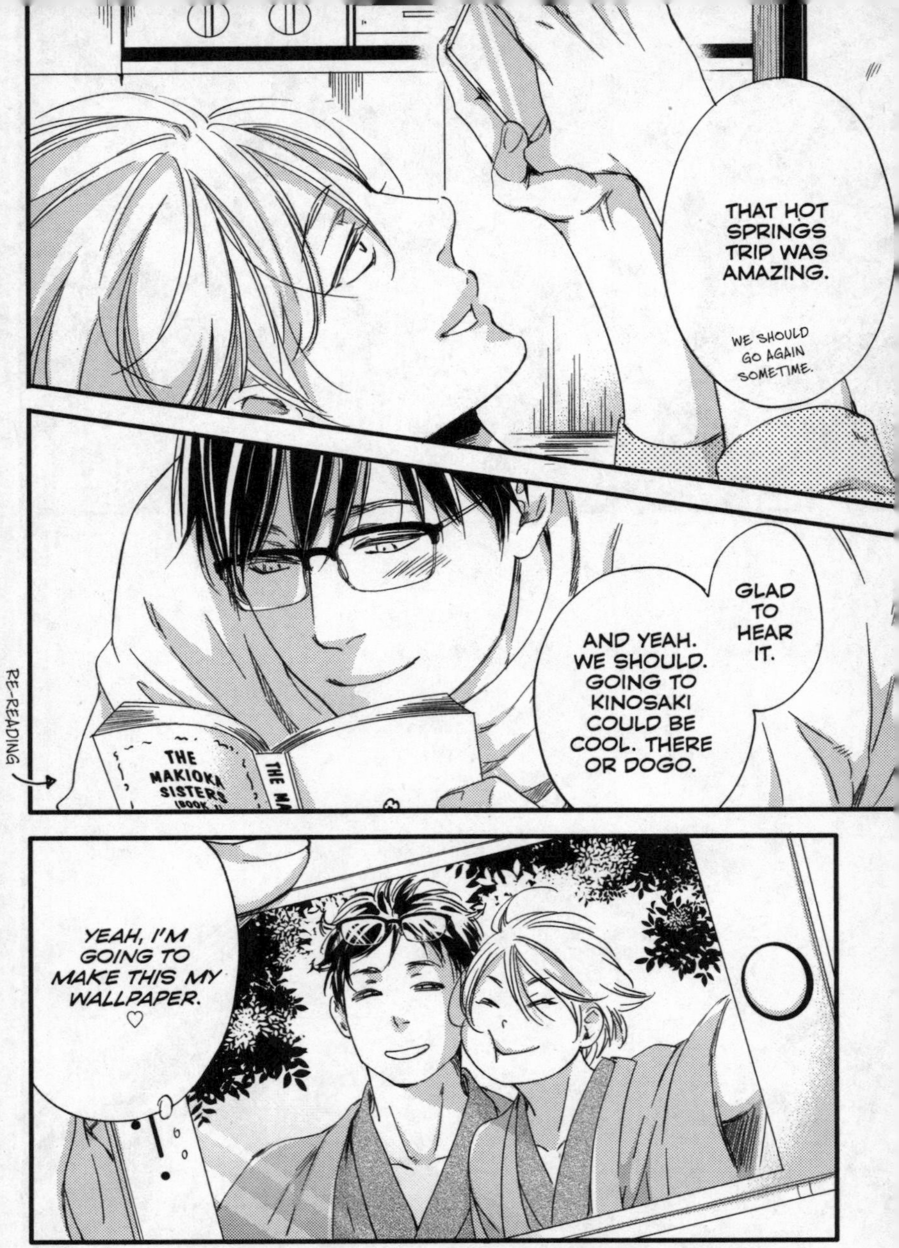
THAT HOT SPRINGS TRIP WAS AMAZING.
WE SHOULD GO AGAIN SOMETIME.
GLAD TO HEAR IT.
AND YEAH. WE SHOULD. GOING TO KINOSAKI COULD BE COOL. THERE OR DOGO.
RE-READING
THE MAKIOKA SISTERS
YEAH, I'M GOING TO MAKE THIS MY WALLPAPER. ♡

End AFTER THE BATH. HIS EYES ARE, OF COURSE, HALF SHUT.

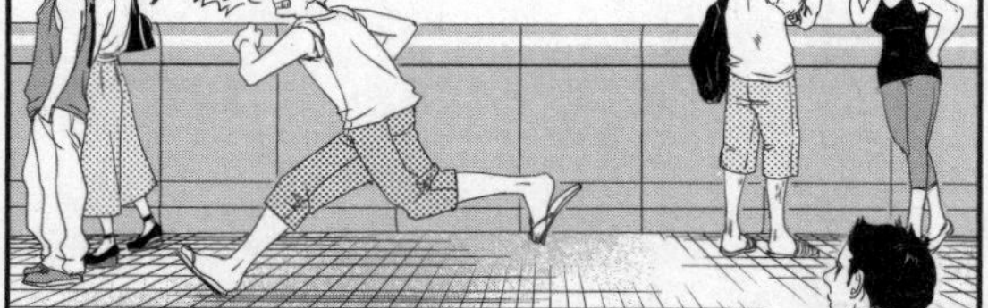
AUGH!

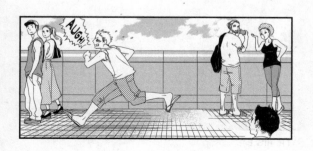

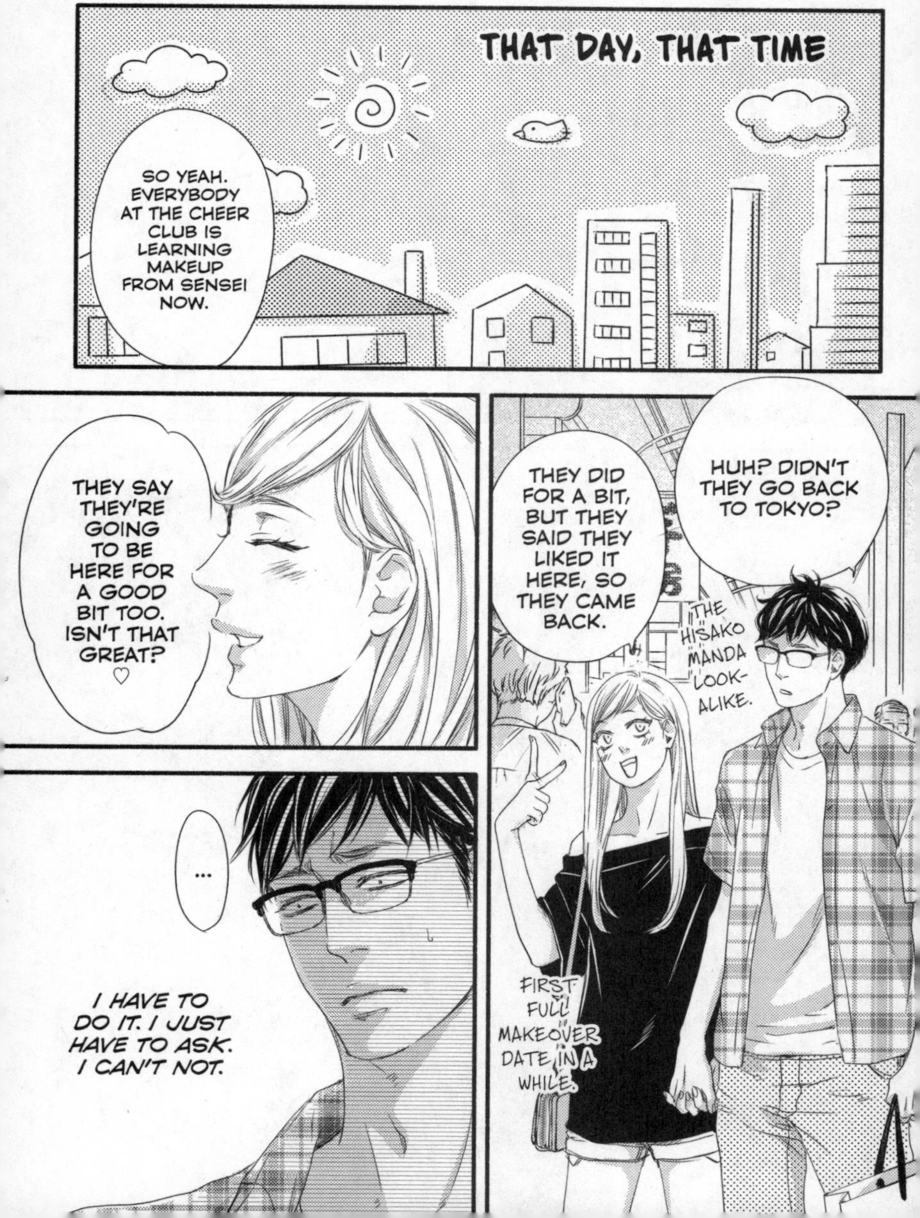
THAT DAY, THAT TIME
SO YEAH. EVERYBODY AT THE CHEER CLUB IS LEARNING MAKEUP FROM SENSEI NOW.
HUH? DIDN'T THEY GO BACK TO TOKYO?
THEY DID FOR A BIT, BUT THEY SAID THEY LIKED IT HERE, SO THEY CAME BACK.
THE HISAKO MANDA LOOK-ALIKE.
FIRST FULL MAKEOVER DATE IN A WHILE.
THEY SAY THEY'RE GOING TO BE HERE FOR A GOOD BIT TOO. ISN'T THAT GREAT? ♡
...
I HAVE TO DO IT. I JUST HAVE TO ASK. I CAN'T NOT.

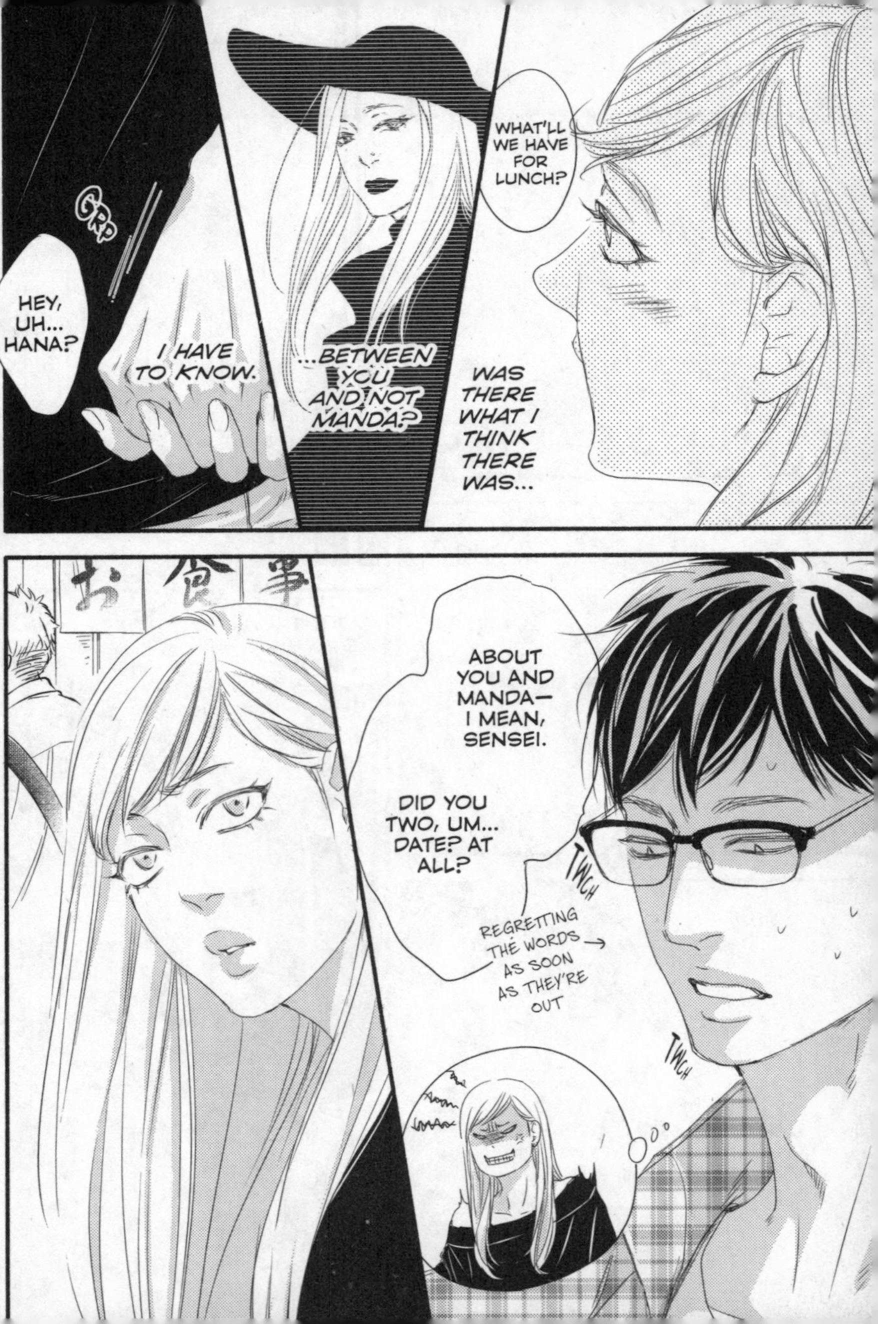
WHAT'LL WE HAVE FOR LUNCH?
WAS THERE WHAT I THINK THERE WAS...
...BETWEEN YOU AND NOT MANDA?
I HAVE TO KNOW.
GRP
HEY, UH... HANA?
ABOUT YOU AND MANDA— I MEAN, SENSEI.
DID YOU TWO, UM... DATE? AT ALL?
TWCH
REGRETTING THE WORDS AS SOON AS THEY'RE OUT
TWCH
お食事

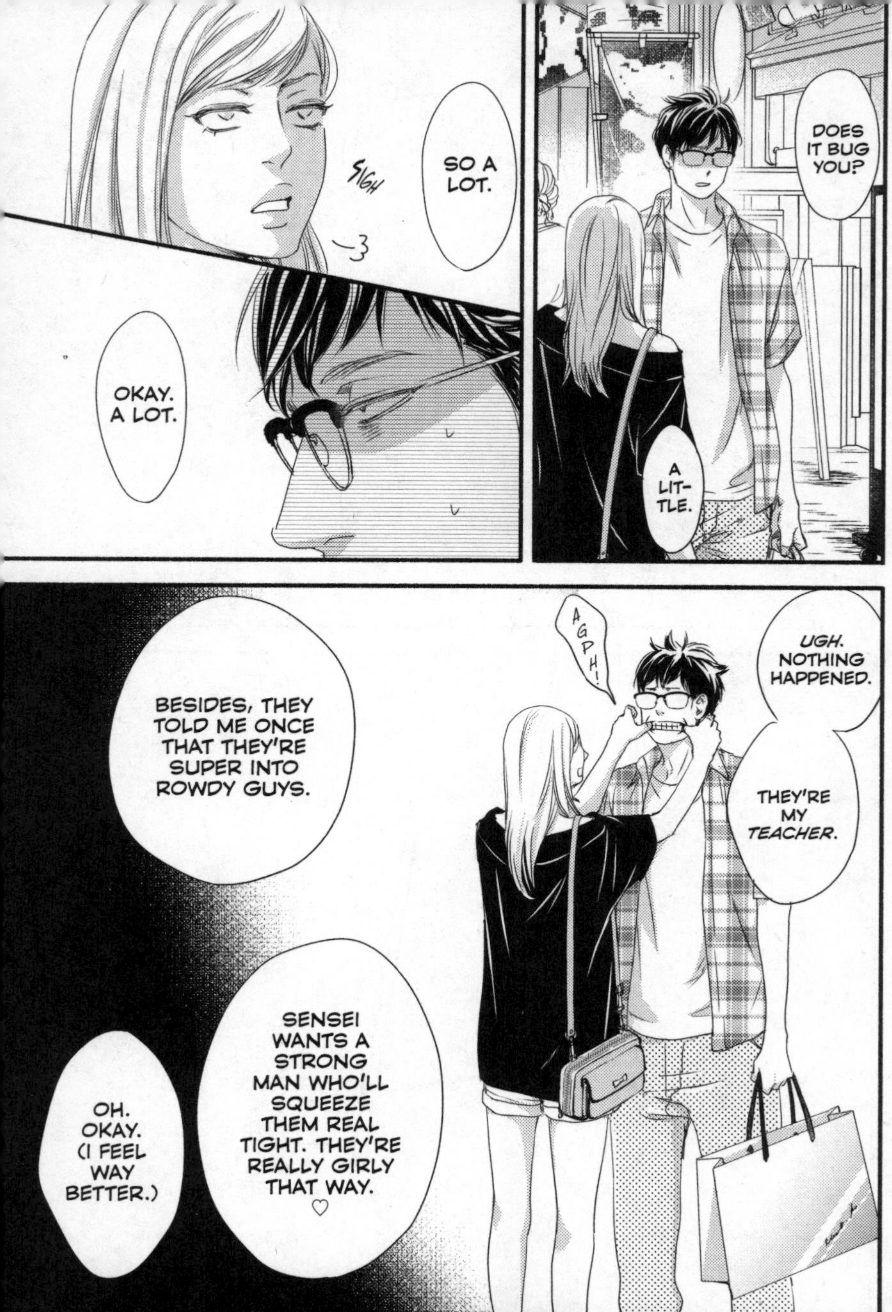
DOES IT BUG YOU?
A LITTLE.
SIGH
SO A LOT.
OKAY. A LOT.
UGH. NOTHING HAPPENED.
AGPH!
THEY'RE MY *TEACHER*.
BESIDES, THEY TOLD ME ONCE THAT THEY'RE SUPER INTO ROWDY GUYS.
SENSEI WANTS A STRONG MAN WHO'LL SQUEEZE THEM REAL TIGHT. THEY'RE REALLY GIRLY THAT WAY. ♡
OH. OKAY. (I FEEL WAY BETTER.)

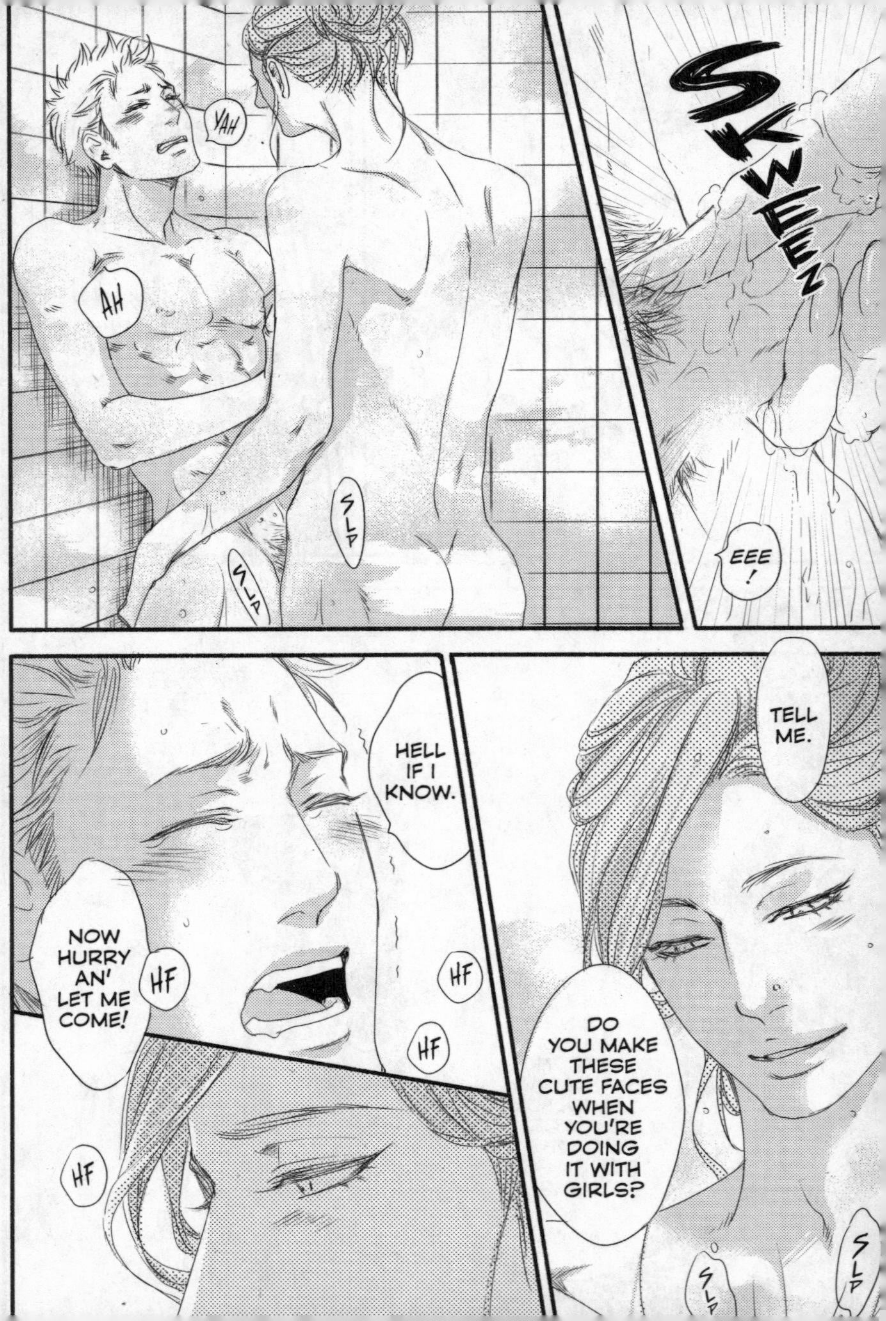
SKWEEZ
EEE!
YAH
AH
SLP
SLP
TELL ME.
DO YOU MAKE THESE CUTE FACES WHEN YOU'RE DOING IT WITH GIRLS?
SLP
SLP
HELL IF I KNOW.
NOW HURRY AN' LET ME COME!
HF
HF
HF
HF

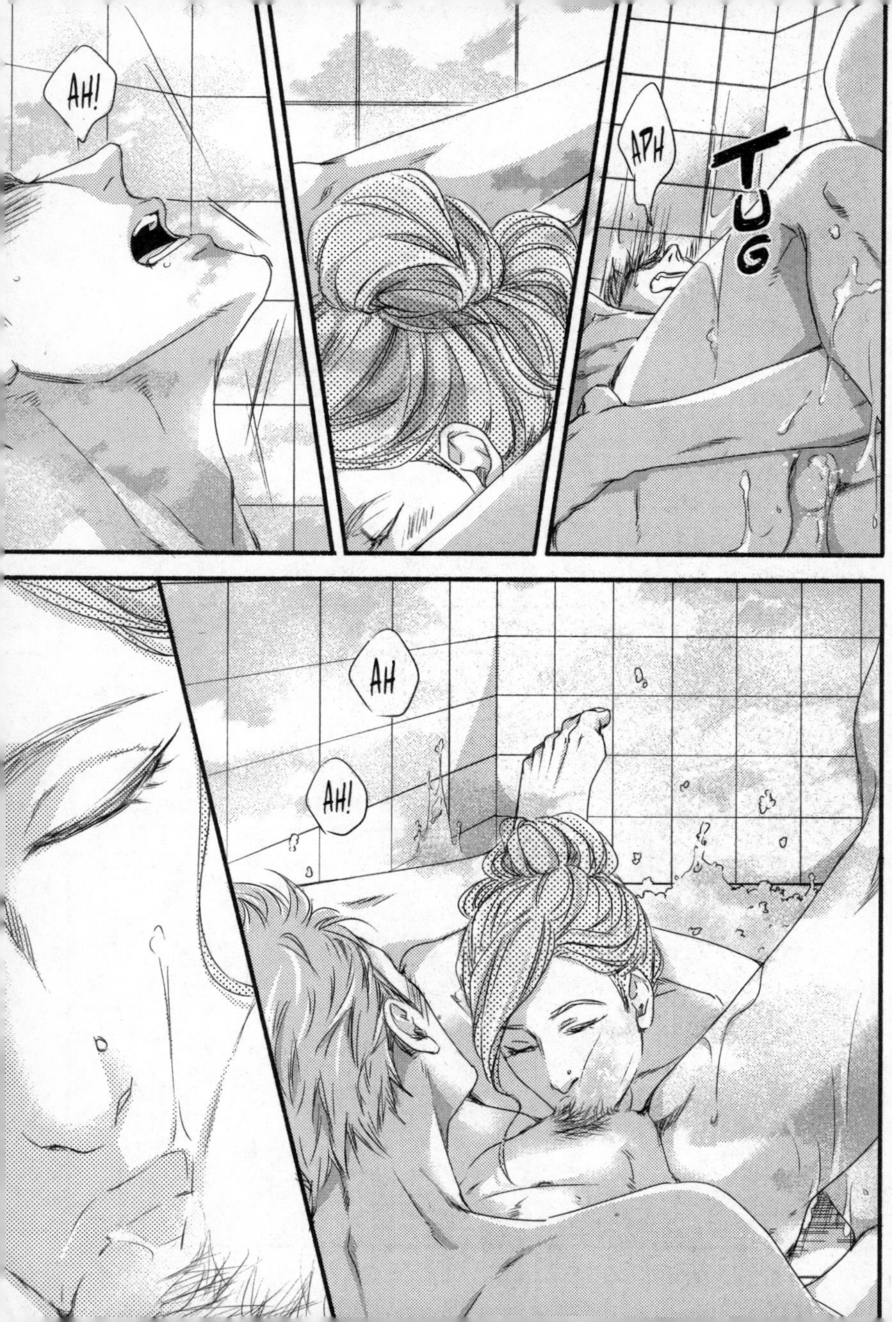
APH
TUG
AH!
AH
AH!

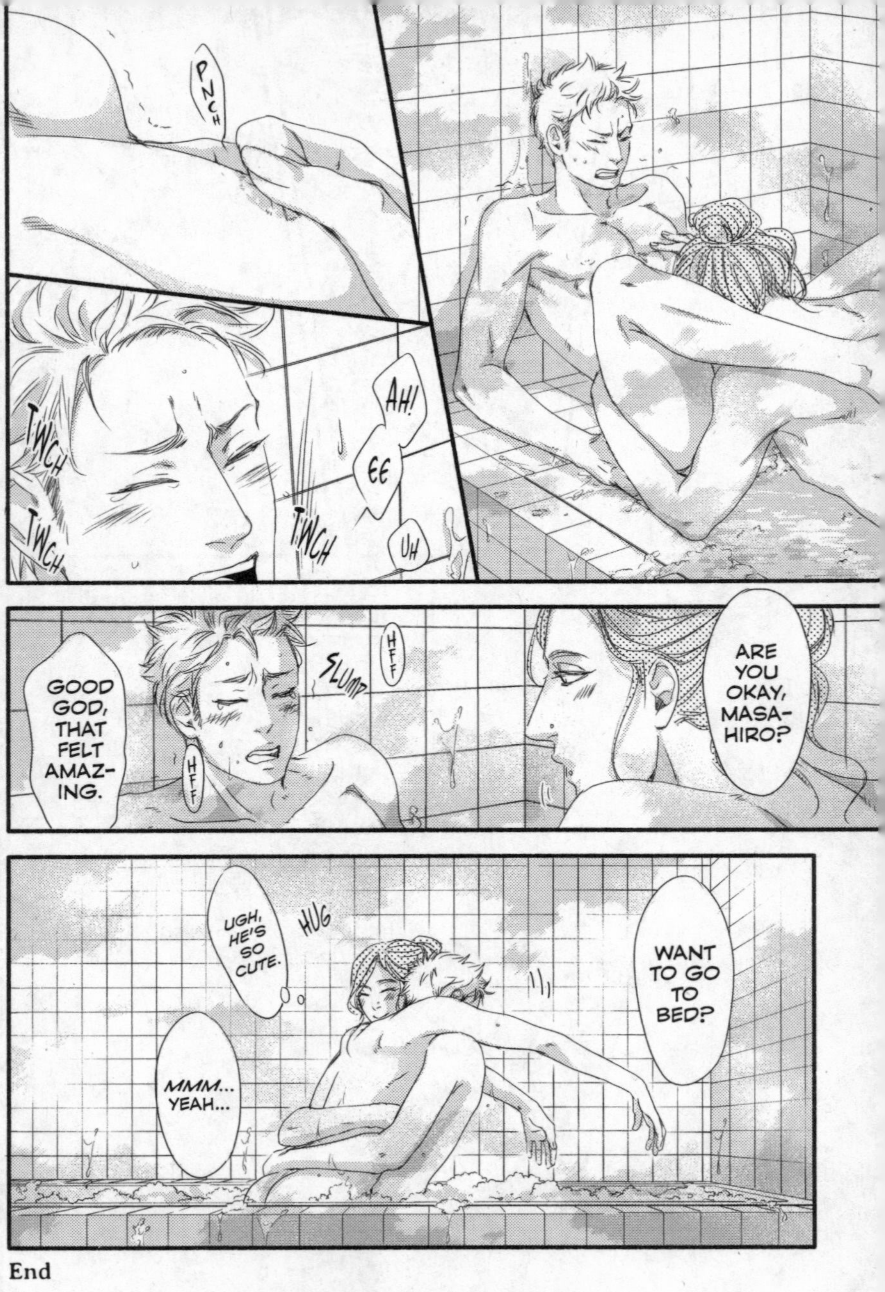
PNCH
AH!
EE
UH
TWCH
TWCH
TWCH
ARE YOU OKAY, MASA-HIRO?
HFF
SLUMP
HFF
GOOD GOD, THAT FELT AMAZ-ING.
WANT TO GO TO BED?
HUG
UGH, HE'S SO CUTE.
MMM... YEAH...

End

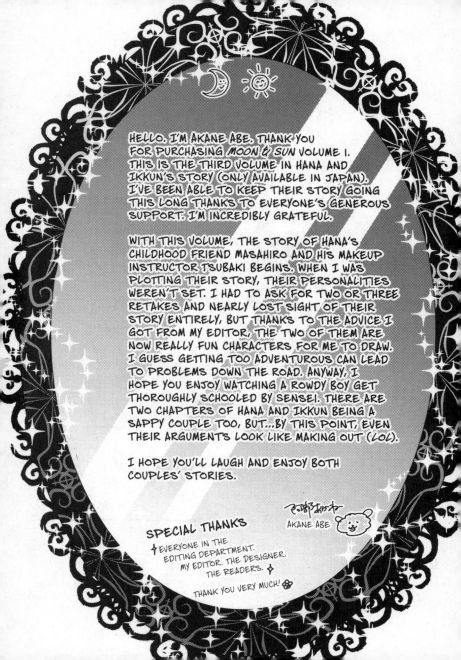

HELLO. I'M AKANE ABE. THANK YOU FOR PURCHASING *MOON & SUN* VOLUME 1. THIS IS THE THIRD VOLUME IN HANA AND IKKUN'S STORY (ONLY AVAILABLE IN JAPAN). I'VE BEEN ABLE TO KEEP THEIR STORY GOING THIS LONG THANKS TO EVERYONE'S GENEROUS SUPPORT. I'M INCREDIBLY GRATEFUL.

WITH THIS VOLUME, THE STORY OF HANA'S CHILDHOOD FRIEND MASAHIRO AND HIS MAKEUP INSTRUCTOR TSUBAKI BEGINS. WHEN I WAS PLOTTING THEIR STORY, THEIR PERSONALITIES WEREN'T SET. I HAD TO ASK FOR TWO OR THREE RETAKES AND NEARLY LOST SIGHT OF THEIR STORY ENTIRELY, BUT THANKS TO THE ADVICE I GOT FROM MY EDITOR, THE TWO OF THEM ARE NOW REALLY FUN CHARACTERS FOR ME TO DRAW. I GUESS GETTING TOO ADVENTUROUS CAN LEAD TO PROBLEMS DOWN THE ROAD. ANYWAY, I HOPE YOU ENJOY WATCHING A ROWDY BOY GET THOROUGHLY SCHOOLED BY SENSEI. THERE ARE TWO CHAPTERS OF HANA AND IKKUN BEING A SAPPY COUPLE TOO, BUT...BY THIS POINT, EVEN THEIR ARGUMENTS LOOK LIKE MAKING OUT (LOL).

I HOPE YOU'LL LAUGH AND ENJOY BOTH COUPLES' STORIES.

SPECIAL THANKS

AKANE ABE

EVERYONE IN THE EDITING DEPARTMENT. MY EDITOR. THE DESIGNER. THE READERS.

THANK YOU VERY MUCH!

I WAS CURIOUS ABOUT THAT

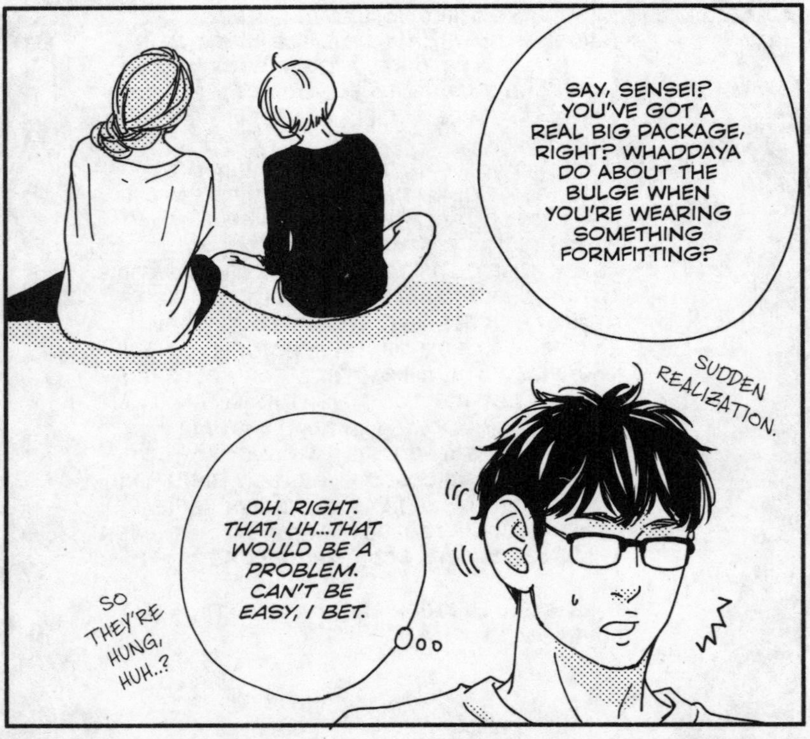
SAY, SENSEI? YOU'VE GOT A REAL BIG PACKAGE, RIGHT? WHADDAYA DO ABOUT THE BULGE WHEN YOU'RE WEARING SOMETHING FORMFITTING?
SUDDEN REALIZATION.
OH. RIGHT. THAT, UH...THAT WOULD BE A PROBLEM. CAN'T BE EASY, I BET.
SO THEY'RE HUNG, HUH..?

I WAS CURIOUS ABOUT THAT

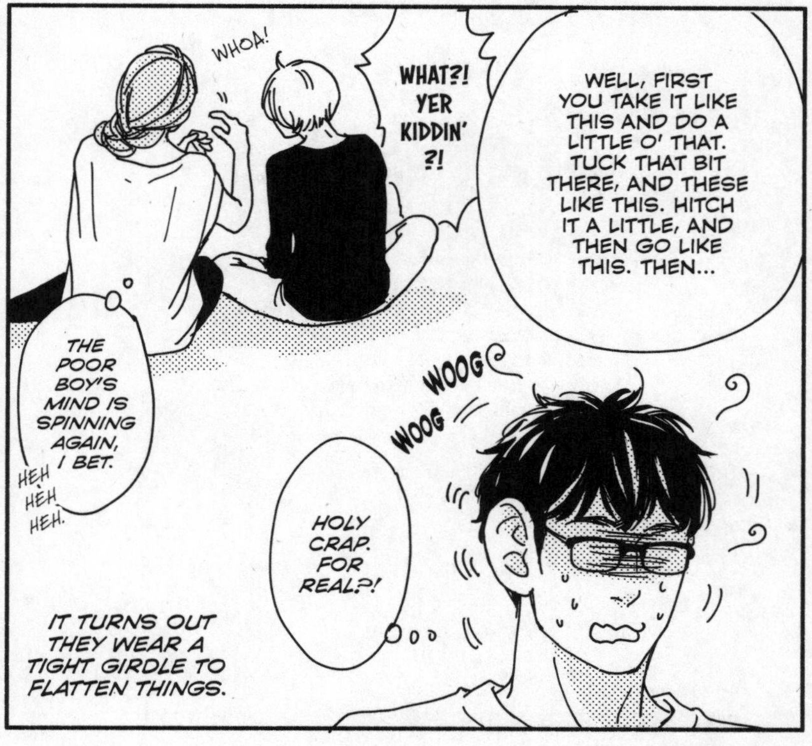
WELL, FIRST YOU TAKE IT LIKE THIS AND DO A LITTLE O' THAT. TUCK THAT BIT THERE, AND THESE LIKE THIS. HITCH IT A LITTLE, AND THEN GO LIKE THIS. THEN...
WHAT?! YER KIDDIN' ?!
WHOA!
WOOG
WOOG
HOLY CRAP. FOR REAL?!
THE POOR BOY'S MIND IS SPINNING AGAIN, I BET.
HEH HEH HEH.
IT TURNS OUT THEY WEAR A TIGHT GIRDLE TO FLATTEN THINGS.

About the Author

This is **Akane Abe**'s third English-language release. Her previous releases include *Hard Rock* and SuBLime's *Am I in Love or Just Hungry?* Born on January 20, she's a Capricorn with an O blood type. You can find out more about Akane Abe on her Twitter page, **@akanebosuke**.

Moon & Sun
Volume 1
SuBLime Manga Edition

Story and Art by **Akane Abe**

Translation—**Adrienne Beck**
Touch-Up Art and Lettering—**Deborah Fisher**
Cover and Graphic Design—**Yukiko Whitley**
Editor—**Jennifer LeBlanc**

© 2018 Akane ABE
Originally published in Japan in 2018 by Shinshokan Co., Ltd.

Printed in the U.S.A.

Published by SuBLime Manga
P.O. Box 77010
San Francisco, CA 94107

10 9 8 7 6 5 4 3 2 1
First printing, July 2022

PARENTAL ADVISORY
MOON & SUN is rated M for Mature and is recommended for
mature readers. This volume contains graphic imagery and
MATURE mature themes.

SuBLimeManga.com

For more information

on all our products, along with the most up-to-date news on releases, series announcements, and contests, please visit us at:

 SuBLimeManga.com

 twitter.com/**SuBLimeManga**

 facebook.com/**SuBLimeManga**

 instagram.com/**SuBLimeManga**

 SuBLimeManga.tumblr.com

J A C K A S S !

STORY AND ART BY **SCARLET BERIKO**

WHEN THE PANTY HOSE GO ON, ALL BETS ARE OFF BETWEEN THESE BEST GUY FRIENDS!

Practical Keisuke's incredibly handsome best friend Masayuki has always rubbed him just a little bit the wrong way. Maybe it's because Masayuki is rich, carefree, and so stunningly handsome that he can, and does, have any girl he wants? But one day, when Keisuke accidentally wears his older sister's panty hose to gym class, it's suddenly his hot friend who's doing the rubbing… on Keisuke's panty hose-clad legs! Has he unwittingly unleashed a secret fetish that will change their relationship forever?

MATURE

SuBLime
SuBLimeManga.com

Finder

DELUXE EDITION

PAIN AND PLEASURE COLLIDE when a sophisticated underworld boss crosses paths with a naive photographer hell-bent on bringing him down!

STORY AND ART BY
AYANO YAMANE

This deluxe edition includes never-before-released material as well as a double-sided color insert and special cover treatment!

Photographer Akihito Takaba takes on a risky assignment trying to document the illegal activities of the Japanese underworld. When he captures its leader—the handsome, enigmatic Ryuichi Asami—in the cross-hairs of his viewfinder, Takaba's world is changed forever.

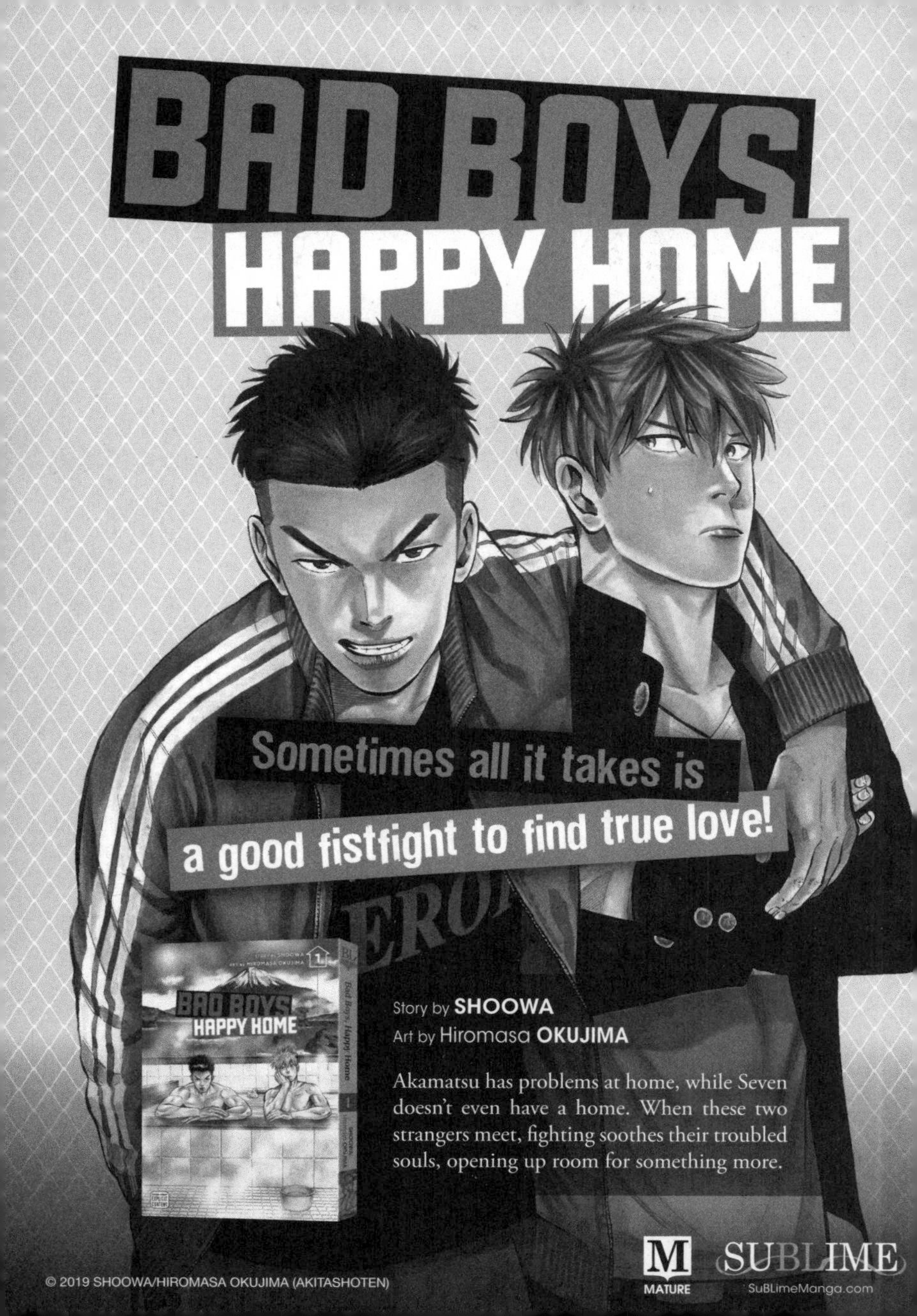
BAD BOYS
HAPPY HOME
Sometimes all it takes is
a good fistfight to find true love!
Story by SHOOWA
Art by Hiromasa OKUJIMA
Akamatsu has problems at home, while Seven doesn't even have a home. When these two strangers meet, fighting soothes their troubled souls, opening up room for something more.
M
MATURE
SUBLIME
SuBLimeManga.com
© 2019 SHOOWA/HIROMASA OKUJIMA (AKITASHOTEN)

A young yakuza boss has a sexy encounter with his wild
side when his family's dirty business becomes personal.

Fourth Generation Head: Tatsuyuki Oyamato

Story and Art by
Scarlet Beriko

The last thing playboy Tatsuyuki Oyamato, fourth-generation heir to a yakuza
family syndicate, wants is any responsibility for running the family business. But
Tatsuyuki's forced to step up both in the sheets and on the streets when a hot
hookup deepens his newfound attraction to men, while also drawing the attention
of a mysterious man who seems dangerously obsessed with Tatsuyuki's lineage...

2015 SCARLET BERIKO / SHINSHOKAN